This is very much a story about sisters and their importance to those lucky enough to have them. I can't imagine what life would have been like without my own sister, Martha McConnell Greer, who is also my best friend. To her this book is dedicated with gratitude and love.

When Gregor Samsa woke up one morning from unsettling dreams, he found himself changed in his bed into a monstrous vermin. . . . "What's happened to me?" he thought. It was no dream.

—Franz Kafka, *The Metamorphosis*

Virginia A. McConnell

Sympathy for the DEVIL

The Emmanuel Baptist Murders of Old San Francisco

PRAEGER

Westport, Connecticut
London

Library of Congress Cataloging-in-Publication Data

McConnell, Virginia A., 1942–
    Sympathy for the devil : the Emmanuel Baptist murders of old San Francisco /
Virginia A. McConnell.
        p. cm.
    Includes bibliographical references and index.
    ISBN 0–275–97054–X (alk. paper)
    1. Murder—California—San Francisco—Case studies.   2. Sex crimes—California—
San Francisco—Case studies.   3. Women—Crimes against—California—San Francisco—
Case studies.   4. Durrant, William Henry Theodore, 1871–1898.   5. Lamont, Blanche,
d. 1895.   6. Williams, Minnie Flora, d. 1895.   I. Title: Emmanuel Baptist murders of
old San Francisco.   II. Title.
HV6534.S3M33   2001
364.15'23'0979461—dc21   2001021648

British Library Cataloguing in Publication Data is available.

Library of Congress Catalog Card Number: 2001021648
ISBN: 0–275–97054–X

First published in 2001

Praeger Publishers, 88 Post Road West, Westport, CT 06881
An imprint of Greenwood Publishing Group, Inc.
www.praeger.com

Printed in the United States of America

The paper used in this book complies with the
Permanent Paper Standard issued by the National
Information Standards Organization (Z39.48–1984).

10 9 8 7 6 5 4 3 2 1

Contents

Map and photo essay follow page 181.

Acknowledgments

Jackson Vance, the librarian at the Clarkston Center of Walla Walla Community College, was—as always—kind, patient, and untiring: kind in listening to my many theories and ramblings about the major players; patient with my many requests; and untiring in her efforts to track down items that were elusive or not subject to Interlibrary Loan. I could not have written this book without her contribution.

Thanks go out to my many "Lovely Assistants," who dug up information for me in far-flung areas: Jeff Crawford of the California State Archives in Sacramento; Margaret Posehn, who researched in the California State Library in Sacramento; Ruth Burkholder and her helpers in Ontario, Canada; Linda in the Lane Medical Library, who sent me Theo's records from Cooper Medical College; and my students in CT 125, especially Carol Driskell, Robynne Therrain, Shawna Fredericksen, Chris Arnold, and Steven Kennedy.

Special thanks to my student Chris Cable, who loaned me the 1882 book on manners, and to internet acquaintance Michael Meade, who sent me the copy of Dorothy Dunbar's *Blood in the Parlor*, which is out of print.

My student Darrell Harman was kind enough to let me pick his brain about embalming, mortuary science, and autopsy procedures.

I owe a special debt to Canadian author Felix Cherniavsky, who inherited Maud (Durrant) Allan's diary, as well as her letters from Theo and their parents, and has published excerpts from them in his book, *The Salome Dancer*. They were invaluable for coming to an understanding of the dynamics in the Durrant family and for better insight into the Theo Durrant not seen by the public.

Professional and personal thanks are due my friend and colleague, Barbara Blasey, who created the 1895 map of San Francisco for the book and generously includes me in her family's holiday meals.

Other "caretakers" who fill my life with delightful and generous gifts are Lisa Greenville, Laurie Austin, my "boss" Devon Gustafson, Orville and Zelda Davidson, Lori Loseth, and Billie Havens.

Heartfelt thanks are due to the families of Blanche Lamont, Tom Vogel, Flo Upton, and Eugene Deuprey, who were kind enough to provide information and photographs.

Many thanks to the volunteers and archivists of the Church of Jesus Christ of Latter Day Saints' Family History Center in Moscow, Idaho, and the library in Salt Lake City, Utah. Their invaluable contributions make it possible for us to access the past.

A very special note of gratitude must inevitably go to the reporters of the *San Francisco Examiner, Chronicle*, and *Call*—especially Alice Rix of the *Chronicle*—who covered the Durrant case from 1895 to 1898 and allowed me to live it through their eyes. Alice Rix's insights into Isabella Durrant and her pen pictures of the women at the trial were especially helpful.

To all you unknown people who so generously contributed your genealogical databases to the internet, a profound thank you for the time and money you save us researchers.

A special thanks to my niece, Kristin McConnell, who read some of the beginning chapters and encouraged me with her "Good job, Gigi!"

Thanks also to my obstreperous pets—Jake, Sammy, Rita, Elijah, and Bear—who forced me to take many breaks, whether I wanted to or not.

My editor at Greenwood/Praeger, Heather Staines, knew exactly what to say to get me past those discouraging writer's blocks, and provided valuable comments throughout the process. She charitably consented to be a sounding board for my many theories, ruminations, and discoveries about the case and the people in it, and never once told me to stop sending those long, pesky e-mails.

Introduction

I first heard of the Durrant case when I was living in San Francisco in the 1970s, and at that time I even visited what I believed to be the murder site: the Emmanuel Baptist Church (it was not the same one). Everything I knew came from commentators who had written about the "Demon of the Belfry," and I must confess that I adopted the same smug, smirky attitude toward it as they. That attitude tended to look on Theodore Durrant not only as a monster and a fiend, but a rather foolish one to have left so much damning evidence behind.

As a matter of fact, my original intention in researching this case was to present Theo Durrant as America's first sexual serial killer. Of course, there had been earlier serial killers—the Benders come to mind, and H. H. Holmes, who was being tried at the same time as Durrant—but these murders were primarily for gain. Durrant was in a different category, and I assumed that he would have continued his new-found "career" had he not been discovered. I also assumed that he was a classic psychopath.

But a funny thing happened on the way to writing this book: I discovered neither a psychopath nor a serial killer, but a genuinely good person whose crimes were a complete aberration. His two tragic deeds aside, I would have been proud to call him "brother" or "friend." My focus, then, became the intriguing question of what might have happened to cause the life of a young man of such great promise to go so terribly wrong. "When did he become a monster?" was the plaintive question asked over and over by one of his defense attorneys, and this book is an attempt to answer that question.

However, there is no way to prove Theo Durrant innocent of these terrible crimes; the circumstantial evidence against him is both mountainous and convincing. To believe in his innocence, it would be necessary to adopt the stance of his parents, his sister, and those who refused to accept the evidence at face value: that he was the victim of a monstrous conspiracy to destroy him and protect the real culprit(s). It is a ludicrous stance, forgivable in a family member or friend, but not in a serious researcher.

But, it is also true that, by today's standards, his trial was not entirely fair. The immense pretrial publicity was so extensive that he should probably have been granted a change of venue (an opinion voiced by at least one member of the California Supreme Court at his appeal and also by Governor James Budd). The police allowed hundreds of curious spectators to mill about the Blanche Lamont crime scene in the belfry before a complete inspection had taken place. They constantly submitted Durrant to one-man line-ups ("This is the man we have arrested. Is this the man you saw?"). Immediately after his arrest, the chief of police declared that he had "enough evidence to convict a dozen men" and hung Theo's picture in his Rogues' Gallery of convicted murderers—before he had even been arraigned.

The role of the press in the nineteenth century was always an important one, but in the Theo Durrant case it assumed an almost unrivaled fever pitch, primarily because of the newspaper wars. In San Francisco in 1895, there were six daily newspapers, all struggling for survival. The Big Three were William Randolph Hearst's *Examiner*, the De Young family's *Chronicle*, and the *San Francisco Call* coming in behind these two. The *Examiner* and the *Chronicle* vied for scoops and subscriptions, each constantly bragging that it had more of each than its rival. The *Chronicle* was more sedate in its approach to the news, and usually more formal, while the *Examiner* focused on sensationalism, gossip, and a more informal, personal "between-you-and-me" style. (The *Examiner* even invited its readers to submit solutions to the crime, which it printed in a special section of each edition.)

The *Call*, which could not compete with these two giants, chose what it claimed to be a higher moral ground in declaring that it would not publish sensational or tasteless items. It omitted the more sordid aspects from Durrant's trial and refused to print pictures of his execution. The *Call* was particularly incensed by the practices of Hearst's *Examiner*, which it referred to as "that yellow rag," and often reached levels of shrill hysteria in exposing what it saw as the evils of that newspaper. Picture a Yorkshire terrier barking frantically at a Great Dane, and you have a good idea of the tone of the *Call* on these occasions. The Great Dane, of course, paid it no attention at all.

The newspapers, then, assumed the status of major characters in the Durrant drama, each with its own distinctive personality.

A handful of women reporters covered the trial, the most notable of whom were Alice Rix and Annie Laurie (pseudonym of Winifred Black, one of the "sob sisters") of the *Examiner*, and Carrie Cunningham, Miss Rouse, and Mabel Craft for the *Chronicle*. Few reporters back then got to use bylines, but the women almost always did. Alice Rix's accounts of the trial, of her time spent with Mrs. Durrant, and of her interviews with Theo are particularly insightful. Young, ambitious Carrie Cunningham got several scoops, a veiled confession from Theo, and threats of a contempt citation from the judge. She was a witness at the trial for two separate issues, thereby symbolizing the indissoluble marriage between this case and the press.

The Emmanuel Baptist murders took place against the colorful backdrop of San Francisco as it approached the twentieth century. Its fears and its dreams of that new century are a constant theme in the newspapers of 1895–1898, and the apparently motiveless deaths of Blanche Lamont and Minnie Williams reflected its citizens' apprehensions about the dawning of a modern age: Is this what the future looks like? Will we abandon all of the standards that make us civilized?

It was an exciting era to live in: Gold was discovered in the Klondike; Oscar Wilde was on trial in England; Emile Zola exposed the Dreyfus Affair scandal; and William Randolph Hearst was promoting American imperialism and pushing war with Spain.

Women were agitating for more rights and more power, and sarcastic digs at the "new woman" show how frightening that was for people back then (not only for men, but for women who felt their traditional roles being threatened). Bicycles had recently evolved from the high-wheeled "ordinary" to the "safety" model that resembles what is in use today. Among the many passionate devotees of this new fad of bicycle riding—now that it had been made accessible to all—were women, who saw in it a sort of emancipation, a freedom not experienced in other areas of their lives. And to make their riding both safe and comfortable, they adopted the wearing of bloomers. It is impossible to overestimate the very raw nerve this touched.

Religion came under scrutiny as well, since the murders happened "right under God's nose," so to speak. Cynics were quick to point out the ineffectiveness of religion in the life of Theo Durrant and the failure of God to protect the two victims in His own house of worship. And the religiously inclined fretted about the ushering in of a Godless era with the new century.

Our story is also one of upward mobility. The young men and women you will meet in these pages were the sons and daughters of tailors and shoemakers, postal workers and cabinetmakers, common laborers and jacks-of-all-trades. They were all looking to improve their own lot in life with career and marriage choices; and, while this was not a primary motive for the murders, it was definitely the motive for the two victims' being at the time and place where they were killed. Ironically, William Makepeace Thackeray's *The Newcomes*, which runs like a leitmotif through the case and was an exhibit at the trial, involves this very concept of moving up the class structure—often to the detriment of those who attempt it.

I encountered three main difficulties in researching this case: the newspapers, previous commentators, and the 1906 San Francisco earthquake. Because of the ongoing newspaper wars and the hysterical frenzy produced by the murders, truth became a commodity that was often hard to unearth. Not only were rumors rampant (and therefore presented to reporters as true), but in many instances it seems that reporters, in the interests of selling papers, made up interviews out of wholecloth. Then the next day there would be an article, usually in a rival paper, in which the quoted individual would deny that he/she had said what was reported, or deny that the interview took place at all. (However, the newspapers helped ferret out the truth in many instances in their constant watchdogging of each other. They hated being scooped, and were quick to question inaccuracies in a rival, although with less frequency than I would have liked.)

I read the three major newspaper accounts (the *Chronicle*, the *Examiner*, and the *Call*), and where information only appeared in one and not the others, I had to determine whether it might have been the result of an exclusive interview with that paper or simply misinformation. I had to weigh everything I knew about the case, including my interpretations of the personalities involved, and decide whether a piece of information was more likely than not to be accurate. It is possible that I may have erred in some of those evaluations, and for that I apologize.

The problem with previous commentaries on this case is that they often rely on each other and not on the existing records. Hence, some of the misstatements later recanted or rumors subsequently proven untrue have been perpetuated as fact by these writers. So I found I could not trust these accounts unless I could verify the facts independently.

Probably the biggest "urban legend" that has survived into the present is the rumor that Theo had enticed various women into the church where he then either undressed completely or exposed himself. These stories were always passed on by "a friend of a friend," often with an actual name for a victim, and no doubt were an attempt to make sense of the kind of person who could commit crimes like these. However, after an exhaustive, months-long search, even the police (who desperately wanted to find one of these women) had to admit that such incidents never occurred and the women never existed.

The San Francisco earthquake and fire in 1906 destroyed many original records, including the official trial transcript. The transcript that was done for the appeal, and which exists in the State Archives in Sacramento, is essentially a summary done by Assistant District Attorney Peixotto, and later published by him in book form. But a summary does not reveal a witness's hesitations or evasiveness or fumbling for an answer. For that, the actual transcript is invaluable.

Luckily, the *Chronicle* and the *Examiner* both published transcripts, so the original flavor of a witness's testimony can be experienced. However, in the interests of good taste, they also refrained from including anything they considered shocking, and this generally meant the gynecological testimony by the physician who conducted the autopsies. Peixotto's summary includes that testimony for Blanche Lamont, but Durrant was never put on trial for Minnie Williams's murder, so we have been deprived of possibly crucial forensic information.

My goal here is to present as nearly as possible what Blanche and Minnie and Theo were really like, and what happened to each of them on those fateful days in April 1895. Some of it will, of necessity, be speculation. However, I have not only indicated those areas of speculation, but I have backed them up with all available evidence, much of which is done in explanatory endnotes. Where there is dialogue, it is either a recreation of what was actually said, a rendition based on a summary, or—in those instances where no one reported the conversation—what most likely would have been said under the known circumstances.

At a distance of more than one hundred years from the events involved, and where there was no admission of guilt by the defendant (at least, none that was ever made public), I have had to rely on the evidence available, as well as what we know today about human behavior. My interpretations of what really happened in the Emmanuel Baptist Church on April 3 and April 12, 1895, are attempts to fit all of those areas of knowledge and come up with plausible answers to puzzling, century-old questions.

It is not my intention to make a hero of Theo Durrant, nor scapegoats of the unfortunate young women who were his victims. However, I would like, in some small way, to set the record straight and present the "Demon of the Belfry" in a fairer manner than has been done over the past one hundred years. It is incredibly easy, and incredibly simplistic, to dismiss him as a monster and ignore the very real difficulties under which he was suffering. Theo Durrant was not a devil, nor were his victims angels. (This is not to say, however, that Blanche Lamont and Minnie Williams are to be blamed in any way for what happened to them; they could not possibly have perceived danger on April 3 and April 12.)

Students of this case will recognize that I have taken some liberties with the chronology of certain minor pieces that do not affect the fabric as a whole. For example, similar events have been lumped together, even if one or two of them happened at a later time. Testimony and evidence that was merely cumulative and not otherwise interesting was omitted, as was that which was not probative of guilt or innocence. This was done to spare the reader from the feeling of drowning in a multitude of facts that often have no real bearing on the main story. To include every single piece of information involved in this case would easily produce a volume of a thousand pages—but one that would not be entirely readable. With this mass of detail, it is inevitable that some minor errors may have escaped my attention. However, I would like to assure readers that the major facts remain intact.

The Emmanuel Baptist murders have always been presented as the beginning of the modern type of violent crime, a psychological symbol of a quaint era of sexual repression and its results. But much more than that, they represent an intensely personal human drama that should not be overlooked. The people you will meet in these pages were real people, with real joys, real griefs, real flaws. Even though they lived more than a hundred years ago, they matter to me as they most certainly did to those who loved them. And I hope they will matter to you as well.

In Plain Sight

She comes—she's here—she's past!
May heaven go with her!
　　　　　—William Makepeace Thackeray, quoted in
　　　　　Trilby by George du Maurier (1894)

Henry Shalmount loved his job. He had been a streetcar conductor
for five years with one of the many railway companies in San Francisco, and he prided himself on keeping exactly to the schedule.
Shalmount knew every inch of the route he covered for the Sutter
Street Railway, and he enjoyed seeing the regulars every day on
their way to work or school. Secretly, he thought of them as "his
people."[1]

Over the past month, since March 1895, an attractive young
woman got on his car every morning at Mission and Ninth Streets
and got off at Sutter and Polk. He knew she was a schoolgirl because she carried books with her, tied together with a leather belt-
like strap. She always wore the same dress and hat, and she always
rode alone. So Shalmount was surprised to see her this morning,
April 3, in the company of a young man. Truth be told, he was
even a little jealous, as he had always taken special notice of her

and felt somewhat protective toward her. The stranger represented an intrusion on their "relationship."

The young woman began to move toward her usual seat at the rear of the car, but the young man took her arm and steered her toward the "dummy," the name given to the outside benches (still coveted by today's cable car riders). This angered Shalmount, especially as the girl seemed to hesitate before making up her mind. Why didn't her escort let her sit where she wanted? "All aboard!" he shouted testily, and the couple went outside and sat on the dummy. The girl took off her gloves.

When Shalmount came around to collect the fares, he noticed that the young man had his arm on the bench in back of the girl, as if to protect her from the hard wooden seat. Between two fingers of his outstretched hand, he held two transfers. Later, the conductor saw that the stranger had the young woman's gloves in his hand and was fooling with them. "He seemed to be talking very sweetly to her," he would say later. They were obviously having a good time, laughing and talking and being "jolly."

As the streetcar approached Sutter and Polk, the young man asked for two more transfers, and when the car stopped, the couple got off. Shalmount didn't know if it was his imagination, but the two seemed to be staring at him as if he had done something wrong, or as if he owed them change. "I don't know what they meant by it, really," he thought, somewhat miffed. All in all, the young man's presence had spoiled his daily enjoyment of the schoolgirl's ride on his car.

Herman Schlageter, 22, was in his final semester at the Cooper Medical College in San Francisco. On the morning of April 3, 1895, he was riding on Henry Shalmount's streetcar when he noticed a classmate, Theodore Durrant, get on at Mission and Ninth with a young lady. They were engrossed in their conversation, so he didn't call attention to himself.[2]

At 3:00 that afternoon, Mary Vogel looked anxiously out her front window for about the twentieth time in an hour. That man was still there! What was he up to? She was so nervous, she couldn't concentrate on her sewing. She was convinced he was planning to rob her.

Mrs. Vogel, 44, lived with her husband, Melchior, at 919 Powell

Street, directly across the street from the San Francisco Normal School. Her parents were German immigrants and, although she had been born in New York City, her German accent was heavy and her English poor.

There had been a rash of burglaries on the Vogels' block of Powell Street, and a friend had recently entrusted them with $300 in cash that he wanted to invest in some stock of the Spring Valley Water Company. So when Mary Vogel spotted the stranger alternately pacing and loitering across the street in front of the school, she determined to keep her eye on him, at one point even getting her opera glasses to see him more clearly. He was a young man with reddish-blond hair and a slight mustache, wearing a dark suit and a hat.

Actually, Mrs. Vogel was not really checking out his clothes so much as his face in case she had to identify him later. She thought he might be waiting for a confederate—he was clearly waiting for *something*, with all his nervous pacing—at which point the two would undoubtedly burst into her apartment and demand the cash. She had first noticed him at 2:07 and was relieved when an hour later the young man ran ("like a boy") to meet some of the girls coming down the Normal School steps. He tipped his hat to one of them, escorted her onto an approaching cable car, and took a seat next to her on the outside bench, all in what seemed to be one fluid movement. ("It was so quick done," Mrs. Vogel would say later.)

As the cable car pulled away and out of sight, Mrs. Vogel could finally relax her vigil.[3]

Nineteen-year-old Minnie Bell Edwards left her cooking class at the Normal School as soon as it was over at 2:55 on Wednesday, April 3. She lived in San Mateo and wanted to get a head start on the long series of streetcars and trains she would have to take to get home. As she left, she joined the new girl, Blanche Lamont, who was also headed toward the door.

Blanche had just enrolled in classes as a special, non-matriculating student that Monday, April 1, but didn't attend any until the following day. Principal Yoder had introduced her to some of the girls, including Minnie, but Blanche was very shy and not terribly outgoing. Minnie decided she would make the effort to get to know her. As they exited the school together and walked down the long flight of stairs toward the cable cars, Minnie talked about commuting from San Mateo and Blanche mostly listened.

As Minnie and Blanche approached the corner to wait for a car, a young man came up behind them and tipped his hat. Blanche seemed glad to see him. She let him take her books, and the two got on the cable car together. Minnie didn't want to intrude, so she sat on the inside, away from the dummy where the couple sat. The school had a strict policy against the young women being escorted by gentlemen either coming to or going from school, and Minnie made a mental note to inform Blanche of it the next day. Being new, she obviously was not aware of the rule.[4]

Over on the sidewalk, strolling leisurely toward Market Street, two other students—May Lanigan and Alice Pleasant—also noticed the faux pas of the new girl. "The new scholar has her young man with her," Alice commented to May; "it won't be long before the principal puts a stop to that." They watched the couple as the cable car rolled slowly along Powell Street and approached the California Street intersection. Here it was necessary for the car to stop, let go of its cable, glide across the intersecting tracks of the California Street line, then pick up its own cable on the other side. Because of this, Alice and May had plenty of time to observe Blanche Lamont and her young man.

The boy had a book open on his lap, and he and Blanche were looking at it and laughing. There was no doubt that Blanche was having a good time. As the car rolled past the two girls on the sidewalk, Blanche's escort looked up at them and they got a good view of his face. He was not bad looking, with a slight mustache and a neat appearance, but his reddish-blond hair was a little too long for their tastes. It was so long in back that it curled up a little at the ends.[5]

Then the car caught its cable and rumbled down the hill and out of sight.

Old Mrs. Crosett was weary. It had been a busy day visiting with her granddaughter on Webster Street and she was looking forward to getting home, where she lived with her oldest son, her daughter-in-law, and their children. Although sharp of mind and eye, 71-year-old Elizabeth Dorrance Foster Crosett had many physical ailments, and the whole ordeal of walking to the streetcars, getting on and off, and transferring from one to the other had worn her out.[6]

Since the death four years earlier of her husband, James Lyman Crosett, the widow spent much of her time visiting her five children. She didn't want to be a burden to any one of them, so, although her permanent home was considered to be in the Mission District with her son, James, in reality the children could never be sure at any given time where she might be.

Her husband, James, Sr., had been one of the original pioneers, a '49er, although most of the money he made from gold was lost through bad investments. Still, he had done quite well in merchandising, and left his widow a tidy sum. James and Elizabeth had been very close, and his death left her feeling rootless and lost. They had shared and suffered and enjoyed so much together; she missed talking to him. Being with her children was not the same, and could never fill the empty void inside.

As Mrs. Crosett sat on the inside of the car headed toward the Mission District, she happened to look at the dummy bench directly in her line of vision. Why, there was Theo Durrant! She tried to get his attention, maybe even hoping to get him to ride with her to 24th Street and help her off the car—she had such trouble with that—but he was thoroughly engrossed in the young lady he was with.

Theo Durrant was almost as familiar to Mrs. Crosett as her own grandson, Jim. For the past four years, Theo and Jim had been close pals, attending the Cogswell Polytechnical College together and then getting up that Independent Telegraph Line for neighbors and friends in the Mission. Mrs. Crosett smiled to herself as she thought of how excited Jim and Theo could get over the telegraph line. They had even hooked her up to it![7] Well, she was a pioneer, wasn't she? She wasn't above learning a few newfangled tricks.

Elizabeth Crosett had been very glad when Jim began to hang around with Theo Durrant. She considered Theo a model young man and thought he would be a good influence on her grandson, who needed a little straightening out at times. She knew that Jim had also been smitten with Theo's sister, Maud, an accomplished pianist, and had even asked her to marry him. But Maud had turned him down, not only because she didn't feel the same way about him, but because she was leaving for Berlin to pursue her musical studies there.[8]

Theo and his companion got off the streetcar at 21st Street and Valencia without noticing Mrs. Crosett. The elderly woman watched as they walked down toward Bartlett Street. She didn't know the girl Theo was with, but she was tall and slender, a good two inches or so taller than he was. The wind was blowing that day and the young lady held onto her hat with her right hand. Her dress was blown against her body, revealing a slim, shapely figure.

When Mrs. Crosett finally got home, she looked at the clock. It was a few minutes before 4:00.

Martin Quinlan, attorney at law, was experiencing a pleasant buzz. He'd been "lying low and sipping slow" all day, starting at breakfast, and was now on his way to his fourth (but not his last) saloon stop of the day: Gionetti's, at the corner of 22nd and Mission, where he was to meet his friend, David Clarke. It was now after 4:00, but Quinlan was in no hurry. He knew Clarke would wait for him. They would probably have a drink or two, then go down to St. Luke's Hospital to visit Clarke's brother-in-law, who had been injured in an accident. In fact, that was the purpose of the meeting: Clarke wanted Quinlan to represent his brother-in-law in a lawsuit.

In his mid-thirties, Martin Quinlan was a widower with three children. His mother had moved in with him to take care of them. Quinlan had no regular office at this time, being somewhat short of funds, and was content to use Lane's Saloon near City Hall for this purpose. As the expression of the day put it, he "carried his office in his hat."[9]

Every morning, Quinlan would wander over to the Police Court to see if any newly-arrested person needed a lawyer, and every noon he would make sure he was back at Lane's for lunch, liquid and otherwise. His past was an interesting one as well, as he had been twice arrested for assault with intent to commit murder and once for seduction, although not convicted on any of these charges.[10]

Quinlan stopped on 22nd Street to watch workmen tear up the street to put in the new electric car line. It was fascinating to see the old-fashioned Nicholson pavement exposed as it was uprooted: it was a uniquely designed combination of wooden blocks, tar paper, and cement that was economical, safe (horses' hooves would not slip on it), and silent.[11] Quinlan had definite ideas on how to fix the streets, and this was another reason he watched the construction.

As the itinerant attorney made his way slowly toward Mission Street, he noticed a young couple coming down Bartlett. The young lady was on the outside, which was unusual (the gentleman usually walked there), but not unheard of.[12] The young man was someone he recognized from the Mission District neighborhood, although he did not know his name. Both of them were so involved in their conversation that they took no notice of Quinlan, who had to step aside a little to let them pass as all three met at the corner. He watched them as they strolled leisurely in the direction of Emmanuel Baptist Church on Bartlett between 22nd and 23rd.

The time was between 4:10 and 4:20.[13]

Mrs. Caroline Leak was getting worried. Her daughter, who lived in Palo Alto, had told her to expect a visit after she completed a shopping expedition in downtown San Francisco, and at 4:15 her estimated noontime arrival was long past due. Mrs. Leak looked out her window one more time to see if her daughter was approaching. Instead, she saw a young couple she recognized.

Mrs. Leak lived in a direct diagonal line across the street from the Emmanuel Baptist Church, where she had been a member for about fifteen years. For the last four of those years, she had known its most prominent young member, Theo Durrant: He was the assistant superintendent of the Sunday school, passed out the hymn books at the services, was an officer in the Young People's Christian Endeavor Society, served as usher on most Sundays, and was a general Mr. Fixit around the church.

Today, April 3, she immediately recognized Theo Durrant as he and his companion approached the church's side gate. Theo was listening intently to the young woman, his face turned toward Mrs. Leak. The girl was looking at Theo as she talked. Consequently, the elderly lady was not completely sure who she was. But from her height (5'7")[14] and her coloring (brown hair), she thought it was either Lucile Turner or Blanche Lamont. Both young women spent time at the church and with Theo Durrant, and both were the tallest girls at Emmanuel Baptist.

Theo held the gate open for the young woman and they walked together down the pathway, where he produced a key to the side door. As they disappeared into the church, Mrs. Leak thought, "What an imprudent thing for her to do!" Although she considered Theo Durrant above reproach, she thought that ugly, suggestive gossip would surely result if anyone knew that the girl had gone alone with him—or with any man—into the church.

Theo and his companion entered the church about 4:30, and Mrs. Leak sat for a while to see when they would come out.

They never did.[15]

George Rufus King was only 18 and still in high school, but he was already an accomplished organist and played at nearly every service at the Emmanuel Baptist Church. George's whole family was involved with the church: his parents; his two sisters, Flora and Nettie; and his maternal grandparents. His father, Dr. William Zadoc King, a dentist, was one of the trustees, and George's grandmother, Charlotte (Mrs. Rufus) Moore, was president of the Ladies' Aid Society. His mother, Ophelia, helped out with the many fairs and benefits, and also directed the choir. George himself, besides playing the organ, was helping Theo Durrant collect and catalog books for the church library.

George King idolized Theo Durrant and treasured their friendship. He admired Theo's many accomplishments and his personal qualities, and hoped he himself could grow into such a man. He liked the way Theo could be religious without being smarmy about it, and the fact that he had a good sense of humor and lots of friends.[16]

George was a senior at Lowell High School (also called Boys' High) and wasn't really sure what he wanted to do after that, although he planned to attend college. Theo, on the other hand, seemed to know exactly what he wanted: After his graduation from Lincoln, he had gotten a degree in engineering from Cogswell Poly and was now in his final semester at Cooper Medical School. After graduation, he planned to do graduate studies in medicine in Europe while his sister furthered her musical career there.

After school on April 3, George headed over to the church to practice the organ pieces for the Easter Sunday services that were two weeks away. One of them was both tricky and odd, selected by the equally odd pastor, Rev. J. George Gibson: *Un Ballo in*

Maschera ("A Masked Ball"), an opera by Giuseppe Verdi whose plot involves forbidden love, betrayal, and murder. A strange choice for Easter Sunday services!

As soon as George unlocked the front door with his father's key and entered what was essentially the basement of the church, he could smell gas. Was there a leak in the gas jet he had recently installed in the library? As he approached the library, he could see that its door was wide open. How could that be? Only he and Theo Durrant had keys to the new lock, which they had just put on a few days previously. It wasn't like Theo to be careless about leaving the library open to vandalism.

The whole point of the second lock on the library door was to prevent theft and vandalism by the boys who came for Sunday school. Most of the losses came at the hands of the janitor's 16-year-old stepson, James Sademan, who often helped with chores around the church. James was an incorrigible thief and found the original lock easy to pick. He took chalk, crayons, notebooks, and other Sunday school items stored there. The second lock, which was one that Theo had at home, was put on primarily to keep James from getting at the supplies.[17]

The library, located in the front part of the church and directly under the steeple, consisted of two rooms: a larger anteroom with a table and some chairs, and a smaller closet-sized room tucked in under the stairs. It was in this closet that the books and supplies were kept, and where George had put in the new gas jet.

George could see nothing amiss in the larger room, and nothing to indicate that Theo might be around somewhere. In the closet, he lit a match and dangerously waved it around the joints of the gas jet to see if anything was leaking out. Nothing. Shrugging his shoulders, he left the library and locked the door behind him.

It was now a few minutes before 5:00. There would be a prayer meeting that night at 7:30, and George also had to be home before 6:00 for the family dinner. He sat down at the piano in the main classroom and began to play the music from Verdi's opera. He had only been playing a few short minutes when a figure emerged through the partially opened folding doors that separated the main classroom from the infants' classroom. It was Theo Durrant in a state of mental and physical disarray.

Durrant was not wearing his coat or hat, and there were dust marks on the legs of his trousers. His hair was mussed up, his face was pale, his eyes were congested, he was shivering, and basically he looked sick.[18] It was such a shock for George to see the always-meticulous Theo in this state that he jumped up from the piano bench. "What's the matter with you?" he asked his friend in a shrill voice as he moved toward him.

"I've been working on the gas jets that light the sunburners in the auditorium and I've been overcome with gas," Theo replied. "I need you to do me a favor: Run down to the drug store and get me a packet of Bromo-Seltzer."

Theo dug a 50-cent piece out of his pocket and gave it to George, who sprinted out of the church and down to Keene's Drug Store at the corner of Valencia and 22nd Streets. He got the Bromo-Seltzer for $.25, then sprinted back with the medicine and the quarter in change. When George entered the church, Theo met him in the lobby[19] and they went back through the classroom to the kitchen, where Theo got a glass of water and took a dose of the Bromo-Seltzer.

"Do you want some of this?" Theo asked George. As he said this, he appeared to become nauseated by the medicine.

"No, thanks," George told him. "It doesn't look all that pleasant."

Theo checked himself in the mirror. "I guess I don't look quite so pale now." The two boys sat together on the classroom platform while Theo rested.

"Why didn't you come get me to help you with the gas jets?" George asked. "I could have turned them on and off while you worked, and then you wouldn't have had to leave them on the whole time."

"As a matter of fact, I was on my way to your house this morning," Theo told him. "But I ran into Blanche Lamont on her way to school and she wanted me to accompany her. She was running late and couldn't wait for me to go to your house first."

"Do you feel up to helping me carry down the cabinet organ?" George asked. He needed it next to the piano so that he could practice his duet with Mrs. Worth, and it was relatively easier to bring the cabinet organ (even though it weighed 200 pounds) down to the piano than to bring the piano up to the main organ.

Theo nodded, and the two boys climbed the winding staircase that led to the organ loft. The gas smell that George had noticed down below was almost nonexistent one floor above. He grasped the organ with his back against it and headed back down the tor-tuously winding staircase, with Theo holding it from behind. There were five sharp turns in this staircase and with a 200-pound organ it would have been a difficult task on the best of days. But Theo claimed that he was still feeling the effects of the gas, and they had to stop several times so he could rest.

At last the organ was in place next to the piano in the Sunday school classroom. George and Theo went back to the library, where Theo took a key out of his pocket and unlocked it. As soon as the door opened, George could see his friend's hat, with his coat neatly folded underneath it; both were on top of a large box that stood taller than the table. It was funny he hadn't noticed them before, he thought, but possibly he was so concerned about locating the gas smell that he had focused only on getting into the closet.

Outside the church, George paused to lock the front door, then joined Theo on the front sidewalk by vaulting over the short fence. It was now a few minutes before 6:00.

"I'd better be moving along," George said; "I'm late for dinner."

"I'll walk along with you for a while," Theo said. "It will clear my head." Both young men lived a few blocks from the church, but in exactly opposite directions. At the corner of Capp and 22nd Streets, Theo said goodbye to George and turned back in the di-rection of his own house.[20] Along the way, he saw some neighbors he knew and stopped to talk with them as their children played in the street.[21]

A few minutes after 6:00 P.M., Theo entered his home at 1025 Fair Oaks. His parents were waiting for him to arrive so they could eat dinner.

"Finally, Theo!" his mother exclaimed as he kissed her. "Why are you so late?"

"I've been at the church, Mamma," he told her. "Some of the gas sunburners haven't been working right, and I fixed them this af-ternoon. Then George and I had to carry a cabinet organ down-stairs."

Mrs. Durrant noticed immediately that something was wrong with her son. Normally he had a healthy appetite, but tonight he looked sick and picked at his food.

"What's wrong, Theo?" she asked in a worried tone. "Are you

coming down with something?" Ever since his near-fatal illness of
the year before, she became alarmed at the smallest sign of sick-
ness in him.

"It's from the gas in the sunburners, Mamma," he told her. "I
think I was nearly asphyxiated from it, so I don't feel so well right
now. I left the gas turned on so I could work on the lights without
having to keep climbing down to shut it on and off. I'll be all
right—in fact, I'm feeling much better already. I took some Bromo-
Seltzer."

"That's good, dear," Mrs. Durrant said distractedly. "Papa, do
you have Maud's letter?"

Theo looked up quickly from his plate. "There's a letter from
Maud?"

"Here it is." Mr. Durrant held it out to him. "Why don't you read
it to us?"

Theo pushed his plate aside and began to read the letter from
his sister, who had left on February 14 to study music in Berlin.[22]
As he read, the horrible feelings he was experiencing fell from him
and his equilibrium came back.

God, how he missed Maud! He never dreamed it could be this
bad without her.[23] If only she hadn't gone away, everything would
still be all right.

Missing!

She is . . . rather taller than the majority of women; of a countenance somewhat grave and haughty, but on occasion brightening with humour or beaming with kindliness and affection. Too quick to detect affectation or insincerity in others, too impatient of dulness or pomposity, she is more sarcastic now. . . . Truth looks out of her bright eyes, and rises up armed, and flashes scorn or denial, perhaps too readily, when she encounters flattery, or meanness, or imposture.
—William Makepeace Thackeray, *The Newcomes*

Tryphena Noble was vaguely annoyed. Professor Schernstein had been waiting for fifteen minutes to give her niece, Blanche Lamont, her weekly violin lesson and she was still not home from school. Mrs. Noble was trying to make polite small talk with him, every minute expecting Blanche to come through the door.[1]

Perhaps the streetcars were running late, she told the elderly musician. And it was remotely possible that Blanche had gotten lost—after all, this was only her third day at the Normal School, and on the first day, Mrs. Noble had accompanied her to get her enrolled as a special student. Blanche herself had rescheduled her violin lesson to 4:00 to accommodate her new classes.

At 4:30 there was still no sign of Blanche, and Mrs. Noble's annoyance was turning to worry. Her niece had suffered a bout of typhoid fever the previous summer before coming to San Francisco. And there were those peculiar fainting spells she had, sometimes even on her way to school. Once, during a stressful exam, Blanche had passed out and remained unconscious for an unbelievable two hours.[2] Maybe she had taken sick on the way home.

Professor Schernstein left, promising to check back later to see what had happened to his errant pupil. This was not like Blanche, who was punctual and serious about her musical studies. She had begun advanced lessons with him shortly after Christmas (she was already quite an accomplished violinist), and in all that time had never missed one. He thought perhaps that in the excitement of starting at the Normal School she had forgotten the rescheduling.

Mrs. Noble sought out Blanche's sister, Maud, who was watching the young Noble boys, Karl and Paul, while their mother entertained the music teacher.

"Did Blanche say anything about doing something after school today?" she asked her niece.

"No, Auntie," Maud replied in a worried tone. "And it isn't like her to miss a lesson. I don't know what to think."

The Lamont girls were the daughters of Tryphena Noble's sister, Julia. Their whole family had moved to Dillon, Montana, in 1881, where David Lamont had first taken a job in a bank and later was appointed postmaster of the Dillon Post Office. The children consisted of Grace Julia, born in 1872; Mary Blanche, born in 1873; Maud Margaret, born in 1875; Rodger David, born in 1887; and Antoinette Marie, born in 1890.[3]

Julia Lamont already had her hands full with this growing family when her husband, David, died unexpectedly in 1892 at the age of 44. Grace, the eldest at age 20, took over as head of the family as far as financial support was concerned, and was appointed as her father's replacement at the post office. Julia helped out as clerk (as did all the children at times) and also took in boarders at their home on Orr Street. Rounding out the family finances was a small pension Julia got for her husband's brief service in the Civil War.[4]

Blanche was very ambitious and had no intention of ending up as a clerk in the Dillon Post Office for the rest of her life. For the school year of 1889–1890, she went back to the Lamonts' native town of Rockford, Illinois, and attended the Rockford Female Seminary (today Rockford College) for the preparatory course it offered to those who wished to proceed to the college-level, four-year course of studies. However, Blanche went back to Montana after that one year and never returned to Rockford for the remaining two.[5] Perhaps she was homesick for her family, or perhaps the Lamonts' financial situation would not permit more.

Still, Blanche was determined to have a career as a teacher. In the summer of 1893, she got a position teaching the miners' children in Hecla, Montana, a company town about thirty miles north of Dillon. That Christmas she attended the state teachers' convention in Butte (probably hoping to line up some job opportunities) and by spring of 1894 had a teaching contract with a district near Dillon for that fall.[6]

Unfortunately, Blanche contracted a serious illness over the summer, probably typhoid,[7] and that finished the teaching job. But she was chafing at the bit in Dillon, where the opportunities for upward mobility were few and the pool of eligible bachelors was both small and undesirable.[8] Her younger sister, Maud, had gone to San Francisco that June to live with their Auntie Noble and get a certificate to teach kindergarten.[9] Blanche wanted to go, too.

Blanche missed Maud, but more than that, she longed to live in an exciting city like San Francisco. And she could get a bona fide teaching certificate and improve her chances of getting a really good job. True, there was a normal school being started in Dillon, but delay after delay had put construction past its anticipated 1894 opening.[10]

Julia Lamont was not sure that Blanche was strong enough to make such a trip, nor that her sister, Tryphena, with growing children of her own, was up to adding yet another young woman to her care. But Blanche begged and pleaded, and for her trump card said that the sea air would be better for her health than the stifling, stuffy air of Dillon in the summer and its bitter winter cold. Julia, broken down in the end by her daughter's relentless pressure, gave her consent and Blanche left for San Francisco in mid-September 1894.[11]

A photographer named Henry Brown, traveling throughout the West in 1893, took two poses of Blanche and her twenty-nine Hecla students ranging in age from 3 to 13 (she herself was only 20), photos which reveal more of the real Blanche Lamont than the rather sickly, bland image that comes through in the "official" picture used for the trial.[12]

The Blanche in the Hecla pictures is attractive, spirited, a little saucy even. It is easy to imagine young men being smitten with her, and somewhat difficult to reconcile this young woman with the taciturn, passive, and passionless girl presented in the newspapers.

In fact, as with the photographs, there were two sides to Blanche Lamont. In new situations and with unfamiliar people, she was withdrawn and kept her own counsel. But with those she knew, she was outgoing and spunky, sometimes sarcastically witty. She was not above criticizing others, although seldom to their faces. Blanche sometimes had a romantic, dreamy side to her, but she was also independent, quick-tempered, practical (her aunt called her "systematic"), and ambitious. Although she was legally an adult, she often acted much younger. In other words, Blanche Lamont was not a boring, uncomplicated, one-sided person (as she is often presented), but a complex, vibrant, and interesting young woman in the process of discovering who she was.[13]

When Blanche got to San Francisco in September 1894, she was still recuperating. She had lost weight during her illness and was determined to get more robust. (In the 1890s, a hefty figure was more attractive than today's slim standard.) Maud took her sister to Dick Charlton's grocery store across the street from their aunt's house and talked the portly grocer into putting his scales on the floor so Blanche could weigh herself. On her 5'7" frame, 112 pounds made her look positively emaciated. Thereafter, the girls went over on occasional Friday evenings at 7:00 (Charlton's business was slow then) so Blanche could see what progress she was making. In late March 1895, the last time she was weighed, the scale registered a little over 115 pounds (although in mid-February—probably as a result of holiday cooking—she had gone all the way up to 121).[14]

Maud Lamont had been in San Francisco since late June 1894, and was attending her aunt's church, the Emmanuel Baptist near the Nobles' home in the Mission District. The Lamonts were Episcopalian, but in San Francisco they would worship with their aunt and uncle. On Blanche's first Sunday there, Tryphena Noble made a point of bringing both girls over to Theo Durrant and his sister, Maud.

"Theo, I would appreciate it if you and Miss Maud would show my nieces around," she told him. "I want them to have a good time while they're here." The Durrants assured her that they would take the Lamont girls under their wing and include them in the social activities of the church's young people.[15]

Gradually, Blanche began to take on more and more social and academic activities until by April 1895, she was booked nearly every day and night of the week. Every morning she took the street-cars to the Boys' High School (Lowell High) for classes in geometry, physics, and English as a special student.[16] Once a week she had violin lessons with Professor Charles Schernstein, and on Friday nights she rehearsed with the Grace Methodist Episcopal orchestra, where she played on Sundays. She was in the Emmanuel Baptist orchestra, too (as the times for services at the two churches were different), and there were rehearsals there as well.

After Emmanuel's services, Blanche stayed for Sunday school, and on Wednesday evenings there were prayer meetings which she sometimes attended. She and Maud joined the Young People's Christian Endeavor Society, with meetings once a week and socials once a month. And she joined a Reading Club, which met on Thursday evenings.

As a result of many of these activities (and surely one of her reasons for joining them), Blanche met several young men. There was Elbert Cowan, a fellow member of the Grace Church orchestra, who often walked her home after rehearsals; Tom Vogel, newly graduated from dental school, who sometimes walked her home from church meetings and also belonged to her Thursday reading group; Clarence Wolfe, whose stepfather was a church trustee and a former member of the city's Board of Supervisors; George King, the church organist (although he was younger and mostly walked home with Maud); and the very attentive Theo Durrant, assistant superintendent of Emmanuel's Sunday school and in his last year of medical school.

Blanche must have been elated at all the attention from such eminently respectable suitors. This was more like it! Even Harry Poindexter, an acquaintance from Dillon studying geology at Stanford University,[17] came to call a few times. But Harry lived too far away to be a serious contender. For all her seemingly calm exterior, Blanche could not repress her excitement over her newfound social popularity. In late March, she eagerly wrote to her sister Grace in Dillon that a dental student (surely Tom Vogel) was teaching her to ride a bicycle.[18] And several neighbors recalled seeing a frequent gentleman caller arrive on a bicycle and spend time with Blanche on the Nobles' porch.[19]

So, when Blanche had still not arrived home by dinnertime on Wednesday, April 3, it occurred to Maud (though certainly not to their aunt) that Blanche might have let her romantic nature get the better of her and eloped with one of her swains. When Auntie, who had to go to the evening prayer meeting to deliver a notice to the pastor, said she would have an announcement made about Blanche's disappearance, Maud was vehement in her attempt to discourage this.

"Don't say anything to anyone," she told Mrs. Noble. "If you do, they'll just gossip and then if Blanche comes back, it will be very awkward. Let's wait until Uncle Charlie comes home and see what he thinks should be done."

Tryphena Noble did not usually go to the Wednesday evening prayer meetings, mostly because her husband worked late and there was no one to watch Karl and Paul. Tonight she was only going because she needed to deliver the notice, so she would have to sit through the service and catch the pastor afterward. She took a seat in a back pew to be as inconspicuous as possible and hoped that no one would attempt to converse with her. She was sick with worry and felt the burden of responsibility for the welfare of her niece. What would she tell Julia?

As Mrs. Noble sat there lost in thought, a slightly built young man slipped into the pew ahead of her and turned around to face her. It was Theo Durrant.

"Will Blanche be coming tonight, Mrs. Noble?" he asked.

Mrs. Noble hesitated. Should she tell him the truth? Theo was such a trustworthy young man, and had been a friend of Blanche's before her niece decided in January that she wanted nothing more to do with him. But she remembered Maud's admonition, and instead she replied, "No, I don't believe she will be."

"I promised I'd bring her a book she needs for class, but I forgot it or I'd give it to you. I saw her this morning and she asked me to accompany her to the Boys' High School. She told me she has to read *The Newcomes* and I said she could use my copy. Tell her I'll bring it to services on Sunday."

"Well, she'll be glad to get the book," Mrs. Noble told him. "I know she's been wanting it." Blanche had come home from school on Tuesday with the literature assignment, but she didn't want to spend the money for it. She had asked her aunt if she knew where she could borrow a copy, and had reminded her again just that morning before leaving for school.[20]

On the way home, Tryphena Noble ruminated about Blanche's disappearance and on what Theo had told her. So, at least her niece had arrived at the school that morning. It was strange that she should ask Theo to escort her, though, as she was sure Blanche was still "on the outs" with him. Maybe the intervening months had mellowed her, and when she saw him she decided to let by-gones be bygones.

Shortly after being introduced to Blanche in September, Theo had begun escorting her and Maud home from church services and meetings. Often, George King would accompany them as Maud's escort (possibly at Theo's request).

Once, Theo showed up at the Nobles' with his sister, Maud, to ask if Blanche could go with them to a concert at the Methodist Church. But after the concert, Maud Durrant went off with some-one else and Theo escorted Blanche home alone.

On one Sunday after religion classes, Theo walked home with Blanche to ask Mrs. Noble if they could ride out to Golden Gate Park on the new trolley line. But no one was home except Maud, so they told her their destination and left. They stayed at the park longer than they intended and didn't arrive back at 209 21st Street until 5:30 or 6:00 that evening. Theo had felt bad about keeping Blanche out for so long, and came in to apologize to her aunt.

Mrs. Noble treated the incident lightly: "I'm not worried about either of you doing anything wrong," she told him. The idea of Blanche's being in any danger with Theo Durrant was laughable!

But around Christmastime, Blanche and Theo's relationship be-gan to change. Theo was getting too serious, and Blanche thought this was inappropriate after such a short time. Finally, on the way home after church one Sunday, Theo brought the matter to a head. He pulled an enormous ring out of his pocket and asked Blanche to marry him.

At first, Blanche thought he was kidding. "Um hmmmm," she said noncommittally, looking at the ring.

Theo pressed her to take it. "I'd better not," she told him. "I'll just lose it." Inside she was laughing at the ridiculousness of it all and the way he was being so ostentatious about the ring. Still, she did not refuse him outright, and he seemed to gather hope from this.

Over the next couple of weeks after Theo's proposal, Blanche heard church members talking about Flora Upton, Theo's fiancée. "The nerve of him!" she told her aunt. "Asking me to marry him when he's already engaged!"

After the Young People's meeting one night in early January, Theo asked Blanche to walk with him to his house on Fair Oaks so he could get a Christmas present he had for her. He had meant to bring it with him that evening, but had forgotten it, he told her. Blanche went with him, not because she wanted the present, but because she expected him to attempt to explain his engagement to Flo Upton. And if *he* didn't bring it up, *she* fully intended to. She couldn't wait to see him squirm over this!

When they arrived at the Durrant home, Blanche refused Theo's invitation to step inside while he got her gift. No one else seemed to be home, and it would be unseemly for her to go into the house of any man with no chaperone.

"Come on," he urged. "You'll freeze out there. You don't have to come all the way in—just to the foyer here." As he talked, he pressed a button and bright gaslight flooded the entryway. Finally, Blanche relented and stepped inside.

Theo dashed into the parlor and came out with a gaudily decorated red lampshade. "Look at the beautiful present someone made for my sister," he said. Then he sprinted upstairs and came down with her present: a padlock! He had bought one for himself also. (Mrs. Noble had thought it a strange sort of gift, but said nothing when Blanche told her.)

As they were about to leave to go back to the church, an odd thing happened: Theo extinguished the lights in the hallway and awkwardly put his arms around Blanche. She protested, and he quickly disengaged himself. "Please don't say anything about this," he begged her. "Did you think I was going to kiss you? Well, let it go; you will not understand it, but it was an impulse that I cannot explain. Forget it."

Back home, Blanche laughed as she related the incident to her aunt. Far from being offended by Theo's artless attempt, she was amused by his discomfiture.[21] But the next time he tried to walk her home, she confronted him about Flo Upton. "You should have told me you were engaged," she said sternly. Possibly she was relieved at having a graceful "out" so she wouldn't have to hurt his feelings with a definite refusal.

But Theo vigorously denied that he was engaged. Flo Upton was only a friend, he said, and busy gossipmongers at the church had joined them together. Yes, he was writing to her at her teaching job down in the Merced area, but only to sing the praises of Blanche Lamont. Blanche didn't believe him—or chose not to—and forbade him to walk her home.

In late January, Theo once more attempted to escort Blanche home, but she turned him away. "Do not follow me!" she said angrily. "From now on, I don't want to see you unless it's in a group!" Blanche did not think it was at all appropriate for her to be alone with another woman's fiancé.

Would Blanche have allowed Theo to court her if Flo Upton had not been in the picture? She did not seem to be serious about him, but possibly was not quite ready to dismiss a potentially desirable suitor (after all, he would soon be a doctor). However, she was often critical of him in speaking to her aunt and sister, making fun of his "so-called intelligence" and scorning what she saw as his lack of vocabulary and poor reading skills.[22] This doesn't sound like a young lady who is smitten with a beau or jealous of a rival.

When Tryphena Noble arrived home from the church on April 3, she could tell by Maud's face that Blanche still had not returned. Charles was home now and determined to go to the police the next morning if his niece was still missing. No one in the Noble household could sleep easily that night.

The next day, Thursday, April 4, Uncle Charlie went to the Police Department to see Chief of Detectives Isaiah Lees. To assure Lees of his reliability, Noble took with him a former city supervisor named Ryan, who asked Lees to supervise a search for Blanche as a personal favor to him. Since Blanche was 21, she would not be treated as a missing person until a longer time had passed. Ryan's influence assured quicker action, however, and that afternoon Lees assigned Detective Abraham Anthony to look into it. Anthony's first action on Friday was to go to the San Francisco Normal School to talk to students and teachers.

Meanwhile, by Friday, Maud and the Nobles had still not told any of their acquaintances of Blanche's disappearance. They were still hoping she would show up safely with no one the wiser. That morning at 8:45 Theodore Durrant came to the Nobles' door with a book in his hand. Maud answered the door, but didn't open it and didn't invite him in.

"Is Blanche at home?" he asked.

"She has to leave for school by 8:00," Maud said truthfully, if evasively. She thought it strange that he would expect Blanche to be home at such a late hour. And didn't he have classes to attend himself?

"I'm sorry to have missed her," Theo went on. "I'm on my way to the hospital and I have a book I promised her. Will you see that she gets it?" He handed her a copy of Thackeray's *The Newcomes.* [23]

Maud took the book and assured him Blanche would get it. Silently, she was wishing more than anything that she would be able to give the book to her sister, and soon.

And what was Maud herself doing home so late on a weekday? The fact is, even though her announced intention in going to San Francisco was to obtain a kindergarten teaching certificate, she had been there almost a year and had never taken a single class! She had taught at the Potrero Kindergarten for a week (probably as a substitute) and had even optimistically listed herself in the 1895–1896 City Directory as a kindergarten teacher, but Maud seems to have spent most of her time babysitting her little cousins and attending church activities. [24]

What is more probable is that Maud simply wanted to get out of Dillon for a while and experience life in the big city, and she (or her mother) felt that a legitimate reason was necessary for a two-year absence. There are some indications that Julia Lamont was not getting along well with her third daughter, and possibly everyone concerned needed a break. [25]

When Detective Anthony came by after his fact-finding mission at the City Normal School, he had news to report: Three students had seen Blanche get on a cable car with a young man. They described him as shorter than Blanche, with reddish hair and a slight mustache. The girls all said that Blanche and the young man seemed to know each other well. The Nobles were puzzled as to who this could be.

"Can you think of a friend who might have an idea where Blanche has gone?" Anthony asked them.

Immediately, the Nobles responded, "Tom Vogel," and off Detective Anthony went to interview him. Only later did they think of Theo Durrant.[26]

Maud and the Nobles felt that once Tom Vogel was interviewed, there would be no need to keep Blanche's disappearance a secret. So that Sunday, they had an announcement made at Emmanuel Baptist and asked for help from the congregation.

On Monday evening, Tom Vogel and Theo Durrant stopped by the Nobles' to offer their sympathy and their assistance in finding Blanche. Their friend, Clarence Wolfe, claimed to have a working acquaintance with houses of ill repute, ostensibly through his days as a lineman with the fire department, and he knew about some that even the police didn't know about. The two boys said they would accompany Wolfe to these. Maybe Blanche had been abducted and sold into white slavery (it was not unknown on the Barbary Coast), or maybe she had been lured there by someone. She was so innocent and trusting, Theo said, that she just assumed everyone else was as good as she was. It wouldn't take much to fool her into going somewhere.

Charles Noble was a little shocked by this talk of houses of prostitution. "I don't think those are appropriate places for young men to be going," he told them. (But later that week, Tom Vogel would go back to the Nobles', this time with the worldly Clarence Wolfe, and restate the offer.)

As Tom and Theo were leaving, Mrs. Noble told them, "Maud feels so bad—this is just awful for her."

Theo put his hand on Maud's arm in sympathy. "You must not give way," he told her. "Blanche will be back soon and everything will be all right. And if you need a friend, come to Emmanuel Baptist Church."

On Tuesday, April 9, when there was still no definite word of Blanche, Maud went down to the *Examiner* and placed an ad in the personals to run for the next few days: "Blanche—No matter what has happened, come back to me. Maud"[27]

The following day, Wednesday, April 10, when Blanche had been gone a week, articles concerning the disappearance appeared in both the *Examiner* and the *Chronicle*. The reporters had obviously found out about the "mysterious young man" seen by the three Normal School students, and Mrs. Noble is quoted as vigorously denying any elopement possibility. According to her, Blanche had few male friends, was not interested in men, and never went out with any![28]

Why would Mrs. Noble make such a statement? It may be that, because Tom Vogel and Theo Durrant had suggested that Blanche might be in a house of prostitution, albeit involuntarily, Mrs. Noble wanted to say nothing which could in any way be construed as insinuating that her niece was "loose." Or it could be that she was really not aware of the extent of Blanche's social life. Most of the information about gentlemen callers comes from Maud, and her cryptic message in the newspaper seems to indicate that she, at least, entertained the possibility that some indiscretion on Blanche's part was the cause of her disappearance.

After his interview with Tom Vogel, Detective Anthony went back to see the Nobles and told them that Vogel had thought the description of the young man seen by the three schoolgirls fit Theo Durrant. What about him? Anthony asked them. Could Durrant have had anything to do with Blanche's disappearance?

"That's not possible," Charles Noble told the detective. "Theodore is not that kind of a man." And, as Anthony was leaving, Mrs. Noble assured him that he was on the wrong track: "Theodore had as much to do with poor Blanche's disappearance as you."[29]

Then, on Holy Saturday, April 13, Tryphena Noble received a strange package in the morning mail. On the outside wrapper was crudely printed "Mrs. Noble, 209—21st St., City," and inside that was a page from the *Examiner*. On various blank sections of the newspaper were written the names "George R. King" and "Prof. Shoenstein" [*sic*] in spidery handwriting as if by an elderly person;[30] and "Geo. R. King" in regular signature format. Inside the newspaper was another, smaller paper, and in this were wrapped three rings.

They were the rings belonging to Blanche Lamont.

The Durrants of Toronto

Turning and turning in the widening gyre
The falcon cannot hear the falconer;
Things fall apart; the center cannot hold;
Mere anarchy is loosed upon the world,

The blood-dimmed tide is loosed, and everywhere
The ceremony of innocence is drowned.
                    —from "The Second Coming" by William Butler Yeats

Like most people in California in the nineteenth century (and, indeed, even today, although to a lesser extent), the Durrants were from somewhere else. California was the land of golden opportunity, and the inhabitants of San Francisco's Mission District in 1895 had their roots in Ohio, Mississippi, Tennessee, New Hampshire, New York, Canada, South America, Germany, and elsewhere.

William Allan Durrant's people were originally from Norfolk, England, but his parents, Thomas and Mary, had emigrated to Toronto, Canada, with their large brood of children in the late 1840s. William was born there in about 1850 and eventually learned his father's trade of shoemaking.[1]

Isabella Matilda Hutchinson was born in Oakville, Ontario, in 1852. When her mother died, she was placed in the home of a woman named Mrs. Dredger and raised by her. The very spirited Isabella and the dour Mrs. Dredger did not get along well. Mrs. Dredger was a strict Presbyterian who did not believe in dancing (which Isabella loved) or in doing any work on the Sabbath—not even washing the dishes or making the beds. The family went to church services twice every Sunday and the children also went twice to Sunday school classes.

Isabella made her escape as soon as she was old enough to be on her own. She moved to Toronto and began working in the Charles and Hamilton shoe factory. There she met William Durrant, and they were married on June 30, 1870.[2]

What the lively, tireless, ambitious Isabella Hutchinson saw in the drab, passive William Durrant is a mystery. Perhaps she saw a project, someone whose life she could direct without his objecting; perhaps she saw in him (erroneously, as it would turn out) her financial security; or, perhaps it was simply the old adage at work: opposites attract.

William and Isabella wasted no time in starting a family. Their first child, William Henry Theodore, was born on April 24, 1871, followed by Ulla Maude Alma (she would later drop the "e" from her second name) on August 27, 1873, and Edward Thomas on December 13, 1876. Little Edward did not live long, dying of what was called "infantile convulsions" on January 6, 1877, at the age of three weeks.[3]

It was about this time that William Durrant became ill and had to go to England for treatment. It is never specified as to what this illness was, but from what is known of William's personality and behavior, it is very likely that he suffered from manic depression.[4] Isabella had to take in sewing to support her family.

When William returned in about 1878, he decided to move to San Francisco, where his parents were then living, and left Isabella and the children in Toronto until he could find a place for them all to live. Once again, Isabella was without her husband for a year, and Theo and Maud were without their father. It probably would have happened anyway because of her very strong and domineering personality, but these prolonged absences on the part of William caused Isabella to focus all her emotional energy on the lives of her two surviving children. Call it bonding, call it imprinting, call it what you will—but the end result was that these two children returned that emotional focus, and Papa was destined to be little more than a bench player in the family dynamics until his son's difficulties in 1895.

Finally, William Durrant was able to send for his family, and in early December 1879, Isabella left for San Francisco with Theo, then 8, and Maud, 6. En route, they had an adventure at a train rest stop in the "Wild West." Isabella had taken the children off the train to see the wares being sold by the local American Indians, but when it was time to get back on the train, Maud was nowhere to be found. A frantic Isabella suddenly caught sight of some reddish-blond hair flowing out from a blanket being carried away by two Indian women, and little Maud was rescued from her would-be kidnappers. Had her hair not been so distinctive in color, Maud would probably not have been noticed.[5]

The Durrants lived at 219 Hayes Street, opposite St. Ignatius College (today the University of San Francisco), for a year or two, at which point Theo and Maud were sent to board in Santa Rosa for six months because of an unspecified health problem of Maud's. William and Isabella rented rooms from a woman at 5th and Jessie Streets during this time, and when the children came back to the city, the whole family moved in with William's parents at 305 Fell Street.[6]

Given William's later sporadic and unsuccessful work history, it is possible that at this time the family finances were suffering, which necessitated their living with the senior Durrants. This situation lasted for about five years, when William and Isabella finally were able to purchase their own home in 1888 (possibly with Thomas Durrant's help) at 1025 Fair Oaks Street in the Mission District.[7]

Theo had attended private school in Toronto, but in San Francisco he went to a public school: the Lincoln Grammar School, from which he graduated with a high school diploma in 1888, just about the time the Durrants were moving into their new home. After high school, he went to the Cogswell Polytechnical College[8] (where Maud joined him after her own high school years) and graduated in 1891. The college was only a few blocks away from the Durrant home, so Theo and Maud walked back and forth together.

At Cogswell, Theo was an average student, doing better at

courses where he could use his hands. He excelled at architectural sketching as well as the electrical and mechanical classes, but did poorly in courses requiring conceptual thinking.[9] Socially, he was well-liked, but quiet and reserved, sharing little about himself.

Theo and two of his classmates, Jim Crosett and Dick Allen, got together something they called the Peanut Line, a telegraph system hooking up their houses so they could get academic help from each other. Other students gradually found out about it, and the boys ended up increasing the line to nearly the entire student body, in essence creating a campus-wide "chat room" for homework assistance.[10]

After graduation, Theo, Jim, and Dick renamed their company The Independent Telegraph Line and did a fairly booming business in the Mission District. (Once people in the Victorian era figured out they could send recipes, homework, or love letters through the telegraph, it became as much a craze as e-mail would one hundred years later, and hundreds of independent companies—service providers—sprang up.) By April 1895, the boys had plans for expanding the line.

Theo was a genius when it came to anything mechanical or electrical, and he wanted to study engineering even after Cogswell. He registered at Stanford University for the 1891–1892 academic year, but did not go back to Palo Alto after that.[11] It was never specified as to why he did not, but once again the family finances might have dictated that he attend school closer to home. In 1893 he enrolled in San Francisco's Cooper Medical College (today the Stanford University Medical School) and was scheduled to graduate on December 5, 1895.

It was not exactly Theo's idea to become a doctor. Left to his own devices, he would have continued in engineering. But Isabella Durrant wanted her children to move up in the world, and she chose this career for him. Her cousin, Dr. Clarke, wanted to enter the ministry, and gave Theo the chance to take over his medical practice. Mamma saw this as a great opportunity for her son to advance in life, so Theo was enrolled at Cooper.[12]

This is not to say that Theo was reluctant to become a physician. He had inherited his mother's ambition and drive, and threw himself completely into his medical studies. And, of course, he wanted to please her. But, ultimately, the choice was not his own, and there were signs that he had gotten in a little over his head. Although he had a 97 percent average in all his courses in April 1895, it was not without a price. It was necessary for him to take extremely meticulous lecture notes (so detailed and thorough were they that other students borrowed them to copy), and then stay up late many nights to go over them. And he became anxious about his attendance, often checking with the professor after the class to make sure he had been counted present so as not to lose points. Even then, he failed some exams and had to repeat them before being allowed to continue. Despite Theo's eventual high grade point average, Cooper was no walk in the park for him.[13]

But he was no stranger to hard work. From the time he was a senior in high school, and all throughout his career at Cogswell Poly, Theo got up early to deliver the *Morning Call*, one of San Francisco's six daily newspapers. He wanted to help out with his education, and he also wanted to buy himself a bicycle.[14]

Theo had fallen in love with the new fad of bicycling, and learned to ride a high-wheeled "ordinary." But they were expensive, even by today's standards, averaging $200–$300. Theo got one for $185, then paid $100 more for the "safety" version that came into prominence in the mid-1890s. The "safety" bicycle, which resembles today's mountain bike, made it possible for women to ride, too, and they took to it in droves. So Theo saved up his money again and bought Maud one.[15]

Theo would frequently ride around the gold country counties of Tuolumne, Amador, and Calaveras (where a tall tale about a frog had jump-started the career of Mark Twain), and soon got to know those scenic back roads as well as the streets of the city where he lived.

One summer, Theo and a friend packed their bicycles and took a long trip to Yosemite, sometimes camping out and sometimes wheedling beds and meals from hotel owners. In typical Theo fashion, he made many friends on the trip, some of whom were still in contact with him in April 1895.[16]

Theo's cycling activities and his generally active lifestyle gave him a lean, wiry body. Physically, he was short, at 5'5" a few inches shorter than the average 1890s male. His feet were small (size 7B) and his head was small and oddly shaped (size 7, but he had to wear soft hats that would mold to his head).[17] His hazel eyes were farther apart than normal (as were his mother's and his sister's), his lips were thick, and his left ear stuck out.

Still, despite his physical shortcomings, Theo Durrant was not unattractive. He had a certain style about him. He had only a few clothes, but they were well-chosen and well-fitting. (When a piece of clothing went out of style, Theo simply wouldn't wear it in public, even if it was still in good shape.)[18] He was particular, even fussy, about his appearance and liked the new pompadour look for his hair. Not only was it fashionable, but the slightly longer hairstyle offset his protruding ear and the odd shape of his head.

Theo earned money for his schooling in other ways besides delivering papers. He worked for the insurance company of Mannheim, Dibbern for a while, and for all his vacations clerked at a large department store called the Golden Rule Bazaar (later merged with The Emporium) on Market Street in downtown San Francisco. If he had any spare time after that, he took on whatever electrical jobs he could get.[19]

However, Theo's ambition did not come from greed. He was generous with his talents and his time, often helping people with electrical problems at no charge. He rewired the home of the Durrants' neighbor, Joseph "Pop" Perkins, as well as that of his parents, so that the gas lights could be turned on with the press of a button. He constructed a back porch for the Durrant home, put in some honeysuckle to grow up its side, and dug out a pond on the property. As a member of the Emmanuel Baptist Church, he was an unpaid handyman, gladly rewiring the church for convenience, building a stage for entertainments, and fixing anything that got out of order. In fact, in the manner of churches everywhere, Emmanuel Baptist took advantage of Theo's good-natured willingness to provide free services.

Theo's kindness, gentleness, and selflessness were hallmarks of his personality from a very early age. In fact, he was so unusually generous as a little boy that one of Isabella's visitors commented that she "never saw such a child for dividing everything he got." When he was older and working, he was constantly bringing gifts home to Mamma and Maud.

On a family trip to the Russian River one summer, Theo taught a little girl how to swim. That same summer, he and Maud saw that two swimmers were in trouble: a large, heavy-set woman and a two-year-old child. Theo rescued the woman while Maud got the toddler. Another time, Theo nursed a duck back to health after it had been badly mauled by a dog.

When Theo's grandparents were in the process of moving to Los Angeles in 1894, they gave Theo a few chickens to raise (eggs were very expensive at the turn of the century, and many people, even in the city, had chickens). He spent hours building a comfortable coop for them, then bought some baby chicks at 10 cents apiece. Not wanting them to miss their mother, Theo concocted a flannel substitute. And, so they wouldn't catch cold, he placed a lamp inside a round container in the center of the box. During the night the lamp overheated, and in the morning when he came down to breakfast, he was informed (one can imagine the casual tone in which this was said and the effect it must have had on him) that "your little chickens are all smothered."

Theo dashed down to the basement to rescue the chicks (why didn't the family member who noticed them do something?) and spent the next hour washing the black soot off their downy little bodies.

In 1893, Theo joined the Signal Corps of the California National Guard as a bugler (he could play several musical instruments). He loved going to the Thursday night meetings and then off with the guys on the occasional weekend training expeditions. And how he loved wearing the full dress uniform! He was very particular about his looks and his clothing, and the uniform made him look terrific.[20]

In the summer of 1894, the Pullman workers' strike spread across the country from Chicago, and paralyzed the Sacramento railroad. The National Guard was dispatched from San Francisco (many of the Sacramento members broke ranks and joined the local strikers) to break it up and get the trains through, and Theo's Second Brigade went up to the capital under the direction of 45-year-old General John H. Dickinson, a San Francisco attorney. At the end of three weeks, they came home when the president sent in federal troops.[21]

In the spring of that same year, Theo came down with a nearly-fatal case of meningitis (called "brain fever" back then). There were no antibiotics in those days, and survival often depended on the luck of the draw. Mamma nursed him with an obsessive devotion that paid off: After seven weeks, Theo turned the corner of the crisis and began the long, slow road to recovery. While he had lain ill, feverish, and hallucinatory, he lost a lot of weight, down from his usual 130 pounds to a mere 90. By April 1895, he was up to

115. But, although his recovery was complete, there was undoubtedly some neurological damage to his brain.[22]

From the time he was very small, Theo showed a religious bent, and by April 1895 was thoroughly involved with the Emmanuel Baptist Church. He was the assistant superintendent of the Sunday school (and was about to be appointed superintendent), an usher at the services, secretary of the Young People's Christian Endeavor Society, singer in the choir (he could sing both tenor *and* bass), a member of the orchestra, and an attendant at three weekly services: two on Sunday and one on Wednesday evenings. Theo went to church more often than his parents, who usually attended only one of the Sunday services. Emmanuel was a second home to him.[23]

Activities for young people at Emmanuel Baptist were numerous, and that included outings with the Sunday school. On one of these, a picnic in Marin County, Theo and his friends commented on the pall cast on the landscape by the ominous buildings of San Quentin Prison, and wondered about the ogres and devils incarcerated there. It represented a world completely foreign to their own reality.[24]

Another one of Theo's favorite pastimes was performing in theatrical productions, preferably musical ones. By the age of 8, he had played a small scene-stealing role in the enormously popular Gilbert and Sullivan comic opera, *H.M.S. Pinafore*.[25]

Also from a young age, Theo became extremely attached to his sister, concentrating his entire emotional focus on her and his mother. Unlike most older brothers, he gladly did everything with his little sister, escorting her to Saturday matinees, to concerts, church, and school. He treated her with great respect, carrying her coat or books, opening doors, pulling out her chair, and in general acting as if she were his date instead of his sister. He even held her hand as they went to the matinees. His behavior toward her was so unusual that people commented on it and said what a good boy Theo was.

Maud was tall, attractive, and musically gifted, whereas Theo was short, bordering on homely (at 23, he was still battling acne),[26] and only average in music. Still, instead of being jealous of his sister, Theo was immensely proud of her, singing her praises to all who would listen. There was nothing that was too much trouble for him to do for Maud.

Together with Maud, Isabella Durrant comprised the very center of Theo's emotional life. Far from being uncomfortable with this, however, Mamma reveled in and encouraged her son's attachment to her. She charted the path of his career, "discussed" with him the best uses of his money, and kept track of his comings and goings. She monitored his social acquaintances to make sure they were "the right kind," and instituted his practice (which he may have wanted to do on his own anyway) of kissing her whenever he left or returned to the house. She gave both her children constant directives for behavior ("Stand up straight." "Keep yourself neat and clean." "Don't use slang.").[27]

As Theo got older, it became increasingly clear that he had become an emotional substitute for Isabella's manic-depressive husband, who frequently could not rouse himself to take care of things, such as ordering coal. In the last months of 1894, Papa was unemployed and the Durrants took in a boarder: 18-year-old Joseph Browder, a messenger boy with the Edison Light Company.[28]

Most of Papa's business ideas proved to be failures (what Theo would charitably characterize as his father's "ill luck or nonsuccess").[29] To make things even worse, Papa came home one day around Christmastime 1894, wild-eyed with excitement over a get-rich-quick scheme proposed to him by a stranger. The stranger assured him he would greatly multiply whatever investment he put into the plan, so Papa took out the equity in the Durrant home, all the cash from the savings accounts, left his family some money for supplies, and took off to meet the stranger, whose name was Nicholson, in Pennsylvania.

Papa stopped at a boarding house in Philadelphia (most likely suggested by Nicholson) and put his money in the family's safe. The next morning it was discovered that the safe had been burgled and the family claimed to have been drugged.

This episode left Papa so depressed that he literally could not get out of his bed for a week. When the mood passed, he managed to track Nicholson down and found out that the get-rich-quick scheme involved a "green goods" scam: passing counterfeit money. Some people in San Francisco were so disbelieving that a man could get into a scheme without knowing what it was in advance that they said Papa had known all along about the counterfeit money. Better to be a knave than a fool.

When Papa got home, without thinking to notify the police back in Philadelphia, it was Mamma who intuited, supposedly through a dream, that the boarding home people were in on the theft with Nicholson. Theo reported the incident to a private detective, Peter Chappelle, in the hopes that something could be done to get Papa's (*their*) money back.

But if Papa was not the emotional focus of the family nor an adequate financial provider, he nonetheless cherished his family. He both loved and feared his wife and seldom crossed her; his dependence on her was absolute. His devotion to his two children never wavered, and there was nothing he would not have done for them. They, in turn, loved their father very much, even if at times he was distracted and difficult.

During the time that William Durrant was away over Christmas, Theo was the man of the house even more than usual. He was on his vacation from Cooper and working every day at the Golden Rule Bazaar to pay his medical school expenses and help support the family. And every day at noon, pretty, buxom, 16-year-old Edna Lucile Turner, a fellow Emmanuel Baptist member, would stop by to see if he had eaten his lunch yet. He hadn't . . . so she would wait for his break and go with him to the nearby Creamerie Restaurant for a 10-cent lunch. (But then Mamma would come by to walk home with him after work, undoubtedly throwing him into a state of guilt and emotional confusion.)[30]

Theo looked forward to Lucile's visits. He felt he could be more himself with her, as she could be both feminine and "one of the boys." She encouraged him to talk about himself, which he didn't always like to do, and her lack of sophistication made him feel more comfortable. She was young, but then so was he, emotionally speaking.

Back home, Mamma was increasing her obsessional hold on her son. Possibly claiming to be frightened with Papa away, she often got Theo to share her bed. Although it is unlikely that any untoward contact took place, it was nevertheless unseemly and highly inappropriate—especially as she and her husband had ceased sharing a bedroom.[31]

Probably the most influential event in Theo Durrant's growth and development around this time was his entry into medical school—which, ironically, had been Mamma's idea. Although he would not be boarding there, he would be attending a school away from his immediate neighborhood and without his sister. There he would get a crash course in how other boys were developing into men. And it would be an eye-opener for him.

When Theo began his classes at Cooper Medical College in 1893, he confessed to his classmate and neighbor, Harry Partridge, that he had no sexual experience. It is probable that there was quite a bit of locker room-style bragging among the medical students, whether of real or imagined incidents, and Theo must have felt himself to be way behind in this regard. He very much wanted to be accepted by his fellows, so he began to brag as well. He talked of intimacies he had supposedly experienced with girls from church and with prostitutes. He talked about women so much that Harry Partridge began to think he had gone "nutty" on the subject. But, as Mamma closely monitored Theo's comings and goings, and as he was quite prudish about women, it is more likely that Theo was a virgin.[32]

It was said at the time that Blanche Lamont was a romantic, and it's possible she was. But Theo Durrant was definitely so, with ideas about women and love that were almost medieval, much of which he gleaned from novels. He seemed to revere women, to put them on a pedestal, and to expect of them—as did many men in the nineteenth century—a higher standard of behavior. He does not seem to have been at all enthusiastic about the concept of the "new woman," independent and enfranchised, that was so heavily discussed in the waning years of that century.

Once, Theo and Karl Partridge (Harry's brother) were walking downtown when two female acquaintances of Theo's approached. They were somewhat bold in asking if he would treat them to a drink, but Theo gallantly escorted them through the back door of a nearby saloon (ladies were not allowed to use the front door). Theo ordered a Queen Charlotte, a prissy drink comparable to today's wine spritzer, and the girls ordered . . . beer! Theo later confessed to Karl Partridge that he was shocked they had drunk beer.[33]

Another time, a fellow worker at the Golden Rule suggested they take some young women to a place called the Grotto, but Theo said this was definitely not a proper place to take a lady. In fact, he went on, if he found out that someone had taken his sister there, he would shoot her![34] It is an interesting choice: shoot HER and not the cad who took her there. The implication is that her reputation would be already sullied, perhaps beyond repair. Better to be dead than disreputable.

Back on the Cooper campus, Theo continued his campaign of seeming worldly. He smoked cigarettes, although he never did elsewhere (even though his father smoked them, Theo must have considered cigarettes unseemly). Smoking was not allowed in the college building, so the boys stood outside at their breaks. One time a streetcar was going by with some of the Emmanuel Baptist church ladies on it, and Theo quickly put out his cigarette. "Do you think they saw me?" he asked his companion. "Who?" the other one asked. "The ladies on the streetcar. I wouldn't have them see me smoking for a good deal."[35]

Teased by someone about all the time he spent at church, Theo said he only did that to "work the room," to get clients for when he would be practicing medicine.[36] This was patently false; no one who was merely interested in business prospects would spend nearly all his spare time in church activities. But the lie made him seem clever, modern, and worldly—an image he wanted to project.

Later, many people would label Theo a hypocrite for his two-sided behavior at home and at school. However, there is little doubt that the "real" Theo was the unsophisticated, innocent boy engaging in the time-honored tradition of attempting to fit in with his peers.

And something else was happening to Theo over the course of his years at Cooper: He was trying out some baby wings of independence in an attempt to create a life apart from Mamma. For one thing, he bought a couple of padlocks to put on his dresser and his desk at home, most likely to keep Mamma from prying.[37] What did he have to hide? Victorian pornographic playing cards? Letters from young ladies? Or was it just the principle of the thing, as it has ever been for young people in their search for individuality?

Whatever reason he had for privacy, Theo seems not to have been able to bring himself to force a confrontation with Mamma by installing the padlocks ("Why is this locked, Theo? What are you hiding in here?"). In the end, he gave one of them as a Christmas gift to Blanche Lamont (who may have been having privacy issues of her own at her aunt's house) and put the second one on the library door at the church.

While at church, Theo spent much of his time hanging out with the young women. Later, people would read sinister meaning into this, but the truth was that Theo felt more comfortable with women. He had never played with boys as a child, limiting himself to his sister's company, and even had many feminine qualities besides his personal grooming. (His bedroom was so neat that a newspaper reporter compared it to a girl's.) Perhaps he felt girls to be less critical of him. And he didn't have to adopt the "worldly" stance he tried to affect at Cooper.[38]

Still, Theo *was* noticing girls. There was, of course, the lovely Lucile Turner (whom one observer termed a "Juno Robusto"), who had come to San Francisco in May 1894, to live with her aunt, Dr. Tom Vogel's mother, after her mother died. Lucile was attending the California School of Mechanical Arts, a kind of technical high school founded by James Lick. She also spent much time at the Emmanuel Baptist Church, teaching in the Sunday school, attending the Young People's meetings, and—beginning in February 1895—helping Theo and George King with the fledgling library.[39]

The church library was Theo's pride and joy. His goal was to make it the best church library in San Francisco, and that goal was very close to being fulfilled. When he and George began in February, they had one hundred books donated by the members. By the time their March drive ended (more like a "push," really), they had amassed nearly four hundred. Theo, George, and Lucile spent much time at the church cataloging all the books and trying to find room for them in the tiny library space.[40]

So Theo and Lucile spent a lot of time together. Did he have a crush on her? Probably not. He seems to have regarded her as more of a sister than a girlfriend, but Lucile may have felt something more for him. She certainly sought him out frequently enough. And she may have been somewhat jealous of the girls he actually courted.

Another young woman who spent a good deal of time with Theo was Flora Upton, an attractive, quiet, and completely nonthreatening girl a year older than he. When Flo's mother, Rosa, died in 1888, Flo and her father, Charles Upton, moved in with her Aunt Roxie Davis and Roxie's husband, George, a physician. Flo had graduated from the San Jose Normal School and after that got a job as a governess and teacher in the small town of Minturn in Madera County (near present-day Chowchilla). She was away from San Francisco a lot, and that probably appealed to an uncertain Theo.[41]

Theo and Flo became semiengaged around the fall of 1893. It was a semiengagement in that nothing was officially announced and there was no wedding date set. The understanding was that, at some point after Theo graduated from medical school and got established in his practice, the marriage would take place. The arrangement must have pleased Theo: It gave him some credibility in the world of grown-up men without actually tying him down or requiring his daily attention to Flo. Despite his admiration for her, Theo doesn't seem to have been in love with her.

Around the same time as his engagement to Flo Upton, Theo met another girl at Emmanuel Baptist, someone totally different from the young women he normally encountered: Minnie Williams, a tiny, feisty, talkative sprite who made her living by working in other people's homes. As a "working girl," Minnie was neither college-bound nor a suitable marriage prospect for an aspiring doctor—as Mamma informed Theo numerous times.[42]

It may be that Minnie's lower-class status was the source of her attraction for Theo. Although she was not an improper young lady, there were aspects of Minnie that might have led him to believe she would allow him to gain that sexual experience he was bragging about at school. And, sad to say, he does not seem to have respected her as much as he did the other young women of his acquaintance.[43]

Theo never intended to make Minnie a serious part of his life. For one thing, Mamma would not have allowed it, and Theo—despite his attempts at independence—would not have gone against Mamma on such an important issue. It was enough of a rebellion simply to date Minnie. Whenever Mamma was around, Theo ignored Minnie, acting as if he didn't even know her. Later he would try to make it up with her, avowing a love he did not feel.[44]

Once during the summer of 1894, Theo saw his chance. He had called for Minnie at her residence in Alameda, across the Bay, to take her on a picnic to a scenic area in Fruitvale. She must have given him some encouragement (for one thing, it was she who selected the location) because it is inconceivable that he would have proposed sexual intimacy out of the blue, but later it would be presented as one more proof of his innate degeneracy.

At any rate, Theo suggested that they take advantage of the scenery and the seclusion, assured her of his love for her, and said that as a medical student he knew how to take care of any "problems" that might arise as a result of the encounter. But Minnie indignantly refused, and Theo meekly backed down. He could have pressed the issue—there was no one around to stop him—but he did not. And, although Minnie later claimed to have been grossly insulted by his proposal, she did not stop seeing him.[45]

On another occasion, during a Young People's social at his house, Theo took Minnie up to his bedroom, a daring thing for him to do with Mamma in the house, and a daring thing for Minnie to do (a lady was not supposed to go alone into a gentleman's bedroom). They did nothing but talk, and Minnie later said she had enjoyed their conversation (and probably the fact that he had singled her out as someone special). Was this another way for Theo to assert his independence from his mother?[46]

Theo continued to see Minnie without his mother's knowledge, but in September 1894, something happened to threaten whatever relationship he had with her: the arrival of Blanche Lamont from Montana. Theo was immediately taken with Blanche, not merely because of her large brown eyes and winsome smile, but because she reminded him of his sister. Like Maud and Lucile Turner, Blanche was taller than the average woman in 1895. And, like his sister, Blanche was shy at first, but full of life and energy when she got to know someone. She captivated Theo completely, and he neglected little Minnie Williams during the time he was pursuing her.

A mere three months after he had met her, Theo asked Blanche Lamont to marry him. He had little romantic experience, and mistakenly thought that waving a large ring in her face would impress her (possibly something he picked up from the many books he read). She didn't give him a definite answer, but she didn't out-and-out refuse him, either. Theo hoped he could influence her to say "yes."[47]

Soon, however, things fell apart for Theo's chances with Blanche. She confronted him about his engagement to Flo Upton and, although he hotly denied it (how he wished he had never consented to that arrangement!), Blanche did not believe him. She turned cool toward him and, by the beginning of January, was not spending much time with him.

Around this time, Lucile Turner was having problems of a gynecological nature.[48] Embarrassed to discuss them with a physician, or even her aunt, she nonetheless went to her buddy, Theo, for advice. Still, she was hesitant to talk about it out loud, so Theo wrote out a series of questions for her to answer. From the information she gave him, he either prescribed some kind of medicine, or got it for her himself; whichever it was, the medicine relieved her problem to a great extent.

One Sunday after church, when Theo was walking Lucile home (Blanche having indicated her unwillingness to have him escort her), he asked if her problem had gone away. No, she told him, she still had it, although not as badly as before.

"You probably need a physical examination to see what's going on in there," he told her. "If you want, I can do it for you. There's a place in the church that will give us complete privacy."

"No, thanks," Lucile said. "I guess maybe I'll have my folks arrange something for me."

Later, Lucile would claim to have been outraged by Theo's suggestion, but all the evidence indicates that she did not take it in any improper light at the time. She didn't slam the door in his face (as she later said she did), she didn't bother to mention it to anyone, and she didn't stop being friends with him. In April, when everyone Theo knew was becoming famous and giving stories to the press, Lucile would barter their friendship for fifteen minutes of fame by regaling newspaper reporters with the story of her "narrow escape" from his clutches.

Was Theo's motive in suggesting the examination completely medical, or was he once more attempting in his bumbling way to gain sexual experience? Blanche's rebuff must have hurt him, and maybe he thought Lucile—whose admiration for him was obvious—would make a good rebound girlfriend. On the other hand, there is nothing in the relationship between Lucile and Theo that ever indicated he had either sexual or romantic feelings for her, and Lucile herself seems to have taken the offer completely in stride at the time.

The year 1895 was not shaping up to be a good one for Theo Durrant. The love of his life was spurning him, and now an even bigger blow was facing him: the departure of his beloved sister, his emotional mainstay. Maud, a gifted pianist, had progressed as far as she could in San Francisco, and her teachers suggested that she go to Berlin to study with the masters. Theo knew this was his sister's big chance, but he didn't think he could bear to be away from her.

So Mamma, Maud, and Theo concocted a plan: After Theo's graduation from Cooper in December, he and Mamma (nothing was ever said about Papa's joining them) would go to Berlin where Theo would do postgraduate medical studies and squire his two "girls" around Europe. Presumably, Mamma's function would be to direct her children's lives, as she had done in San Francisco. It was a plan that Theo kept before him always, as it helped lessen the pain of Maud's absence.[49]

Maud left for Berlin on February 14, 1895, and a small group of friends and family gathered to see her off. Among those friends was Minnie Williams. Theo gave Maud a diary to make sure she would write down her experiences. Brother and sister hugged each other tightly in farewell, and Maud whispered in his ear: "Be a good boy, dearie, and be sure to graduate."[50]

Soon after Maud's departure, Theo began to go across the Bay again to visit Minnie Williams. Minnie was a little miffed at his neglect of her during his Blanche phase, but she accepted him back. From her point of view, a good marriage prospect should not be tossed away lightly.

One night in late February, Lucile Turner arrived at Emmanuel Baptist for Sunday evening services and noticed Theo sitting in a pew with his head on his hand and his face hidden. He looked so despondent that she slipped in beside him and tried to joke him out of his mood, but he would not respond. So she resorted to their old method of corresponding on the flyleaves of hymnals.[51] She wrote:

"Are you sleepy or broken-hearted? Either or both? You are not yourself for some reason or other that I can't divine." She passed it over to him and he wrote underneath it:

"I know it and I can't help it."

Lucile knew that Flo Upton had made a very recent and very brief visit to the city, and assumed this was the cause of Theo's sadness. So she wrote back:

"Because she has gone, do you mean?"

"That is a natural course of events now, the going away part."

"Money matters or love, one or the other I know it is," Lucile responded on the flyleaf.

"No; it is something 100-fold greater in importance to me."

At the time, of course, Lucile assumed it referred to Flo Upton. But that wouldn't make sense, with his comment about "the going away part" being in the "natural course of events." If they were to be married, eventually there would be no going away. And his statement that what was bothering him was more important than love would militate against that, too.

Lucile would later attempt to place this conversation at a time after Blanche Lamont disappeared, and try to insinuate that it must have referred to this.[52] However, the time was later accurately determined to be late February or possibly early March—a month or more before Blanche's disappearance.

What would be "100-fold greater in importance" to Theo than love or money? What "going away" would be in the "natural course of events"? The answer, of course, must be Maud's departure for Berlin. They were growing up and getting on with their lives, and Theo must have realized that this separation was only a prelude to the time when they would no longer live together under the same roof. It was natural, of course, but that didn't make it any easier for him to take.

That Maud's absence from his life had set Theo helplessly adrift can also be seen in his inexplicable series of letters to a local actress, Helen Henry, whom he had only met a couple of times.[53] He explained to her that his sister had left for Europe and he longed for someone to take her place, to be a sister to him. (Minnie Williams couldn't fill the bill, and Blanche Lamont wouldn't.) He asked Miss Henry to be that person, and allow him to call on her after her performances and escort her home. Although the letters are completely aboveboard in tone, and thoroughly gentlemanly, his whole approach here is not entirely sane. Theo was a man without moorings.

Meanwhile, Flo Upton, for reasons never divulged, wrote Theo a "Dear John" letter in March. Had he said or done something wrong during her February visit? Had she heard of his attentions to other young ladies? Whether it was something specific, or whether she thought the long-distance thing wasn't working out for either of them, the so-called engagement was broken off.[54]

And then, on a bright, breezy morning in early April, on his way to George King's house to set up a time to carry down the cabinet organ that afternoon, Theo happened to see Blanche Lamont waiting for a streetcar.

The Little Quakeress

Minnie was a smart girl in concocting plans and she generally
carried them out well.
—Jennie Turnball, friend of Minnie Williams

The last time Susan Morgan saw Minnie Williams, she was wrapping paper around the Morgans' furniture on the morning of Good
Friday, April 12, 1895, so that they could have it sent to their new
house in the state of Washington. Clark Morgan, the 60-something
former head of the California Casket Company had resigned to
take a similar job in Tacoma, and Minnie, their hired girl, would
most likely be following them there in a week or two.[1]

"Hired girl" was not an entirely accurate term for 21-year-old
Marian Elora ("Minnie") Williams. Although she had served that
function in other homes, in the Morgans' Alameda household she
was mostly treated as a member of the family. Part of this was due
to her tendency toward illness[2] and part of it was due to the way
they felt about the diminutive spirit who added such zest to their
home.

In fact, for the first several months Minnie was living with the
Morgans, she did no work at all and did not pay any rent. Later,

when she began feeling stronger, she went to work sewing shrouds in Clark Morgan's California Casket Company. By early 1895, she had quit this job (probably at the urging of Morgan) to help Susan with the household chores.

Weighing only ninety pounds and standing well under five feet in height, Minnie was often mistaken for a child. When she worked for the Morgans' neighbor, John Young, people used to joke with him that he had hired a doll to do his housework.[3]

That Minnie had to do housework at all, however, was in part due to her own penchant for "concocting plans."

Like Theo Durrant, Minnie Williams was from the province of Ontario, Canada (her middle name, Elora, is a town there), where she was born in August 1873. Her parents, Mr. and Mrs. Albert E. Williams, immigrated to the United States with their four children after 1880 and settled in the Mission District in San Francisco. Albert Williams was something of a wheeler-dealer, making money in all sorts of ventures, primarily real estate and sales commission work. Unlike Theo's father, William Durrant, Williams was successful in his enterprises, and by 1892 had amassed a fair amount of property and moved his family over to the upscale East Bay island town of Alameda.[4]

However, Minnie began to suspect that her father was not faithful to her mother, and somehow discovered who the other woman was.[5] This woman had a daughter about the same age as Minnie's younger sister, and Minnie went about setting a trap for her father by using these two little girls. The younger Williams girl was commissioned to befriend the daughter of Albert's mistress and get information about how often the unsuspecting Williams was visiting there. The little spy duly reported this back to Minnie.

Minnie learned that on a particular Sunday, her father and his mistress would be at church services. She arranged to have her mother accompany her to the same services, where she pointed out her erring father and his new love interest. Mrs. Williams quickly obtained a divorce, and Williams suddenly found himself out in the cold. Moreover, since he had not told his mistress that he was married, she wanted nothing more to do with him. And she refused to give him back the large amount of property he had transferred to her. Albert Williams's days of prosperity were over.

After the divorce, Mrs. Williams was forced to earn her living as a seamstress. She moved her family (sans Minnie, who stayed in Alameda to work) back to the Mission District and struggled hard to make ends meet. In the fall of 1893, Minnie moved back to San Francisco to stay with her mother, but the whole ordeal had been too much for Mrs. Williams emotionally and financially. She wanted to go back to her home in Beamsville, Canada, where she still had family.

The generous members of the Emmanuel Baptist Church raised funds to send Mrs. Williams and her three youngest children back to their home in Ontario. Minnie enjoyed the San Francisco Bay Area and had many friends there, so she elected to stay rather than go back to the small town of Beamsville. Although she claimed she didn't want to be an extra burden on her mother, she must have known that she would have been a tremendous help to her, not only with the younger children, but by providing another income; so Minnie's real motives were undoubtedly her unwillingness to trade big-city opportunities for small-town boredom, and her reluctance to give up her acquaintances.

Albert Williams, in the meantime, had to go back to work himself. He blamed Minnie for his predicament (apparently choosing to ignore his own part in the breakup of his home) and refused to speak to her or give her any money to support herself. This would change in the last year of her life, but it must have been a bitter pill for Minnie to swallow.

On her own in the world, Minnie became even shrewder than she had been before. It was what she used to survive. She resented the humiliation of being a servant,[6] and she probably also realized that her health problems would not allow her to work full-time. Consequently, Minnie was ever on the alert for a suitable marriage prospect. In the Mission District, she focused her attentions on two young professionals: the dentist, Dr. Tom Vogel; and the medical student, Theo Durrant.

There was at least one other San Francisco man she was seeing at one time, and in 1893 she had also gone out with a much older man: a 42-year-old employee of the Singer Sewing Machine Company, who lived in a hotel. At that time, she asked her friend Jennie, "If you were going to marry and you had two chances—one a young man and the other a man of 42 years—which would you take? Would you take the man of 42 or would you wait for the young man?" So she must have received a proposal from the 42-year-old, but wanted to hold out for the young man, who was possibly a reluctant Theo Durrant.[7]

After her death, there were two schools of opinion about Minnie: those who swore she had never been anything but completely proper in her dealings with men (some of these said she *had* no gentlemen friends!) and those who gossiped that Minnie fell far short of that ideal.[8] The truth, as it often does, fell somewhere in between.

Once called a "little Quakeress" by many of her friends because of her prudish manners toward men, Minnie seems to have become bolder in the years she was on her own after her parents' divorce.[9] Perhaps she felt she did not have the luxury of reserved, passive behavior now that she had to rely on her own devices. For example, once she got off the train in Alameda at a fairly late hour and spied beat patrolman Dennis Welch. Unhesitatingly, she appealed to him in her little-girl manner: "Mr. Policeman, will you walk me home? It's dark and I'm afraid." Welch, who was charmed by her approach, did so.[10]

Although Minnie was a virgin until immediately before her death, and was careful to avoid any semblance of improper behavior that would be noticeable to her employers, she was not always as prudent as she should have been for a young woman of that era. She admitted to her friend Jennie Turnball that she had seen the 42-year-old's hotel rooms, and declared them as "very handsome."[11] In the 1890s, it was considered extremely improper for a young woman to visit a man in a hotel room, even if nothing happened there.

And it was Minnie who took Theo to the isolated location in Fruitvale in the summer of 1894.[12] His "infamous proposal" to her there, repeated so often as a proof of his degeneracy, could easily have been prompted by what he perceived as the signals she was sending out, not the least of which was her decision to take him there in the first place. Perhaps he felt that such was expected of him under those circumstances. That Minnie did not stop seeing him after that is further proof that she was not as insulted as she let on.

Minnie was corresponding with at least one young man in San Francisco, for when she left the Henry Lippman home in the fall of 1893, she left behind a letter. In it, the suitor begged, "Why don't you come to San Francisco?"[13]

Yet another aspect of Minnie's impropriety can be seen in her relations with the elderly Clark Morgan, who seems to have been smitten with her, although in a passive sort of way. His obsession with Minnie began from the first moment he saw her working at John Young's house. Then, when the Morgans' own servant became ill, they enticed her to work for them, which she did for six weeks. It is not known why she left after such a short time, especially as she seems to have gone from there to another Alameda home. At any rate, the Morgans told her to come back if she ever needed a home—which she did in May 1894.[14]

Clark Morgan even tried to adopt Minnie, since she was, as he said "worse than fatherless." He was appalled that Albert Williams could neglect this darling girl in such atrocious fashion. Williams had no objection to the adoption scheme, but the law forbade the adoption of anyone over the age of 18. What Morgan expected to accomplish by the legal adoption of a 20-year-old girl is puzzling. And why Mrs. Morgan consented to go along with it is even more bizarre.

Minnie's motives, at least, are understandable: A legal adoption by the Morgans would assure her of financial security during their lifetimes and at their deaths. However, Morgan was old enough to be Minnie's grandfather; indeed, this is exactly what she called him: "Grandfather."

While Minnie was dating Theo, she apparently regaled Clark Morgan with tales of their relationship. She complained that he ignored her when his mother was around and that he was also interested in other girls. And she told him about the Fruitvale incident. The fact that she chose "Grandfather" Morgan to confide in for such a highly personal incident instead of his wife, Susie, gives a hint that possibly Minnie's stories were designed to appeal to Morgan's prurient interests.

In November 1894, the Emmanuel Baptist Church put on a reception for its newly appointed pastor, Rev. J. George Gibson. Although she was then living in Alameda, Minnie was still a member of the church and even went over for services twice a month. Clark Morgan stopped by the church when the reception was nearly over so he could escort Minnie back to Alameda, and was introduced

to some of the parishioners—including Tom Vogel and Theo Durrant.

On the way back to Alameda, Minnie coyly asked him, "How did
you like the boys?" Morgan replied that he thought Tom Vogel
looked like a fine young man, but that she should stay away from
Durrant: There was something about his looks he didn't trust. Of
course, Morgan himself is reporting this after Theo's arrest, so it
could fall under the category of "I knew it all the time" hindsight;
or it could represent some jealousy on his part, as Minnie's emotions seemed to have been more engaged by Theo than by Tom
Vogel. And there is always the possibility that Theo's looks really
were off-putting. He was somewhat foppish in his dress and manners, and Morgan may have been reacting to this.

It was around this time that Albert Williams made peace with his
daughter, and Minnie began visiting him at his various abodes.[15]
As she had done with Clark Morgan, she told her father of the
various gentlemen she was seeing (carefully omitting, however, the
Fruitvale incident). Williams was alarmed to hear that one of these
was a man his own age, so he did some investigating and discovered that the man had a wife and children back East. Minnie was
hurt and angry at her suitor's deception, but Williams congratulated himself on saving her from even more distress later on. (And
it's not hard to detect his smugness at paying back his daughter
for her role in the breakup of both his marriage and his love affair.)

When Blanche Lamont arrived on the scene in September 1894,
Minnie confided to her friend Jennie that she was hurt by Theo's
immediate dropping of her to chase after Blanche.[16] She must have
felt that this was at least partly due to the class difference—after
all, Blanche did not have to work as a servant to support herself,
and she was also going on in her education. Minnie may have even
tried to befriend Blanche, a shrewd move that would accomplish
two objectives: keeping tabs on Blanche's relationship with Theo
and allying herself with someone of a higher class. However, Blanche does not seem to have reciprocated.

Minnie's best friends in San Francisco were Miriam Lord, who
had also been born in Canada, and, in the last year of her life, the
vivacious Lucile Turner. She often stayed overnight with one or the
other when she was in San Francisco and it was too late to go back
to Alameda. With Lucile Turner she shared a love of intrigue and
gossip, and it is probable that she received most of her information

about Theo's activities from her, as Lucile spent a great deal of time with him in the library.

Minnie is supposed to have told several people that the relationship between Theo and Blanche "was of a nature to startle anybody," but this could not have been based on reality and was more likely to have been a combination of gossip from Lucile Turner and Minnie's love of shocking people. It cannot have come from Blanche, as it is hard to imagine that she would have selected Minnie as a confidante. As any relationship between Theo and Blanche that went deeper than friendship existed only in Theo's head, it is possible that he may have voiced some wishful thinking to Lucile, and Lucile—ever one to embellish—passed it on to Minnie in its newer version.[17]

When Maud Durrant left for Berlin in February 1895, Theo (who had alienated Blanche with his proposal of marriage while he was engaged to Flo Upton) began going over to Alameda again to see Minnie. Dennis Welch, the Alameda policeman who had escorted Minnie home one dark night, noticed them walking together several times, and also occasionally saw Theo alone at the Park Street station as he waited for the train to the ferry. In fact, on February 24, Theo missed the train and asked if he could spend the night at the police station. They let him sleep on a bench there.[18]

Minnie went to San Francisco on Friday, April 5 (two days after Blanche Lamont disappeared), to see Mrs. Amelia Voy at 1707 Mission Street about staying with her family until she should catch the next steamer to Tacoma to live with the Morgans. Later that afternoon, she visited with her father at the photography studio where he had an office as their commission agent, and that night they went to dinner and the theater.

During their time together, Williams urged his daughter to let him put her up in a hotel for those two weeks, instead of staying at Mrs. Voy's where she would have to pay rent. But Minnie said she would rather be among friends and in a family setting. She would be too lonely in a hotel, she told him.[19]

The following day, Saturday, April 6, Officer Dennis Welch saw Theo over in Alameda in front of the Park Street Hotel, a place he had frequently seen him with Minnie. On Monday, April 8, the day after Blanche Lamont's disappearance was announced at church, Theo got Harry Partridge to answer for him and skipped his classes at Cooper to go across the Bay to Alameda yet again. Dennis Welch did not see him that day, which was election day in Alameda, but two of the Morgans' neighbors saw Minnie on the porch with a young man who looked very much like Theo. And a woman named Frances Willis, who knew him from the Mission District, sat with him on the return train at 3:00.[20]

Minnie later recounted her April 8 conversation with Theo to Clark Morgan, as she so often did.[21] Durrant had wanted her to go with him to the theater in San Francisco that evening, she told "Grandfather," as he needed to talk to her. Minnie did not want to go to the city. "You can talk to me right here," she told him. But Theo insisted that he needed to discuss something with her.

"If it's on the same topic as the last time," Minnie said, "I'm not interested." Theo assured her it was on an entirely different topic. For one thing, he would be going to Germany to pursue his studies—though, what relevance this had to anything was not offered by Minnie when relating the conversation to Morgan. Minnie finally consented to see Theo and talk with him, but not until Friday, when she would be going to the city to attend her final meeting of the Young People's Christian Endeavor Society. She had received the invitation, sent out by Theo as secretary, and would use the opportunity to say goodbye to all her Mission friends and see if she could—finally—get them to take her name off the books.

Minnie had to be careful with her money, since she was on her own, and she became very frugal in her last years.[22] Since she was living in Alameda and wasn't able to attend many Young People's meetings, she didn't want to have to pay the dues. Still, although she had asked many times, her name was still listed and her unpaid dues kept accumulating. She simply could not afford it, and was anxious to get this matter settled before leaving.

When Clark Morgan testified at the inquest in April 1895, he was asked what Minnie meant by scolding Theo about "the same topic as last time." He assumed it referred to the Fruitvale incident, but it could not have been that: Minnie and Theo had gone out many times since the summer of 1894. She was most likely referring to a conversation that would have taken place on April 6, or possibly on April 5 when she was in San Francisco—whichever was the last time they had seen each other. Minnie had probably wanted Morgan to ask the same question asked at the inquest—"What was the topic you didn't want to discuss again?"—but he failed to follow up. And this brings us to yet another facet of Minnie's personality.

Despite the many reports of Minnie's reserved, quiet manner, she must have been a veritable chatterbox. At some point, people just turned her off. A common theme emerges through all the interviews with those closest to her—the Morgans, her father, Jennie Turnball, Mrs. Lippman, Miriam Lord—and that theme is: "I wasn't really listening." "I wasn't paying attention." "I never asked what she meant by that."[23] There is a consistent failure to pay complete attention, a consistent failure to ask the follow-up questions they were obviously meant to, which would indicate that Minnie told a lot of stories. Whether these stories were real or exaggerated, there must have been many of them; nothing else explains the lack of curiosity on the part of her father and her friends, or their lack of attention when she spoke of topics that could be considered "juicy."

Minnie decided that when she went over for the Young People's meeting and social at Tom Vogel's house, she would begin her stay at Mrs. Voy's. The Morgans would be moving out of their Alameda home on Saturday and, until their departure for Tacoma on Monday, would be staying with their daughter and son-in-law, the Gotts, who also lived in Alameda. So there was nothing for Minnie to come "home" to.

She must have been excited about going to the party, and surely the anticipated presence of both Tom Vogel and Theo Durrant made her take extra care in her appearance. At 2:30 on Friday afternoon, Minnie had her hair done, then picked up a new dress she had had made for the occasion. Asked by her hairdresser if she would have an escort for the party, Minnie said she wasn't sure; she might be going alone. Later, the dressmaker would say her little client seemed pensive and worried, but this doesn't jibe with either the Voys' recollection ("buoyant and happy") or with that of other witnesses. Maybe she just didn't feel like talking to the hairdresser.[24] Or, something might have happened to elevate her mood before arriving at the Voys'.

Back at the Morgans', and running a little late, Minnie gathered up some flowers, put on her cape, arranged her turban, bade goodbye to an attentive Clark Morgan, and sped out the door—just in time to catch the 4:05 train to the ferry.

Over at the San Francisco Ferry Terminal, Southern Pacific Detective Peter S. Chappelle saw someone he knew waiting at the landing: Theo Durrant. Chappelle thought him an odd duck. Durrant was always coming up with some idea or other—his mind never seemed to stop—and his latest thing had been to become a railroad detective like Chappelle. Theo had even gone so far as to get the application forms, and then a week later told Chappelle that he had changed his mind!

So, when Chappelle saw Durrant watching the passengers get off the East Bay ferry at 3:00 that Friday afternoon, he did not call attention to himself.[25]

At 3:30, East Bay residents Charles Dukes and Clarence Dodge were waiting to catch the ferry home after another day at Cooper Medical School. They recognized a classmate, Theo Durrant, waiting also, and hailed him. Dodge kidded him about his name being connected with the missing Blanche Lamont in the newspaper: "Durrant," he called out, "what have you done with that girl you made away with?"

Theo seemed glad to see Dukes and Dodge, whom he knew better than most of the other students because of their alphabetical seating arrangement at lectures. He told them he was waiting for some of his Signal Corps mates to come over, at which time they would go to the armory and get ready for their outing the next day. His National Guard weekend would begin then and he asked both young men if they would answer for him at the hospital clinic the next day. Students were not supposed to answer for each other during roll call, but it happened with a fair amount of regularity. Classes were usually so large—seventy-five in those that Theo was taking—that it was impossible for the professors to know who was really there and who was not.[26]

Another person at the ferry terminal that afternoon was 45-year-old Frank August Sademan, the janitor at the Emmanuel Baptist Church, who was watching for his stepson and silently fuming. Sixteen-year-old James was becoming more and more incorrigible, until Frank and the boy's mother, Mary Agnes, were at their wits' ends as to what to do with him. Possibly the young man resented Frank's intrusion into the family, through either the death of his father or the divorce of his parents, as well as the new little Sademan children coming along: Charlotte and Frank, Jr.

Whatever his reasons, James had turned into a thief. Sademan had tried to help his stepson earn some money and keep out of trouble by paying him to clean portions of the church; but then James got into trouble stealing Sunday school items from the library and forcing Theo Durrant to put a second lock on the door. Now, on Good Friday, the boy had stolen $15 from his home—a goodly sum of money in 1895, and intended for the monthly rent—and had run away. Sademan was down at the ferry looking for James at the suggestion of his wife when he happened to see the very man he had just been thinking of: Theo Durrant!

"What are you doing down here, Mr. Durrant?" Sademan asked the young man.

"Well," Theo said importantly, "I've just received a clue that Blanche Lamont will be leaving the city and going over to the East Bay. I'm watching to see if I can spot her. The detective hired by the Nobles is absolutely worthless. First of all, he wouldn't do a thing until they paid him $50; and after that he asked only a few basic questions, then declared they shouldn't be worried about a girl that old!"

Sademan commented on the disappearance of the Emmanuel Baptist regular, which by now was common knowledge throughout the city, and Theo said that her friends should be doing as much as they could to look for her, as the authorities didn't seem to be doing much. He also mumbled something about having another reason for being at the ferry as well, but Sademan didn't pursue it. After ten minutes of conversation, the two said their goodbyes and Sademan continued his search of the wharf. It was now about 4:15.[27]

Adolph Hobe, 23, arrived at the ferry terminal at 5:05, just ten minutes before he would have to catch the boat to his home in Oakland. As he made his way to the landing, he happened to notice an old high school classmate, Theo Durrant, who had graduated with him from Lincoln. After high school, when Hobe was still living in the Mission District, he would occasionally run into Theo on the street and they would chat for a few minutes. So, he could not be mistaken as to the identity of the young man, whom he saw engaged in conversation with a very short woman wearing a turban and a cape. On his way past, Hobe tried to catch Theo's eye to say hello, but Theo never looked up from his companion's face.[28]

When Minnie Williams arrived at the Voys' house shortly before dinnertime on Friday, August 12, she was "buoyant and happy," and looking forward to the Emmanuel Baptist social that evening.[29] As she helped get dinner ready and arranged the flowers she had brought, Minnie talked cheerfully with Mrs. Voy and her daughters Annie, Florence, and Genevieve. In spite of her good mood, however, there seemed to be one thing uppermost in her mind: Tonight she would definitely take care of the dues problem and get her name taken off the membership list.

While Minnie and the Voys were eating dinner, Minnie's trunk arrived, having been shipped out earlier that morning from Alameda. Curiously, the young woman didn't change into her new dress after all, although she did put on a new waist (a vest-like garment) for the social. As she was leaving for Dr. Vogel's at 8:00, Amelia Voy gave her a key to the house so she could get back in after they had gone to bed and locked up.

"I probably won't need it," Minnie said. "I should be home earlier than that." But Amelia told her to take it just in case, and Minnie headed up Howard Street. If she was meeting anyone, or going anywhere except to Tom Vogel's, she never let on.

Dr. Philip Perkins, 26, a dentist and also Theo's friend and Signal Corps sergeant, was on his way to the streetcar around 8:00 Friday night when he met Theo outside his house. Phil had borrowed a blue flannel uniform shirt of Theo's and Durrant needed it back. He told Phil that if he would give him the key, he would go to the armory and get it out of the dentist's locker. They waited on the corner together until Phil's streetcar came at 8:05, and then Theo took off in another direction—which was strange, Phil thought, as this was the streetcar that went by the armory.[30]

Mrs. Mary Ann McKay was bone tired after her day of doing other people's laundry.[31] Not only was it hard work, but she was getting on in years and didn't have the energy of her youth. As she walked down Bartlett Street to her home at about 8:15 that Friday night, her pace was so slow it was taking her forever to get there. She wanted more than anything to be home so she could collapse in her favorite chair and put up her throbbing feet, but she just couldn't make herself move any faster.

Approaching the front of the Emmanuel Baptist Church, Mrs.

McKay saw two young people engaged in deep conversation. The girl, who was very small and dressed in a cape and turban, was leaning close to the boy and seemed to be coaxing him to do something. Her gloved hand was outstretched toward him, palm up, and she moved it up and down in emphasis. ("The hand haunts me," Mrs. McKay would say later.) She didn't get the impression the girl was angry, but just pleading.

As the old lady passed, she heard the boy say, "Oh, you're a coward," and she smiled to herself. "Them do be lovers," she thought whimsically, "and the girl is afraid to go home."

Charles T. Hills's reversals were making him paranoid about his wife.[32] He was unemployed and unable to find work, so his wife—to his great humiliation—was forced to get a job cleaning houses. It seemed unnatural to him to be home during the day while his wife worked, and he felt emasculated by the whole thing. He began to imagine her carrying on with other men and this thought preyed on him all day.

On the evening of Friday, April 12, when his wife had still not arrived by 8:00, Hills went down to the corner of Bartlett and 23rd Streets to watch for her. (By chance, he happened to be in front of a liquor store and possibly made a purchase there to ease his pain.) Across the street in the gloom, he could just make out a neatly-dressed man standing under a tree and looking down Bartlett as well. Was this man waiting for Hills' wife, too?

Pretty soon a short, small woman came along and the man across the street hurried to meet her. She gave Hills the impression that she had been expecting to meet this man, as the two took hold of each other's arms and walked briskly down the street. He still couldn't tell whether the woman was his own wife, so he crossed the street to follow them. The couple moved so fast he had a little trouble keeping up. Hills judged it was about 8:20 when the couple entered the side door of the church. Instead of going through the gate after them, he walked along the fence border to see if there was an opening, but couldn't find one.

Hills walked back to the gate and cautiously opened it, then went down the path to the side door. He tried the door and found it unlocked. He hesitated, then slowly turned the knob and opened the door. It was pitch black inside, and Hills had qualms about following the couple into a dark building. He heard nothing, but then another thought occurred to him: What if it was his wife and she knew he was following them? She might quickly leave by another door and hurry home before he could catch her.

Hills closed the door and ran home, intending to catch his wife just entering. She was there when he arrived just as the clock struck 8:30, and claimed she had just gotten in after walking up from Mission Street. Hills was not placated, and may have fueled his fire with a purchase from the liquor store. He told her what he had seen and accused her of being the woman in the church. Moreover, he went on, he would go back the next morning to see if she could have left by another exit.

Two young men, brothers named Friedlander, were riding their bicycles to the California Cycle Club, where they were members. As they approached 23rd and Bartlett Streets, one of them lost control of his bicycle and took a spill. Picking himself up, he noticed a man on the corner closest to the church. The man had a small mustache, and wore a soft hat and a long, single-breasted overcoat. The time was approximately 8:10.[33]

James P. Hodgdon, a Southern Pacific claims adjuster, liked his cigar in the evening after dinner, and sometimes two. His habit was to walk up and down in front of his house while he smoked it (his wife no doubt forbade him to smell up the house). On Friday night at about 8:15, he was on his way to the corner store to buy a Havana—possibly the same liquor store Hills was waiting in front of—when he saw what he thought was a young man "taking liberties" with a girl of 15, trying to get her to do something she didn't want to do. Hodgdon even crossed the street to interfere, but then he noticed that the young lady was not a child at all. As he approached, she took the young man's arm, so she obviously wasn't in any trouble and she didn't ask him for help.

The young man looked right at Hodgdon as he went by, but the claims adjuster didn't stop. When he bought his cigar and came out on the street again, the couple was nowhere in sight.[34]

At 8:30, 16-year-old Albert McElroy was waiting near the Baptist church to meet his friend, Bert Minner, 18. As he waited, he saw a couple approaching whom he would later identify as Theo and Minnie. As they walked by, the young man seemed to be trying to shield the woman's face from Albert's view. Later, when Bert Minner arrived, both boys noticed a light moving in one of the church's back windows on the ground floor.[35]

Alexander Zenger, a Russian immigrant, had lived for many years in the Mission District and on the same street as the Emmanuel Baptist Church, to which his wife belonged. He had known Theo Durrant since the young man was just a boy, and had also known Minnie Williams in the days before her parents divorced. So when he saw the couple on Bartlett Street just after 8:00 that Friday, April 12, he knew immediately who they were. He watched them as they entered the church gate and disappeared through the side door at the end of the pathway.

Zenger had heard rumors afloat in the neighborhood about possible scandalous behavior on the part of the young people of Emmanuel Baptist. There were stories about a bed in the pastor's study and young men and women entering the church together at all hours. Consequently, when Zenger saw Theo and Minnie go into the darkened church after 8:00 P.M., he determined to watch and wait. At 9:00, Theo came back out the side door . . . alone. Zenger shrugged his shoulders and abandoned his post; undoubtedly there were others in the church and Minnie was with them.[36]

It is curious that not one of these witnesses, who should have been fairly tripping over each other between 8:00 and 8:30, mentions seeing any of the others. Little Bartlett Street had probably never seen such an onslaught of foot and bicycle traffic in its existence! Moreover, there are contradictions in their stories. Mrs. McKay and James Hodgdon saw the two engaged in some kind of conversation where each was trying to coax the other to do something. Mrs. McKay said it was the girl; Hodgdon said it was the boy.

Hills, who had a stronger motive for noticing than Mrs. McKay or Hodgdon, says he saw them from the first moment they met, and that they hurried right along to the church. On the other hand, he may have omitted the stop along the way where there was some hesitation to enter on the part of the girl. Also, he may have been sipping from a bottle as he waited and was none too clear about what he actually saw. He would not have wanted to reveal this. It does seem improbable that, while other witnesses could clearly see the faces of one or both people, Hills could not be sure if the woman was his wife.

But didn't any of these adults see the two boys, or the young man who fell off his bicycle? Didn't Alexander Zenger, standing in the gloom of his house and spying on the doings at the church, see Hills following the young couple or Hodgdon approach them, or Mrs. McKay pass by at her weary pace? These are questions they were never asked at the inquest, and they should have been. Zenger didn't come forward with his story until many months later, so never testified under oath and was never subjected to cross-examination.

At 9:15 that Friday night, two sets of sisters were out for a walk in their Mission District neighborhood: Louisa (13) and Emma (17) Struven, and Maggie (15) and Cecelia (16) Fitzpatrick. As the girls approached 22nd and Mission Streets, just a few blocks from the Baptist church, they noticed a young man standing there, lost in thought. Their presence seemed to rouse him from his reverie, for as they went on down the block, he ran after them, yelling excitedly, "Flora! Flora!"

The girls were so startled by this that they stopped and turned around. The young man cried out again, "Flora!" and went up to Louisa Struven. "What did you say?" she asked him. "Don't say anything, Lou," the other girls told her. "He's just trying to get us to talk to him." As soon as he got close to Lou, however, the young man realized his mistake and went back the other way. But the Struven sisters had recognized him: Theo Durrant, who used to walk by their house every day with his sister when the Durrants were attending Cogswell Poly.[37]

Commentators since then have wondered why Theo called out "Flora!" Did he mistake one of the girls for his ex-fiancée, who was a year older than he? Not likely. In a wild flight of fancy, one writer even claimed that "Flora" was a pet name Theo gave Minnie, even though her middle name was Elora.[38] Even if this were true, why would he think he saw her outside the church at 9:15 when he had already entered the church with her an hour earlier? We know that Minnie never came out of the church alive, and Theo would be the last person to think she might be walking by him with a group of girls.

Who, then, was Flora? She was George King's 14-year-old sister, and a natural mistake for Theo to make in the April gloom when a group of similarly-aged girls walked by.[39] Perhaps, as with her brother on April 3, Theo felt compelled to explain his presence at the church. Under the circumstances, it would have been extremely ironic if the girl really *had* been Flora King.

At 9:30, Tom Vogel opened his door to Theo Durrant's knock. "You're just in time to be too late!" he told him.[40] As secretary of the Young People's Society, Theo should have been there for the business meeting that started at 8:00. When he hadn't been, the group appointed Lizzie Marshall to stand in for him.

Vogel noticed that Theo was somewhat disheveled: perspiration dotted his forehead and his hair was mussed up. "I had trouble catching my horse at the armory," Theo explained. "Could I wash up before going in to the others?"

"Of course," Tom told him, and showed him to the washroom off his dental parlor. As Theo washed his hands and face and combed back his hair, he made a strange request: "Please don't tell the young people that I had to wash up first." Tom assured him he wouldn't, possibly thinking that Theo was carrying fastidiousness just a little too far.

The social part of the meeting was just underway as Theo entered the room, and that meant refreshments, chatting, and parlor games. No one noticed anything strange in his behavior—he was, if anything, "more lively than usual," as Dr. Gibson related afterward.[41] He entered into the boisterous talking and took turns reading a longish letter from his sister in Berlin. One of the girls started the letter, and Theo completed it.

The young people of the Emmanuel Baptist Church played two social games that evening: "Coffee Pot" and "Wink."[42] In "Coffee Pot," a form of Twenty Questions, a person is chosen to be "it" and leaves the room. The others decide on an action verb that "it" must guess. When called back into the room, "it" must then discover what the verb is by asking questions. The word "coffeepot" is substituted for the unknown verb, as in "Do I coffeepot every day?" "Does it cost money to coffeepot?" There is no limit to the number of questions that can be asked, and it's easy to see that this game would be a real icebreaker.

A more ominous game, under the circumstances, is "Wink." All the players draw from a pack of cards that contains only one jack.

The person who draws the jack is the murderer, and "kills" the others by winking at them. When a player is winked at, he or she must die in a really obvious manner, so everyone else knows it. Any player can accuse anyone else of being the murderer, but a wrong guess (false accusation) is instant death to the guesser. Eventually, the winner is either the player who guesses correctly . . . or the murderer, who manages to kill everyone off without being accused.

Did Theo draw the jack that night?

Around 11:30 the party began to break up. Some of the young people walked the pastor home, probably rightly guessing he might be afraid of the dark. Theo walked home with Elmer Wolfe and Elmer's date of the evening, Miriam Lord.[43] They talked about the weather, which Theo hoped would be sunny for the Signal Corps' heliographing experiment over the weekend: A team from on top of Mount Tamalpais in Marin County would send a Morse code message to Theo's team on top of Mount Diablo in Contra Costa County by using the sun on mirrors. Theo's team would then relay the message to a third team in Sacramento.

At Miriam's corner, Theo tactfully excused himself, saying he had to get up early the next day to go over to Mount Diablo. Miriam and Elmer walked toward her house on Capp Street, and Theo walked down 24th.

Elmer Alonzo Wolfe was in something of a dither. He had looked forward all day to escorting Miriam Lord to the church group social that night, even though he did not belong to it himself and thought it might be boring. But for Miss Lord he could endure it.

Wolfe worked for his stepfather, Charles Taber, as an accountant at the Guadalupe Dairy Company in South San Francisco. Sometimes he lived at the ranch and sometimes he lived with Taber, who was a former city supervisor and currently a trustee at Emmanuel Baptist. Even though Elmer was only 25, he was already married and divorced, and the father of a 5-year-old son. He had gotten married when he was just 19, but it hadn't worked out— mostly because of Elmer's temper and his constant attentions to other women. In the divorce proceedings, his wife accused him of being abusive.[44]

Now Wolfe was courting 22-year-old Miriam Lord and trying to mend his ways. In fact, he was so distracted by thinking of her after saying good night that Friday that, after changing clothes at his stepfather's house, he went to the wrong stable for his horse![45] He usually left his horse at his brother's stable, but when he got to Clarence's, he remembered that this night he had left it at the Dairy Company stable instead. He would have to hurry to catch a cable car out that way, as the cars would be closing down at midnight.

When Elmer Wolfe was running down Bartlett Street, he saw a figure standing on Bartlett near 24th. Elmer was on the opposite side of the street and had no time to stop, but as he ran past, he thought to himself, "That looks like Theo. What's he doing there?"

Holy Week Horrors

The analogy with the murderous career of Jack the Ripper in London will at once suggest itself. The unexampled crimes of that unknown red-handed fiend—unexampled up to this time—have never been explained. Is the same bloody drama to be repeated in San Francisco?

—*San Francisco Examiner*, April 15, 1895

The Reverend J. George Gibson simply could not take that infernal racket one more minute. The pastor of Emmanuel Baptist Church had come over to his study early on Holy Saturday to write his Easter sermon, but there had been a constant stream of interruptions. And now the piano tuner was filling the air with discordant sounds. To Gibson, it was like nails on a blackboard.[1]

Before going back home, however, he thought he'd better check on the library. Earlier that morning, the janitor's stepson, James, had come to him to report that "the lock on the library door is busted." Sure enough, when Gibson got down there he could see that someone had wrenched the lock away from the wood. Cautiously, he opened the door and looked in. Everything seemed in order: the table and chairs were upright and the door to the little book room was closed. Paper and pencils were on the table as usual. Maybe George King or Theo Durrant had forgotten his key and had to break the new lock. Without investigating further, Gibson closed the outer library door and went on home to finish his sermon.

Scottish-born John George Gibson, 37, had only served as Emmanuel's pastor for five months. His previous pastorates had been in St. Andrew's, Scotland, and more recently in the northern California towns of Red Bluff and Chico. Among his parishioners in Chico was George King's family: his parents, his paternal grandparents, and several aunts and uncles. Now located in San Francisco, the Kings remembered the dynamic young minister with the Midas touch when it came to parish fund-raising, and when the pastorate of Emmanuel Baptist became vacant, Dr. William King—a trustee—asked the board to extend an invitation to Gibson.[2]

George Gibson was eccentric, to say the least. Extremely effeminate in both speech and manner, he was nonetheless enormously popular with the women in his parish. However, he much preferred dealing with women in groups and went out of his way to avoid spending time with them individually. Gibson, unmarried, could devote all his energies to his church, and this was undoubtedly one of the secrets of his success. It was a good thing that he *was* successful, for he did not handle adversity well; he was nervous, easily excited, and tended to fall apart when things did not run smoothly.[3]

Gibson's sermons were well written and dramatically delivered. Often, he would sing a solo from the pulpit in his beautiful baritone voice, and his tastes in music were unusual for a minister: He liked to include what was considered secular music in the services, and for Easter Sunday 1895 he had chosen selections from the operas *Rigoletto, A Masked Ball, Tannhauser*, and *Cavalleria Rusticana.*[4]

In conversation with those he did not know well, Gibson often affected a pose, as if he were delivering an address: He used a somewhat formal and stilted vocabulary and held his right arm out at a forty-five-degree angle.[5] His study in the church contained a set of maxims which he tried to live by and obviously hoped others would emulate. Most had to do with minding one's own business and reveal a misogynistic man with a strong distaste for personal questions:[6]

RULES FOR ALL

1. Never say anything you cannot *prove*.
2. Never ask a question you would not like *to be asked*.
3. Never think a man is *bound* to answer your question. He is not.
4. Never allow your conversation to be *all questions*, for that would reveal both your *curiosity* and your *ignorance*.
5. Never ask what 'so and so' said about you, unless you want to reveal how small your mind is, that it thinks so much on *self*.
6. Never think the one who asks questions *is loved*. He is not, because he is too *self-interested*.
7. Never think you can ask questions and not show people your character. Every question is a window through which people see your mind.
8. Never ask a *woman* her age. It will make her angry, and anger in a woman means more than passion usually—confusion.
9. Never ask a woman about her life before marriage. It might be unkind. Women are as pure as men—more, vastly more.
10. Never ask young persons about their fathers and mothers. They were born. That is enough. *You were no more*.
11. Never *ask to see things*. Wait until you are shown them.
12. Never *enter a room* unless invited to do so.
13. Never spit on the floor.
14. Never get angry.
15. Never sulk.

J. GEORGE GIBSON

That Holy Saturday morning, J. George Gibson walked back to his rooms, which he was renting from George King's maternal grandparents, Rufus and Charlotte Moore. For his first Easter service at Emmanuel Baptist he wanted to impress his parishioners and reassure the trustees that they had made the right choice in selecting him. But he would need peace and quiet to write the perfect sermon, and it didn't look as if he would be getting it at the church.

At 9:30 that morning, 15-year-old Lila Berry entered the Emmanuel Baptist library and sat down to read while she waited for the other decorators. Once everyone arrived they would begin arranging the many flowers the parish members had been bringing for the festive Holy Day. Just before 10:00, the other women came into the library together: Miriam Lord, Catherine (Kate) Stevens, and Mrs. Herman Nolte, the only middle-aged one in the group. The four chatted for a few minutes, when Mrs. Nolte, who did not belong to Emmanuel Baptist, commented that it was a pretty strange library that had no books.[7]

Lila Berry stood up and went to the little closet. "The books are kept in here," she told Mrs. Nolte as she opened the door . . . and jumped back with a scream. There across the threshold lay the figure of a small woman with blood on her face and what looked like blood on the floor, the walls, and the table. The skirt of her dress was pushed up around her knees and one of her legs was bent under her body. The waist of her dress was partially open. Lila ran out into the lobby, then slowly crept back for another look.

"Is it real?" she asked. The other women could not be sure. What lay before them was so far removed from the world they lived in that they thought it might be a wax doll placed there by the janitor's son to frighten them. "Or it could be Blanche Lamont," one of them said.

But they were scaring themselves now, and Mrs. Nolte quite sensibly sent the girls home while she went to find the pastor. On their way out, Miriam and Kate saw James Sademan. "Did you put that thing in the library closet?" they asked him. But James had no idea what they were talking about, and the girls cautioned him: "Don't go in the library or you'll get the fright of your life!"

Mrs. Nolte did not find Rev. Gibson in his study or anywhere else in the church, so she went around to his rooms on Valencia Street and told him he'd better come see the figure on the library floor.[8]

"I can't tell if it's a real person or a dummy, Dr. Gibson," Mrs. Nolte said. "You'd best come and decide for yourself."

"Is the clothing, er, disarranged?" Gibson asked her. "Are the limbs exposed?" He was clearly discomfited by the prospect.

"Yes, the dress is pushed up a little bit, and the waist has been torn open."

George Gibson had never in his life seen a woman without her clothes on, and he did not intend to put himself in the compromising position of witnessing his first one in the presence of another woman. On his way back to the church, he went around to get George King's father, the dentist, to accompany him, and together the three—Dr. King, Rev. Gibson, and Mrs. Nolte—proceeded to the church library with some trepidation.

Nothing in their lives had prepared them for this moment. The figure, that of a small woman, was definitely real, and the three stood watching in silence for a few minutes. Dr. King picked up the woman's cape from the floor and put it on the table, careful to avoid the blood there.

It is indicative of George Gibson's personality that he thought he could keep this from the police, and consequently from the public, and that life could go on as usual with no further interruptions. Instead of contacting the authorities, he locked the church door and took Dr. King with him to the Golden Gate Undertaking Company a few blocks away. The owner, George Keeler, was away, but his son-in-law, a young man named Harry Snook, was on duty.[9]

"Someone has died at the Emmanuel Baptist Church," Gibson told him in classic understatement, "and we need to have the body removed. Please do not tell anyone about this, as it will just disturb the congregation."

"Was it a sudden death?" Snook asked.

"No, I shouldn't think so," was Gibson's strange response.

Eventually, Snook understood the situation and explained to the pastor that the police would have to be notified. He made the phone call from the mortuary and went back to the church with Gibson and King.

When Lila Berry arrived home from the church that morning in a high state of excitement and reported what she had seen, her mother sent her right over to Dr. Tom Vogel's to fetch him.[10] Lila told Tom that either the body of Blanche Lamont or a wax figure had been found at the church, and he accompanied the young woman back to her house to get her mother. Tom and Mrs. Berry then went to the church.

Outside the church, which was now locked, Clarence Wolfe and his sister, Daisy, were waiting impatiently, flowers in hand. They had heard nothing of the excitement of the morning, but had come to decorate for Easter services. When Rev. Gibson finally arrived with Dr. King and Snook, the undertaker, he unlocked the door and all went inside.

The first thing Gibson wanted was for the undertaker to wash the blood off the girl's face, and then he wanted the body immediately removed from his church.[11] He seemed incapable of understanding that nobody could do anything until the police arrived.

Tom Vogel approached the body cautiously so as not to disturb anything. The broken handle end of a regular table knife lay on the victim's chest. He saw the blue skirt of the dress, and instantly recognized it as that of Minnie Williams. He knew the blue dress very well. Next, he noticed a mole under her neck that he had seen many times. After his identification of the corpse in the closet, Tom Vogel went back home.

What the young dentist's feelings were at this point have never been made public, but he must have been very distraught. Minnie Williams was not only his patient but his good friend, and possibly he had courted her as well. Mrs. Morgan said that Minnie liked Tom Vogel quite a lot, and at the November reception for Dr. Gibson she had especially introduced him, as well as Theo Durrant, to Clark Morgan, and later asked his opinion of them both.[12]

The police and the coroner arrived at the church a little after noon, and immediately sent again for Tom Vogel. As Minnie's dentist, he would recognize his work on her teeth, and they wanted a more substantial identification than the blue dress and the mole. Vogel came back and peered into Minnie's mouth to examine her teeth.

"Yes, these are Minnie's teeth. Why, there's something caught in her throat!" he exclaimed. Tom stepped aside as the coroner's deputy reached in and pulled out several strips of lace-covered cloth.[13]

"These were torn from her underclothing," the deputy said grimly.

Underneath the body, they found a stick with a sharpened end. It had obviously been used to shove the rags down the victim's throat, but where had it come from? An examination of the little room revealed that the stick had originally been glued inside the library table and served as a runner for the drawer. Whoever killed Minnie had wrenched it from the table and sharpened it, possibly with the kitchen knife.

With the kitchen knife and the drawer slide and the unlocked side door, the evidence was growing that the murderer was very familiar with Emmanuel Baptist Church. This was no crime committed by a passing tramp or a "footpad" (the nineteenth-century term for a mugger).

The tiny eight-by-ten room was a bloody mess. There were pools of it on the floor where the victim had lain, pools of it on the small table, and streaks of it on one wall. There was the outline of a right foot on the floor. Strangely enough, despite the carnage, there was not a drop or streak of blood in the room adjoining the closet. The murderer had obviously gotten blood on at least one shoe; did he take them off when he left so as not to leave a trail?[14]

Minnie had a gash on her forehead that went down to her nose. Although it was superficial and far from fatal, it must have bled quite a bit, as head wounds always do. Her tongue had been cut by the sharpened stick that pushed the cloth strips down into her esophagus, and her killer had slashed both her wrists so deeply they had almost been severed from the arms. On and under the left breast were several stab wounds with pieces of the broken kitchen knife still sticking in them.[15] Could a dull table knife account for these terrible wounds?

It was later determined that—except for the gash in the forehead—most of Minnie's wounds were postmortem. The wrist slashing had been done either after or at the point of death, but the heart stabbing was definitely done after death. She had been raped just before death and had been a virgin up to that time. It was estimated that she had been dead eight to ten hours before she was found, which would place her time of death at midnight (although a later analysis of the stomach contents would revise the time to 8:30 P.M.). The cause of death was determined to be asphyxiation due to strangulation.[16]

When the police and the morgue officials arrived at the church, so, too, did a host of newspaper reporters. Reverend Gibson had disappeared, and could not be found either in the church or at his home. Some time later he returned to Emmanuel Baptist and issued an edict that would affect how the press would present him from that time on: The church was to be locked and no reporters were to be let in for any reason (the police, of course, did not honor this). And when he was asked for interviews, he sent word that he would see no newspaper people at any time.[17] Gibson's response to disaster was to hide, ostrich-like, and pretend that nothing had happened. It was the worst decision he could have made.

At the Charles G. Noble house, the undertaker's wife, an Emmanuel Baptist member, had rushed over to tell Aunt Tryphena and Maud Lamont that a body had been found in the church, but that it was not Blanche. The two women were somewhat relieved because it still left open the possibility that Blanche would be found alive, but it was not a good sign that a dead woman was found in the same church where Blanche had spent so much time.[18]

Moreover, that very morning they had received the package of rings in the mail. Instead of being comforted that Blanche might have sent them as a sign that she was all right, Mrs. Noble knew her niece would never have addressed the wrapper simply to "Mrs. Noble," but would have put her complete name: "Mrs. Charles G. Noble." Secretly, she was beginning to think that Blanche would be found dead, too.

That same thought was in the mind of Detective Edward Gibson (no relation to Rev. J. George Gibson), who had come to the Noble house to examine the wrappers and the rings. When he found out about the discovery of the body at Emmanuel Baptist, his immediate thought was that the same man had killed both girls and that Blanche would be found in the church.[19]

In the meantime, policemen had been dispatched across the Bay to inform Clark Morgan of Minnie's death and to question him regarding her associates. Morgan, though overwhelmed and reeling from the news, was reluctant to become involved as a witness. He had tickets for Tacoma in his pocket and was scheduled to depart on Monday. He did not relish being held up in northern California for an inquest and a trial.[20]

Besides, Morgan told them, he didn't know anything about it. Minnie had no gentlemen callers that he knew about—except for Theo Durrant, on occasion. And come to think of it, Minnie told him that Durrant had just been over to see her that week to ask her to accompany him to the theater. She didn't want to go to the theater, but told Theo she would see him at the youth social on Friday evening.

The police were very interested to hear the name of Theodore Durrant in connection with the murdered Minnie Williams, as he had also been the last to see Blanche Lamont before she disappeared. Mr. Durrant would definitely merit a closer look.

When Chief of Police Patrick Crowley heard Clark Morgan's statement, he had a warrant issued to search Theo Durrant's home and to bring the young man in for questioning. And he authorized Detective Gibson and his men to close off the Emmanuel Baptist Church and look for the missing Blanche Lamont there.

At the Durrant home on Fair Oaks, a shocked and indignant Isabella Durrant heard the policeman at her door say that Minnie Williams had been murdered at the Emmanuel Baptist Church and that her son was suspected of the crime. Mamma had no choice but to let them in, but then she followed them around with a steady stream of commentary—most of it concerning the outrageousness of such a charge. It had to be a conspiracy on the part of people who intended to injure Theo's good reputation.[21]

To the newspaper reporters who came in with the police, Mamma pleaded Theo's case, stating (untruthfully) that her son hardly knew Minnie Williams: "I cannot understand why they should connect our boy with this crime," she told them. "He has too many young lady acquaintances of his own class and social standing to be under the necessity of paying attention to a little servant girl."

In Theo's neat, Spartan bedroom, they found a well-used phrenology chart hanging on his wall and a mandolin lying on the desk. A photograph album contained two pictures of Minnie Williams. In the closet, they found one pair of shoes and another shoe with no mate. "He has only one pair of shoes besides the ones he's wearing," Mamma told them. The searchers unfortunately never asked her about the mateless shoe and did not take it with them; nor was there any indication in the newspapers as to which shoe it was. The outline of a right shoe had been found in Minnie's blood on the library floor—had that bloody shoe been destroyed or thrown away?

The police confiscated the blue cheviot school suit[22] Theo had

worn on April 3 and on most weekdays, and on their way downstairs Sgt. Burke noticed a hat and coat hanging on a rack in the
entranceway.

"Do those belong to your son?" he asked Mamma.

"Yes," she told him, "but let me look through the pockets first
before you take it away."

But Sgt. Burke was quicker than Mamma and grabbed the coat
before she could begin her search. "I will look through the pockets," he told her firmly. He found nothing until he got to the inside
pocket. He pulled out the contents and held it up: It was a
woman's purse. No purse had been found in the library closet with
Minnie, and Florence Voy was positive that the young woman had
carried one with her when she left their house on Friday evening.
The discovery of a purse in Theo's pocket looked like a significant
find.

Mrs. Durrant reached out her hand eagerly. "Let me see what's
in there," she insisted. Once more, Sgt. Burke remained businesslike and unintimidated. "I will look through the purse," he said,
"and will show you whatever is in it." When he opened it, however,
it appeared empty. He turned it upside down and shook it, and a
small piece of red cardboard fell out. It was an old horsecar ticket,
not used since San Francisco had switched to cable and electric
streetcars.[23]

In the church, policemen were searching every nook and cranny
for any indication of the presence of Blanche Lamont. As some of
the burlier members of the force crept gingerly along the false
ceiling, their legs fell through, scattering plaster dust below and
creating gaping holes that could be seen from the main floor.[24]

Around midnight, the exhausted searchers climbed the stairs to
the last unexamined place: the belfry, which despite its name had
never contained a bell. Its upper regions were not even used for
storage because they were such a nuisance to get to, although a
few items were housed on its lower landing. About the only use
the belfry got was for ventilation. When the church proper got
unbearably hot and stuffy, the janitor would open the door for the
draft to swirl down from above. Mostly, though, he kept the door
closed and locked to keep out the boys who liked to run up and
down the stairs.[25]

Another usage the belfry got was for young people, possibly in couples, to go up and look at the view of the city through the wooden slats—or look at each other, since there was not much viewing to be had through the narrow openings. Either way, the names of dozens of young men and women were carved there in memory of the time they visited.[26]

When the policemen arrived at the door to the belfry, they found it locked. It was very late and they were loathe to break down the door, so they decided to resume their search the next morning with the aid of a key from the janitor. It had been a long, traumatic, and tiring day for everyone, and they were eager to end it.

Easter Sunday morning dawned, and Emmanuel Baptist church-goers arrived to find their church closed tight. A sign read "No Services Today." Today of all days! Little by little, news of Saturday's gruesome find was spread around the crowd, which had multiplied to the hundreds. George King, the organist, wandered around the edges of the crowd with his music under his arm, lost and forlorn. The name of his best friend, Theo Durrant, was being mentioned in connection with the murder of little Minnie Williams.[27]

Upstairs in the church, Detective Edward Gibson, Patrolman Arthur Riehl, and janitor Frank Sademan had returned with a key to the belfry. But it was no use. Someone had disabled the lock in such a way as to render it unresponsive to any key. There was no choice but to batter the door in. The husky young Riehl put his shoulder to it and the door shattered easily.[28]

Sademan stayed below while Gibson, followed by Riehl, climbed the narrow, twisting stairs. At the top level (a twelve-by-twelve platform covered with old papers, leftover pieces of wood, and layers of dust), Gibson paused on the last stair. Over in the corner he saw what he was looking for: the naked body of a dead woman, most likely Blanche Lamont.

In the dusky belfry light, the body glowed like a piece of white marble. There was no mark of violence that Gibson could see, and the young woman had been laid out as if by a conscientious funeral director. Although she was naked, there was a reverential air about the way her killer had left her. Her legs were placed together and straight out, her hands were crossed at her breast, and her long hair had been lifted from beneath her so that it flowed across the rough boards "in a shiny, silken stream." Her eyes had been closed by whoever had murdered her, and he had taken two blocks of wood from the belfry floor to keep her head propped up at the neck. Nonetheless, one of the blocks had shifted and the girl's head had fallen over slightly to the left.

Modern criminal profiler Robert Ressler calls this kind of treatment an *undoing*, an indication that the killer knew the victim and felt some remorse at what he had done: "[H]e engaged in these rituals for the purpose of undoing the crime in a sad attempt at restitution."[29]

Detective Gibson needed help processing the crime scene and he wanted to get it before tramping over the platform. He directed Riehl: "Stay here and don't let anyone up until I get back." Then he went to the 17th Street station and called Chief Crowley with the news.

While Gibson was gone, Blanche Lamont's uncle, Charles Noble, had come to the church in a weird coincidence—not because he had heard of the discovery of the body, but because he had mistakenly received a telegram intended for Sunday School Superintendent Philip Code. He thought Code might be at the church, but when he got there he was taken instead to see if the body in the belfry was that of his niece.[30]

Up in the belfry, Noble sadly confirmed what the police had suspected: The dead girl was Blanche Lamont. Amazingly, conditions in the belfry had preserved the body to such an extent that there was no discoloration and no odor, even after ten days. However, when the morgue attendants came to remove it (they had to borrow a tablecloth from the church kitchen to negotiate the winding stairs with the body), the change in elevation resulted in an immediate transformation. As soon as the body reached the lower levels of the church, the pent-up process of decomposition released itself all at once, and by the time they got to the ground floor, the body that had reminded Gibson of a piece of white marble had turned black. The sharp stench of decayed flesh permeated the area. And they could see what had not been visible upstairs: a series of bruises around the neck bearing the distinct indentations of fingernails.

John Sheridan Barrett, M.D., Cooper Medical School Class of 1893 (two years ahead of Theo Durrant), had been out sailing on the Bay all day Sunday and had heard nothing of the sensational discoveries in Emmanuel Baptist Church.[31] When he got back to shore, however, he was informed that two bodies awaited his immediate attention as autopsy physician at the morgue. Barrett went as soon as he could, making his way through the throng of people who endured the smell of the morgue's alley in the hopes of seeing something sensational. Inside, the young doctor began his examinations of two of the thirty-four unexplained deaths waiting for him: Case No. 5643, Marian Williams, age 21; and Case No. 5662, Blanche Lamont, age 21.[32]

Before the arrival of Dr. Barrett and while the two bodies lay in the morgue, people tried any trick they could think of to get inside and see the murdered girls. In the beginning, many claimed to be friends or relatives of the coroner, William J. Hawkins, until the police guards finally figured out that Hawkins had an unusual number of acquaintances and put a stop to it.[33]

A distinctly odd occurrence was the request of the police that the three Normal School classmates of Blanche Lamont come down to see if they could identify her body! Blanche's uncle had already identified her, and her aunt and sister—reluctant to look at her blackened face—had lifted up the sheet on her foot and recognized the deformity she had from birth (the second toe on the left foot was turned under). What possible use would be served with an identification by three schoolmates who had known Blanche for approximately an hour? Today, even close relatives are spared such encounters by looking through glass windows or at video monitors; the thought of three 20-year-old women being forced to look at the decomposed body of an extremely casual acquaintance is repulsive—all the more so because it was completely unnecessary.[34]

At Emmanuel Baptist, crowds of people swarmed over the two crime scenes. Several women almost fought to see the blood-stained library closet where Minnie Williams had met her death, and it was estimated that at least twenty people (and probably many more) made the trip up to the belfry to stare at the spot where Blanche Lamont was found. In sad contrast to the grim scene was the large cross of calla lilies that adorned the pulpit in anticipation of the festive Easter services that never took place.[35]

Finally, the police kicked everyone out of the church and set a guard on the door, but it was too late to preserve the crime scene in the belfry. And, although it was probably impossible to gather any recognizable footprints because of all the papers and wood chips strewn on the top floor, no attempt had been made to do so.

After the church had been cleared of civilians, the police began a search for the murderer's bloody clothes (they thought he could not have sliced up Minnie so thoroughly without getting any on him) and for Blanche's hidden garments. Several of them searched the belfry, led by a young man with a name that sounds like the heroine of a romance novel: Starr Dare. Son of the Police Court's prosecuting attorney, Dare had come to help his father, and also to be involved in the most exciting thing to happen in San Francisco since James Marshall discovered gold at Sutter's Mill in 1848. Young and athletic, Dare climbed up into the rafters and among the crossbeams, encouraging the others to do the same.[36]

They were rewarded for their perseverance. After two hours of searching among the cracked lumber, between the timbers, and behind crossbeams, the men produced the missing clothing of Blanche Lamont. It had been ripped off her body, as if the murderer was in a hurry to get it hidden. In at least one instance, in the removal of the waist, the killer was obviously frustrated with the complicated hook-and-eye arrangement that held it shut and did not want to bother undoing each one.[37]

Under normal circumstances, the body of Blanche Lamont might never have been discovered until it had become an unrecognizable skeleton. This was undoubtedly the reasoning behind the concealment of clothing that could identify her—and possibly point to her killer.

Probably the most important find among the beams and rafters was the discovery of Blanche's schoolbooks. Still held together with her leather carrying strap, a pencil stuck in one for a bookmark, the textbooks were silent proof that Blanche had gone right from school to the church: Shute's *Practical Physics*, Wilson's *Elementary Geometry*, a paperback *Syllabus*, and a notebook.[38]

Throughout Blanche's books there were scraps of paper, most having to do with geometry problems or sentence structure. But in one there was a very different kind of insert: a pamphlet from May Duncan's School of Delsarte and Dancing.[39] Was Blanche planning to add interpretive dancing to her repertoire of talents? If so, she never said anything to her sister or her aunt about it. It is these occasional revelations that give us a brief glimpse of a more complicated Blanche Lamont than was presented in the press.

On the inside cover of the physics book was a list of maxims that eerily echoed those in the study of Rev. J. George Gibson. However, there is a mocking air to them, as if the writer had his or her tongue planted firmly in cheek. Did Blanche put them there? Or did she buy the book used and find them there? Could this be what she and Theo were laughing about on the cable car as they perused one of her books? Possibly they were remembering Gibson's maxims as they read them:[40]

Learn what the book tells you. Do not expect anyone to explain any thing to you. No one will. Use common sense. If you have none take the consequences. Do not ask any questions. You may be taken for an idiot. You may be one. If you cannot make an experiment keep still about it. No one will know the difference.

On San Francisco's Telegraph Hill, a group of Signal Corps soldiers was foreseeing possible trouble. They knew that Detective Abraham Anthony was on his way to Walnut Creek to arrest fellow soldier Theo Durrant for the murder of Minnie Williams. Durrant was immensely popular with his Signal Corps comrades, and the Telegraph Hill contingent, getting ready to participate in the heliographing experiment, thought that the Mount Diablo brigade might cause trouble for Anthony. To prepare them for this and forestall resistance, the Telegraph Hill group sent their first heliograph message to Walnut Creek: "Bugler Durrant is to be arrested. Police on the way." (Later, this was determined to be the first nonmilitary use of the new heliographing technique.)[41]

Over on Mount Diablo the signaler could not believe the message he was getting. Durrant to be arrested? He asked for a repeat. Yes, it was true: "Hold Bugler Durrant for police." No reason for the arrest was given, however, and the young men—including Theo—assumed it was a joke and treated it accordingly at first. They went on with their experiment as planned, as the hours of sunlight were limited, and sent the required messages to Sacramento. That afternoon, they wended their way on horseback down to their jumping-off place: Fred Moses' ranch in Walnut Creek.

As they approached the end of the trail, Detective Anthony

stepped forward and asked for Theo Durrant. "Here I am," Theo answered.[42]

"I've come to arrest you for the murder of Minnie Williams," Anthony told him. Theo paused, then asked, "Who told you to arrest me?" "Chief Crowley of the San Francisco Police Department," Anthony said.

"Well, I'm innocent," Theo said as he got off his horse. Anthony showed him some of the articles that had filled all the San Francisco papers that day (Anthony did not know at this point that Blanche Lamont had been found, and there was no mention of it in the newspapers). Theo looked at them and turned pale.

"I'm sorry only for my mother," he said. "How can she stand it?"

The Prince of City Prison

As I walk along the Bois Boulong
With an independent air
You can hear the girls declare
"He must be a millionaire!"
You can hear them sigh and wish to die,
You can see them wink the other eye
At the man that broke the bank at Monte Carlo.
—"The Man That Broke the Bank at Monte Carlo" by Fred
Gilbert (1892).[1] Tune whistled by Theo Durrant on his
way to court.

As predicted by the Telegraph Hill Signal Corpsmen, there was some resistance to Theo's arrest. Lieutenant Boardman told Detective Anthony that he had brought ten men over from San Francisco and he intended to take ten men back with him.[2] After the unit was dismissed, Anthony could then arrest Bugler Durrant. Besides, Boardman argued, the National Guard was a federal unit and thereby had precedence over a municipal regulatory body.

However, Anthony stood his ground and insisted that he was taking charge of Durrant then and there. Theo himself averted a showdown by agreeing to go with the detective.

Although Theo Durrant was thought of as "the criminal of the century" in San Francisco, it was obvious that Detective Anthony did not consider him much of an escape risk. Instead of handcuffing his charge, Anthony allowed him to go alone to the Walnut Creek post office to pick up his mail while the detective ordered a drink at Rogers' Hotel and waited for him! It was an attitude that was to prevail throughout the duration of the case against Durrant as he was transported to and from hearings and trial proceedings. Somehow they knew that as far as escape was concerned, in the words of one guard, "he [wa]sn't that kind."[3]

One of the reasons Theo would not have attempted to escape was undoubtedly his intense desire to "settle this thing." He worried about what his mother might be thinking (rarely does he mention his father in this regard) and was anxious to present his alibi so the police could declare him innocent. From the outset, he seemed oblivious to the real trouble he was in, and was unable to do what all attorneys tell their clients in similar circumstances: Theo Durrant could not keep his mouth shut. The statements he made on this, his first day as a captive, would come back to haunt him and his defense attorneys for the next seven months.

On the train from Walnut Creek to Oakland, Theo tried to exonerate himself. First he said he had not seen Minnie Williams in six months, then changed the time to several weeks. How did he explain her purse in his coat pocket? She had given it to him, he told Anthony, at Christmas or New Year's—he couldn't remember which. (Oftentimes women, having no pockets, would give their purses—which were about the size of today's wallet—to their escorts, and just as often would forget to get them back at the end of the evening.)[4]

When the reporters got on the train at Martinez, however, Theo had a different story to tell about the purse. After the Young People's social at Dr. Vogel's, he said, he was walking down Bartlett Street near the church (what he was doing there he did not explain) and a shiny object in the road caught his eye. Upon further examination, it turned out to be a small mirror which had obviously fallen from the purse that was nearby. He picked up the purse, put it in his own overcoat pocket, and thereupon forgot about it.

Theo told this story in a strange, halting manner, as if he were walking gingerly across a minefield—which, of course, he was. He seemed to be making it up as he went along, and his story began with a device which he would use continually: that of an almost passive dissociation from reality. "It came to me in a most mysterious fashion," he told reporters. "I happened to find it in my pocket." What did that mean? they asked him. Had someone put it there? "No, of course not," Theo said, "I put it there myself." Then he went on to tell them about his chance encounter with the mirror that Friday night. As he talked, he plucked nervously at his military coat.[5]

But one of his responses to a question seemed completely genuine to the reporters. Had he heard that Blanche Lamont was found dead? "Dead!" was his completely astonished reply, and then a stunned silence. Detective Anthony's notes say that Theo turned red as he told the newsmen he would like to get her killer alone in a room for about a half hour.[6]

Was Theo faking this response? Was he that good an actor? More likely, he was unprepared for such a quick discovery of Blanche. Why should the hacked-up body of Minnie Williams in the church library lead the police to search the belfry for the missing Blanche Lamont? He was probably caught off guard by this, in which case his astonishment would have been very real.

The fact that he was now associated with *both* these crimes should have been enough to warn Theo to say nothing more to anyone, and certainly not to reporters. But he couldn't stop talking even then. He said that on April 3, the date of Blanche's disappearance, he had arrived at the Emmanuel Baptist Church at 4:30 P.M., having left the medical school after his last lecture, and there proceeded to fix the sunburners until he was overcome by gas. (He would later come to regret locking himself into this time.)

Whenever he got to a sticky section in his story, or when reporters asked him an uncomfortable question, Theo decided to clam up and save his story for Chief Crowley. But, he assured them, the facts were on his side and would demonstrate his complete innocence. He had nothing to worry about. All the same, he burst into tears several times on his way back to San Francisco.[7]

The Durrants had not been idle while their son was being brought across the Bay from Walnut Creek. They went to Abraham W. Thompson, an attorney and close friend, and asked him to help Theo when he was brought to the city prison. No doubt they all felt the situation was only a temporary one and that Theo would be released from custody as soon as he could tell his story. Otherwise, Thompson would probably not have accepted the case, as he was not familiar with criminal law or procedure. A small, nervous man with a timid voice and a white "Smith Brothers"-type beard, the elderly attorney had evidently not done much adversarial trial work, either. He had been a judge at one time, and was often referred to as ex-Judge Thompson—or, in one instance, as "Ancient Judge Thompson, the Populist Lawyer."[8]

Detective Anthony, who had intended his arrest of Theo Durrant to be consummated quietly on the San Francisco side, could not have been prepared for the immense crowds at the Oakland ferry landing.[9] How did they find out what train they would be on? As soon as he saw them, however, Anthony knew there might be real trouble. Already people were yelling "There he is!" and attempting to crowd into the train compartment to get a look at the "Demon of the Belfry."

Police officers from San Francisco had been sent to Oakland to escort Anthony and his prisoner to the city on the ferry, and these surrounded Theo as he exited the train. They bustled him onto the boat with the crowd in full pursuit, took him up to the porter's office, and locked the door. As the boat approached the San Francisco Ferry Terminal, Theo was brought out in full view of the crowd, which swelled forward to see him. They pushed against the rope barricade and the police could barely keep them back. No one would be allowed to exit the boat until Theo was safely in the police wagon.

But there were new problems on land, as hundreds of people stood waiting for the most famous criminal in California history to get off the ferry. Although the police got Theo into the carriage successfully and the hackman whipped the horses into a fast clip toward the prison, the crowd came distressingly close to the back of the wagon. Cries of "Get him!" "Hang him!" (and other things that were unprintable) could be heard almost all the way to the prison.

It was an unnerving experience for Theo, but once inside the prison office he regained his composure. He was greeted there by Chief Crowley; his new attorney, A. W. Thompson; Papa Durrant; and a host of reporters from the six San Francisco newspapers: besides the *Chronicle*, the *Examiner*, and the *Call*, there were also the *Evening Post*, the *Daily Report*, and the *Evening Bulletin*. His first stop was Crowley's office, to make his statement there.

Unfortunately, in his exuberant desire to prove his client innocent, Thompson allowed Theo to make a statement to the newspapers as well. As he sat holding Papa's hand for comfort and courage, Theo once again presented a timeline he would not be able to sustain later (claiming, for example, that he had arrived at Tom Vogel's house at 8:55).[10] The detailed and often convoluted itinerary he laid out now prevented his attorneys from later taking advantage of witnesses who claimed to have seen him elsewhere and at times inconsistent with his committing the murders.

The Emmanuel Baptist murders and the arrest of Theo Durrant opened a veritable floodgate of rumors, theories, wild stories, and overall hysteria. People who knew Theo on any level fell into two camps: those who "knew all along" that the odd little guy was capable of this, and those who refused to believe that the polite, gentle young man they were familiar with could have committed these atrocities. There didn't seem to be any middle ground.

Other crimes were now laid at Theo's door. He was blamed for the unsolved murder of a young drugstore clerk, Eugene Ware, who had been killed on the job the year before.[11] Stories began to circulate that Theo and Ware had been friends (they didn't even know each other), that they had been in the Signal Corps together (Ware was handicapped and would not have been accepted into the National Guard), that Minnie Williams had lived in the same boarding house as Eugene Ware and dated him (neither was true), and that Ware and Theo had fought over Blanche Lamont (also false).

The disappearance of a 20-year-old married woman, Ella Forsyth, was likewise blamed on Theo. People just "knew" Mrs. Forsyth would be found hidden somewhere in Emmanuel Baptist Church, even though she was not a member of that congregation. (Mrs. Forsyth eventually turned up in San Jose, where she had run away with another man.)[12]

A few days after the murders hit the front pages, a drunken man and his equally inebriated mistress had a late-night fight after leaving a Tenderloin saloon. The man waved his gun at her and shouted what he evidently thought was the ultimate threat: "I'll fix you like Durrant fixed Blanche Lamont!"[13]

An enterprising company, Baldwin & Hammond Auctioneers, capitalized on the murders a mere two days after their discovery by incorporating them into their ads: "HORRIBLE CRIMES OCCUR in all large cities. . . . The recent atrocities are deplorable, but they should not prevent you from attending our great auction"[14]

A young Wells Fargo employee, Joseph E. McGlinchy, went home from work on Easter Monday and read the newspaper accounts of the murders, then took the articles with him to the cellar and hanged himself. The inquest jury concluded that "the deceased had no cause to commit suicide and . . . his mind was in an abnormal condition from reading the accounts of the crimes committed in the Emmanuel Baptist Church." When told of the incident, Theo commented that McGlinchy must have been crazy to commit suicide over someone else's difficulty. "Time enough to kill himself when he has his own trouble," he said.[15]

Not even Blanche Lamont escaped the gossipmongers. The prevailing theory was that Theo was performing an abortion on her, botched it, and she either died or he killed her to prevent her from telling anyone what had happened. Minnie Williams had somehow found out about it and this is why she was killed.[16]

There were reports of young men and women using the church at all hours of the night for a trysting spot and of a bed in the pastor's study. (Actually, there *was* a lounge there, one that Gibson had brought with him from Chico, but supposedly the rumors had been extant before that.) It got so bad that church trustee Charles Taber wrote an open letter to the newspapers denying the charge and stating that any young people seen entering the church at night were there for legitimate activities.[17]

Hypnotism was one theory as to how Theo got his victims to go into the church with him (proponents of this idea apparently assumed that the girls would otherwise have figured out in advance that he intended to kill them there). This was undoubtedly an offshoot of the immensely popular novel *Trilby*, in which the villain Svengali mesmerizes the title character into living with him and also transforms her into an international singing sensation.[18]

But by far most of the theorizing addressed itself to causation: How does a mild-mannered, respectable young man turn into a depraved devil? And how could we not have noticed this earlier? The medical students at Cooper had recently been assigned the reading of Dr. Richard von Krafft-Ebing's controversial and scandalous work *Psychopathia Sexualis*, translated into English three years earlier. Filled with detailed case histories of sexual perversities, the book was deemed too strong for young, susceptible minds like Theo Durrant's, and was considered responsible for turning him into a homicidal maniac.[19]

On the other hand, it was possible that Theo was a homicidal maniac from birth, and this could be determined by the science of physiognomy: the divination of personal and moral characteristics by examining an individual's physical features. Theo's wide-set eyes, thick lips, and strange head shape somehow presaged his eventual incarnation as the Demon of the Belfry.

An entire half-page spread in the *Examiner* showed Theo's hands with the screaming headline "THE HANDS OF THEODORE DURRANT WHICH STABBED MINNIE WILLIAMS AND STRANGLED BLANCHE LAMONT" and a "professional chiromancer" was asked to examine the sketch. Notwithstanding the fact that the palm reader had only the *backs* of Theo's hands to look at, he nonetheless ventured this analysis:[20]

The ends of the fingers indicate a mind that would not be inclined to weigh the consequences of an act. They are what I should call 'mean' fingers, indicating a petty and spiteful disposition. There is plenty of animal courage in these hands—they belong to one who does not know what fear is, and they are the hands of one who would not be a good boon companion. . . . The thumb of this hand indicates great will power and a great deal of brute force. The fingers are those of a man who possesses an exceedingly critical mind—one who is inclined to be fastidious about many things. The backs of these hands do not indicate a brutal nature, but the ball of this thumb shows a disposition to use brute force rather than cunning or calculation in accomplishing his purpose.

If physiognomy could alert us to the killers in our midst, then there must be some noticeable physical similarities among homicidal maniacs. The *Examiner* presented a sketch of a normal ear next to the ears of Theo and two other contemporary "monsters": Martin Thorn (who with his mistress Augusta Nack had killed and dismembered Mrs. Nack's other suitor, Willie Guldensuppe, in New York) and H. H. Holmes (who had dispatched men, women, and children for their insurance money in Chicago and Philadelphia). The ears of the three killers were shriveled-up little organs, obviously meant to reflect their shriveled-up little souls.[21] (However, all the pictures and sketches of Theo's ears show them to be perfectly normal in shape, even if his left ear stuck out slightly from his head.)

Other theories had to do with "bad blood." A man from New York City sent a telegram to Coroner Hawkins advising him to check Theo's racial heritage: "Misses Williams-Lamont horrors suggest negro diabolism. Is Durrant clear-blooded? Majority of negroes are Baptists."

In January and February 1894, Theo had suffered from severe pelvic pains and a high fever (104 degrees), which a physician diagnosed as "ulcerous degeneration in the tissues of the pelvic region," possibly due to being jarred while riding a bicycle on rough roads.[22] Asked if this indicated that Theo had "bad blood," the doctor quite sensibly responded that it did not.

Most of the students at Cooper Medical College were of the opinion that Theo could not possibly have killed the two young women. The janitor wept when he was interviewed, saying that Theo was "the quietest and nicest boy in the whole crowd here" and that a terrible mistake had been made with his arrest.[23] But there were others at Cooper who claimed Theo behaved peculiarly (without, however, giving any examples); that he took a malicious, cold-blooded delight in dissecting corpses, especially female ones (his professors said his behavior was perfectly respectful and businesslike, and that the students seldom got female bodies to dissect);[24] and that he regaled them with tales of raping and killing an Indian woman (even if he did say this, there is no evidence that it actually happened). The president of the senior class said that he always considered Theo a gentleman—but, he added (apparently in his eagerness not to appear naïve, and unaware of the inconsistency), one of "low caliber."[25]

A San Francisco prostitute related tales of wild, drunken orgies at her "house," where the prisoner was known as "Crazy Theo."[26] It was never substantiated that "Crazy Theo" (if such a person existed) and Theo Durrant were one and the same—nor, with Mamma's overprotective supervision, was it likely.

With such conflicting information, the mystery of Theo Durrant deepened: Who was he really? Could he have done this thing? What was his motive? Adding to the mystery was the behavior of Theo himself at City Prison. For the most part, he seemed unconcerned, nonchalant, at times as if he were actually enjoying himself. Disdaining prison fare, he sent to a nearby restaurant for his meals, then distributed his prison ration to other inmates. His mother sent down a bed and a rocking chair for his cell, and he spent time cleaning and decorating his little cubicle. He fussed over and worried about his appearance ("I wouldn't like my looks to go against me").[27] He laughed and joked with visitors as if he were not facing the gallows. Shouldn't he be more concerned about his fate?

Actually, while Theo often *did* act blasé about his situation, there were many times when he indicated depression, distress, and worry. But reporters placed him in an awkward position: When he was unconcerned, they said he was hard-hearted, unmoved by either his own plight or the terrible thing that had happened to the two girls who had been his friends (thereby indicating his guilt); when he cried or was morose, they said it was his guilty conscience and his fear of being hanged. So he was damned if he did and damned if he didn't.[28]

For example, for two nights in a row, Theo had screaming nightmares a few hours after falling asleep. He thrashed around, made motions of fending someone off, and yelled "Help me! Help me!" The guards and the other prisoners were frightened, as they thought he was having some kind of seizure or convulsion; but, after a few minutes the fit subsided and Theo slept calmly—without ever having awakened. Rather than view this as the sign of either a guilty conscience overcome with remorse or an innocent man oppressed by his predicament, the police thought he might be faking it to set up an insanity defense.[29]

There were also times when Theo talked about Blanche and expressed sorrow for her death (interestingly, he never mentioned Minnie by name, except as one of "those poor girls," and never indicated any sadness over her murder). In every such case, he made the connection to his sister, Maud: Blanche was like his sister, so "lively," so beautiful, so full of fun; he said he thought of Blanche as he thought of his sister. It would seem that Theo was incapable of thinking of Blanche without, at the same time, being reminded of Maud.[30]

However, just as often, Theo seemed to have forgotten why he was in prison. He had the capacity to disengage himself so totally that he was able to relax, to laugh with his visitors, to sleep soundly (apart from the two nightmares), and to act as if he were in his own living room.

It would not be until his mother began showing up in court that observers would see yet another clue to the stoicism of Theo Durrant.

In the Mission District, the tongues wagged nonstop. There was a story of a female boarder at the Durrant home who had awakened the night of Minnie Williams's murder and smelled something burning in the stove, the obvious inference being that Theo was destroying his bloody clothes. The problem with the story was that there *was* no female boarder at the Durrants' at that time.[31]

To explain both the absence of bloody clothes and Theo's innate degeneracy, a story emerged that he had enticed other women into the church, excused himself, then reappeared in a state of total nudity. The women this happened to were too embarrassed to report it (although they somehow managed to convey it to the talebearers). This rumor proved the most tenacious, sending the police throughout the state on a wild goose chase of several months before concluding that the so-called "mysterious woman" (sometimes called Annie Wilming or Welming, and sometimes called Ida Clayton) was a myth. Even today, most accounts of the case include this legend as a fact.[32]

Policemen assigned to guard the Emmanuel Baptist Church at night dreaded this duty. They said they could hear strange sounds that might have been the ghosts of the murdered girls, and they imagined they could see things in the dark.[33]

A very real threat came, however, not from things that go bump in the night, but from an irate citizenry who wanted the church burned to the ground. It had been desecrated beyond redemption and had been bad luck from the time it was first erected on the former site of a haunted house. Several of its pastors had brought disgrace down on its head: One had committed suicide, another had been discovered acting shamefully in some unspecified way (which must have meant something sexual, since nobody seemed to hesitate to speak of suicide and murder), and a third had killed Charles De Young, cofounder of the *San Francisco Chronicle*.[34]

This last scandal was one of San Francisco's juicier events. The flamboyant and controversial Reverend Isaac Kalloch (to whose church the Durrants belonged when they first came to San Francisco) ran for mayor on the Workingmen's ticket in 1879. (The Workingmen's party was dedicated to excluding the Chinese from California, since they were a ready source of cheap labor.) Charles De Young used the *Chronicle* to attack Kalloch and his party for their stand on Chinese exclusion, and dug up a sex scandal involving Kalloch back in the Midwest. Kalloch responded by saying equally nasty things about De Young, which so enraged the editor (although he had started the fight between the two) that he went after Kalloch with a pistol and shot him. However, he only wounded the minister, and the result was such an outpouring of sympathy for Kalloch that he was eventually elected mayor of San Francisco.

De Young, not having learned his lesson, continued his attacks on Kalloch in his newspaper. Isaac Kalloch's unstable son, Milton, who was at that time the pastor of the Emmanuel Baptist Church, became so unhinged by all this (and possibly by his overindulgence in alcohol as well) that he sought out Charles De Young in the *Chronicle* offices to avenge the name of Kalloch, Sr., and shot the newspaper owner to death. This was in April 1880.

Now, fifteen Aprils later, came the coup de grace of a double murder within the confines of the church itself. It didn't seem as if Emmanuel Baptist could ever raise itself up from this latest scandal. Best to torch it and start over.

This persistent talk of burning the church to the ground reached Emmanuel Baptist's insurance companies, and they notified the trustees that they were considering cancelling their policies. The trustees were doubly upset at this prospect; not only would the church be financially unprotected, but a $10,000 balance remained on the mortgage.[35] However, the church remained unused and the talk of razing it remained just talk.

At the Golden Gate Undertaking parlors, the bodies of Blanche and Minnie were placed in identical white coffins for public viewing. Blanche was too far decomposed for an open casket, but the undertakers had done a fine job of erasing the marks of violence from Minnie's face. People lined up for blocks to shuffle solemnly past the two biers. Many of these, mostly women, got back in line for a second viewing. It was estimated that four to five thousand viewers walked through the mortuary in a four-hour period.[36]

Blanche's body was sent to her home in Dillon, Montana, for funeral and burial, accompanied by her sister. The train was met by a large contingent to escort Maud and the body to the St. James Episcopal Church for the services. Among the voluminous flower arrangements was one from the Emmanuel Baptist orchestra in San Francisco.

Almost the entire city of Dillon was present at the funeral, which was estimated to be the largest ever held in the city, with eighty carriages lined up at the church. All businesses were closed during the services, and afterward the Dillon brass band led the cortege to the burial site in Mountain View Cemetery, where Blanche was buried next to her father.[37]

Minnie's funeral, held at the First Baptist Church in San Francisco, was packed to the walls, although most of the people there had never known her in life. Among her pallbearers were Clarence Wolfe, Dr. Tom Vogel, and George King (who also played the organ). Mrs. King sang a solo. The minister, Rev. M. P. Boynton, used his sermon to talk about the increasing violence in San Francisco and to warn young women not to go out with young men without a chaperone they could trust—namely, a father or a brother. But, in the waning days of the Victorian era at the dawning of the twentieth century, no doubt this advice fell on deaf ears. After the services, Minnie was interred in Laurel Hill Cemetery.[38]

A couple of days before the funeral, Albert Williams tried to make peace with Clark Morgan, who had been openly critical of him. Williams put out his hand, and Morgan at first refused to take it. Then he relented, saying, "If the girl was living I would not touch your hand, but she is dead, and that makes the matter different."

"You misjudge me, Mr. Morgan," Minnie's father said.

"I wish to God that I could misjudge you," Morgan replied sadly.[39]

The Rev. J. George Gibson did not take part in Minnie's funeral service, although he was present on the altar with Mr. Boynton. Gibson's peculiar behavior after the tragedy had singled him out for negative comment, and there were many in San Francisco who felt he may have been guilty of the crimes himself—either as a lone wolf or as Theo's accomplice (how else could Theo have carried Blanche's body up all those stairs to the belfry?). Under the circumstances, it was deemed more appropriate that Gibson's role in Minnie's funeral be an inactive one.[40]

Gibson had nearly suffered a nervous breakdown after the discovery of the murders hit the front page. Ill-equipped for crises and abhorring the answering of questions (*vide* the maxims in his study), he had hidden himself away from reporters. Since he would not listen to their questions, they speculated as to his answers; since he would not grant them interviews, they took free rein in depicting his oddities in their newspapers. And his querulous complaints that the police had caused too much damage to the church in their search for Blanche Lamont came across as unfeeling and self-serving.[41] There must have been many in San Francisco who felt that the strange, reclusive minister made a better villain than the more prepossessing Theo.

Caught by a *Chronicle* reporter outside the church, Gibson was asked why he wouldn't talk to the press or admit them inside. He ventured some statements, such as that he was miffed at being misquoted, but whenever he got uncomfortable he invoked his mantra: "You are asking questions," insinuating that he would continue to talk if there were no questions asked. The man positively had a phobia about questions![42]

At another time when Gibson deigned to speak to a reporter, he cast aspersions on the honesty of the newspaper profession. The reporter took offense and let loose with some unprintable expletives. One of the two struck a blow and the other returned it. This was as far as it got, as at that point, Gibson's sister entered the fray and put an end to it. But Gibson was so overwrought as a result of the confrontation that he took to his bed with "nervous prostration."[43] (He had obviously forgotten Maxims 14 and 15: "Never get angry. Never sulk.")

Enough was enough. In a panic, Gibson sent a telegram to a young man he had known in Chico, asking him to drop everything and come be his personal secretary (and, primarily, his press liaison). Hence, not quite a week after the gruesome discovery in the church, another character entered the Durrant drama: 19-year-old Robert Newton Lynch.[44]

Lynch had been born in Sharpsville, Pennsylvania, on December 18, 1875, and moved with his family to California in 1881. He must have been a precocious young man, as he served in the state senate as a stenographer in 1889 and as a page in 1891. In April 1895, when he was sent for by J. George Gibson, Lynch was teaching stenography in Chico.

Despite his youth, Robert Lynch was more than equal to the task ahead of him and infinitely more resourceful than Gibson in dealing with the vagaries of notoriety. From the time he arrived on the scene, he became Gibson's official mouthpiece, giving interviews and writing letters to the newspapers in the name of his employer.

Gibson and Lynch were more than employer and employee, however. They had been "intimate friends" in Chico (despite the nearly twenty-year age gap), they lived together in Gibson's rooms, and the minister went nowhere without his young protégé. (As eager as reporters were to present the minister in a bad light, it is surprising that they did not make more of this.)

From prison, Theo bemoaned the fact that many of his so-called friends had deserted him, and seemed particularly aggrieved at the absence of Gibson, his own pastor. Was it not the Christian thing to visit an imprisoned man and give him spiritual comfort? But Gibson, who *did* want to visit his parishioner, was paralyzed by indecision. There were, after all, those insinuations in the press and the letters to the editor saying "look to the minister." If he went to see Theo, would it look as if the "Cahoots Brothers" were collaborating to get their stories straight?

Then, as Gibson wavered back and forth—should I go? should I not go?—Mamma Durrant solved the problem for him by writing an open letter to the *Call* that stopped just short of naming the minister as the guilty party. She asked the police to arrest *everyone* who had a key to the side door of the church and pointed out Gibson's bizarre behavior in avoiding public contact, as well as the fact that Minnie had a boyfriend in his forties (no one knew for sure how old Gibson was at this point, but he was assumed to be about 40).

After this pointed accusation, Gibson felt himself excused from the charitable act of ministering to Theo Durrant as he languished in City Prison.[45]

Theo's anticipated exoneration after telling his story to Chief Crowley was not forthcoming, and it was obvious that ex-Judge Thompson, well-meaning and devoted as he might be, would be inadequate as the legal defender of the monstrous Demon of the Belfry. So, entering the fray on Theo's side were two attorneys with much trial experience: General John H. Dickinson and Eugene Nelson Deuprey.

John H. Dickinson, 46, was born in Virginia and brought to California while still an infant. He had practiced law (primarily civil cases) since 1873, and in 1879 was elected state senator for the Republican Party. As a young man, Dickinson joined the California National Guard and rose through the ranks until he was appointed brigadier general in 1891. He was the commanding general of Theo's Second Brigade, and had been at its helm during the Pullman strike in the summer of 1894.

When Dickinson read in the newspapers that one of his men was in legal trouble and had been arrested while on Signal Corps duty, he quickly sought out the officers in Theo's company. All of them spoke highly of him and thought that, from what they had seen of him, he was innocent of the charges against him. Dickinson was also told that the Durrants didn't have a lot of money for their son's defense, and that was all this highly honorable man needed to hear. He offered to help Thompson with the case.[46]

Eugene N. Deuprey, also 46, was a native of New Orleans and, like Dickinson, had been brought to California at an early age. A highly ambitious man, Deuprey was already a successful criminal lawyer. Dickinson, undoubtedly recognizing his own deficiencies in this regard, convinced Deuprey to join the defense team.[47] It would turn out to be the best decision made on Theo's behalf.

Theo's lawyers would have an uphill climb. Not only was all available evidence (albeit completely circumstantial at this time) against him, but the police did not seem interested in pursuing anyone else—even though there were at least three others who legitimately qualified as suspects: J. George Gibson, Elmer Wolfe, and the janitor Frank Sademan. Chief Patrick Crowley stated emphatically, however, that he had "enough evidence [against Durrant] to hang a dozen men" and had Theo's picture hung in his Rogues' Gallery of convicted criminals—two months before his trial![48]

The police had also employed what is today termed the "one-man lineup," whereby witnesses are told, in effect: "We have arrested this man for the crime. Is this the man you saw?" In our modern system, this would be enough to overturn a conviction, but in 1895, it was undoubtedly thought of as more of a convenience for both police and witnesses.

On Monday, April 15, the day after Theo's arrest, the three Normal School students—Alice Pleasant, Minnie Edwards, and May Lanigan—were taken by Detective Gibson to Chief Crowley's office and told that the man arrested for their classmate's murder would be coming. If they recognized him, they were to say so; if they did not, they were to keep still. Then Theo was brought in.

Gibson had Theo turn at all angles so the young women could get a good look at him. They were so nervous, they misunderstood their instructions, and the police escort had almost gotten back out the door with the prisoner before the girls said anything. After they identified him as the young man they had seen with Blanche Lamont on the afternoon of April 3, Theo was brought back into the room and asked if he had anything to say. He looked at the three girls: "I have to say that I was not there," he told them. Still, all three noticed that he had given a flicker of recognition when he first saw Minnie Edwards, the girl who had walked to the cable car with Blanche.[49]

Similarly, the Fitzpatrick and Struven sisters were brought to the chief's office and told they would be going to another room to look at the man in custody for the murder of Minnie Williams. Theo was there with his hat and coat on, facing the witnesses. Celia Fitzpatrick asked the detective to have him turn his back and pull his collar up to duplicate what she had seen that night, and Theo obliged. All four girls identified him as the one who had come up to their group near the Emmanuel Baptist Church on the night of April 12.[50]

Only a very few days after Theo's arrest, the prosecution was ready to present its case to see if there was enough evidence to hold him for trial in the murders of Blanche Lamont and Minnie Williams. In California in 1895, the mandatory sentence upon conviction, absent a recommendation of mercy by the jury, was death by hanging.

The Inquest, and a Trial
by "Noose"paper

I live for those who love me
  Whose hearts are kind and true;
For the heaven that smiles above me,
  And awaits my spirit, too;
For all human ties that bind me,
  For the task that God assigned me,
For the bright hopes left behind me,
  And the good that I can do.
    —Author unknown; poem sent by Theo Durrant as a mes-
                          sage to his loyal friends.

In the year 1895, people were well aware of—and focusing on—
the new century just around the corner. As we in the 1990s worried about the Y2K bug wiping out our technology, our predeces-
sors in the waning years of the Victorian era worried that the New
Age would bring with it an erosion of cultural and moral standards.
Heading their list of dreaded events was the emergence of the New
Woman.

Women had been agitating for enfranchisement for many years,
and the looming twentieth century inspired them to turn up the

heat on these demands. An article in the *Chronicle*, entitled "If Women Went to Congress," supplied quotes from around the United States which encompassed a mixture of the ridiculous and the sublime.[1]

Elizabeth Cady Stanton said that the presence of women in Congress would bring "Justice, Liberty, and Equality for women" and would also "lighten the burdens of men." Most people, male and female—including Susan B. Anthony—thought that the female presence would "clean up" Congress by getting rid of the cigar smoke, vulgar language, tobacco juice on the floor, and feet on the desks. A senator from South Dakota unchivalrously asserted that women in Congress would bring chaos, and one from New Jersey said the whole exercise was a meaningless speculation: *Real* ladies did not want to be in Congress, nor did they want to vote. A woman from Indiana claimed that women "would do more work in less time than men do, and do it better." And a very diplomatic senator from Oregon, John H. Mitchell, blandly stated that "it would be beneficial in all respects."

There seemed to be a pervading fear that women doing traditionally male jobs would result in the abandonment of their femininity in dress and behavior. A joke in the newspapers purporting to represent the year 2000 had a married couple getting ready to go to the opera and the wife calling downstairs, "Honey, where did you put my collar buttons?" [2] (While they could accurately predict the change in women's garb and the relations between the sexes, they apparently thought it too much of a stretch to imagine men not wearing detachable collars 105 years later.) Given this atmosphere, then, it is not hard to see why the bloomer craze caused such a flap.

Amelia Bloomer had introduced her Zouave-type pants for women in the 1850s. In the 1870s and 1880s, when walkathons were a big fad for both sexes, many women chose to wear the new bloomers during the mostly indoor contests. When the introduction of the "safety" bicycle in the 1890s brought cycling to the masses, women responded with a fervor that equaled that of the men. And for safety, comfort, and convenience, they preferred the bloomer costume for their riding garb.[3]

Unlike the walkathons, however, bicycle riding was done outdoors and in the public eye: on city streets and country roads, in parks and in velodromes. Riding was not done only in competition, as walking had been, but for exercise and recreation. Bicycles were also used for transportation. (A cartoon of the time, entitled "The New Era," shows a line of horses headed for the slaughterhouse while farmers, women, children, old men, dandies, and even a dog cycle by in a steady stream.)[4] Despite their high initial cost, bicycles were more economical than horses (they didn't have to be fed and didn't need stables or tack), less messy (no excrement in the streets), and accessible to all.

But the offshoot of this craze was the problem of women riding in public in garments that were perceived to be just a step away from men's pants. Where would it end? There was constant debate about it (including sermons from the Sunday pulpit), and in a protective move the City and County of San Francisco passed a regulation making cross-dressing a crime![5] Bloomers would be allowed, but they must be sufficiently baggy. Nonetheless, the bicycle craze marked the beginning of more sensible clothing for women, and the heady sense of unchaperoned freedom experienced while riding a bike meant that there was no going back to the old ways. (Susan B. Anthony would say later that "the bicycle has done more for the emancipation of women than anything else in the world.")[6]

But if bloomers and bicycles indicated that civilization was going to hell in a handbasket, they would pale in comparison to the murders of Blanche Lamont and Minnie Williams. More to San Francisco than just unspeakable crimes, they touched chords of concerns as California neared the twentieth century: How would the rest of the world view the Golden State? What could be done about the increasing tendency of women to go about unchaperoned? Were these "lust murders" a signal that the modern era would be a conscienceless, depraved, irreligious one?

The official closing of the frontier had been declared only five years earlier, and San Francisco was sensitive about its Wild West image in the eyes of the world. (It was this same sensitivity that was responsible for the rapid rebuilding of the city exactly eleven years later. If Chicago could put itself together quickly after its devastating 1871 fire, then San Francisco would beat that record after its 1906 earthquake.) Would the rest of the world see these murders as being fostered by the climate of bordellos and bad guys?

And there was no overlooking the fact that, despite their status as "pure girls" above reproach, both Blanche and Minnie had met their deaths through actions that could only be described as imprudent by 1895 standards. Blanche went back and forth to school on the streetcars unescorted, and not even in the company of other young ladies; her final act of indiscretion was to enter an empty church alone with a young man. Minnie evidently traveled all over the Bay Area with no escort, often returning to her Alameda home late at night. She met her fate through the same indiscreet behavior as her companion in death. Was the emancipation of women to bring their wholesale slaughter as well?[7]

Finally, there were the murders themselves, perceived as committed out of the unbridled lust and depravity of their perpetrator. Certainly, the old motives made more sense: anger, revenge, greed, the elimination of an intolerable or inconvenient spouse. The Emmanuel Baptist murders, on the other hand, were similar to the savage butcheries of Jack the Ripper seven years earlier, only worse: Not only were they closer to home, but the prevailing opinion was that the Ripper's victims—all prostitutes—had no one but themselves to blame for a high-risk lifestyle that brought them into contact with a fiend. Why, Jack the Ripper was a gentleman compared to Theo Durrant![8]

The crimes themselves were unexplainable, yet there *must* be an explanation. In this post-Darwinian era, there were many who smugly pointed out the ineffectiveness of religion (the young man arrested for the murders had been prominent in his church) and the noticeable absence of God in His failure to prevent the unspeakable from happening on sacred ground.

Ministers scrambled to defend God and religion from such attacks. It was a cheap shot, they asserted, to use these horrible crimes as proof that God did not exist or that religion had no power. The fault instead lay at other feet: at a failure to follow the Ten Commandments, which modern big business seemed to think were hopelessly old-fashioned; at a "soft on crime" approach in San Francisco (since 1890, more than 150 murders had been committed, and the only person executed so far had been a Chinese man); at an approach that proved that "a murderer who has money back of him could not be convicted here"; and at a "need of more motherly influence and protection" (an ironic statement in the case of Theo, who actually had need of a good deal less of it).[9]

Such were the musings of some of the ministers preaching the

Sunday after the discovery of the crimes. But there were lighter moments, too. A wag (or a nut) calling himself "Harry the Hacker" left a woman's glove and a lock of brown hair in a box outside the main police station. The hair was stained with red ink and a note was found inside the glove: "You are on the wrong trail. Got the wrong bird. My handywork. HARRY THE HACKER. Find me if you can."[10]

And a saloonkeeper named Briese thought of a novel way to get even with the city for passing an ordinance against side-door entrances in saloons by filing a petition demanding the closing of all side doors of churches. The board of supervisors refused to take it seriously, calling it a "cheeky joke," even though Briese showed up for the hearing with a lawyer.[11]

At the center of everything—the horrible, the mundane, the irreverent, the jokes, and the gossip—there were the newspapers. Their role cannot be overestimated. In 1895, they were THE primary source of news; the other source was word-of-mouth. To an audience that did not have access to the scenes and events reported, the journalists became its substitute. So good were they in describing these that one hundred years later it is possible to "hear" the barely suppressed gasps in a courtroom; to "smell" a room rank with the mixture of cigar smoke and too many people; and to "see" the nervous licking of the lips by a pale young man with acne brought before the court to enter his plea.

The newspapers did more than this. They lived and died by the news they could dig up, by the scoops they could get on their competition—so their reporters became detectives, many of them more competent than the police. In the Durrant case, many of the most important witnesses were discovered by reporters snooping around Mission neighborhoods.

But the down side of this was that, in their eagerness to bring news to their readers and best the competition, newspapers did not always adhere to the truth. Interviews and events were sometimes manufactured in the minds of reporters, or statements falsely attributed to those who *had* been interviewed.

For example, on the day after the discovery of the crimes, when Theo was over on Mount Diablo with the Signal Corps (and had been since early Saturday morning), the *Examiner* published an entirely fictitious story involving a mad chase through the Mission by the police after an escaping Theo. According to the article, the police had put a guard around the Durrant home, and at midnight on Saturday, Theo had attempted to sneak back into the house. Discovered, he supposedly fled on foot and at the time of publication was still at large.[12] It not only made for more thrilling reading than the mundane truth, but undoubtedly sent frissons of delightful terror through many readers who imagined Theo skulking about their own neighborhoods in search of fresh victims.

Another gimmick was the printing of the wild rumors that sprang up throughout the Mission without checking their validity—or, if the story was checked and found to be false, the article would refrain from revealing this until the end. It was a kind of bait-and-switch routine where readers were lured by headlines (and headlines in those days were stacked four and five deep in descending font sizes), regaled with the titillating gossip, then told at the end that it turned out to be untrue. Readers who didn't stick with the article to the end would never know the punch line. Readers who did often ignored it.

Two such stories (which would later emerge as part of the mythology of the Durrant case) concerned Theo's relations with preteen girls. In one instance, a man told a reporter that his niece, who had attended Emmanuel Baptist Sunday School, said that several of the girls had complained that Theo often tried to kiss them. It made them uncomfortable and they didn't like it. At the end of the article was the real truth, which the reporter discovered when he interviewed the niece herself: It wasn't Theo who was trying to kiss the little girls, but Allen Church, the janitor who was Frank Sademan's predecessor.[13]

Another story named a woman who was disturbed at Theo's close attentions to her granddaughters, and who had allegedly told her daughter-in-law not to leave them alone with him. The grandmother was interviewed the next day by a rival paper and was very upset at this report. She had neither said nor implied any such behavior on Theo's part. What she *had* said was meant to be a compliment to him: that he had been very encouraging to the little children who had performed in a musical recital.[14]

That people tended to remember the rumor and not the retraction—and still do today—reflects the very human tendency to find a clue as to why someone would commit atrocities. It makes sense to us that a monster would leave a trail of slime, and a look at his past should be a reliable indicator of future depravity. It is confusing and unsettling to read about a Theo Durrant who was kind to animals and little children; it doesn't tell us what we need to know.

Because of this great discrepancy between Theo's character and the murders, as well as that between his victims' reputations and the indiscreet behavior of each on the day of her murder, there were many more questions than answers. Readers, both male and female, sent ideas, questions, solutions, and suggestions to the newspapers. Never one to miss an opportunity to sell papers, William Randolph Hearst had several issues of his *Examiner* devote a whole page to these letters, and encouraged people to continue sending them in, claiming that they were performing a public service in doing so: Maybe Durrant was innocent, or maybe there was even stronger proof of his guilt that had yet to be discovered.[15]

Many of the letters are, to no one's surprise, kooky. Reflecting a popular myth, one reader urged the exhumation of the victims to see if the image of their killer was imprinted on their eyes. Another advocated the use of a hypnotist to work on both Durrant and Rev. Gibson—but, the reader cautioned, the hypnotist selected had to be "free from all corruption by the influence of money." There were suggestions for making Theo confess: prod him with sharp instruments or hot irons, or—even better—lock him up in the church belfry with just bread and water. One creative reader wove the unsolved mystery of Eugene Ware's murder into his theory: Theo had killed Eugene Ware and Blanche was with him at the time. Blanche then told Minnie, so Theo killed them both to shut them up.

The result of all this theory, speculation, and rumor-mongering, however, was the potential poisoning of the minds of future jurors. Readers who had been told from the very first day that Theo Durrant was being sought for the Emmanuel Baptist murders and that the chief of police had declared he had enough evidence to hang a dozen men might find it difficult to put this aside in their examination of the evidence as jurors. One reader characterized what was happening in the newspapers as "pressecution."[16]

At City Prison, Theo continued to be the main attraction. As he visited through the bars with his parents and friends, the police sent potential male witnesses to walk by and see if they could identify him (for female witnesses, he was brought into the chief's office). As he sat reading or writing, reporters and the curious constantly interrupted him. Eventually, the police put a stop to the stream of gawkers by refusing admission to anyone Theo did not wish to see. However, this only made people more creative in the ruses they invented to get a look at the criminal of the century.

Many women said they were physiognomists who could determine Theo's guilt or innocence by touching him, or spiritualists who had messages for him from Blanche and Minnie. A well-dressed married couple claimed they lived by Cooper Medical College and might have some important information in the case; but they would have to see the prisoner first to identify him. They were taken to his cell, but after staring at him for a long time, declared he was not the one they had seen. Their smug looks on leaving gave away their real intentions. Others pretended to be looking for lost children, or relatives who might have been arrested for public intoxication.[17]

Most of Theo's visitors consisted of his parents (usually separately), occasional young ladies from the church who came with Mamma, members of the Signal Corps, and classmates from the medical school. Mamma brought him flowers (she was the only woman allowed to do so), fruit, and other items. Once she slipped Theo a mirror through the bars, claiming it was fruit when she was challenged. (Prisoners were not allowed anything that could be used as a weapon for suicide or aggression.)[18]

Their son's arrest and subsequent vilification in the press had galvanized Mamma and Papa Durrant, and their days were now devoted to Theo's cause. Papa went to George King and asked him to change the story he had told to the police: Instead of saying that it was *definitely* Theo he had seen in the church on April 3, could he please say that it was a man who *looked* like him? [19] As George was a good friend of Theo's and saw him nearly every day, there was no likelihood that he could have been mistaken in the encounter. Papa's attempted subornation of perjury, which was duly reported to the police by a friend in whom George had confided, did Theo's cause no good.

In the meantime, Mamma was busy voicing her various theories through interviews and letters printed in the newspapers. She was constantly berating the police, denouncing their evidence, or issuing mysterious statements about newly-discovered evidence that would free her son. For example, she said that a man and woman were seen entering the church while Theo was at Tom Vogel's. She was not at liberty to discuss this, but at the proper time they would be brought forward. They never were.[20]

THE INQUEST ON MINNIE WILLIAMS[21]

In California in 1895 there were two prerequisites to be accomplished before a suspect could be tried for murder in the superior court. First came the inquest, conducted by the coroner in front of a special jury gathered for that purpose. Its sole purpose was to determine how the victim had died and, if through homicide, at whose hands. As this was not considered an adversarial proceeding, attorneys for the suspect could not ask questions. Jurors, however, were allowed to ask questions of the witnesses. Once a verdict of homicide was reached and a suspect named, the case went to a preliminary examination in the police court.

The purpose of the preliminary examination, which was held before a judge only, was to determine whether the prosecution had enough evidence to proceed against the suspect—in other words, whether there was probable cause. The trick here was for the district attorney to present just enough evidence to convince the court without, at the same time, revealing all the cards in his deck: He wanted to be able to spring some surprises at trial and catch the defense off guard. (Today, there are rules requiring the prosecution to share discovery with the defense.)

At this hearing, the defense was allowed to cross-examine witnesses and could, if it chose, put some of its own on the stand. There was a fine line to walk here, too: An attorney would be trying to discover as much as he could about the state's case without revealing what defenses he would be pursuing. (Oftentimes, however, the prosecution could figure this out by the line of questioning during cross-examination.) Once a verdict of probable cause was rendered by the police court judge, the suspect became a defendant. On the other hand, if the judge thought there was not enough evidence against him to warrant taking him to trial, the suspect was released.

Because Minnie Williams had been found first, even though she had not been killed first, the inquest on her death was held before that of Blanche Lamont. It was scheduled to begin at 10:00 A.M.

on Tuesday, April 16—a mere three days after her body had been discovered in the church library. Hours before that time, hordes of people crowded around the entrance to the morgue, hoping to be allowed to view the spectacle. Even after the police, with much difficulty, forced them back from the doorway, they milled around on the sidewalk for the whole day, hoping for glimpses of the witnesses. They were rewarded for their patience when Detective Gibson arrived with Theo himself.

Theo was not expected to attend the inquest. His attorneys had told him not to, and he had no desire to go. However, Chief Crowley—who probably wanted to do what he could to rattle his prisoner—insisted that he should be there to hear the witnesses against him. Theo at first refused, but Jailer Sattler told him he could go the easy way or the hard way, and so he went along docilely enough. Part of his reluctance was due to the ever-present threat of mob violence, and just the whole ordeal of being stared at and scrutinized constantly. Another part may have been due to a fear of the possibility of being confronted with the body of Minnie Williams.

Dressed neatly in a business suit and bow tie, with a Signal Corps pin in his lapel, Theo looked more like a clerk or even an attorney than the suspect in San Francisco's most famous murder case. He greeted his father and his attorneys, then took a seat at the very back of the room against the wall, hoping to be as inconspicuous as possible. Throughout the testimony he nervously chewed gum and, so he would not have to look at anyone, picked up a book on medical jurisprudence from the coroner's desk and engrossed himself in it. Occasionally, he took out a pocket comb and ran it through his hair. That this inattention was feigned was revealed when the pastor, Rev. Gibson, was on the stand and at a loss to supply the name of a parishioner. Without looking up from the textbook, Theo volunteered the name from the back of the room.

On the stand that first day, Clark Morgan revealed his pique at having to testify instead of proceeding with his move to Tacoma. Chief Crowley had assured him that his testimony would be of no value to the coroner's jury—so why was he here? Morgan also told the story of the red horsecar ticket found in Minnie's purse, a story which served to identify as hers the purse found in Theo's coat pocket: At the beginning of Holy Week, Morgan had emptied out a tin box on the dining room table to sort out its contents and throw away what was no longer useful. Minnie immediately spied the red ticket, which Morgan had kept for nineteen years, and picked it up. "What's this?" she asked. When he told her, she exclaimed, "I am going to try to see if I cannot ride on it in Oakland!" Morgan told her to go ahead and take it.

Although Morgan could not identify the purse as Minnie's, he was sure the red ticket was the one he had kept for nineteen years. He was so sure, in fact, that to a juror who questioned this he responded that he was willing to pay $100 if it were *not* the right one.

The other witnesses that first day were Officer Arthur Riehl, Detective Peter Chappelle, and Frank Sademan. But the one who really livened up the proceedings was the Reverend J. George Gibson. Gibson was extremely ill at ease on the stand, and tried to overcome it with a flippant, sarcastic attitude. At times, he was downright rude. This was always his response to uncomfortable situations, and it did much to alienate his interrogators and insure his position in the mythology of the Durrant case as an accomplice or an alternate suspect.

When he was first called to the stand, Gibson made a dramatic sweeping bow before taking his seat. He seemed to expect a response, which no one gave, and sat down looking a little embarrassed.

Gibson stated that he had been in his study at the church until 7:30 P.M. on Friday, April 12. At that time, he left and walked the two or three blocks to Tom Vogel's house for the meeting of the Young People's Christian Endeavor Society. When he arrived approximately five minutes later, Tom's mother answered the door. "Well, Mrs. Vogel," he said to her, "I do not know whether I am early or whether I am late, because my watch is not keeping good time." "You are in lots of time," Mrs. Vogel assured him as she led him to their upstairs flat.

Gibson first said Theo came in that night between 9:30 and 11:30, then later stated it as 9:30. When Coroner Hawkins asked him about the discrepancy, Gibson got huffy: "I do not understand you. Please make it a little clearer." The coroner repeated his question, and Gibson told him haughtily, "You are under a wrong impression, I think." "Just correct it then," Hawkins said tersely.

With regard to another issue, Gibson got testy over the way Hawkins was asking the questions: "Put your questions directly to me, and I will answer them directly." The coroner responded with, "Mr. Gibson, you will please let me conduct this examination as I see fit." A question-and-answer segment on the locks (where Gibson was referring to the library lock and Hawkins was referring to the lock on the side door) is reminiscent of Abbott and Costello's "Who's on First?" routine, and just as frustrating for those involved. Gibson was a trying witness, but they weren't through with him.

The next day, Gibson reinforced his image as a pastor who was curiously ignorant of his own church. Not only had he never been to the belfry before Blanche's body was discovered, but he never even knew the church *had* a belfry! He didn't know who had a key to the side door, and had been obliged to buy his own. Asked about his congregation, Gibson had to resort to the book of names, addresses, and dates of membership given to him by Theo when he was appointed pastor in November 1894.

Gibson was hypersensitive to criticism, and at this point in the proceedings probably felt he was coming off badly as the shepherd who was supposed to guard his flock. When a juror asked for clarification, Gibson turned on him:

Juror: I understood, yesterday, if I am not mistaken, that the lady who saw the body first, in the excitement of the moment, said that she didn't know whether it was male or female, or whether it was made of wax, or what it was—she could not make out anything. That is what I understood from the testimony of the witness. Today the testimony came in that she had covered the body, so that it should not be ex-posed. Now, is that a mistake, or should it be simply a correction to be made?

Gibson: May I ask the gentleman a question?

Coroner: Certainly.

Gibson: Does he imply that I was trying to hide the sex of the individual?

Juror: No. I simply want to understand it because as we are jurors, we want to get every particle of evidence that we can. . . . Maybe I am mistaken but it is the duty of the jury to get a particular explanation for your protection, or for the criminal's protection; we want to know just the exact statement.

Gibson: I did not say anything to carry the impression that Mrs. Nolte did not know of the sex of the figure. Mrs. Nolte did know the sex of the figure, but I did say Mrs. Nolte did not know whether the figure was wax or real.

If Gibson thought he got rough handling at the inquest, he was in for a good deal more of it at the preliminary examination.

Mrs. Amelia Voy and her daughter, Florence, both testified that Minnie told them the social would be at Tom Vogel's that night, which scotched the theory that Theo had misdirected Minnie into thinking that it would be at the church. It also reveals that Minnie deliberately avoided telling them about meeting Theo at the church first. Why wouldn't she want them to know this if it were an entirely innocent "date"?

Mrs. Voy, who must have felt some vague guilt at the fact that Minnie was killed while staying at her home, blurted out at the end of her testimony, "Poor child. She was a splendid girl, one of the best I ever knew."

Tom Vogel's inquest testimony was a masterpiece of considered, thoughtful responses. On the one hand, he wanted to be absolutely truthful; on the other, he wanted to be absolutely fair to his former friend. He was scrupulous in his answers, peppering them with a liberal sprinkling of "I think" and "it seems to me" and "if I am not mistaken." When Tom had first been questioned about Theo's excuse for lateness, he said it was that he was out with the corps and had trouble catching his horse. Now, he could not be sure exactly what had been said, and he refused to state positively. Overall, he came across as a highly credible and fair witness, if an overly cautious one.

Vogel's testimony is important for illuminating two incidents, both involving his cousin, Lucile Turner. The first incident concerns the gynecological examination. Tom testified that Theo "suggested in a gentlemanly manner that he would prescribe for her" and that Lucile agreed to take the medicine. As far as his cousin's being so insulted by Theo's proposal to examine her that she slammed the door in his face, Tom now said, "I think it is a little different from the way Lucile told me. She says now that she did not shut the door in his face." (It is not hard to imagine Tom questioning her very closely about this and her finally admitting the truth.)

The second incident is another that has entered the lore of the Durrant case, and concerns Minnie's suspicions of Theo. On this second day of the inquest, Coroner Hawkins asked Tom Vogel if Minnie had ever told him she was suspicious of Theo. His response was, "She never told me that." Pressed further as to whether he knew of her telling anyone, he said, "I don't know that I have heard *her* say so. . . . I heard a young lady say so, but then I do not know whether it is true or not." He admits that the young lady in question is Lucile Turner, but his statement strongly hints that Lucile does not always tell the truth: In other words, just because Lucile says so doesn't mean it was actually said or, if said, was actually true. (Reading between the lines, one senses that Tom Vogel was fed up with his cousin!)

Even if the statement were true, there is no indication as to when it might have been made. In all likelihood, Lucile is the one who revealed to Minnie that Theo was going out with other girls (as related by Jennie Turnball), and Minnie may have made the statement at that time. The statement about suspicion probably did not have any connection with the disappearance of Blanche Lamont and, as we shall see, in order for it to be so connected, would require that Minnie be in contact with Lucile sometime between April 3 and April 12, which she almost certainly was not. (See chapter 12, infra.)

Tom Vogel finished his testimony by concluding that "I always took Durrant for a perfect gentleman. He always seemed so to me."

Miriam Lord told of the last time she had seen Minnie, which was the day of the reception given by the Christian Endeavor Society for Rev. Gibson: Friday, March 22, three weeks before her death. Miriam claimed that Minnie had never talked to her about Theo—a strange thing, if true, in that the two young women were very close friends. Could Theo have told Minnie to keep their relationship a secret from the Emmanuel Baptist people? Still, she must have discussed him with Lucile Turner, and it was with Lucile that she spent the night on March 22 after the reception for the pastor.

Clarence Navarre Wolfe, age 22, was a newspaper carrier. He had known Theo for four or five years and had last seen him the morning of Saturday, April 13 at 23rd and Bartlett Streets (near the church) between 6:30 and 7:00. Clarence had finished delivering his papers and Theo was outside a blacksmith shop waiting for his horse to be shod so he could join his outfit at the armory. Theo had said nothing about Minnie Williams during their conversation, but pointed out an article in the *Examiner* about Blanche.

When Clarence first saw Theo that morning, the latter was walking from 23rd Street. The coroner, obviously wanting to present the insinuation that Theo had just come from finishing up his butchering of Minnie, asked Clarence: "Would the direction bring him from the corner of the church?" Clarence, who had previously stated that Theo had come out of the blacksmith shop and resented the hint that he was lying to protect him, gave the coroner a smart response: "No, sir, it might have brought him right out of the door where his horse was standing."

With the exception of Lila Berry and Charles Dukes, Clarence Wolfe was the only one of Theo's former acquaintances who acknowledged him in court that day.

Other witnesses were William A. Frodsham of the Second Regiment, who had been in the armory the night of April 12 but hadn't seen Theo (although he admitted it was possible for him to have been there and not be seen); Elmer Wolfe, whose peregrinations that night would bring him much grief in the police court; Dukes and Dodge, who saw Theo at the ferry and whom he had asked to cover for him in class; Miss Frances Willis, who had ridden with Theo on the train in Alameda on April 8 (and whose beauty caused the young coroner to stumble over his words in examining her); and, finally, the police and medical witnesses. (Theo was called to testify, but his lawyers said they had advised him not to.)

Sergeant William Burke's testimony at the inquest reveals a little of how rumors get started: He stated that on the morning the body of Minnie Williams was discovered the police had received a message from the coroner (who in turn had gotten it from the Golden Gate Mortuary) that a Dr. Gibson was in the act of dissecting the body of a young girl at his office on Bartlett Street! Burke assumed Gibson was a medical doctor, but when he got to Bartlett and saw the large crowds and the morgue wagon outside the church, he realized the message referred to the *Rev.* Dr. Gibson, and that there was no dissection taking place.

Deputy Coroner McCormick stated that the police hadn't gotten to the church for about an hour. When they did, they and McCormick searched the area, and in the larger library room adjoining the smaller one where Minnie had been killed, McCormick found papers scattered on the floor. Among them was the library card of the then-missing Blanche Lamont. He began to think there might be a connection between the two cases.

McCormick was also of the opinion that the blood on the walls, which consisted of big, thick clots in most places, had been put or thrown there.

Dr. John S. Barrett's autopsy report gave two causes of death: from asphyxiation caused by choking to death on the rags, and bleeding to death from the cuts in the wrists. Since he could not tell for sure which had preceded which (although he was fairly sure the wrist wounds were inflicted slightly before or at the time of death), he hedged his bets.

The lacerations in both wrists severed the radius, the ulna, and their arteries. There were three wounds in the chest around the heart, all inflicted after death. One of them would have been instantly fatal if done while the victim was still alive. The two wounds in the forehead were just above the nose and slightly less than one inch in length. They were superficial, involving the scalp but not the skull. The victim had been raped, and prior to that had been a virgin (a "pure girl").

It was not reproduced in the newspapers (because it was not considered proper reading material), but Barrett may have indicated that Minnie was raped *after* death as well. Only one newspaper makes any reference to this ("outraged before and after death"), which is not sufficient to consider it a fact. However, in his summary of the Williams case at the end of his book on the trial of Blanche Lamont, Assistant District Attorney Edgar Peixotto states it as a fact, and it must be assumed that he had access to the autopsy report.[22] And in the Blanche Lamont trial, when a friend of Theo's from Cogswell, a funeral director, came forward as a character witness, the prosecution asked him several questions concerning the number of times Theo had visited his funeral home, the degree of interest he had taken in the job, etc.[23] So there must be some validity to the assertion. (Another question, however, would be whether the killer, in fact, knew Minnie was dead at the time.)

What would a modern criminologist make out of this crime scene and the autopsy report in attempting a profile of Minnie Williams's killer? First of all, the guilty party had to have been very familiar with Emmanuel Baptist Church: entering through the locked side door, finding a knife in the kitchen (which was not adjacent to the library), using a runner from the table drawer, and basically navigating around the church in the dark with just a candle or a lamp. As only Theo and George King had keys to the lock on the library door and as that lock had been broken off, this could indicate that it was someone other than one of these two who took Minnie there that night. But keys can be forgotten and locks can be broken to deflect suspicion.

The crime scene itself was highly disorganized: everything seems to have been improvised on the spur of the moment, and the killer didn't bring any "tools" with him as he undoubtedly would have if he had planned this in advance. He probably struck Minnie in the forehead first—possibly a blitz attack as soon as they got in the library—to keep her from screaming as he tore off the rags from her undergarments, dislodged the runner from the drawer, went to the kitchen for a knife, and sharpened the stick. So it must be assumed that Minnie was unconscious during these activities. The rags were shoved down her throat to keep her quiet if she should wake up, and also to suffocate her.

But, assuming the same man killed both Blanche and Minnie, why did he not strangle her manually, as he had done with a much larger Blanche Lamont? What would have been the purpose of taking all that time and trouble to get the rags down her throat? It is possible that manual strangulation was originally intended—after all, it had been successful with Blanche and there would be no reason to change that MO—but Minnie's response might have been such that he lost control of the situation. Although there were no clear signs of a struggle and Minnie had no defense wounds, she may have been very vocal—thus, the strike on the head, either by some weapon or against a table. While she was unconscious, possibly he got the idea to rape her, in which case he wouldn't want to kill her first—the idea of having sex with a dead body is repugnant to most people. But if he had planned the rape from the beginning, why didn't he bring a gag with him, and the means to shove it down her throat? Therefore, the rape is possibly an afterthought, and may even have been committed—or faked—for staging purposes.

The killer showed absolutely no respect for this victim, treating her more or less like a rag doll. The rape itself is a sign of disrespect, and the way he mangled her body when it was not necessary is another. Possibly he was even angry at her, but his anger was not directed at women in general because he didn't mutilate her sexual organs. He did stab her in the breast, but it was only the *left* breast and it was only to get at the heart (at least one of the cuts was *under* the breast). He didn't bother to pull down her dress completely, but neither did he pose her in an obscene attitude (as the Ripper had done with some of his victims) or cause her to be exposed.

The slashing of the wrists could have been done to insure death, especially if she exhibited any signs of life after the rags were inserted in her throat. Or, it could have been that, unable or unwilling to take her up to the belfry with his other victim (he had probably locked himself out), he decided to stage the murder as the act of a tramp or a "footpad."

This killer did not think he would be suspected, and this is why he felt he could confidently leave Minnie's body in the open. The slashing of the wrists and the excess stabbing of a heart already stopped, plus the "decoration" of the wall with postmortem blood, indicates staging. He wanted it to look like an absolute butchery, the kind of thing that only an uncivilized tramp or sex fiend would do. He trusted that his own good reputation would prevent him from being seriously considered as a suspect.

The coroner's jury was out for only a half hour and, to no one's surprise, came back with a verdict charging William Henry Theodore Durrant with the murder of Minnie Williams. In dismissing the jury, the coroner said, "Gentlemen, in this case I approve of the verdict."

They could now proceed to the preliminary examination in the police court.

THE PRELIMINARY EXAMINATION IN THE DEATH OF MINNIE WILLIAMS

On Monday, April 22, 1895, the first day of the preliminary examination, San Francisco citizens—who had been excluded from the inquest—turned out by the thousands for their first chance to view the proceedings. The hearing would take place in what was referred to as New City Hall at the corner of Larkin and McAllister Streets, completed the previous year. (Shoddily constructed with cheap materials to provide kickbacks to politicians, the new structure would be totally disintegrated by the 1906 earthquake.)[24]

In the basement of New City Hall was housed the prison, and it was estimated that six hundred people lined the McAllister Street entrance to watch Theo being brought to the courtroom upstairs. However, the guards took a different route and the crowd was disappointed.

Up in the courtroom, seats were packed an hour before the scheduled hearing and another large group milled around outside in the hallway. Newspapers criticized the numbers of women and girls in attendance—most of them young and well dressed—as lacking in modesty. These women took the best seats and some even boldly climbed into the prisoner's dock to get a better look at Theo. Although the police were concerned that the large crowds were there because of animosity toward the prisoner and feared an attempt to harm him, it turned out that the primary motive of the attendees was simple curiosity.

Theo himself may have felt some anxiety about the crowd's intentions, as he seemed to be made of stone that first day. He neither spoke with his attorneys nor exhibited any expression. He looked as if he hadn't slept well the night before, with bloodshot eyes, pale face, and twitching mouth.

Papa Durrant got to court too late to get a seat and spent the first day standing by the prisoner's dock. He looked more anxious about the proceedings than his son did.

Theo's attorneys were the same, but with a slight difference: General Dickinson would be the attorney of record, with Deuprey and Thompson listed "of counsel." Eugene Deuprey might have been having second thoughts about what must have at first seemed to him an entirely winnable case. After the inquest testimony, he undoubtedly had a clearer view of the holes in his client's story.

(An attorney "of record" cannot step down from a case without a court order, even if he or the client wishes it. And if the court thinks the client's best interests would be harmed by the removal, the order will not be issued.) There was also the matter of payment: General Dickinson might have been willing to work *pro bono*, but Deuprey certainly wasn't.

The prosecuting attorney in the police court was Ernest H. Wakeman. However, since it was practically assured that the case would be eventually tried in the superior court, Wakeman would take an assistant's role to the 30-year-old district attorney, William Sanford Barnes.

Barnes had graduated with honors from Harvard in 1886 and finished up his legal education at Columbia. He was admitted to the California State Bar in 1887 and went into partnership with his father, General William H. Barnes, an attorney who was also well known for his oratory. After four years of private practice, the younger Barnes was elected district attorney in 1892, and in April 1895, was earning a yearly salary of $5,000—more than Police Chief Patrick Crowley ($4,000) or Mayor Adolph Sutro ($4,200).[25]

Barnes was a large, balding man of 250 pounds with a florid face, and looked older than his 30 years. He was also a man of large ambition, and he instinctively knew that the Durrant case could make him famous if he were successful. (He had aspirations to be governor, and had unsuccessfully sought the nomination in '94.) Barnes had an excellent legal mind and had inherited his father's oratorical skills. No doubt he intruded himself into the police court examination so he could evaluate his opponents' strengths in these two areas.

The presiding judge for the police court was Charles T. Conlan, a relatively young man recently appointed to that position and anxious to establish himself as someone who could not be trifled with in a courtroom. As a result, he was austere and somewhat short of temper. With the Reverend Gibson, he became caustic and critical, barely disguising his contempt.

On that first day, a photographer named Stewart Merrill took the stand to identify the picture he had taken of Minnie in the receiving vault at the Laurel Hill Cemetery. The undertaker had stripped the body to the waist and propped up the coffin so Merrill could get a picture of the wounds suffered by the victim. The photograph, which had been enlarged for the courtroom proceedings, was a ghastly sight: The stitches of the coroner's Y incision were starkly prominent, as were the discolored wounds on Minnie's breast and forehead. The picture was passed along to the defense attorneys and, as they examined it, Theo peered over their shoulders. Reporters were horrified to note that he had absolutely no reaction to the grotesque photo. He might as well have been looking at a law book, they said, for all the interest he showed.

The Morgans were called to the stand and asked to identify the person in the photograph, which neither could do. What possible purpose their identification would serve was never made clear, and seemed entirely irrelevant to the proceedings.

April 22 was a hot day in San Francisco, and inside the courtroom the temperature was intolerable. The windows had been closed against the noise on Larkin Street, and it was estimated that there were 500 people packed into every nook and cranny of the courtroom. The rotund District Attorney Barnes was suffocating from it all, and asked Judge Conlan if some windows couldn't be opened. Conlan obliged, and welcome drafts of air wafted in.

But then another problem arose. Down below on Larkin Street the cable whirred in its slotted housing, cable cars rattled up and down, and horse-drawn trucks rumbled over the cobblestones. Added to this ruckus was the roar of the milling crowd out in the corridor and the buzz of the whispering women in the front rows of the courtroom. Witnesses could not be heard, and Wakeman complained to the court. Immediately, Captain William Y. Douglass, a large, beefy policeman dressed in his brass-buttoned, double-breasted parade uniform, jumped up and bellowed at the crowd, "Silence in the court!" Douglass had a voice that matched his size, and after this edict, the only sound that could be heard was from busy Larkin Street.

That same day, Douglass achieved some prominence by physically ejecting a lawyer who was not part of the proceedings, but insisted on standing in the passageway to the judge's chambers. Conlan had ordered this area to be kept clear, and when the attorney refused to move, Douglass grabbed him unceremoniously by the collar, danced him to the door of the courtroom, and threw him out into the hallway—all to the immense amusement of the crowd. (The humiliated attorney would later file suit against Douglass in the amount of $299 for what he termed "undue force and violence.")

There was to be even more entertainment that day for the throngs lucky enough to get inside the courtroom. When the bailiff called the name of A. E. Williams, Minnie's father, a well-dressed woman of about 30 came up to the stand instead. Thinking she was a witness, the clerk prepared to swear her in.

"This is not Mr. Williams," Barnes said.

"Who are you?" asked the judge.

"My name is Williamson," the lady replied, and in a rambling statement declared an end to this and all future proceedings against William Henry Theodore Durrant, whom she—Lucy Laura Gould Williamson—declared to be innocent pursuant to a revelation given to her by Jesus Christ.

"Get this woman out of here!" roared Judge Conlan. As policemen approached Lucy Williamson, she climbed up to the desk where the judge was sitting and threw a letter at him. (It turned out to be a declaration demanding Theo's release, per the Almighty.) Refusing to be escorted out by policemen ("Unhand me, sir!"), she strode out of the courtroom on her own, head held high. "I thought this would crop up," Conlan muttered, referring to the appearance of "cranks," or nut cases, at the trial.

A new witness at the hearing this first day was a young baker from Alameda, Frank Arthur Young, who had known Minnie for three years. She had often bought bread at his bakery, and on Thursday, April 11, had stopped in to say good-bye to him, as she would be going to San Francisco to live for a couple of weeks before moving to Tacoma with the Morgans. Minnie had a little notebook, which had been found in the compartment on the outside of her purse (and therefore missed by Sergeant Burke in his examination of it at Theo's house), and Young's name and address were written in it. The baker now testified that Minnie had asked him to write them there.

The elderly laundress who had walked past Emmanuel Baptist on Friday night provided some unintentional humor because of her slight deafness. Mrs. McKay testified that as she passed the couple near the church, she heard the young man say, "Oh, you are a coward."

| *Mrs. McKay*: | I says to myself, "That's lovers—." |
| *Deuprey*: | We object to what she said to herself. |

Mrs. McKay (ignoring him):   I says to myself, "That's lovers and she's afraid to go home, don't you know."

When they tried to get her to estimate the time she had seen the couple, she went into a maddeningly confusing routine where she attempted to detail the comings and goings of herself, her employer, and her employer's daughter in order to pinpoint the time. Then, she and Deuprey came to cross-purposes regarding blocks of pavement versus blocks of streets.

Eventually, Day One was over, and William Barnes had come away with some very valuable information regarding Theo's defense attorneys: They put him on notice that they would contest even the smallest point and would cross-examine every witness with vigor.

Captain Douglass, who had distinguished himself in court on the first day, was in charge of bringing Theo to court and guarding him there. Newspaper sketches exaggerated Douglass's bulk compared to the prisoner, who was short and slender. Reporters, who probably had a long history with the good captain in previous cases, poked some gentle fun at him and his newfound importance, saying that he gave the case "the appearance of weighty dignity."

During one lengthy cross-examination, reporters had noticed Douglass nodding off. After it was over, he awoke with a start and quickly checked to make sure Theo was still there. Douglass was probably completely unaware that he was being observed, but in the next day's paper a cartoon appeared featuring a giant Douglass and a doll-sized Theo: The policeman fell asleep and dreamed that Theo had escaped, whereupon he awoke with a start, saw his prisoner still in his chair, then picked him up and cradled him in his arms so he could go back to sleep without worrying.

As the days of the hearing went on, Theo seemed to take more interest in the proceedings, even coaching his attorneys at times. He was obviously more at ease with his defense counsel. One reporter noted that, even though Theo might *look* as if he were indifferent, he was really not. That Wednesday, the third day of testimony, he turned 24.

Some new witnesses were brought forward as well. Theo's friend and classmate, Harry Partridge, testified that he had answered

"Present" for Theo—at the latter's request—at Dr. Hirschfelder's clinic at the City and County Hospital on Monday, April 8. The time of this clinic was 10:30–11:30 A.M. Another classmate, George Burgess, testified that Theo was also absent from Dr. Hirschfelder's clinic on Friday, April 12 (the day of Minnie's death) and from Professor Ellinwood's lecture later that day.

From across the Bay in Alameda came three important new witnesses: Annie Moisant, Edith McKean, and Officer Dennis Welch. Miss McKean lived next door to the Morgans and both young women knew Minnie Williams by sight. At 2:10 on Monday afternoon, April 8, they were on Edith's porch and saw Minnie on the Morgans' porch talking with a young man who looked very much like Theo Durrant.

Dennis Welch testified that he had known Minnie by sight for about two years and had often seen her with Theo Durrant. The last time he had seen them together was March 30 or 31 on Park Street in Alameda. But he had often seen Theo over there alone, most likely on his way to or from seeing Minnie, and the last time was on Saturday, April 6. Didn't he mean Monday, April 8, election day? he was asked. But Welch stated emphatically that it was *not* election day, but the preceding Saturday.

Welch had come over to San Francisco during the coroner's inquest to look at Minnie's body and see what kind of a butchering job had been done on her (but probably mostly out of curiosity). On the stand, he told Dickinson that he didn't get to see her because "one of the fellows in the Morgue" wouldn't let him in. Dickinson must have been in need of a little entertainment himself after his hours of cross-examination of Welch, or else he was so tired he couldn't think straight—hence, this exchange:

Dickinson: One of the fellows in the Morgue. Was he dead or alive?
Welch: He was alive.

Lucile Turner's testimony reveals her sense of importance at being a figure in the Durrant case. She was treated with respect by both sides, and the reporters thought she "made a fine appearance on the stand." Still, Lucile was picky about the way Barnes asked her the questions she must have been told to expect: "Please explain yourself," she said once in an offended tone, and at another time asked somewhat indignantly: "In what manner do you mean 'what occurred'?"

Judge Conlan tried to help the process along by getting Lucile to give her testimony in narrative form, but she didn't want to do that: "I cannot make a statement of the conversation. If you will ask me questions I can answer them." When she attempted to dole out her information piecemeal, Conlan interrupted impatiently: "Can you not state all the conversation that occurred about it? What did he say about it? What did he say to you and what did you answer?" The judge was obviously frustrated with Lucile's attempt to prolong her stay in the limelight.

On cross-examination, Lucile fell into Dickinson's trap. Seduced by his pleasant manner in asking questions, she blithely talked about her relationship with Theo before and after the "insulting proposition." Had she seen Theo after that? Oh, yes, she had seen him almost every Sunday after that, had met him at different places, and had been in his company. Had she spoken with him as usual? Well, of course she had. As she had been in the habit of doing? And then Lucile realized her mistake. She attempted to backpedal, but it was too late: "Well, I don't hardly think so. I spoke to Mr. Durrant the same as usual, and treated him so I thought people would not notice anything had happened between us. I don't think I felt as free with Mr. Durrant as I did before."

Lucile admitted to having "flyleaf conversations" with him after the incident, as she had often done before, and said that the first time she told anyone about what had happened was when she told her aunt on the day Minnie's body was found. All in all, then, despite the sensational nature of her testimony, Lucile gave the impression of having invented her feeling of insult and possibly even embellishing what actually occurred. It is significant that, even when the defense later opened the door at the trial by putting Theo's good character in issue, the prosecution did not call Lucile Turner to repeat her story.

As he had at the inquest, John George Gibson came in for more than his share of abuse on the stand—this time not only from the defense, but from the judge. The pastor wore a caped coat and, when his name was called, he strode in, took his place at the witness stand, and dramatically flung the ends of the cape over his shoulders. His neck was quite seriously scarred (he never said from what) and the redness of these old wounds betrayed his nervousness. His friend and secretary, Robert Lynch, took a position next to the prisoner's dock to give him moral support and maybe calm him down a bit.

Gone was the flippancy and "pertness" of the inquest as Gibson proceeded to answer Barnes's questions. (Lynch had probably told him this was not an attitude designed to win public support.) But he had not gotten very far before Judge Conlan took a hand, ostensibly for clarification. After Gibson stated that he didn't know who had keys to the church and that no one had asked his permission to put the new lock on the library door, Conlan became both angry and sarcastic: "Don't you think as pastor you should know this? Isn't it your duty to know what goes on?" Gibson was unflappable, and this riled Conlan further. "May I draw your attention, Judge, to one mistake?" But Conlan didn't want to hear it: "You had better answer the question. I want to know this!"

Gibson added to his impression as a pastor ignorant of his own church by admitting he knew nothing about the side gate, did not know for sure who the trustees were, did not know who had sent for the piano tuner, and had no idea how the library worked "because I did not manage it."

Conlan (disbelieving):   Did you not know, Dr. Gibson, what was done with your Sunday school library while it was in your church, the church of which you were pastor?

Gibson (repeating):   I did not manage it.

When Gibson got to the part about James Sademan's report of the "busted" lock and his own cursory investigation of the library, Conlan was at him again. Did Gibson mean to say that he hadn't opened the door where the books were? The judge couldn't let it go. He kept coming back to the fact that Gibson hadn't opened that door and made him say again and again what his reasons were. Nor could he abandon the idea of Gibson's not having a key to the new lock: "Well, a man who was pastor of a church ought certainly to know something about it!" Around and around they went, and at certain points in the testimony, the judge would jump back into this question.

Gibson was deflated by the end of the morning session on his first day at the preliminary examination, but by the afternoon when he took the stand again, he had regained some of his composure and also indulged in some of his accustomed flippancy. His attitude was maddening: He was literal, obtuse (possibly deliberately so), and overly cautious:

Dickinson: How do you know what time it was?

Gibson: By my watch and the clock in the study.

Dickinson: Did you look at your watch?

Gibson: Not particularly.

Dickinson: Did you look at the clock?

Gibson: Not particularly.

Dickinson: What did you do on returning to your study?

Gibson: I studied.

On the second day of his testimony, Gibson tangled with Dickinson over the pastor's handwriting. Peeved at the way he was being treated, Gibson refused to give a handwriting sample there in court. There was plenty of it around the church, he rejoined— you can go look for it yourself. Eventually, Gibson relented, but then disdained the pens they were offering him because they were not the kind he usually wrote with. What kind did he write with? A Waverley, he told them, and off they went to hunt up a Waverley. Finally they found one, and Gibson happily settled down to write his sample. Even though they were giving him the same words found on the wrapper sent with Blanche Lamont's rings, he seemed nonplussed by it. Possibly he felt that the distress he had caused everyone over the course of two days was well worth it!

Elmer Wolfe came to court wearing an overcoat very similar to Theo's: long, dark blue, and with a velvet collar. He carried a dark slouch hat (a soft fedora-like hat) that was also like Theo's. This was an unfortunate choice on the part of a witness who must have gotten an inkling at the inquest that the defense was going to try to put him forward as the young man who was seen by all those witnesses on the night of Minnie's murder.

At 5'8" and 160 pounds, Wolfe was both taller and heavier than Theo. Still, the similarity of the overcoat and hat could not be overlooked. As the wily Deuprey cross-examined him closely on his movements that day and night, and his reasons for them, Elmer chewed gum furiously. When Deuprey wanted him to stand up and take off his coat, he refused. He thought the lawyer was going to make him put on Theo's coat, but when he found out this was not the case, he relented. Deuprey put the two overcoats together so that Conlan could see how alike they were.

After the intense cross-examinations of Gibson and Wolfe, it was obvious to all that the defense would present them as more likely suspects than Theo.

Another gum-chewing witness was Charles Hills, who seemed completely unaware of what his testimony revealed about his domestic affairs. There was tittering in the courtroom as he related following the young couple to the church in the April gloom, convinced that his wife was having an assignation with another man. A few days after his testimony, distraught over losing a job he had just started because of having to appear in court, and weighed down by his marital problems, Charles Hills attempted suicide by slashing his wrists. The attempt was unsuccessful, and Hills later said he had been drunk at the time. It could not have helped his situation that all of this was being reported in six newspapers![26]

Dr. Barrett's autopsy report, somewhat cursorily delivered at the inquest, came in for vigorous cross-examination at the preliminary examination. Deuprey was something of a medical expert, and relished his role in picking apart the young coroner. Barrett was *very* slow and *very* deliberate with his answers, sometimes pausing so long that the question was repeated two or three times. When the response finally came, it was delivered in a halting, jerky fashion that was painfully tedious for everyone to listen to.

Deuprey challenged every finding in a nit-picky way. For example, the report of the condition of Minnie's lungs took *one-half hour*. When Barrett admitted that the autopsy notes he had in court were not the originals, but that he had copied them right after the autopsy from those stained with blood and guts, Deuprey made him go get the gory ones. (However, when he came back from the morgue he had to confess that he couldn't find them and must have thrown them out.)

Deuprey's main goal in his cross-examination was to show Barrett's incompetence with regard to this particular autopsy, and also to suggest alternative theories. He wanted Barrett to state that it was the cuts on the wrists that had caused Minnie's death rather than strangulation because this would mean that the killer must have had blood on his clothes—which Theo did not. Deuprey went around and around on the difference between asphyxiation and strangulation, and at one point asked about death by hanging. At this inartful reference to his client's probable future, everyone looked at Theo for his reaction. But he was ready for them, and had his stone mask firmly in place.

Barrett admitted that he had no help during the autopsy except from Tom Smith, the morgue janitor, who occasionally aided in lifting bodies, holding instruments, etc. Deuprey repeatedly emphasized Smith's position as janitor. Moreover, Barrett had neglected to analyze the contents of Minnie's stomach, which would be probative in determining exactly when she had died. He tried to put a brave face on it by claiming it was not a standard procedure, but his failure in this regard came across as incompetent. (After court that day, the defense got an order to exhume Minnie's body to have the stomach analyzed. The progress of the digestive process caused the time of death to be moved back from midnight to 8:30.)

When Barrett got to the gynecological portion of his report, the judge warned the women that they were getting into embarrassing territory, unfit for feminine ears. But, while several women left, there were about thirty who stayed throughout the exhaustive report and cross-examination. Deuprey made the coroner go into detail as to how he determined that Minnie had been a virgin until shortly before her death, and finally got the doctor to admit that, although he still held this opinion, he couldn't be absolutely sure that she was. The defense was obviously trying to insinuate loose living on Minnie's part and that more than one young swain could have wanted her out of the way.

Barrett also revealed that Minnie was poorly nourished, which meant she was not getting enough of the right kinds of food. Since it was not likely that the Morgans were starving her, this could have been the result of the organic illness she was supposed to have had (an illness, by the way, either not revealed by the autopsy or not mentioned in the report).

On Wednesday, May 1, Judge Conlan declared that Theo would have to be held for trial in the superior court, as the evidence unequivocally showed him to be guilty of Minnie Williams's murder, in the judge's opinion a more heinous crime than that of Jack the Ripper because of the purity of the victim. It would now be time for Blanche Lamont's day in court: first the inquest, then the preliminary examination.

THE INQUEST ON BLANCHE LAMONT[27]

Minnie Williams's inquest and preliminary examination had taken almost two weeks of testimony. In contrast, the inquest for Blanche Lamont took a mere three hours and the preliminary only two days. It was as if both sides understood that they would be locking horns over the latter case at the trial level and were anxious to get there. And Blanche's preliminary examination would have been even shorter had the prosecution not produced three surprise witnesses, thereby necessitating much cross-examination on the part of the defense team.

After the Nobles and the Normal School girls told what they knew, George King was called. His testimony gave notice, albeit subtly, that he would be a reluctant witness for the state and that he would, as much as possible, remain loyal to his friend Theo. It is almost certain that the young organist never revealed all that he knew about Blanche's murder.

King repeated his encounter with Theo on the afternoon of Wednesday, April 3 (the encounter that Papa Durrant had tried to get him to "forget"), and said that he had not seen Theo and Blanche together for the previous three months. Asked about any conversations regarding the two victims, George replied that Theo had a very good opinion of Blanche, but did not seem to care much for Minnie. However, he refused to be more specific as to what exactly had been said, claiming (as he would several times throughout the case) that he simply could not remember.

George went on to say that Theo had not restricted his friendship to those two young women, but was on "fairly intimate" terms with many others in the church, especially Lucile Turner and Flo Upton. But when he was asked to name some of these others, George had that memory block again. In fact, he claimed, at the moment he could not name *any* of the other young ladies in the parish! It was plain to all that George King would not willingly put the rope around his friend's neck.

John West, a conductor on the Powell Street cable car line, had come forward to say that his car was the one that Blanche and Theo had ridden to Market Street on the afternoon of April 3. However, he was so confusing in his testimony and so contradictory to what had been observed by the Normal School girls, that no one believed him. The newspapers slyly insinuated that he was just trying to be part of the hoopla surrounding the case: "West either had a rush of imagination to the brain or mistook another couple for Durrant and Miss Lamont." When asked to point out the man he had seen on his cable car, West paused, looked around the courtroom for several dramatic moments, then pointed to Theo.

The surprise witness produced by the prosecution at the inquest was the bibulous lawyer, Martin Quinlan, who had practically bumped into Theo (whom he knew by sight) and a young lady on Bartlett Street at about 4:15 that afternoon. And to bolster up Quinlan's testimony, his friend David Clarke was able to pinpoint the day because of the visit to his hospitalized brother-in-law.

As Quinlan described the young couple he had seen that day in precise and believable detail, Theo slid down in his chair as if he wished to disappear.

If Dr. John S. Barrett had not been exactly sure what caused the death of Minnie Williams, he had no difficulty determining this with Blanche Lamont: asphyxiation due to strangulation. There were no other marks or wounds on the body except for the bruising around the neck and what Barrett had determined were fingernail marks—seven on the right side and five on the left. (Obviously, the strangler had shifted the grip on one hand.) The larynx and trachea were compressed and the brain and lungs congested, consistent with strangling.

Barrett said that it could not be determined whether Blanche's neck had been grabbed from the front or the back, but this makes no sense. If she had been grabbed from the front, the fingernail incisions would be close to the back of the neck; if from the back, they would be toward the front of the throat. The written record is maddeningly unenlightening on this point. (See chapter 9, infra.)

Blanche was just finishing up her menstrual period when she died, so there were some blood spots on her underpants. Barrett did not check for seminal fluid because he did not think that it could have survived in the rank, foul discharge that he felt certain came from the body itself and not from an outside source. Moreover, the internal organs were not very decomposed, and he was able to determine that Blanche had *not* been raped either prior to or after death.[28]

As with the death of Minnie Williams, the murder of Blanche Lamont demonstrates the killer's complete familiarity with the church. He not only knew about the belfry, but was also aware of an alternate exit from it after he had disabled the door to prevent anyone else from entering. The absence of any sign of activity on the platform of the belfry indicates that it was *not* the place where the murder occurred.

But this crime scene was a totally different one from that where Minnie was killed nine days later. There was a respect shown for this victim that was not shown for Minnie: The only mark of violence was from manual strangulation, there was no rape, and Blanche's body was laid out lovingly. Although Minnie was left dressed and Blanche was stripped of her clothing, the latter was most likely done to prevent identification if someone should chance upon the body. The killer was hoping that Blanche would have turned into a skeleton by the time anyone thought to go up to the belfry, and the absence of all identifying clothing meant that no one could be completely sure who it had been in life. He must have felt that the victim's identity could lead to him, and this would be the primary reason for his hiding everything connected with her.

Despite the haste in the presentation of evidence by the coroner (who was guided in this by District Attorney Barnes), the inquest jury came back with the decision that Blanche Lamont had met her death at the hands of Theodore Durrant.

THE PRELIMINARY EXAMINATION IN THE DEATH OF
BLANCHE LAMONT

Thursday, May 2, 1895—the first day of the preliminary hearing—brought more throngs of people to New City Hall to view the spectacle. Theo, pale and hollow-eyed, looked as if he had slept badly the night before.

The Nobles came forward once more to tell what they knew of their niece's relationship with the young man accused of killing her, and Blanche's three classmates (whom she had not known at all in life) recounted their last glimpses of the "new girl" and her "beau" on the cable car.

John West, the cable car conductor, attempted to establish himself once again as a piece in the puzzle, but his story was neither believable nor helpful to either side: The prosecution would have to discount the three Normal School students in favor of West's testimony, and the defense would have to admit that Theo was with Blanche that afternoon. Hence, he was useless to either side. (West insisted that Blanche and Theo sat *inside* the cable car, and that Theo got on with another young man after Blanche was already on.)

But before they let him go, they had a little fun with him. At the inquest earlier that week, West had looked around the courtroom before pointing out Theo as the man he had seen with Blanche. When Dickinson now asked him why he had done this (insinuating that maybe he didn't really recognize Theo), West sheepishly admitted that he thought it would look better if he made it seem as if he were really trying hard to do a good job in identifying him. "Yes," said Dickinson contemptuously, "you thought you would make it more dramatic. Good-by." As West left the stand, District Attorney Barnes echoed his opponent's sarcastic "Good-by," and then Judge Conlan chimed in with his own. Spectators erupted in laughter, and even Theo had a smile on his face.

The next day brought even more excitement for the crowd and more worries for the defense. The afternoon session was so packed with people that there was literally no room for anyone to stand.

Dickinson took Martin Quinlan in hand for forty-five minutes and had him recount every establishment he had visited on Wednesday, April 3. Quinlan was forthright and unapologetic about his bar-hopping, most of which was done after he saw Blanche and Theo. Each time Dickinson asked "What kind of business was that?" and Quinlan answered "A saloon," the courtroom crowd roared with laughter. At one point, the defense attorney asked him, "Have you pursued the same course of living since, in regard to taking drinks?" and Quinlan smoothly replied, "Whenever I feel like taking a drink, I take one."

Martin Quinlan made a good witness because he refused to be bullied, did not get angry, and told his story in a straightforward way. He could not be shaken from it no matter what tactics Dickinson tried, and came across—despite his propensity for saloons—as truthful and reliable.

Quinlan had testified at the inquest, so the defense had a little time to get ready for him on cross-examination. But now the prosecution had a bombshell to drop on Dickinson and Deuprey in the person of a pawnbroker who had come to court that day during the recess to look at Blanche's rings. He had seen them in the newspaper, he said, and his wife had insisted he come forward with what he knew.

Adolph Oppenheim had a pawnshop on Dupont Street in a somewhat seedy section of the downtown area. Sometime between April 3 and April 10 (but probably before April 8, which was his birthday), a young man who looked like Theo entered his shop around 10:00 or 11:00 A.M. Business was slow and Oppenheim had been reading a German novel. He put it down to attend to his new customer, who was dressed in a dark slouch hat and a long dark overcoat with a velvet collar. He also noticed the young man's thick lips and slight mustache.

Oppenheim's impression was that the customer was a pimp because of the way he was dressed and because there were several of them in the neighborhood. The young man had a ring in his hand, which he now showed to the pawnbroker, and asked, "How much for this?" Oppenheim examined it, determined that it was a cheap, mass-produced item, and replied, "I do not want it." The young man asked again, "How much for this?" and Oppenheim repeated that he didn't want it because it wasn't worth very much—probably $2.50 when purchased new—and the little chip diamond was too small.

Disappointed, the customer walked to the door, looked up and down the street as if undecided where to go, then walked in the direction of California Street. Oppenheim went back to his chair to continue reading his novel.

When the sketches of the rings returned to Blanche Lamont's aunt appeared in the newspaper, Oppenheim recognized the chip diamond immediately. Although it was mass-produced, he had never carried this particular ring before, and so he remembered its distinctive qualities. Later, when Theo's picture also appeared in the paper, Oppenheim (whom the *Examiner* insisted on calling Oppenheimer) realized that he was the one who had attempted to pawn the ring.

But the pawnbroker didn't want to get involved. He thought they had enough on Theo Durrant without his testimony. Finally, his wife convinced him that he should let the district attorney decide whether he had valuable information or not, so that noon— the second day of the preliminary examination—Oppenheim went down to City Hall and asked to see the rings firsthand.

Nor was Barnes finished with his surprises for that day. Theo was contending that he had been at Dr. Cheney's lecture at the medical college on the afternoon of April 3, and therefore could not have been the man seen with Blanche on the streetcar. Professor Cheney's rollbook did not indicate that Theo was absent from class for that hour (3:30–4:30), but the effectiveness of his roll-taking procedure was suspect. Still, no one could be found who would admit to having answered for him, and so far there was no way to show that he *hadn't* been there.

But now Edward F. Glaser, a senior classmate of Theo's, took the stand to tell about an incident that had occurred on Wednesday, April 10, the week after Blanche's disappearance. The professor whose lecture occupied the slot before Cheney's had cancelled, and the students found themselves with an extra hour. Edward Glaser and Theo went into an empty classroom to cram for the quiz they were sure to have in Dr. Cheney's class on the lecture from the preceding week: infant feeding and the sterilization of milk.

Glaser could not be sure who suggested what, but he himself read from his notes of that April 3 lecture and Theo—who, despite his legendary prowess as a notetaker, did not seem to have any of his own—copied them down. The nervously eager Glaser bounced around in his chair as he testified, leaning forward to hear each question and looking at the ceiling before answering. Then he would stroke his slight blond beard and throw his foot across his knee—looking for all the world as if he were "made of bedsprings endowed with feeling and sitting on tacks."

It was one more link in the chain of circumstantial evidence against Theo.

After the inevitable verdict of guilty, Theo's status changed from that of suspect to that of defendant, and his address changed from City Prison to the county jail. His attorneys dug in to strategize their defense for the trial and their cross-examination of the witnesses, especially those recently sprung on them: Martin Quinlan, David Clarke, Adolph Oppenheim, and Edward Glaser.

They did not yet know about Mrs. Leak and Mrs. Crosett.

Knee-deep in the Hoopla:
The Road to Trial

> Don't you know that this is a world of chance and change?
> Very few things appear in their true light at first. It is impos-
> sible that things can remain long as they are, and public opin-
> ion will just as surely change as it is true that I am here.
> —Theo Durrant, May 1895

The first thing Theo Durrant did upon being found guilty at the
pre-trial level was to request a shave and a haircut. He had been
asking for these for some time, but police wanted to be sure that
all possible witnesses had a chance to identify him as they would
have remembered him. So, before being transported to his new
home in the county jail, city prison officials arranged to have a
local barber come in to relieve Theo of his long locks and the
mustache he had begun growing in March. The barber, mindful of
a promotional opportunity, took a lock of the hair to hang in his
shop.[1]

Theo left not only his hair behind, but also the bed and rocking
chair that his parents had sent to him. Now that he was officially
a defendant and not merely a suspect, his privileges would be few.
His privacy, such as it was, was gone, too: Over at the county jail

he would share Cell 28 with another criminal, a bigamist named Shear. The bewildered bigamist was overwhelmed by all the publicity surrounding his new cell mate, and was even interviewed himself as to what kind of a guy Theo was.[2]

Instead of bars, such as were on the cells at City Prison, the county jail doors were solid except for a small wicket that could be dropped down to receive food trays. This meant that Theo would be able to hide from nosy people, but it also made it harder to talk to visitors, as he had to lean down to look through the narrow wicket.

At the end of May, Chief Jailer A. J. Sattler took his charge from the jail, boarded a streetcar, and escorted him to City Hall for his arraignment. Nobody recognized Theo with his new haircut, shaven upper lip, and impeccably creased trousers. Sattler had taken him an hour before the scheduled time to throw off the curious spectators who inevitably lined up to see the famous Demon of the Belfry whenever he had to make a court appearance, and from that time on it would be a constant challenge thinking of ways to thwart the multitudes.[3]

In the courtroom, waiting for the proceedings to begin, Theo wandered over to look out the window. A reporter expressed surprise that he was allowed to do this, as it would be an easy matter for him to jump out and escape. Sattler and the bailiff laughed at the idea that Theo would even attempt it: "He isn't that kind," they told the reporter.

That day, Theo entered his plea in both cases, although the prosecution had already determined to try him for Blanche's murder first, which was thought to be the stronger case.[4] When Blanche's name was mentioned in the indictment, Theo averted his eyes and mumbled, "Not guilty." However, in the count for Minnie's murder, his voice was clear and strong, which probably says much about how he viewed his level of involvement in each case.

Trial was set for Monday, July 22, 1895, in the matter of *People v. Durrant*.

There were signs that Theo was becoming increasingly dissociated from reality. He told a friend that he wanted to send condolences in the form of a card and flowers to Blanche's family in Dillon. And when, before going from City Prison to the county jail, Chief Crowley had him sit for his "Rogues' Gallery" picture, Theo—

alone of all those who had ever suffered this indignity—preened and posed and asked for copies. It was his defense attorneys, not Theo, who objected to this and threatened to sue Crowley for libel.[5]

Theo was generally even-tempered, but there were a few times when he flew into rages over real or imagined slights. Once he went into a tirade against a prison officer about having his slop bucket used as a toilet emptied more frequently, and it took Mamma—who was visiting at the time—several minutes to calm him down. Another time, he went off on reporters and others looking at him as they would an animal in a cage. Although these tantrums were rare, they provided an insight into a different aspect of Theo's normally placid personality. Had Blanche and Minnie seen this side of him?[6]

Moreover, he was making statements against his interest. Despite his attorneys' pleas to say nothing to anyone about the case, Theo was talking to people who were then reporting to newspapers or the police. A classmate at Cooper, Gil Graham, came to see him with a friend who was a freelance newspaper reporter. During the visit, Theo asked the friend to step aside so he could talk privately with Graham, at which point he asked Graham if he could borrow his notes of Professor Cheney's April 3 lecture!

When Graham seemed reluctant, Theo suggested a way that he could smuggle the notes in and not get caught: He was to go to his home and ask Mamma for Theo's notebook, then tuck his own notes inside and bring the notebook to the jail. And if he didn't want to do that, he could just give a copy of the notes to Mamma, and she would bring them. Or, he could commit them to memory and dictate them to Theo at the jail. Theo now admitted to Graham that he had no notes of his own (he had either forgotten about those dictated to him by Edward Glaser or had not copied them sufficiently) and, consequently, that he needed them to establish his "alibi," a word he used himself. Graham was greatly disturbed by this whole encounter ("You are very foolish to make such a request," he told Theo), and at first determined to say nothing to anyone about it; eventually, however, he went to the district attorney.[7]

To his friend George Maline, Theo confided that he had *walked* to Emmanuel Baptist from the medical school on April 3, and that nobody had seen him. It was a dangerous lie because, by his own admission, he had been at the church by 4:30; and he had been seen by George King at 5:00. If he had been at Cheney's lecture, which ended at 4:15 that day (Cheney finished early because he had an appointment), then walked to Bartlett Street, he would never have arrived until well after 5:00—in fact, he could barely have gotten there by 5:00 even on the streetcars.

Maline, in his eagerness to show that his friend did, indeed, have a defense, told a reporter what Theo had said, thereby undermining the so-called surprise Theo claimed he had wanted to spring on the prosecution (and possibly on his own defense team as well, as they probably knew nothing about this).[8]

June went by with few ripples in the surface of the Durrant case. In mid-July, a week before the trial was to open, Emmanuel Baptist Church was in the news again when it was reconsecrated and open for services for the first time since the discovery of the murders.[9] It was hoped that the horrors of April would be behind them and that blessing the church anew would wash away the evil that had visited. To prevent a curious public from climbing to the belfry, the gallery was kept locked. Elmer Wolfe, who had not attended church much before the murders, passed the collection basket. Rev. J. George Gibson, happy to be back in his own church after guesting at other Baptist parishes, sang a baritone solo.

Among the former members who did *not* return to the church on Bartlett Street were the Nobles and the Kings (except for George). Dr. William Z. King had remained a staunch supporter of his son's former friend, and frequently brought him magazines at the jail. The defense had lined him up to appear as a character witness at the trial.

On July 21, the day before jury selection was to begin, Theo's attorneys announced that there would be no change of venue motion, as they would prefer to try the case in San Francisco and were not afraid to do so. In fact, however, they were at that time preparing affidavits for just such a motion—a motion they knew would probably not be granted, but whose refusal would give them their first grounds for appeal. Dickinson and Deuprey knew that their only hope of saving their client, unless some heretofore unknown witness were to step forward, lay in preserving the record for an appeal from errors at the trial court level. Their plan was to contest *everything*; surely something would cause a reversal in the event of conviction.

The first day of the trial was like the opening of a much-anticipated play, and both actors and audience showed the excitement. So many spectators attempted to cram themselves into the little courtroom that eventually the judge would move the proceedings to a larger one.

Judge Daniel J. Murphy was within two years of retirement, and this would be the biggest case in his most distinguished career. Bald, heavily mustached, and of ample girth, "Hizzoner" (as he was frequently referred to by the press) brooked no nonsense by attorneys or spectators. There would be no berating of witnesses, either, as there had been in the police court; Murphy was protective of them and, while he considered them fair game for tricky cross-examination, would not allow them to be ridiculed or unduly harassed. (The modern-day objection to "badgering the witness" was not available in 1895.)

In fact, Daniel Murphy was probably the best judge possible to sit on this case. Close to retirement, he had no judicial mark to make for his future and had already presided over several high-profile trials. His near-phobia about being reversed on appeal led him to be scrupulously fair, even to the point of deciding doubtful questions in favor of the defendant. Theo's best chances of getting a fair trial would be in the courtroom of Judge Murphy (despite the judge's insistence on mispronouncing his name to rhyme with "currant" instead of correctly accenting the last syllable).[10]

Leading the prosecution was District Attorney William S. Barnes, assisted by Edgar Davis Peixotto in his first big case. Peixotto was young (at 27, just slightly older than Theo), short, and—also like the defendant—a stylish dresser. He wore his hair in the current fashion of "football bangs," or curls dangling from his forehead in the manner of varsity gridiron heroes. In court that Monday, he could barely suppress his excitement.

Papa Durrant was there, as he had been for all Theo's court appearances to date. He was nervous and fidgety, pulling at his mustache, chewing on a toothpick, and shuffling his feet back and forth as he sat. Theo was as sartorially resplendent as Edgar Peixotto, with his black cutaway coat, striped trousers, and light scarf;

but his face had broken out and he looked pale and tired. He sat quietly with his hands folded in his lap, paying little attention to anything.

Captain Isaiah Lees was there, calmly chewing tobacco and commenting to the press that he thought Theo was the "cleverest criminal of modern times."

Theo's three attorneys came in with a private detective, Harry Morse, who was working with them on the case. They shook hands with their client and began pulling folders out of the boxes of material they had brought in.

Finally, District Attorney Barnes arrived, bowing to everyone, including Theo, who returned his greeting with a smile and a nod.

The curtain could now be raised on Act I.

Judge Murphy's first point of business was to ask the attorneys if the jury pool could be divided—half today and half tomorrow—so that all 150 men would not be kept from work. He wanted their consent so that no one would raise it as an objection later. General Dickinson, who was ready to present the motion for a change of venue, thought that should come first, as a decision in their favor would render moot any jury pool in San Francisco. He told Murphy that he had a motion to make first, and after that would respond to the proposition of splitting the jury panel.

Judge Murphy was testy: "*This* is the first matter," he told Dickinson. "I want to take care of this first." In the courtroom there was a low hum as spectators fearfully discussed the possibility of losing their "drama" to another jurisdiction.

Dickinson remained firm. "I think a change of venue should come first, and then we will assent to your proposition." But Murphy would not be mollified by Dickinson's indication of the defense's consent to the splitting of the jury pool: "That is not the matter I am speaking about!" he thundered, his jowls shaking.

"I have no objection to it," Dickinson responded meekly.

Murphy was still not finished asserting his authority. When Deuprey came forward to present the defense's motion for a change of venue (normally done with a brief oral argument and a submission of the supporting material for the court to read at its leisure), the judge told him to *read* it. Deuprey gulped in astonishment. "Your honor, it will take all day and maybe more to read all of this," he said, indicating the great sheaf of papers in his hand. "I can't help it," Murphy replied ("as unfeelingly as a town pump"). "And you'll have to read a little louder than usual because I have a bad cold and am a little deaf."

Deuprey took a deep breath and valiantly began to read from the newspaper articles that the defense claimed had constituted unfair pretrial publicity for Theo. At the prosecution's table, District Attorney Barnes perused a copy of *Psychopathia Sexualis*. Everyone else in the courtroom stared at a stonelike and impassive Theo throughout the proceedings.

When Deuprey, hoarse and tired, got halfway through the articles and affidavits, he begged the judge for mercy. "Your honor, couldn't we just submit the rest of these without reading them?" But Murphy was unmoved by Deuprey's plight: "Keep reading," he ordered. Whenever the lawyer's voice got too low, Murphy would tell him to speak louder. At one point, the judge wanted to know what page he was on. When Deuprey began to count the unnumbered sheets, Murphy asked roughly: "Haven't you got it paged?"

Judge Murphy's motive in forcing the defense to read everything in support of its motion was probably to establish his authority in the courtroom and also to discourage the filing of motions which were not likely to be granted. Murphy had presided over the trial of Alexander Goldenson for the murder of 13-year-old Mamie Kelly, a highly inflammatory case from 1886,[11] and had denied a change of venue there as well. As he had been upheld on appeal, he would not be inclined to grant Theo's motion, and the defense attorneys should have realized that. Still, they were doing everything they could to create a record in the hopes that a higher court might disagree with the trial judge.

One of the items read by Deuprey in support of the motion was the subscriber numbers for each of the six daily newspapers. For several months, the *Examiner* had been taunting the *Chronicle* to open its books for an independent count of the number of subscribers, and offered to do the same with its own books. The *Chronicle* had been bragging that it had more subscribers than the *Examiner*, and Hearst wanted to know where they were getting their figures. He insisted that his own paper was on top and that the *Chronicle* was either lying or somehow tweaking the numbers to make them look like more. In fact, the *Examiner* was even offering the *Chronicle* $500 if it would allow this audit of its books, regardless of the outcome.[12]

Now, in the Durrant trial, Eugene Deuprey was proving Hearst's point with the subscriber figures:

Post	17,500
Report	40,000
Bulletin	30,000
Call	47,000
Chronicle	68,000
Examiner	75,000

In its report of the trial the next day, the *Examiner* crowed triumphantly that the announcement made its victory part of the court record, and therefore official.

The *Call*, a distant third, announced that it would not print a verbatim transcript of the trial, which both the *Examiner* and the *Chronicle* had said they would do. Instead, the *Call* would print a synopsis only, so it wouldn't take all day to read the reports, and would precede each article with a one-minute summary of the highlights. Moreover, the *Call* would avoid all references of an unseemly or sensational nature, unlike its competitors (although, in fact, *none* of the papers printed gynecological information). The *Call* was hoping that its moral stance and its summaries would boost sales, since it knew it could not prevail in head-to-head competition with its rivals.

"Sob sister" Annie Laurie (pen name of Winifred Sweet Black), a reporter for the *Examiner*, attended court that first day to give the woman's perspective, but she spent most of her article criticizing the women who came to watch the trial, the majority of whom had "fought like wildcats" for their places in the courtroom. They were there to see Theo, and craned their necks to observe him throughout the day as he sat—"a queer little machine"—with a distant, daydreaming look on his face. The women all seemed to be well dressed and, according to Annie Laurie, "looked like women who had someone who ought to have made them stay at home." So much for the New Woman.

At the lunch break, Jailer Sattler and Deputy Sheriff Fitzgerald took Theo to a restaurant near City Hall, and Papa joined them a few minutes later. The defense attorneys were not there, and their absence was symbolic of an attitude that would run throughout the Durrant trial: Theo was almost never consulted about any aspect of his trial, and his attorneys rarely kept him informed as to what they were doing. Part of this, of course, was undoubtedly due to Theo's habit of running off at the mouth; but another part surely had to be that he had little to offer them in the way of help: no real alibis, no witnesses, no exculpatory evidence whatsoever. It was Theo's word against all those people who had seen him with Blanche on April 3, and his attorneys had almost nothing to work with. They would have to manufacture a defense because in reality there *was* none.

Back in court for the afternoon session, Deuprey droned on with his reading of the affidavits and the newspaper headlines. Theo tried to avoid the sketch artists (who had nothing else to focus on) by turning his back on them—but eventually he gave up and submitted to the inevitable.

Toward the end of the afternoon, Judge Murphy mercifully stopped Deuprey and indicated that court would convene again the next day. As he was intoning his adjournment speech, however, spectators got up to leave. "Take your seats!" bellowed Murphy and, like guilty schoolchildren, everyone quickly obeyed. He gave them a little speech about rudeness and told them they had to wait for the words "Court is adjourned" before they could leave. As Murphy had the power to exclude people from the courtroom, they were anxious to stay on his good side.

At the end of the first day of *People v. Durrant*, then, one thing was crystal clear: Judge Daniel J. Murphy was firmly in charge of his courtroom.

The second day of the trial brought new excitement for the spectators with the first appearance of Isabella Durrant. Small, stylishly dressed, and smiling, she would be at her son's side until the end of the trial, looking for the most part as if she were attending his graduation or his wedding.

It became evident to everyone as they watched Mamma over the progress of the case that Theo had inherited—or adopted—her sanguine attitude. Instead of being impassive, however, as was her son, Mamma spent her days in court smiling and chatting with

Theo, old Mrs. Thompson (the attorney's wife, who usually accompanied her), or other friends—with everyone, that is, except Papa, who was noticeably excluded from the group and usually sat by himself a row behind them. His role from that point on would be the running of errands.

Mamma came to court every day cheerily dressed and carrying flowers for her son to put in his lapel. She kissed him on the lips (sometimes "lingeringly"), arranged his flower for him, and at breaks and adjournment helped him on with his coat. At times he would play with the gloves she had removed, forgetting that this intimate gesture was the very one that had struck Henry Shalmount when he observed Theo and Blanche on his streetcar the morning of April 3. At other times he held her hand while conversing with her.

Women in the courtroom were in an absolute frenzy to see Mamma close up, and some were rude and unmannerly in their attempts to do so. Two women told the bailiff that "we want to look at her," pushed their way forward until they were very close, then stared her up and down. Mamma tactfully took no notice of them.

For the most part, Mamma Durrant acted as if she were giving a reception and everyone in the courtroom had come to help her celebrate something. She chose her clothes and accompanying corsages with care, and never frowned or looked worried at the day's testimony. Mamma wanted everyone to see how much she believed in her son's innocence, and felt that to be less than bright and cheerful would somehow indicate that she was not confident in the outcome of the case. She was probably oblivious to the somewhat ghoulish effect this attitude produced.

Mamma's courtroom presence, however, is no doubt the key to Theo's own. Whether or not it was his nature to appear unmoved and unworried, it is almost certain that she had told him not to let the public see any sign of doubt or weakness, to act as if he had no worry about the trial because he knew himself to be innocent.

Both the *Chronicle* and the *Examiner* wanted Theo to pose for photographs after court on the second day, but Dickinson initially refused. After Deuprey talked to him, he relented. Deuprey, much more astute when it came to public relations, probably guessed that Theo's cooperation with the newspapers would result in more favorable coverage by them. He needn't have worried about Theo's reaction: He was eager to have his picture taken and anxious about his public image. He had been complaining about the way the sketch artists were presenting him, and he hoped these photographs would make him look better.

Theo fixed his hair and sat down in the courthouse law library. Papa told him to look pleasant, and he replied, "Oh, I always look pleasant." Then he directed the photographer: "Take the pictures so the books show—it will look as if I'm sitting in my library."

When Mamma came in, wearing a corsage and carrying a small bunch of carnations and a boutonniere rosebud, she exclaimed, "Well, I declare! Being photoed, Theo? If I had known that, I would have brought your Prince Albert. It looks so good on you." Like Papa, she encouraged him to look pleasant. He grinned at her: "Don't josh the actors." They might all have been at a photographer's studio, with not a care in the world.

Mamma wanted Theo to wear the rose in his lapel for the pictures, but he preferred to hold it: "I think it looks far prettier to hold it in one's hand," he explained primly. And so, along with the bust shots that appeared in the *Examiner* the next day, there was one of a dignified-looking, self-confident young man, somewhat haughty even, legs crossed, with a folded newspaper in his lap and a rose held lightly in his hand. More than anything else, this photo probably best signifies how Theo tried to face his situation with aplomb. But what did not show up in the photo was that the hand holding the rose shook "as if with palsy."

When the photo session was over, Theo asked for copies to send to his friends and some to hang up in his cell "to liven it up."

In jail, Theo was reading the works of Bunyan and keeping up with his medical studies. He still hoped to graduate in December and had been depressed at not being allowed to take his final exams in the spring. If necessary, he intended to enroll at Cooper for another semester to finish up. Asked about his predicament, he said that he didn't think about it—he let his attorneys do that for him. His conscience was clear and he trusted that God would take care of him. "My alibi is perfect," he told reporters. "I simply told my story to the attorneys the day after my arrest and on that slight statement they have built their case!"

Mamma kept Theo's cell in flowers, which he arranged on a shelf with the books he was reading. The cell was very narrow and his cot took up most of the width (he had been moved to Cell 29 by this time, which he had all to himself). Lighting was poor for reading and writing, which was how Theo spent most of his time when not in court.

If the sheriff had not forbidden it, Theo would have had many more bouquets of flowers than those brought by his mother. Young women were constantly bringing them to the jail, along with other gifts for the famous prisoner, but the sheriff didn't want to encourage the kinds of women who lionized criminals.

One of these women began showing up in court every day and sending loving looks Theo's way. She also sent bunches of sweet peas, and once he even wore one in his lapel, bending down occasionally to sniff it. Known as the Sweet Pea Girl, the attractive young woman entertained reporters, spectators, and policemen alike with the mystery of who she was. The speculation went on for days: Was she a friend of Theo's? Was she a crank? Would she be a witness at the trial?

Police detectives attempted following her after court sessions, but she always managed to give them the slip. Finally, a clever reporter tracked down the clues that were coming from the East Bay and discovered that she was Mrs. Rosalind Holland Bowers of Oakland. Her husband, a salesman, had no idea his wife was going to the city every day to moon over Theo Durrant, and scoffed at the idea. Finally, however, he was forced to the realization that his wife was the famous Sweet Pea Girl.

At first charmed by her attention, Theo eventually became disturbed by it and thought it would prejudice the jury against him. He asked his attorneys to keep her out of the courtroom, and they did. To his credit, he never responded or gave any reaction to the Sweet Pea Girl or any of the other women who attempted to flirt with him in court. Later, he would acknowledge that Mrs. Bowers was sending him gifts of books and even hinted that he had known her before his arrest, but this lie may have been to protect her from being labeled as one of "those" women who hang around the trials of young men accused of murder.

Theo needn't have bothered protecting Mrs. Bowers's reputation, however. After her discovery by the press, she left her husband and moved into a hotel. Her husband made a veiled reference to some trouble in her past, and judging from her be-havior during and after the trial, that most likely meant prostitu-tion. But the Sweet Pea Girl, who provided everyone with such welcome distraction during the dreary days of jury selection, has remained an inextricable part of the Durrant case.[13]

Witnesses old and new also occupied the attention of the press during July and August while the jury was being selected. Alice Pleasant, one of the Normal School students who had seen Theo and Blanche together on the cable car, had married since her tes-timony at the preliminary examination, and was now Mrs. George P. Dorgan. She had received a letter threatening that she would suffer a worse fate than Blanche Lamont if she didn't keep quiet about what she saw. Signed only with the initials J.T.H., the letter was almost completely unintelligible because of the illiteracy of the sender. When Alice finally figured out the message, she destroyed it without contacting the police. She never heard from "JTH" again.

Other witnesses, primarily those who would be involved in the Minnie Williams case if it came to trial, had left town to avoid being interviewed. And the Cooper medical students intended to leave for vacation as soon as they finished their exams so as to avoid subpoenas that would cause them to miss out on their holidays.

There were also a few new sensations in the witness department. Mrs. Mary Vogel, who lived on Powell Street across from the Nor-mal School, came forward to say that she had seen Theo pacing up and down in front of her home and had watched him for an hour, thinking he was a burglar. And a man named Charles Clark had supposedly contacted the defense from Boston, saying that he could supply Theo with an alibi: He had seen Blanche Lamont on a Valencia Street car on the afternoon of April 3. She was accom-panied by a young man, someone other than Theo Durrant.

But who was Charles Clark?[14] He claimed to be a commissioned salesman for the Italian-Swiss Colony Wine Company and was trav-eling through the New England states to drum up buyers for the wine. But Italian-Swiss Colony had never heard of him, and Clark didn't appear in any of the city directories. He said he knew both Blanche and Theo, but neither Blanche's family nor Theo had any idea who he was.

If Clark had such valuable information, why had he left town without saying anything to the police? Even his own wife was baffled. They had talked quite a bit about the case, she said, and he never mentioned anything about seeing Blanche. She could not figure out how he knew either the victim or the defendant. Clark's mother, who lived out of town, said that on April 3 her son had been visiting her, as she had been ill.

Clark's intrusion into the case was a big mystery, especially since he indicated that he would not be returning to San Francisco anytime soon. The prosecution began preparing pages and pages of interrogatories for him, to determine exactly what he knew and how he knew it. The district attorney accused the defense of dirty tricks. And he was probably right.

It turned out that Charles Clark was actually a friend and neighbor of Eugene Deuprey. Supposedly, he mentioned to Deuprey that he had once seen Blanche Lamont on a streetcar on some undetermined day, but even this may not have been true. What probably happened is that Deuprey, knowing that Clark would be out of the state and therefore unavailable for close questioning, concocted this story to confuse the prosecution, at least for a while.

There were witnesses coming out of the woodwork to testify for the state, but nobody had come forward to help Theo. Deuprey probably felt he needed to counteract this barrage and make it seem—at least for a short while—as if there were some alibi witnesses out there, and let the public see that it was not as one-sided a case as it appeared to be. Would Deuprey have allowed Clark to perjure himself? Probably not. But he had come close to crossing the line of what was considered ethical behavior.

However, an even bigger surprise was in store for both sides: the discovery of Caroline Leak, who had actually witnessed Theo and Blanche entering the church on April 3.[15] She had not come forward earlier because she hadn't wanted to get involved (which for most people meant a reluctance to be in the spotlight and bothered by reporters, as well as a fear of testifying in court). When Blanche had come up missing, Mrs. Leak remembered what she had seen and wondered if Theo knew anything about it. She had no thoughts of murder, but it did occur to her that the young lady might have run away and that Theo knew where she was.

When Blanche's body was discovered in the belfry, Mrs. Leak realized immediately that she had important information. Still, she said nothing because of her fear of having anything to do with the case. It bothered her, though, and she told her best friend, Mrs. Henry, and swore her to secrecy. Mrs. Henry was not as timid as Mrs. Leak, and went right to the police with the information. The prosecution was delighted to discover this very important eyewitness, and intended to keep her as a surprise to prevent the defense from preparing anything to counteract her testimony. And this plan would have worked but for the reporter Carrie Cunningham.

Carrie Cunningham, 34, was very ambitious and fancied herself as something of a Nellie Bly (the famous nineteenth-century investigative journalist). She was at that time working for the *Chronicle*, having also served a stint with the rival *Examiner*, and scoured the Mission daily for news and clues. Carrie had heard the story of the witness placing Theo and Blanche at the door of the church, and hunted it down relentlessly. Hence, only a very short time after Mrs. Leak had given her information to the police, Carrie Cunningham's scoop hit the front pages of the *Chronicle*. The police reluctantly admitted that the story was true, and the *Chronicle* boasted that it had beat its competitors—notably, the *Examiner*.

Carrie's next assignment was to befriend Theo and see if he would confide more in a woman than in the many male reporters who had interviewed him from all six newspapers. Nearly every day, then, from about the middle of August, Carrie visited Theo at the county jail, bringing him whatever she was allowed to by the authorities: gum, fruit, newspapers, books. She was so short she had to stand on a box to talk through the wicket.

Theo enjoyed her visits and became more relaxed with her than he normally was with reporters. Of course, he had always felt more comfortable with women. For Carrie's part, what started out as an assignment soon turned into something more: She genuinely came to like him, and the more she saw of him, the more she thought he might be innocent.

Carrie even got to go inside Theo's cell one time, something even Mamma hadn't been able to do. He was painting his walls in an elaborate fresco design that would make him feel as if he were in a garden in classical Greece or Rome instead of a prison cell, and Carrie brought along a *Chronicle* sketch artist to reproduce it for the paper. Theo explained how he loved architectural and mechanical drawing and in the past had gotten so caught up in it that he frequently found himself up as late as 2:00 A.M. without even being aware of the passage of time.[16]

As a result of her friendship with Theo, Carrie was able to get many little tidbits for the *Chronicle* that he did not share with the other newspapers. And then one day he shared the biggest secret of all.

When Carrie came to the jail that day Theo showed her a bulging, sealed envelope on which was written "To my attorneys: To be opened if I am convicted, and returned to me unopened if I am acquitted."[17] Theo had a tendency to be dramatic and mysterious, and Carrie wondered if this would be one of those times. He made her promise that she would never print the story unless he gave permission, and she consented. On that day, and over the ensuing days when he brought up the subject again, she took verbatim notes to protect them both.

Theo claimed that when he was fixing the sunburners at the church on April 3 he heard a noise. He went to check it out and "ascertained that Blanche Lamont was murdered on the second landing." The murderers—there were two of them—found him and threatened him that if he ever revealed what he had seen they would go after his mother: "They even threatened violence to my loved one—to my mother. They said they would make way with her—would spirit her away. I could not stand any threats against her."

Then, Theo claimed that the murderers (he hinted that they were Rev. Gibson and either Elmer Wolfe or George King) put some kind of a spell on him: "No, not hypnotism, I don't believe in hypnotism. . . . Why, do you know, from the afternoon of April 3d until the day I was arrested I was like one in a dream. I did not realize what I was about—I did not know what I was doing."

Theo told Carrie that he had not told anyone this story, not even his parents. The reason he was telling her was for some kind of independent corroboration in case he needed to use it to exonerate himself. If she were to tell the story first, then it would not only verify its existence prior to *his* telling it (i.e., that he was not just making it up right then and there), but would also give him "permission" to tell it without fearing reprisals against his mother. (Though he doesn't seem to have thought about the fact that the alleged murderers would immediately know the source of Carrie's information, even if she presented it as a rumor!)

Carrie promised not to print the story just yet ("But you have to admit it's a corker," she told him) and asked him some questions about what he had seen. He told her he had walked across the false ceiling over to the belfry and peered through some holes in the plaster to see Blanche's body lying on the second landing. "She was murdered on the second landing," he said again. When Carrie spoke of blood dripping down from there, Theo got very agitated. "There wasn't any blood; not a bit. There wasn't any blood at all." The absence of blood seemed important to him, although the police *had* found a small amount of it—and it was on the second landing.

"When you looked onto the second landing," Carrie asked him, "was Blanche Lamont dead or was she being strangled?" This question unnerved Theo completely. "Don't, don't!" he cried out, in visible distress. "Oh, I can't say—I can't answer—don't! don't!" He shook as if with chills and began to cry. "I'm sorry I made you feel so bad," Carrie said. "I can't talk of her," Theo said after a while. "Please don't ask me anything about it. One thing I cannot endure is to talk of her. I thought so much of her. . . . Her death affected me as much as would that of my own sister. . . . No one knows what I suffer in court. Why, when her name is mentioned I can hardly keep up. It seems to me sometimes as if I would scream out." Once again, there was the connection in his mind between Blanche and his sister Maud.

Carrie Cunningham kept her word and did not publish the story until after the trial. However, she began to worry about her involvement in this cover-up, if indeed someone other than Theo Durrant had killed Blanche Lamont, and eventually she approached Edgar Peixotto. (She probably felt more comfortable talking to him than to the formidable Barnes.) And, true to their friendship, she told Theo that she had talked to Peixotto, as she did not want to go behind his back. He seemed undisturbed by it.

Throughout the interminable weeks of jury selection—six of them in all—the press dug frantically for Durrant news to fill pages. One of the stories that was unearthed was destined to become a permanent part of Durrant lore: the picnic picture.[18] A former acquaintance of Theo's had gone to Chief Crowley to give him a photo that had been taken on a hayride picnic (this is sometimes referred to as a "straw ride") that Theo, the friend, and several other young people had been on "three years ago"—which would make it about 1892, when Theo was 21.

It's unclear why the picture was initially offered (probably for publicity), but the police kept it to see if they could get a clue to Theo's character by "studying" it. With this in mind, then, they eventually looked at it so long that they began seeing what they wanted to see.

But before the police came up with their brilliant conclusion about the photo, the *Examiner* published a sketch of it along with a story that Theo had insulted the ladies so horribly in some un-specified way that no one would speak to him from that day on. Nothing about the photo itself was mentioned in the article and, in fact, it is hard to tell from the sketch which one is Theo.

Both the police and the press contacted people who had been on this picnic, and no one could remember if Theo had done any-thing objectionable. All denied refusing to speak with him after-ward. Theo himself said that the source of the story was a young man whom he once "licked" at school for insulting a girl Theo was with, and that if the picnic chaperone were to be asked, she would tell a different story. As far as is known, no one asked her—if, indeed, she was ever found.

Theo further clarified that the picnic had *not* occurred three years before the trial, but six years before—which makes it about 1879, when he is 17 or 18. And he goes on to tell enough about the circumstances surrounding the picture to identify him as the one standing in the forefront between two girls. He is leaning against the wagon wheel in a casual pose, a piece of straw in his mouth, his wide-brimmed hat tilted back on his head, and his coat folded in front of him. Theo and the girls are holding some weedy-looking things he identifies as bulrushes, which he picked to "show to advantage."

The picture comes down to us in the Durrant mythology, not because of an incident which may or may not have occurred, but because of a comment made by Thomas Duke in his 1910 book, *Celebrated Criminal Cases of America*. Duke became the chief of police in San Francisco sometime after the Durrant trial, and ap-parently the photo remained in the police files and survived the earthquake. Here is what he says at the end of his chapter on the Durrant case:

The author has a photograph taken of Durrant at a picnic when he was only sixteen years of age, and the position in which he posed proves conclusively that he was a degenerate even as a child.[19]

There can be no doubt that Duke is referring to the picnic picture sketched in the *Examiner* (there was no other picnic), but what can he possibly mean by his "degenerate pose"? To a twenty-first-century viewer, this is puzzling: Theo is very casual, but he is not touching the girls. A clue as to what Duke probably meant can be found in *The Killers Among Us: Book II* by Colin and Damon Wilson (1995). The Wilsons are unaware of the picture referred to, but presume that "Durrant had his hand in his pocket in a position that suggested he was holding his penis."[20] In the photo, Theo has his hands folded around his coat, held at the level of his groin, and Duke jumped to conclusions. For, if his pose was considered truly degenerate, why would the photographer go ahead with the picture? And why would the *Examiner* publish it without comment?

Yet, since 1901, Duke's unchallenged statement has survived as one more proof (along with the "mysterious woman" to whom Durrant allegedly exposed himself in the Emmanuel Baptist Church) of Theo's innate evil.

A lighter kind of libel occurred in the form of an opportunistic play that was to be presented at the Alcazar Theater by William R. Dailey. Entitled *Crime of a Century*, it was a thinly-disguised rendition of the belfry murder, complete with the devil who appeared on occasion to direct the actions of the Theo character with pitchfork, brimstone, and wicked cackle.

As jury selection was still going on, both prosecution and defense were afraid that the play would be unduly prejudicial to the defendant, and accordingly joined in a motion to prevent its performance. Judge Murphy, incensed that someone would have the audacity to interfere with "his" trial, issued an injunction and declared that if the play went on, the actors, the writer, and the producer would all be arrested.

Dailey fired a volley in return: The injunction was a violation of the First Amendment, he claimed, in that speech could not be enjoined before it even happened. The play would go on, and Dailey would fight this all the way up to the U.S. Supreme Court if necessary. (He had hired an attorney, Carroll Cook, who would later serve a long and distinguished career as a judge.)

The result of all this controversy was publicity for a play that probably, if left alone, would have attracted very few patrons. (Edgar Peixotto, who had been sent two complimentary tickets by

Dailey, said it was the worst play he had ever seen.) People showed up in droves just to see the actors being arrested after they began performing. Police lined up along the sides of the theater, prepared to begin making arrests as soon as the chief sent word. When it came, everyone was arrested for contempt of court and dragged out to the police wagon.

Murphy let the women and an elderly man go home, but put the playwright (Dailey) and the men in jail for the night. The next day they were all released pending the appeal by Cook on behalf of Dailey. (In 1896, the California Supreme Court overturned the injunction, declaring that it had been an abridgement of free speech.)[21]

The play and the injunction had provided a humorous respite during the interminable voir dire proceedings. Still, the selection of jurors also contained some amusement with the creative attempts of the veniremen to avoid serving on what they accurately foresaw would be a long trial. To no one's surprise, Judge Murphy had denied the defense's motion for a change of venue (after putting the attorneys through the torture of reading it for two days) and now the jury pool would have to be available each day. For the first time in California history, two alternate jurors were to be selected in addition to the regular twelve. Just put in effect that January, the law provided for the alternates in order to prevent a mistrial if a juror were to become ill or die.

There were the usual objections of those in the jury pool to imposing the death penalty in a case of circumstantial evidence, and the claims of previously-formed opinions that could never be shaken. There was no way to judge the sincerity of people asserting these.

But there were also a fair number of prospective jurors who claimed various stages of deafness. After Judge Murphy had heard several of these, he tried the trick of making his voice progressively lower as he asked questions of the current "deaf" man. Oblivious to Murphy's purpose, he blithely continued to answer, even though at the end the judge was practically whispering. The laughter of the spectators alerted the venireman to his mistake, and he sheepishly retreated after the judge excused him in spite of his not really being deaf.

Another man got caught in this same trick of Murphy's, but when he heard the crowd's laughter, remembered to make the judge talk louder. And when a prospective juror claimed he was deaf in one ear, Murphy growled unsympathetically, "Well, we'll talk in your other ear, then."

Judge Murphy got more and more short-tempered with the excuses of citizens to escape their duty. He said he had never heard of so many deaf people before, and was not at all sure that everyone claiming scruples against circumstantial evidence really had them. Another gimmick used to avoid serving was the payment of a $50 fee for an honorary membership in the National Guard, which entitled the bearer to an exemption, and Murphy declared this to be a travesty of justice.

One day, Murphy, fed up with how long it was taking to find jurors (by August 1, they had only four), made a little speech about how all citizens had to sacrifice in order to perform their duties and give the defendant a fair trial. It was hard on everyone, he told them, but it was necessary for a free and democratic society. After the speech, which he had expected would shame them into staying, he asked for anyone who had an excuse to come forward. Almost all of the day's panel "rose as one man" and approached the bench!

To spice up the daily court reports during the six-week process of jury selection, the newspapers took to entertaining their readers with comments on the idiosyncrasies of the veniremen. One was called "a dark weird man with thin hair and an aggravated case of mustache," and another was made fun of for saying he was "sot in his mind" about Theo's guilt. A man of German descent was "dark enough for a Russian and built like a wrestler," and one who obviously enjoyed a drink had "acquired a fine Burgundian glow." Jacob Martenstein was compared to Father Wayback, a character in the funny papers, and Addison Mizner was called "the king of the brownies" (this was obviously a contemporary reference that readers back then would have understood).

Finally, on August 29, twelve jurors sat in the box. It had been such a long, drawn-out process that the two sides decided against being the first trial to use the two alternates. Twelve would have to do. It had taken six weeks and 1,300 men from the jury pool to accomplish,[22] but the case of the *People of the State of California v. William Henry Theodore Durrant* was at long last well and truly under way.

The Case for the Prosecution

The pure and simple truth is rarely pure and never simple.
—Oscar Wilde

Alice Rix could not take her eyes off Isabella Durrant. She wasn't exactly sure how she thought the mother of a man on trial for his life should act, but she knew it wasn't *this* way. Mrs. Durrant's almost buoyant gaiety was—well, unseemly.

A star reporter for the *Examiner*, Alice Rix had been sent to the trial to write an observation piece on the players in the drama and their spectators—primarily the women.[1] Rix had arrived at the courtroom early, but still had to rely on her press credentials to force her way through the already massive crowd jostling and bumping in the hallway for the chance to sneak a peek when the door opened, or—for the real prize—a place inside.

Despite her status as a journalist, Mrs. Rix was not exactly a proponent of the "New Woman." She didn't approve of bloomers, for example, and thought many women wouldn't know what to do with independence.[2] Her experience in the hallway outside the courtroom merely bolstered her opinion that women didn't know how to work together to achieve a common goal (in this instance, getting to a prime vantage point to see the trial), whereas men did. Instead of joining together, the women were fighting each other and not getting anywhere. And they were impolite, lacking the respect and courtesy they showed to men.

Inside the courtroom, Alice observed nothing but silliness, and she was embarrassed for her sex. The younger girls simpered and giggled throughout the proceedings, and the older women stared rudely at Theo and his family. One elderly crone actually had the audacity to stand within fifteen feet of them and pull out a foot-long pair of binoculars! The Durrants pretended not to see her, but eventually a bailiff made her put them away. What was it, Alice asked, that made women want to be so near crime? And, of course, there was the Sweet Pea Girl, actually sending flowers to the defendant. What caused this kind of behavior?

By chance, Rix sat next to the Sweet Pea Girl that day. "After a moment, I decided that I would like to slap her," she wrote later. The melodramatic heaving and sighing and clutching her handkerchief to her face were more than the reporter could stand. Rix branded her "a poor, limp, tear-stained, hysterical, perverted little simpleton."

As for Theo, Alice thought that he probably reveled in being the center of attention, even though most of that attention was negative. At the same time, she didn't believe what everyone else was saying about his being so cold and indifferent; anyone with half an eye could see that the young man went through "sleepless nights and anxious days."

But when Mamma came on the scene, Alice Rix ceased looking at anyone else. It was like being hypnotized by a snake: She was repulsed, but she couldn't look away. "A small, swift, alert, birdlike woman," Mamma swept in past the whispers of "Here she is!," kissed her son, arranged herself and her finery in her chair, and looked at the crowd "as the sort of woman who feels it a distinction to sit in a private box at the theatre will look over lesser folk who must be content with orchestra chairs."

Rix had nothing kind to say about Mamma, with her "cold, dark eyes," her "affected little smile," and her mischievous, almost flirtatious, tilting of the head at her son. It would not be the reporter's last encounter with this strange mother, and little would happen to change her initial impression. And Papa? She felt sorry for him, as she thought he was more real in his misery, more dignified in his silence.

After the interminable jury selection, the trial was delayed even more by a controversy surrounding Labor Day, not yet a federally mandated holiday. The prosecution's case was scheduled to begin on Monday, September 2, and the holiday had been observed in a half-hearted way by the county the previous year. Judge Murphy saw no reason why the case could not proceed, but Barnes wasn't so sure. If they went ahead, the defense might use it as a point of error on appeal. Finally, both sides agreed to honor the day and begin on September 3 instead.[3]

District Attorney Barnes's opening statement on Tuesday, September 3, was a calm, orderly recitation of the facts the state would prove. There was only one sticky moment, when he got to the discovery of Minnie Williams's body in the library closet, which was the reason Blanche's body was found at all. However, in California at that time a defendant could not be tried jointly for multiple crimes, and all references to the Williams case had to be eliminated for fear of prejudice (as if the jury knew nothing about Minnie's murder!). So Deuprey objected and the judge determined that Barnes should refer to "a certain something" found in the library rather than to a body.

While Barnes was giving his statement, Theo paid nervous attention. He chewed his lip, fingered the new mustache he was growing, and swallowed frequently. Gone for now was the indifference of his previous court appearances.

As soon as the opening statement was concluded, both sides joined in a motion to have the jury travel to the crime scene and go through the Emmanuel Baptist Church. Murphy was very reluctant to do this, as it would expose the jurors to outside influence—a spectator might say something to them or engage them in conversation—and could result in a mistrial. After all the time and trouble it took to get twelve jurors, Murphy most definitely did *not* want to risk a mistrial.

Still, the lawyers were firm in their demand and the jurors expressed a desire to see the site for themselves. They felt it would help them understand the testimony better. Murphy relented, and after warning the jury not to speak to anyone or let anyone speak to them, they all piled on streetcars and headed for Bartlett Street.

Theo had been taken in the jail wagon and got to the church before the jurors, as did the lawyers. He seemed to be in a good mood, possibly enjoying an outing (notwithstanding its gruesome intent) after being cooped up in jail since April. Barnes was looking pretty spiffy that day in a new coat, and as they waited outside for the jurors to arrive, Theo joked about it: "Take a snap of that," he said to a reporter with a camera.

The "gossip telegraph" had somehow spread the word that the jury would be making a field trip to the church, and by the time the court party was ready to go inside, there were thousands of people hanging out in the doorways, the windows, and the streets of the church neighborhood. Moreover, school had just let out and several hundred children stood around watching and jeering Theo. (Years later, one of those children would remember how the adult women in the crowd shook their fists at the prisoner.)[4]

Across the street, a neighbor was visiting Mrs. Leak in her apartment. Hearing the commotion outside, the two women went to the window and looked down at the crowd milling around the church. "Why, there's Theo Durrant!" cried Mrs. Leak. It was a hazy day, and her spontaneous comment, later reported by her visitor, would show not only that her eyesight was keen, but that she had no trouble recognizing the defendant—two points that would be contested by Theo's attorneys.

Inside the church, the jurors, the attorneys, the judge, and the prisoner were guided by Patrolman George Russell, who had previously taken extensive measurements in order to construct a model of the belfry to be used in court and was therefore very familiar with the building. He had been instructed not to make any definitive statements, but to say "This is claimed to be" before everything shown the jury. The formulaic statement became humorous in parts, such as with "This is claimed to be a door" and "This is claimed to be the entrance to the church." At times, Russell's "claimed to be" phrases were not put in the right place—they were either too early or too late—and everyone laughed, including Theo.

In the tiny library room where Minnie's body had been found (Robert Lynch had ordered the blood cleaned up), on the belfry stairs, and up in the belfry, Theo seemed unmoved. However, he probably knew that everyone would be looking at him in those places (especially reporters) just to see a reaction, and would have steeled himself against this. Outside the church at the end of the tour, Theo smiled and nodded at people he knew in the crowd, then got back into the police van. As it sped toward the county jail, it was followed by taunting, hissing schoolboys.

The first day of trial was over.

Once the "real" trial was under way with the taking of testimony, conditions in the courtroom became unbearable. Five hundred people crammed themselves into every available space in a room designed to hold fewer than half that many. There were even spectators sitting on the judge's platform! At breaks and at recesses, men were allowed to smoke in the courtroom, and the air—already stuffy with the heat and odor of people who didn't bathe daily—became saturated with the smoke and smell of cigars, cigarettes, and pipes. On top of that, the windows in the courtroom were being kept closed because it was almost impossible to hear witnesses over the clatter of trucks and cable cars on the street below.

Juror Horace Smyth had endured enough. He sat through this hell for a few days without saying anything, but no longer could he keep silent. One day after a recess he stood up and scolded the judge for allowing these insufferable conditions. He would not continue to serve as a juror, he said, until his demands were met: No more than two hundred were to be allowed in the courtroom (its designated capacity), there was to be no smoking inside, and the windows should be opened, at least at recess, for fresh air. And while he was at it, he demanded a constant supply of ice water.

From that time on, Juror Smyth was labeled as the ice-water-and-fresh-air fiend, a small but outspoken man who had managed to extract a meek agreement from Judge Murphy that existing conditions were, indeed, unacceptable. As a result, smoking was banned, admittance to the courtroom was limited, fresh air was provided, and ice water was always on hand. Juror Smyth became a hero to many, and one of the more amusing scenes was that of a corpulent William Barnes in the undignified position of standing on the ledge outside the courtroom window, his bulk outlined against the light, puffing on a cigarette during a break.

Smyth would make himself prominent also for his interruption of the testimony to ask a witness a question, or a series of them, and in one instance his demand that a witness be recalled so he could interrogate him further. But he was not the only juror to ask questions of witnesses, and nobody ever objected, so it was undoubtedly a standard occurrence at nineteenth-century trials.

Dr. John S. Barrett, the autopsy physician, knew from the police court proceedings that he would be in for a grueling cross-examination at the trial. And he was right.

Barrett testified on direct examination that Blanche had died of asphyxiation due to strangulation. The marks that he took to be fingernail incisions—seven on the right and five on the left side of the victim's throat—were deep and extended down to the larynx. As they were all the same size, and as the marks would have changed somewhat with the decomposition process, Barrett did not measure them. However, he felt that the fingernails that made them were cut straight across, as the marks had no curvature to them. The depth of the wounds probably indicated that a struggle had occurred. There was some blood found around the lips and nose, and some found inside the nose, but this was postmortem blood and a natural result of death by strangulation.

Although Barrett demonstrated in court what he thought to be the most likely position of the killer's hands, the written record never describes this accurately for the reader who was not present at the time. (Today, an attorney or the judge will say, "Let the record reflect that . . ." and then spell it out for transcript purposes.) However, the doctor's usage of the word "throat" and his description of the incisions as reaching down to the "collarbone" strongly indicate that Blanche's murderer strangled her from behind (although it is possible that both approaches were used—front and back).

The exterior of the body was somewhat advanced in decomposition: blebs (blisters of decay) had appeared, the skin had ruptured in some parts, and maggots were present. But the interior organs had not decomposed to a very great extent, and Barrett was able to examine these with no trouble. Blanche had just finished her menstrual period, and this fluid was found in the vaginal canal and in the womb. All her organs were healthy and normal, except for the congestion in the larynx, lungs, and brain that comes from asphyxiation.

Eugene Deuprey, an expert in dealing with medical witnesses, undertook the cross-examination of Dr. Barrett, and contested absolutely everything in his report. Because Theo had square-cut fingernails, Deuprey tried to get Barrett to say that the incisions could have been made by other things—by pieces of wood, or pieces of ivory, for example, or even by some material *shaped* to resemble fingernails. He disputed the verdict of asphyxiation, and even posited the possibility that Blanche could have committed suicide!

Dr. Barrett was on the stand for two hours, most of it for cross-examination. However, he did say one thing that the defense would latch onto as a linchpin of their case: Although he had not weighed the body, Barrett estimated Blanche's live weight to have been 140–150 pounds. In reality, of course, this was much heavier than Blanche had ever been in her life, but the defense wanted to take it as gospel because it was unlikely that a man of Theo's weight (115 pounds at his arrest on April 14) could have carried a woman of that size up the 105 stairs from the library to the belfry.

When the *Chronicle* reprinted the trial transcript of Dr. Barrett's report, it omitted the gynecological and sexual areas, as did the other newspapers. However, someone in the editing room must have dozed off while reading it, as parts of Deuprey's cross-examination referring to those omitted parts (concerning the presence or absence of sperm in the vaginal canal) were inadvertently left in. The *Examiner*, which also printed a verbatim transcript, had not done this, so it was obviously a mistake on the part of the *Chronicle*. Hence, readers in 1895 were able to discover that Barrett did not test for semen ("spermatozoa") because he did not think it could have lived in the foul vaginal liquid—nor did he think the liquid came from anywhere but the victim's own body.

Patrolman George Russell's belfry model was a masterpiece of engineering, and after his testimony on September 4, it remained behind for the convenience of later witnesses. Its very size dominated the front of the courtroom, and Judge Murphy couldn't wait to get rid of it. (Periodically, he would ask in a hopeful tone, "Are we finished with this yet?") At a height of 11 feet, 2½ inches (a scale of 1½ inches per foot), the model stood next to the jury box and sometimes interfered with the judge's ability to see. Nonetheless, it was an extremely helpful visualization tool for the jury and the spectators.

When Detective Edward L. Gibson took the stand to detail his discovery of the crime scene in the belfry and the steps he took in his investigation, the defense once again showed its determination to contest every single element of the state's case. General Dickinson was in charge of the cross-examination of this witness, and tried to show incompetence in the police methods of preserving evidence—including an objection to the admission of the wooden blocks holding up Blanche's head because they had not been properly identified. At one point, an exasperated Judge Murphy cried out: "Gentlemen! Gentlemen! We'll all die of old age if we do not get along more rapidly with the case." There was appreciative laughter from the spectators, and for once the judge did not rebuke them.

During the testimony concerning the discovery of Blanche's body, the *Examiner* reporter noticed that Theo was yawning and that it was obviously forced—as if in exaggerated indifference because he knew everyone was watching him. However, yawning is also a sign of nervousness and, although many throughout the course of the trial thought Theo was blasé about what was going on, there were indications that this was not the case. After the trial, he showed a friend the inside of his lip, chewed raw from anxiety.[5]

As the trial went on and continued to monopolize the newspapers and people's conversations, the wealthier and more distinguished elements of society began to make their appearances. It became a fad to get together "Durrant parties" and go to the courtroom in a group, and it seemed as if everyone in the Western states who held some kind of title—judge, ex-judge, senator, congressman—came to watch the show for at least a day. Many of these notables were invited to sit next to Judge Murphy on the bench. (Gold Rush millionaire John Mackay was surprised when he saw the Demon of the Belfry: "He's a bit of a weakly, effeminate-looking chap," he said with obvious disappointment.)

The most distinguished visitor to grace the inside of Department 3 and sit next to Judge Murphy was a presidential candidate on his first visit to California: William Jennings Bryan, whose "Cross of Gold" speech in support of silver would be known to every schoolchild for decades thereafter.

On the day that the testimony centered around the discovery and identification of Blanche Lamont's clothing, the crowd was electrified by the appearance of a police officer carrying in a dressmaker's form with the victim's clothes on it. As the model made its way to the front of the courtroom carelessly tucked under the officer's arm, its dress brushed against Theo. If he was aware of it, he gave no visible reaction.

The effect of the dressmaker's form was eerie, as if the ghost of the dead girl had entered the courtroom to stand before the young man accused of her murder. The audience drew in its breath audibly, as if it were one person. The huge rips had been pinned together so the clothing would stay on the model, but they could still be seen.

Deuprey and Dickinson were on their feet in an instant, vigorously objecting to the form. The clothing could stay, they said, as it was part of the case; but the form itself was not, and they wanted it gone. It was obvious to all why it was so objectionable: Not only was it a visible reminder of the once-vibrant victim (who is often lost in big murder trials), but it also showed the jurors just how small Blanche really was—not the 140-pound, "full-figured" woman erroneously presented by Dr. Barrett. Judge Murphy overruled their objection, stating that it was ridiculous. So the dressmaker's form remained, along with the belfry model.

Theo was usually brought to the courtroom early in the morning, before the crowds began to show up and even before the attorneys were there. One morning, alone in the room except for a reporter, he stood before the dressmaker's form, lost in reverie for about five minutes. What must his thoughts have been? Or did he know the reporter was watching, and pose for effect?

Everyone who had found a piece of clothing in the belfry got on the stand to testify to that and identify what was found, but most of the items were discovered by the acrobatic Starr Dare. The basque (a jacket-like garment with a short skirt) and the waist were stuck down in the rafters, he said, with sticks on top (probably to hold them there). The corsets were dangling from the top of a platform, and had most likely been pushed down from an upper level. They were actually visible from the lower part of the belfry, so they weren't hidden well.

Some items were stuffed in crevices and others were carelessly strewn about the upper regions. Buttons with cloth still attached were found on the floor near the body, indicating that the victim had been undressed up there. Another thing that pointed to this was the discovery of a glove, overlooked by the killer, on the platform where the body lay, whereas the other glove had been hidden with the rest of the clothing. As Dare retrieved the items that day, he handed them down to a man named John Daly. Daly was a milkman by trade, and this was the only way he was ever referred to: Milkman Daly.

Dare's testimony also reveals that what we consider a very modern phrase—"and stuff"—was already in currency back then, with his reference to "dust and stuff" on the belfry landing. Part of this "stuff" was a missing hatchet that had belonged to the janitor. Theo and George King had borrowed it in late March to install the new lock on the library door, but Sademan had not seen it since then. Now it had appeared in the belfry with Blanche Lamont, and this led to speculation that Theo—a medical student with practice in dissecting bodies—intended to cut up the corpse and eventually dispose of it.

Tryphena Noble and Maud Lamont gave their testimony after this, to identify Blanche's clothing, books, and rings, and to tell what they knew of the relationship between Theo and Blanche. After they finished, they sat in court every day until the verdict, silent and hostile representatives of the victim, to make sure that their loved one got justice. (Blanche's little brother, 8-year-old Rodger, had come back with Maud from Dillon for the duration of the trial, but never went to court.)[6] Maud could often be seen glaring fiercely at Theo, and at other times crying softly into her handkerchief.

Until the time of their testimony, however, they were excluded from the courtroom, as were all witnesses. The purpose of this rule (available to whatever side wishes to invoke it) is to prevent someone from altering testimony to fit that of a previous witness.

Consequently, when a visibly distraught Tryphena Noble was shown *two* leather straps by the defense and asked to determine which had belonged to her niece, Maud Lamont was not in court to witness her aunt's confusion. The duplicate strap looked exactly like the one presented by the prosecution as having secured Blanche's schoolbooks, except for two things: it had BLANCHE LA-

MONT printed on it[7] (which the prosecution's did not) and it lacked a string on the buckle (which the prosecution's version had).

The defense, mysteriously silent for now as to the origin of the duplicate strap, but insinuating that it would be of import, tried to show faulty identification on the part of Blanche's own family, which could taint their assertion that the clothes found in the belfry were Blanche's. (What good this would do, even if they could succeed, is not clear: No one was disputing that the victim was Blanche, which would seem to be a more important point. And the books had Blanche's name in them.) Aunt Tryphena could not remember whether Blanche's strap had her name printed on it— she rather thought it did not—but of one thing she was sure: it had a string on the buckle, which had probably held a railroad tag when Blanche arrived from Dillon. So the defense's ploy failed with Mrs. Noble. Would it work with Maud?

Maud came in looking like a schoolgirl, with her rich, red hair worn in a braid down her back (a style not used by adult women). She was dressed in black, and from the start showed her determination not to cooperate with the defense. Maud even claimed that, although she and Blanche shared the same bed in their aunt's house, her sister never talked about what she was studying in school. And it was a long, drawn-out process getting her to name Blanche's various gentlemen friends.

But Maud was ready for the duplicate strap. Her aunt had just enough time to say something to her in the witness room before she came out to testify, so Maud was reluctant to commit herself to anything regarding either strap. She did say, however, that Blanche frequently printed instead of writing in cursive, and that the name *could* have been written by her sister.

Theo did not look at Maud Lamont while she was on the stand, and when she stepped down and walked by the defense table, he averted his eyes.

The prosecution was getting ready to put on the series of witnesses that would place Theo in Blanche's presence from the Normal School to the door of the church, when Christmas came early for the state. Old Mrs. Crosett, the grandmother of one of Theo's closest friends, had agonized over her decision (for the sake of Mrs. Durrant) and now came reluctantly forward to fill in the last piece of the puzzle: the sighting of Theo and Blanche on the street-car from Market Street to 21st, where they would thereafter be seen by Martin Quinlan and Mrs. Leak.

The gap that had existed was not a fatal lack of evidence, but Elizabeth Crosett's testimony would make the people's case almost unassailable, as only she and Mrs. Leak actually knew Theo Durrant by sight *and* by name. There could be no possibility of mistaken identity. And, even if the defense somehow managed to impeach Mrs. Leak's testimony, Mrs. Crosett's would be a strong backup. The prosecution was elated.

And the press was elated, too, because the stories of the other witnesses who had come forward so far had already been told, and would soon be told again in court. They were old news. Mrs. Crosett's story was fresh meat for a hungry press. As with the discovery of Mrs. Leak, the new "surprise" witness for the state was unveiled in the newspapers, to the dismay of Barnes and Peixotto.

This was a hard blow for the defense. Mrs. Crosett had been like Theo's own grandmother, and the effect of her testifying against him would be almost the same. After the story hit the newspapers, Mamma went to talk to Mrs. Crosett's daughter-in-law, while Papa talked to her son (the parents of Theo's friend Jim). They begged the Crosetts to convince their mother not to testify or, in the alternative, to be less sure in her identification of Theo. It was not the first time the Durrants attempted to sway the state's witnesses, and it would not be the last.

Theo must have been unnerved by the emergence of Mrs. Crosett because right after this he began complaining about a 30-something man with bulging eyes who was trying to hypnotize him in the courtroom. He wanted the mysterious stranger removed, as he felt himself "in mental conflict" with him. The incident is noteworthy because it was the second time Theo had brought up the subject of hypnotism: first in his story to Carrie Cunningham and now with the mysterious stranger. Was he thinking of setting up a defense involving hypnotism now that things were going against him? Or was he simply falling apart?

The testimony of the "three little girls from school" was straight-forward and convincing. Each story corroborated the others and the defense was unable to shake the witnesses in cross-examination—although it *was* successful in keeping out the reason

why Alice Pleasant Dorgan and May Lanigan had taken special notice of Theo and Blanche (the rule forbidding escorts). It probably
didn't matter, though, as this had been covered in the inquest, at
the police court, and in the papers.

When Mary Vogel took the stand to tell what she had seen looking out her window across the street from the Normal School on
April 3, the proceedings livened up considerably. Mrs. Vogel (no
relation to Tom's family) had been born in New York City, but her
German accent was so thick that it provided rich entertainment for
an audience used to low comedy theater skits featuring immigrant
dialects. Although both the *Chronicle* and the *Examiner* printed
the day's trial transcript, only the *Examiner* reproduced Mary Vogel's accent for its readership, an incident that says worlds about
how each newspaper viewed its journalistic purpose.

The prosecution made sure that witnesses were specific in identifying Theo as the man they had seen, and usually required them
to step down from the stand and point him out. This process of
having to come so close to the defendant while being watched by
a crowded courtroom often unnerved witnesses, and they sometimes made their identification somewhat melodramatic. Mrs. Vogel did not disappoint her audience. She "fairly swooped down"
on him like an avenging fury (probably remembering the tension
he had put her through when she thought he was planning to rob
her) as the crowd stood up to see Theo's reaction. "Dat man dere
mit de old rose," she said, almost touching him with her outstretched finger. "I vatch him too long."

Judge Murphy had a hard time controlling the crowd while Mrs.
Vogel was on the stand, but even he had to laugh when, in response to a question as to whether she or her husband owned the
property, she said, "Vat he got is mine. Vat I got is his." When
asked how she knew her husband had done something, Mrs. Vogel
retorted, "How I know? I know everything vat he does."

But in spite of the comedy, which Theo also enjoyed, Mary Vogel's story rang true. The defense tried to confuse her as to the
day she had seen him, but she was firm in placing it: It was the
day her husband had received a double-cancelled postcard, and
when he brought it home to show her, she talked about the
strange man who had waited and paced so nervously that afternoon. She told the court of getting her opera glasses so she could

see the man better, and how fast he had gotten himself and the girl on the cable car ("It was so quick done, quicker than I can tell you."), and how she became frightened when she recognized his picture in the paper a few days later. In fact, she was so upset that her husband forbade her to read the newspaper accounts of the murders.

Occasionally, Mrs. Vogel would get rattled in answering defense questions and it was hard to understand what she was trying to say. "Keep cool," Judge Murphy told her. "Everyone will treat you nicely here."

A witness who was not always treated so nicely was the very dangerous Mrs. Crosett, coming forward to tell her story under oath for the first time. She was old (71) and infirm (lung and heart problems), but her mind was clear and her story was convincing. Mrs. Crosett was helped to the stand by her granddaughter, Charlotte McKee and Charlotte's husband Clarence ("Clancy"), who then sat where she could see them for moral support. Charlotte was the granddaughter she had been visiting on the day she saw Theo and the young lady on the streetcar.

Mrs. Crosett remembered quite a bit about that day for a number of reasons. First, she had lunched with her granddaughter. Then, her daughter, Ellen, Charlotte's mother, had escorted her to the streetcar; Ellen lived in the East Bay and wasn't always in the city.[8] The next day, Mrs. Crosett went to Ellen's home in Alameda for an extended stay. Hence, her ability to pinpoint the exact day when she saw Theo was not at all vague or flimsy, and try as they might, the defense could not get her to back down from this certainty.

Mrs. Crosett had left Charlotte's house at 3:20 P.M., then—accompanied by her daughter—walked her usual slow pace to the first of two street cars that would take her to her son's home on San Jose Avenue and 25th Street in the Mission District. At the convergence of Haight and Market, she said good-bye to Ellen and got on the Valencia car, where Theo and Blanche were already sitting on the outside dummy. She got home just before 4:00, and the two young people had gotten off before she did—at 21st or 22nd Street; she couldn't be sure which.

Eugene Deuprey attacked Mrs. Crosett's sense of timing, her health, and her eyesight. But the elderly woman was firm in that she had left her granddaughter's house on Washington Street at

3:20 and arrived home a few minutes before 4:00. (Deuprey would have two of Theo's Signal Corps buddies retrace her route, and it took them about the same time: forty-five minutes.) Her testimony here was crucial because Theo was now claiming that he did not leave the college until 4:15. His presence on a streetcar before 4:00 undermined his assertion that he had attended the 3:30 lecture.

Mrs. Crosett's health was poor, but it in no way interfered with her mind. She took a battery of homeopathic (natural) remedies, such as belladonna, aconite, and ferrum phosphate (all of which she was able to recite from memory), but had taken nothing on April 3—so she couldn't be said to be under the influence of anything.

Deuprey was running out of options with Mrs. Crosett and becoming more and more frustrated. This was obvious when he began asking her about different times when she had seen Theo, and after one response, the beleaguered attorney said sarcastically, "That is, you *imagine* you have seen him?" Judge Murphy was furious: "You have no right to interject 'you imagine you have' in the witness's statement. I say that this witness and all witnesses in this court are to be treated fairly." To Deuprey's assertion, "I did, sir, treat this witness fairly," Murphy responded sharply, "The Court does not believe you have. Propound your next question, sir."

There was no getting around it: Mrs. Crosett's definitive identification of Theo, told in a calm, unrattled manner, was extremely damaging to the defense.

After the somewhat heavy seriousness of Mrs. Crosett's testimony, everyone was ready for comic relief. It came in the person of Martin Quinlan. Quinlan, "newly barbered and smelling of bay rum and bear's grease," must have girded himself after his police court grilling because not even General Dickinson's sneering insinuations ("Oh, you visit only the police courts") caused him to lose his temper.

Quinlan was vulnerable to attack because of his lack of a real office, his police court practice (which meant he represented petty criminals whose business he obtained by a kind of ambulance-chasing technique), and his frequenting of saloons. Dickinson's questions on these matters were designed to imply that Quinlan's testimony was not only unreliable, but that possibly he was too drunk to identify anyone on April 3. Fortunately for the prosecution, most of Quinlan's imbibing took place from 4:30 on—*after* he had seen Theo and Blanche.

Gionetti's Saloon[9] was less than a block from Quinlan's house, and at 7:30 on the morning of April 3, he and his houseguest, David Clarke, walked down to have a drink. They went back home for breakfast, then returned to Gionetti's for cigars. If there was more drinking, Quinlan did not own up to it. Even so, there must have been many in the courtroom who shuddered at this early morning routine, all of which took place in the space of an hour.

Quinlan's next stop was City Prison to drum up business among the recent admittees. There were no takers there, so he went to his unofficial "office"—Lane's Saloon—to get his shoes shined and buy another cigar. After ten minutes or so, he went over to the police court, then back to Lane's for his regular noontime drink. He remembered that day specifically because "himself" (Lane) was there.[10]

Quinlan could not remember going to any other saloons before heading back to the Mission in the afternoon to meet Clarke once again, but he was asked to name the establishments in the area of City Hall that he frequented. When he had trouble coming up with the name of one, Judge Murphy helpfully volunteered "Hartnett's," and everyone laughed at Hizzoner's familiarity with a groggery.

It was after Quinlan had seen Theo and Blanche that he and Clarke began a prodigious tour of the Mission saloons on their way to and from seeing Clarke's brother-in-law at St. Luke's Hospital. They must have hit every one and there must have been plenty of them in the area. Sometimes Clarke treated and sometimes Quinlan treated. After a while, Quinlan lost track of exactly what time it was or how many drinks they had at each stop, but whenever Dickinson asked (as he had at the preliminary examination) "What kind of establishment was that?" and the attorney answered "Saloon" the crowd would laugh harder than the time before.

By the end of the Quinlan-Clarke saloon tour, everyone knew that Martin Quinlan had drunk quite a lot and that the only thing he had eaten since breakfast was a plate of oysters in yet another bar. But it all counted for nothing: He wasn't drunk when he saw Theo and Blanche, and he remembered it perfectly. All Dickinson did with his post-sighting questions was to provide the audience with entertainment; he did nothing to undermine Quinlan's very positive and very crucial testimony.

David Clarke was questioned next, to corroborate Quinlan's recollection of the day on which these events happened. Clarke remembered it quite well, in spite of his participation in the bar-hopping, because he was living in Guerneville (Sonoma County) at the time. He had come over to San Francisco on Tuesday, April 2, to meet Quinlan, who had been a high school classmate of his in Bodega. But Quinlan never showed up for their appointment, so Clarke spent the night at the attorney's house and made another appointment for the next day. The whole object was for Quinlan to talk with Clarke's brother-in-law, who had been injured in some kind of accident and was recuperating at St. Luke's Hospital.

Clarke was waiting for Quinlan at Gionetti's that Wednesday afternoon and, as his friend was late, he kept looking at the clock. Finally, at 4:15, when Quinlan was fifteen minutes overdue, Clarke went outside to look for him. His impatience is obvious in his testimony, and he probably thought he was going to be stood up again. But then came the dawdling Quinlan, ambling down from 22nd Street as if he had nowhere to be, and the two went back into Gionetti's together where "Mr. Clarke treated."

At the police court hearing, Clarke had sported a large mustache. Today, however, he was clean-shaven, and Dickinson seemed to think this was pursuant to some kind of subterfuge (though what it could be he never made clear). Clarke revealed that he had the mustache taken off about three weeks before his testimony, and Dickinson—again, with no clear point—asked "Where?" "In a barber shop," was the witness's smart remark, to the raucous delight of the crowd. ("This laughing must cease!" Murphy shouted in vain while pounding his gavel.)

Whenever the spectators laughed during the presentation of evidence, Mamma and Theo almost always joined in. But Papa never enjoyed himself in court. It was as if he alone of the family was cognizant of what was really going on, and of what the ultimate stakes would be.

Like that of Mrs. Crosett, the testimony of Mrs. Caroline Leak was strong and definitive evidence against Theo. Her sighting placed him inside the church with Blanche Lamont, whose very schoolbooks were mute witnesses to the fact that she never emerged from there alive after her day at school. Consequently, the defense would have to do everything it could to impeach her. This they planned to do by attacking her on three major points: her eyesight; her possible mental illness or "confusion" as a result of an acrimonious divorce some years previously; and—the most valid of all—the fact that, during a condolence visit to Mrs. Noble after Blanche's murder, she had never said anything about having seen her niece with Theo.

In fact, Dickinson and Deuprey had a theory as to why Mrs. Leak had kept strangely silent at a time when she would have been expected to speak out. They suspected that the sighting story had been made up out of wholecloth by Rev. J. George Gibson to incriminate Theo and throw the mantle of blame from himself. And then he had gotten old Mrs. Leak, who lived across the street and was a loyal member of his church, to tell the tale he had himself invented.

Mrs. Leak, 66, was a small woman with an enormous nose. In its sketches of her, the *Chronicle* downplayed her most prominent feature, but the *Examiner* did not.

When Mrs. Leak began her direct testimony, she almost gave District Attorney Barnes a heart attack. Somewhat hard of hearing, she misunderstood his question "Did you happen to see the defendant that day?" to mean "Did you happen to see the defendant *at church* that day?" and answered "No." Barnes was visibly disconcerted at this, and probably thought that one of his prime witnesses was about to change her testimony. But it was soon straightened out, and Mrs. Leak admitted she had seen him.

Caroline Leak had known Theo for four or five years, and as she attended Emmanuel Baptist twice each Sunday, as well as the Sunday school and the Wednesday evening prayer service, she was very familiar with him indeed. And when she saw him on the afternoon of April 3 between 4:00 and 4:30, he and his companion were *sauntering* as they talked. Their leisurely pace gave Mrs. Leak plenty of time to watch, and there could be no doubt that it was Theo Durrant.

But Mrs. Leak was not exactly sure who the young lady was. She knew it was someone tall—tall for a woman and taller than Theo Durrant—but whether it was Lucile Turner or Blanche Lamont, she could not say. The girl was facing Theo as she talked, and he was looking at her, listening intently. But she never turned in the direction of Mrs. Leak as she observed them from her window across the street. Theo's companion was wearing a dark dress and a large light-colored hat—that much Mrs. Leak could see.

On cross-examination, Deuprey quizzed the witness about her eyesight, which she claimed was good. As a matter of fact, she sewed for a living and wore glasses only for reading.

Deuprey then asked about her "personal problems" (regarding her separation from her husband), inferring that they would have caused her mental distress, and Mrs. Leak told him that it had all taken place too many years ago to be of any consequence to her now. But Deuprey wanted particulars as to what caused the breakup, and this angered Mrs. Leak: "Well, I say, I don't know as I was called here to rehearse my private affairs," she said. "That is going pretty deep into private affairs." Judge Murphy agreed with her and disallowed the question.

A more serious concern, however, was Mrs. Leak's failure to come forward earlier with her information. She had even paid a sympathy call to Mrs. Noble after the Minnie Williams funeral— and still said nothing about having seen Blanche with Theo on what was now known to have been the last day of her life. It looked very much as if Mrs. Leak had kept silent because she had not really seen anything, and was only saying this now to cause trouble for Theo.

No, Mrs. Leak said, that wasn't it at all. She had never talked to Rev. Gibson about it, and did not give any interview to Carrie Cunningham. She didn't say anything to Mrs. Noble because she thought the police had enough information without hers and— quite frankly—she didn't want to get involved. When she talked to Mrs. Henry, she was vague and noncommittal, telling her that she "supposed" she had seen the one who killed Blanche, but never giving his name. As soon as she had said this, however, she regretted it and begged Mrs. Henry not to tell anyone. But Mrs. Henry had gone to the police, and was probably the one who had spoken with Carrie Cunningham.

After Carrie's story broke in the *Chronicle*, reporters began hounding Mrs. Leak, knocking at her door at all hours. Consequently, she hid out, not answering the door and not going any-where at all—not even to church, which must have been a great sacrifice to her. She used to go to her landlord's house to borrow his copy of the newspaper, but after her story became public, she didn't go there, either (he kindly delivered it to her apartment instead).

Mrs. Leak was an intensely private person, and her account of the very unwelcome publicity she received as a result of the story merely reinforced her reasons for not having come forward in the first place. The defense was unsuccessful in shaking her story and, despite her age, the witness came across as "bright and snappy." And, while Theo had enjoyed Martin Quinlan's saga, he looked down when Mrs. Leak pointed him out from the stand.

To prove that it was Blanche Lamont who had accompanied Theo to the church on April 3, and not Lucile Turner, the prosecution called Lucile to testify that she had not been with Theo at all that day, nor had she gone to the church. Lucile mistakenly raised her *left* hand to be sworn, and when the clerk corrected her, she got embarrassed. But on the stand, she was strong and clear (unlike many witnesses who could not be heard), and the newspapers sounded regretful that the "pretty young lady with the fine figure" could not stay longer. There was no cross-examination.

Young George King presented a problem to Barnes and Peixotto. They would call him as their own witness because of the value of his testimony in placing a distraught and disheveled Theo inside the church at the precise time when Blanche must have been killed. But he had remained friendly with the defendant and had visited him in jail at least twice. George's father, Dr. King, was a staunch supporter of Theo, sending him magazines and socializing with his parents. George, then, could not really be considered a prosecution witness and they would have to manage him carefully on the stand.

Right from the start, there had been indications that the young organist would be reluctant to testify against his friend. George and several of Theo's other friends had been called down to the police station after the bodies were discovered, and asked if they knew anything that might be helpful. George had answered "No," the same as the rest, but a few days later he "remembered" the

Bromo-Seltzer incident and went back to the police station. It was his father who was instrumental in this: After the insinuations began appearing in the newspapers implicating George as an accomplice, Dr. King insisted that his son go back and tell his story. But George wasn't happy about it.

In fact, Detective Seymour had seen George at the July rededication of Emmanuel Baptist and told him it looked bad for him to be so friendly with the defense when he had been called as a witness for the prosecution. "I don't give a damn what you people think of me," George told him.

All went well during the direct examination until that portion of the narrative where George came back from Keene's Drugstore with the Bromo-Seltzer and found Theo . . . lying on the Sunday school platform. Lying on the platform? Barnes hurriedly consulted his transcript of George's testimony at the preliminary examination and then read it to the witness: he had clearly stated at that time that Theo had met him *in the vestibule of the church*. The lying down on the platform did not occur until after he had taken the Bromo-Seltzer. Was George now changing his story?

Eugene Deuprey objected on the grounds that the district attorney was trying to impeach his own witness, but this was overruled because Murphy thought that Barnes was merely trying to "refresh his recollection." George was now saying that Theo could have been in the vestibule or could have been lying on the platform, but "after thinking about it" he was fairly sure he was lying on the platform.

What made him think about it? Barnes wanted to know. Well, it was that question the defense had asked on cross-examination at the preliminary. Then it was those consultations in Dickinson's office and those visits with Theo at the jail—someone had suggested it to him, and he rather thought they were right. It was obvious why the defense had "suggested" this to him: If Theo were lying on the platform, it gave credence to his assertion that he was ill from the effects of the gas; but if he had been in the vestibule, it supported the state's theory that he had merely wanted to get George out of the way while he attended to something—for example, putting his coat and hat in the library room.

During cross-examination, George was cooperative and compliant. He assented to the defense's "suggestion" that Theo's hat and coat could have been in the library all along and that he just hadn't noticed them (even though he had been certain at the time that they had not been there). And he changed what he had said on direct about what happened when he first saw Theo appear before him in the Sunday school room: George had told Barnes that he remained at his piano stool while Theo came over to him; but now he told Deuprey that they both walked toward each other and met halfway.

In essence, then, George King was more of a defense witness in the way he was treated and in the way he responded—in spite of the fact that much of what he said was harmful to Theo's cause.

At the noon recess, George stepped down and immediately went over to the defense table to shake hands with Theo. "Well, old man," he said, grinning, "were you worried when I was on the stand?" To Barnes, it smacked of collusion—yet he did nothing about it in his redirect examination the next day, much to the disappointment of the spectators, who had been thoroughly prepared by the newspapers for a "roast" of George King by the prosecution. Nor did Barnes question him about the contradiction concerning the encounter in the Sunday school room.

At the time of the trial, and since then, observers of the case have felt that George either did not tell all he knew or lied about parts of his testimony. What was it that Theo's friend never divulged?

As the evidence against Theo piled up with each witness, everyone wondered how the defense could possibly counter it. Dickinson and Deuprey were very close-mouthed about it, yet were full of bravado about the results. "Wait until next week," they would say with a knowing wink, "and you'll all change your minds about his guilt."

In truth, however, the defense *had* no strategy; their cross-examinations were endless fishing expeditions launched out of a desperate desire to find something, *anything* they could use to raise a reasonable doubt in the mind of just one juror. Theo had given them nothing to work with, and the little bit he had provided—Dr. Cheney's attendance roster, the notes he had taken in class—was vanishing before their eyes like a dream upon awakening. Did they dare even put him on the stand?

Frank Sademan, the former Emmanuel Baptist janitor (not rehired at the church for various derelictions of duty), cleared up a

point of mystery in his testimony: the source of the gas smelled by
George King when he first entered the church on April 3. Many
people thought George might have been lying about smelling gas
in order to back up Theo's story, but it turns out there was a
supposedly harmless but smelly leak from the large chandelier in
the vestibule. It was right outside the library, which explains why
George thought it might be coming from there, and also why he
didn't smell it on the floor above when he and Theo went to get
the organ.

Sademan testified that there was nothing wrong with the sunburners or any of the fixtures on April 3, and to his knowledge
nobody had asked Theo to attend to them. (At the same time, it
was probable that he had told Theo about the leak from the chandelier.) As a matter of fact, some gasfitters had been in the church
on April 2 to put energy-saving devices on each gas fixture.

Sademan had seen Theo down at the ferry landing on April 12,
while the former janitor was looking for his runaway son. At that
time, Theo told him he was acting on a tip received from someone
that Blanche Lamont would be taking the ferry to the East Bay and
that he was watching to see if it were true.

On cross-examination, Dickinson asked Sademan about his familiarity with the belfry (obviously hoping the jury would think
him a more "desirable" candidate for Blanche's murder than
Theo), and also showed that there were many times when he had
found the doors to the church unlocked (implying that anyone
could have walked in off the street at any time). An important fact
was that Sademan had often consulted Theo about things that
needed fixing around the church, particularly those of an electrical
nature, and understood that he had charge of those items. This
was a point for the defense, as Theo could easily have assumed
responsibility in such matters without being asked. For example,
he had moved the whole electric lighting apparatus from down
beneath the church to where it would be more accessible up near
the janitor's room. And another time, Sademan had seen Theo
working on the very things he claimed to be fixing on April 3: the
sunburners over the auditorium.

When his testimony was finished, Frank Sademan went over to
chat with the Durrants.

One of the gasfitters, a man named William Sterling of the Fault-
less Gas Saver Company, testified to the process he and his work-

ers had gone through in installing the new devices on all the gas fixtures on April 2, the day before Blanche's murder. An interesting point was that he had come back on the morning of Thursday, April 4, and tried to take a shortcut through the belfry door. However, he couldn't open it, so he went around another way. At that time, Sterling said, the porcelain knob was off the door, but he could see that the shaft was still in place. He did not notice any chisel marks, either, which means that the total disabling of the door (shaft removed and chisel used) took place *after* that, most likely when the killer came back to hide Blanche's clothing.

One of the witnesses called by Barnes backfired on the prosecution: Dr. Charles Farnum of Cooper College, who they hoped would testify that the medical students used wooden blocks to support bodies during dissection. Since Blanche was found with small wooden wedges holding her head up at the neck, the state wanted to show that it was most likely done by a medical student. However, Farnum said the blocks were never used at autopsy for holding the head, but were sometimes put *under* various parts to elevate them and provide air flow to slow down the decomposition process.[11]

Adolph Oppenheim, the pawnbroker, had received two anonymous letters since coming forward at the preliminary examination. The first, sent in July, sounded suspiciously like the approach used by the Durrants in calling on the state's witnesses: be less positive in your identification and say you can't swear that Durrant is the man you saw. The letter-writer went on to say that Oppenheim would receive $250 if he complied, but that a failure to cooperate would put his life at risk. (Bribes and threats do not seem to have been part of the Durrants' MO, however.)

The second letter, which Oppenheim received two weeks before his trial testimony, called the pawnbroker a liar (and other insulting epithets) and threatened him with a "sudden and violent death" if he continued to tell tales on the witness stand. There was no offer of money with this one, and it seemed to have a different origin from the first. Captain Lees did not believe that either of the letters came from anyone connected with Theo's case, and undoubtedly thought they were from "cranks."

Oppenheim's testimony was the same as it had been at the preliminary examination, except for one particular. Since that hearing, a cigarmaker named William J. Phillips had come forward to say that he had been on Dupont Street that day and saw Theo standing in the doorway of the shop, with the pawnbroker about three feet behind him. However, Oppenheim had originally stated that he went back to his chair when Theo walked to the door, in which case there would have been no way for Phillips to have seen him. Now, however, like George King, Oppenheim had "refreshed his memory" and recalled that he had, indeed, followed Theo to the doorway. ("I plumb forgot it, but I reflected in my memory, and I know I did," he said.)

Like Mrs. Vogel, Adolph Oppenheim probably had an accent, as there was a great deal of amusement on the part of the spectators during his testimony. Finally, Judge Murphy was forced to deal with it: "I desire to say to the audience, if there is any more laughing or giggling the courtroom will be cleared. If anybody desires to laugh and enjoy themselves there is plenty of room on the outside of the courtroom to do it in." And that took care of it.

Oppenheim was still unsure of the exact date when Theo came into his shop to pawn the ring, but seemed to think it was probably April 5 or 6. He placed it as between April 4 and April 10 because he knew it was around his birthday, which was the eighth (the same day as Dickinson's, as the attorney pointed out to him). When the young man had come in, the pawnbroker was reading a book in German, a collection of Russian court stories entitled *Hopgeschecten* by Sachor Maroth, and this further helped him place the date. Also, he wasn't very busy that day and, as he dealt in secondhand clothes as well as jewelry, made it a point to notice the customer's nice-looking overcoat.

On cross-examination, General Dickinson took the witness through every step of his day, even requiring him to look at his watch to time the so-called two and a half to five minutes that Oppenheim claimed Theo had been in the store. Witnesses almost always overestimate time, so this is a standard directive on cross-examination; but Oppenheim's guess had been a good one: the transaction had taken two and a half minutes by the pawnbroker's in-court timing experiment.

The defense theory was that Oppenheim had not seen Theo at all, but somebody who looked very much like him; and there was also the possibility that the witness was exaggerating or making things up. Could anyone really have that good a memory? Consequently, Dickinson and Deuprey were hoping to trick him. First, they had sent several members of Theo's Signal Corps outfit to Oppenheim's store to present various items for pawn: a silver corkscrew, a watch chain, and two watches. Next, they had a jeweler prepare a duplicate of the ring that Oppenheim claimed Theo had tried to pawn.

Dickinson questioned Oppenheim regarding each item brought to him by the young men of the Signal Corps: When was it presented? What did the man look like? What was he wearing? And in each case, Oppenheim did a creditable job of remembering. (As a proprietor of a jewelry store in a seedy neighborhood, he was extremely vulnerable and would have been a fool not to pay close attention to customers.)

When it came time to present Oppenheim with the fake ring, however, Dickinson blundered. As with the duplicate leather strap, the defense's goal was to force the witness to choose the right one and also tell why it was different from the other. Dickinson handed Oppenheim the ring Theo had supposedly taken to the pawnshop, but instead of the duplicate, handed him *another* of Blanche's rings. When the witness had no trouble telling them apart (they weren't anything alike), Dickinson blurted, "I guess I have given him the wrong ring. I withdraw that question," and handed him the right one (the fake). But Oppenheim was forewarned now and, although he was able to distinguish easily between the two rings, the possibility of tripping him up had been ruined by Dickinson's mistake.

Even with the element of surprise gone from the duplicate ring, however, it was a tough cross-examination for Oppenheim. "Life is not all beer and skittles on the witness stand in this case," as one newspaper philosophically noted. The defense would concede nothing without a fight, and made every witness go over and over and over the same ground. (The objection that a question has been already "asked and answered" does not seem to have been available back then, although on occasion Judge Murphy would ask, "Haven't you gone over that once?")

The *Examiner* expressed some doubt about Oppenheim's credibility, saying that he looked "shifty" and blinked his eyes a lot; plus, there was that changing of the testimony, which looked altogether too convenient. There was also a reference to the pawnbroker's "black and tan" appearance, which may have been an anti-Semitic slur. Still, the writer of the article admitted, it was hard to conceive of someone's wanting to send a man to the gallows just for a little publicity for himself.

The last major witness for the state was William J. Phillips, a man of many occupations, to back up Oppenheim's testimony. Phillips had been a meat dealer, a cigarmaker, a shoe company sales representative, and at one time the proprietor of a hotel in Victoria, British Columbia. In April 1895, he was staying at his mother-in-law's lodging house on Pine Street, and every morning between 10:00 and 11:00 would leave there to go to the Shoe Last Company. Phillips had been in a saloon in May when one of the patrons read an account of Oppenheim's testimony at the preliminary examination, and when he saw the picture of Oppenheim in the paper, the whole thing came back to him.

Phillips had been on his way to work one morning in early April when he noticed a sharply-dressed man standing in the doorway of Oppenheim's pawnshop. The man attracted his attention for several reasons: First of all, he was just standing there, as if unsure of where to go next; secondly, his attire made Phillips think he was a "mack" (a pimp), as there were several houses of prostitution in that neighborhood; and, finally, the young man made a strange motion with his lips, one that Phillips had never seen a man make before. In court, Phillips noticed that Theo made the same weird movement with his lips and had no trouble recognizing him.

Asked to point out Adolph Oppenheim, Phillips was able to do so—even though at first he could not find him in the courtroom, as Oppenheim was standing over near the jury box and almost hidden in the crowd. Thus, Phillips was a highly credible witness, even if Oppenheim had not been, and his testimony did much to shore up that of the pawnbroker.

As the prosecution announced it had completed its case in chief, there was great speculation as to what Theo's defense team would outline in its opening statement. How could they possibly controvert all this testimony against him? Had they found any alibi witnesses?

Rumors ran amok for two days. But no one was prepared for what Dickinson and Deuprey actually came up with.

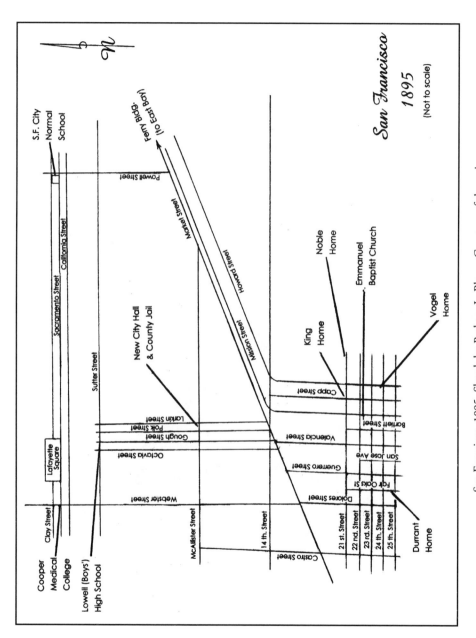

San Francisco, 1895. Sketch by Barbara L. Blasey. Courtesy of the artist.

Emmanuel Baptist Church, 1895.

Theo poses for his portrait. Sketch by Haydon Jones for the *Examiner*.

Isabella Durrant. Sketch by Haydon Jones for the *Examiner*.

Blanche Lamont at age 17. Courtesy of the family of Blanche Lamont.

Blanche Lamont with her class in Hecla, Montana. Image number 1995.108.192 from the Henry Brown Collection, Whatcom Museum of History and Art, Bellingham, WA.

Close-up of Blanche Lamont from class photo. Image number 1995.108.192 from the Henry Brown Collection, Whatcom Museum of History and Art, Bellingham, WA.

Minnie E. Williams.

George R. King. Sketch by George Lyon for the *Chronicle*.

Dr. Thomas A. Vogel. Sketch by George Lyon for the *Chronicle*.

Edna Lucile Turner. Sketch by George Lyon for the *Chronicle*.

Flora S. Upton. Courtesy of the family of Flora Upton.

Rev. John George Gibson (*right*) and his secretary, Robert N. Lynch.
Sketch by George Lyon for the *Chronicle*.

Lower hallway of the church. The library room can be seen to the left of the staircase.

Corner of room in which Minnie Williams was found.

Top landing of belfry where the body of Blanche Lamont was discovered.

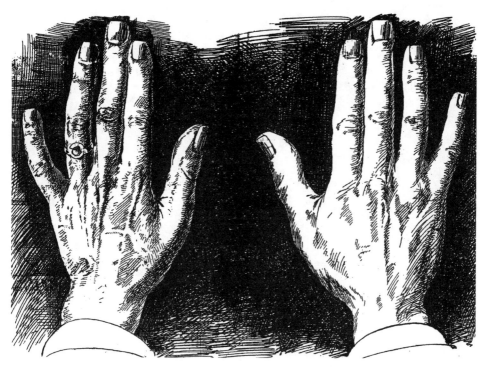

Theo's hands, reproduced life size, took up the entire top half of the front page of the *Examiner*.

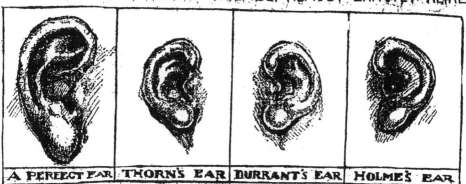

THE EARS OF THE GREATEST OF MURDERERS, THORN, DURRANT AND HOLMES, ALMOST EXACTLY ALIKE

| A PERFECT EAR | THORN'S EAR | DURRANT'S EAR | HOLMES' EAR |

The physiognomy craze—but Theo's ears were normal! Sketch from the *Examiner*.

The so-called "degenerate" picture, taken when Theo was on a picnic around the age of 16. He is the one in the front leaning on the wheel between two girls. Sketch from the *Examiner*.

Mamma and Papa Durrant with Theo at the trial. Sketch by Haydon Jones for the *Examiner*.

The scene in the corridor as the deputy sheriffs took Durrant downstairs from the courtroom.
Sketch by Haydon Jones for the *Examiner*.

Superior Court Judge Daniel J. Murphy. Sketch by Harrison Fisher for the *Call*.

General John H. Dickinson, defense attorney.

Eugene N. Deuprey, defense attorney.

Williams S. Barnes, District Attorney.

Edgar D. Peixotto, Assistant District Attorney.

Mamma breaks down in Theo's arms during the prosecution's closing argument.
Sketch by H. Nappenbach for the *Examiner*.

Defense attorney Eugene Deuprey got up from his sickbed to make a closing argument.
Sketch by R. L. Partington for the *Call*.

William Henry Theodore Durrant, SQ Prisoner No. 17260, San Quentin Prisoner Photographs, San Quentin Mug Book. Department of Corrections Record Group. California State Archives.

Theo in prison stripes at San Quentin. Sketch by H. Nappenbach for the *Examiner*.

DURRANT HANGS!!

The brutal slayer of two young girls,

BLANCHE LAMONT

AND

MINNIE WILLIAMS,

in San Francisco, is sentenced to die November 12.

---THE UTICA---

SATURDAY GLOBE

of November 13 will contain a full account of his remarkable
crime and of his Jekyll and Hyde life, together with
special photo-engravings illustrating the horrible
story of murder at which the whole
world stood aghast.

Killed His Victims in a Church,

where all three worshipped, and then sought to implicate
the pastor.

FOR TWO YEARS HIS CASE

was fought in the courts and now with two days' notice he
must hang.

Order a Copy of the GLOBE Agent.

A broadside announcing one of the execution dates, put out by the
Utica (NY) *Globe* to promote their big "execution issue."

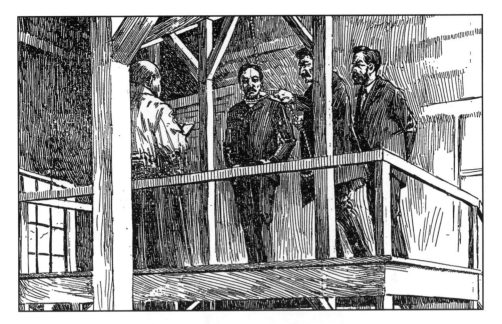

The execution. Father Lagan reads Theo the last rites while Amos Lunt arranges the rope.
Sketch by George Lyon for the *Chronicle*.

Papa Durrant cries out to his son at the execution. Sketch by George Lyon for the *Chronicle*.

Maud Durrant in her new life as Maud Allan.

Maud Allan as "Salome."

Theo Takes the Stand

From first to last the strongest witness against Theodore Durrant has been himself.
— *San Francisco Chronicle*, October 20, 1895

"Durrant-mania" continued to abound in California. An Oakland man claimed that his wife pestered him daily to read to her the verbatim transcript of the trial, even to the point of insisting that he follow her around with it while she did her household chores. The reading was taking up half his day, and he finally "went on strike": he would read the introductory summary presented by the newspaper, he told her, but he refused to read the entire transcript.

One day, the man came home from work to find half his furniture missing, and a note from his wife saying she was leaving him because she was "dissatisfied with her home and wanted a change." Three weeks later, he found that his wife had gone to the home of her sister in Wausau, Wisconsin, and that she had convinced the sister to leave *her* husband as well! The husband in Oakland said his wife had left him because he wouldn't read the Durrant transcripts to her anymore.[1]

A San Francisco man, quite drunk, became convinced that the moon was telling him to jump into the Bay, at the bottom of which he would find Blanche and Minnie, who would then give him the name of their killer. He was rescued as soon as he went off the wharf.[2]

There is an old saying in the law profession that all criminal defenses can be boiled down to two: the WHOME ("Who, me?" to indicate a false identification) and the SODDI ("Some other dude did it," to indicate alibi). Theo's lawyers would attempt both.

There had been speculation (sometimes presented as a definite fact) that the defense would put the "Sweet Pea Girl" on the stand, who would then testify that she was the one seen with Theo on April 3.[3] But, if Dickinson and Deuprey ever entertained this desperate move at all, it never materialized.

As the better orator of the two, Eugene Deuprey was given the task of presenting the opening statement for the defense.[4] At long last, their theories would be revealed. As expected, Deuprey indicated that they would contest the identifications made by the key witnesses on the basis of defective vision (by the "three elderly ladies"), inadequate vision (by the "three young women"), and suspect credibility (on the part of "a pawnbroker, a Victoria hotel-keeper, a Police Court shyster and his corroborant").

Deuprey contended that the prosecution had not proved beyond the shadow of a doubt that Theo had killed Blanche Lamont. Nor had it answered some crucial questions: Where and when was she killed? Who killed her? What was the cause of her death? And—a very important issue—what motive did Theo have to kill her?

The shocker came when Deuprey got to the "Some other dude did it" part of his statement. The defense would show that there was much incriminating evidence that pointed, not at Theodore Durrant, but at the minister, Rev. John George Gibson: The chisel that fit the marks made on the belfry door was found in his office, and the handwriting on the wrapper containing the rings was just like his. "We have a right to show you," Deuprey told the jury, "that others are open to like suspicion, and worse suspicion."

The defense attorney caused another stir when he indicated that Theo himself would testify to explain his movements from dawn until dusk that day. Public discussion about this had been rampant since his arrest: Would his attorneys dare put him on the stand

and expose him to cross-examination? Theo was asked about it constantly, and claimed he did not know. And he probably didn't, for a couple of reasons. First of all, his attorneys must have figured out that he couldn't be trusted to keep his mouth shut. Secondly, they undoubtedly hoped they could avoid putting him on the stand, and must have decided at the last minute that there was no other way out.

There really *was* no other way out, as they had no convincingly exculpatory evidence in their arsenal. Juries are not supposed to hold it against a defendant if he does not take the stand, as the Fifth Amendment gives him the right to abstain, but there is always that nagging question as to why an innocent person would not come forward to tell his story. As defendants go, Theo was an unusually personable, articulate, and presentable one, so the decision made by his defense counsel is understandable. But it would be one they would come to regret.

Deuprey's grand finale summoned Blanche Lamont from the grave. By the end of the defense's case, he assured the jury, it would be as if the dead girl herself had come forth and ordered Theo's release: "Let him stand out; set him free, for he harmed me not."

It was an impressive beginning.

When Rev. J. George Gibson was approached about Deuprey's pointing the finger at him in his opening statement, the pastor—for once—consented to be interviewed with only a minimum of pleading on the reporter's part.[5] However, he laid down strict rules to be followed, and kept Robert Lynch close by his side for consultation.

Gibson seems to have been entertained by the whole thing. His approach was sarcastic and an attempt (largely unsuccessful) at a sly humor. He claimed he was disappointed in Deuprey ("such a brilliant lawyer and so clever in producing duplicate rings and straps"), who claimed to know so much but didn't tell the jury the name of the person who had sold Gibson the copy of the *Examiner* that he was supposed to have used for wrapping the rings.

And so it went, the minister trying to be cute and obscure, and the reporter occasionally leading him on. Underneath some of Gibson's remarks there is a bitterness at what he saw as subterfuge on the part of Theo's attorneys (he had blithely told them to take whatever they wanted from his study, and they took the chisel and a "bloodstained" shoe that they were now planning to use against him). In a rare moment of seriousness, he told the reporter that the defense's nitpicking was hurting Theo's chances: "Every technicality is a curse they throw in the face of the friend they profess to defend. No witness has done so much against W.H.T. Durrant as the actions of his attorneys."

But, then, this statement was made before Theo took the stand.

The first witness for the defense was Isabella Durrant, who was asked many questions about the Durrant family background, Theo's various jobs, and his movements on April 3, 1895. Papa was not asked to testify, probably because his morose manner would not have come across well, and because the boy's mother would normally be expected to be a more sympathetic figure to the jury. The defense was trying to show that Theo came from an upstanding, hardworking family, not the kind of family that would produce a Jack the Ripper.

Other than background, Mamma had very little to add of an evidentiary nature, except that Theo had worn *dark* pants that day, not light ones as Mary Vogel had claimed. And she asserted that he had not worn an overcoat at all in April, as Oppenheim and Phillips had said he did.

Mamma does, however, reveal an interesting dynamic within the Durrant household. She said that after dinner on the night of April 3, she and Theo were upstairs in their respective rooms—hers at the front of the house, and his in the rear, about fifteen or twenty feet away. As she got ready to go to a musicale, she talked with her son, walking back and forth between the two rooms as he tried to study. Asked if anyone occupied the room between hers and Theo's, she at first said "No"—twice. Then, in an afterthought, Mamma remembered: "Oh, yes; my husband occupied that room."

At about 8:15, Mamma was ready to go to the musicale, accompanied by a young woman who lived next door. Yet, even though she had a companion and even though the streetcar stop was only a block away, she called to Theo to escort her there. (After that, he went on to the church for the remainder of the Wednesday night service, where he would talk to Mrs. Noble about Blanche and his promise to loan her *The Newcomes*.)

That Mamma's testimony was not considered significant by the prosecution is evident in their not cross-examining her. But that she was obsessed with her son to the exclusion of her husband can be seen from just that one glimpse into the Durrant family household on April 3.

The biggest gun in the defense arsenal, the one they were most counting on, was Dr. William Fitch Cheney's[6] rollbook, which did *not* have Theo marked as absent for the 3:30–4:30 lecture that day (which actually ended at 4:15 on April 3 because the professor had an appointment). Dr. Cheney's method of taking attendance was this: A senior student, Frank Gray, was assigned to be in charge of the rollbook, and at the end of the lecture he would call out the names of each of the other seventy-four students. If he heard "Here" or "Present," Gray did nothing. If he heard no response, he marked a lowercase "a" for "absent" next to the student's name for that day.

Because there was no "a" next to Theo's name for the April 3 lecture on infant feeding and milk sterilization, the defense felt confident that Professor Cheney would be their star witness. In fact, Cheney had led them to believe that he *knew* Theo was present on that day, which meant that he could not have been the man seen with Blanche Lamont.

The prosecution, however, did not put much stock in the rollbook for two reasons: it was taken at the end of the class when there was a lot of noise and confusion (and, indeed, it turned out that one student present that day, Charles L. Garvin, was marked absent); and the medical students admitted that on occasion they answered for each other (Harry Partridge had answered for Theo on April 8, and Theo had asked Dukes and Dodge to answer for him on April 13). Still, if Cheney could be positive in his testimony, it would go far toward creating the "reasonable doubt" in at least one juror's mind—and one was all they would need to save their client from the gallows.

But when Dr. Cheney took the stand, he collapsed the hopes of the defense team. He had no personal recollection of Theo's being there, he said, nor had he ever told them that. What he *had* said was that his rollbook constituted his official attendance record and he would put his faith in it. Moreover, as soon as the attendance issue came up back in April, Dr. Cheney had quizzed each student individually as to whether any of them had answered for Theo that day. As no one said he had, Cheney felt his rollbook was correct. It was hardly the ringing endorsement of Theo's presence the defense was hoping for.

And when Frank Gray, the student assigned to take roll, took the stand, an even worse revelation occurred: The register they were using wasn't the original record! Wednesday, April 3, was the first lecture of the new month and Gray had not had time to make up the attendance page for April. So he used the column for Sunday, March 31 instead, as there was no lecture or clinic that day. Then he wrote on it, "See April 3" or some such notation. The following week, when he made up the new April page and transferred the attendance from March 31 to its correct slot on April 3, he then *erased* the March 31 column.

A close examination of the erased column revealed a faint mark in the line next to Theo's name, which might have been an "a." On the other hand, it might have been part of the written notation "See April 3," and Gray rather thought it was. However, the rollbook evidence was effectively destroyed by the testimony of both these witnesses, and Theo's defense attorneys must have been mightily discouraged. Their big gun was shooting blanks.

While Theo was in jail, he had sent for three medical school classmates to see if they could remember incidents he claimed happened on April 3. Because he usually sat next to Charles Dukes (seats were assigned in alphabetical order), Theo would often entertain him with cartoonlike sketches during the lectures, and sometimes the two young men would write something in each other's notebook. When Dukes came down to the jail, Theo asked him to check his notebook to see if there might not be some sketches or other marginalia that would jog his memory as to his presence that day. (Theo had either forgotten that he told reporters he had come in late that day and therefore did not take his accustomed seat, or was now abandoning that story.) As Dukes recalled it, the conversation went like this:

Theo: Don't you remember I was there?

Dukes: No, I can't remember whether or not you were.

Theo: I wish you would remember it as a favor to me. I wish you would remember it so that you could state it as a fact.

As for student Charles V. Cross, Theo reminded him of a conversation they supposedly had outside the lecture hall that day right before Cheney's class was to begin. He tried to get Cross to come up with a conversational topic on his own, probably guessing that he would have a better chance at Cross's "remembering" something that way than if Theo presented him with a topic that he might not recall at all. But Cross could not remember any such event.

With Frederick Ross, however, Theo hit pay dirt—sort of. Ross finally remembered that he and Theo had, indeed, taken a walk together around lunchtime on a day when Professor Stillman had posted a note saying he would be late for the class that was to begin at 1:30. The two students walked down to Broadway and sat on a bench for a while, then walked back to school and arrived there about 1:15.

There were two problems with Ross's testimony, from a defense point of view. First of all, on the stand and under oath, he could not swear that the incident had occurred on April 3. He knew it was around that day, but couldn't be positive. For another thing, even if the walk *had* taken place on April 3, a 1:15 arrival back at Cooper still gave Theo plenty of time to get to the Normal School by 2:00.

Ross thought the walk occurred on the same day that the tardy Dr. Stillman (Theo thought the whole lecture had been cancelled) gave a lesson on blackheads, or comedones. This word is pronounced "kummaDOneez," but either Ross wasn't paying close attention or the professor was mispronouncing it: all the reporters wrote it down as "a lecture on comatose," as did the court reporter.

In desperation, Dickinson and Deuprey subpoenaed the entire Cooper senior class. One by one, the students took the stand to answer two basic questions: Did you answer for the defendant at Dr. Cheney's lecture on April 3? Did you see the defendant at the lecture? And one by one, they each answered "No" to both questions. ("Never in the history of medicine were so many doctors agreed," the *Examiner* commented wryly.) In his cross-examination, District Attorney Barnes respectfully addressed them as "Doctor," even though they were two months from graduation. If they had taken notes of the lecture, Barnes asked them to drop them off at the courthouse. (He was sure Theo would produce notes, whether he had actually attended the lecture or not; but he wanted to compare them with those of the other students to see if they were in the right order, or perhaps plagiarized.)

After their testimony, most of the students came over to the defense table to talk with Theo, an indication that they did not believe him to be guilty.

Throughout the course of the trial, the attorneys, the judge, and Theo were receiving lots of mail. Most were anonymous, and those for the attorneys came in the form of suggestions. Barnes estimated that he had received about 1,000 letters by the beginning of October, and Judge Murphy said he was getting six a day. Even Dr. Cheney got one, sent in care of the judge.

Theo's letters were mostly of support and sympathy, and came from all over the world. A group of students at Ohio State University's Starling Medical School wrote to wish him good luck and assure him that they were behind him. Soon, they assured him, he would be back in class and sweating over his studies, just as they were now doing.

He was also receiving many admiring letters from women. Several offered him money for his autograph (one in England offered him 25 pounds, equivalent to about $50—a staggering sum for 1895), and several wanted to "comfort" him. It brought up the same question asked by Alice Rix: why do women fawn over criminals? To Theo's credit, he dismissed all of this as unseemly and a sign of unbalanced minds: "I wish women would stop making fools of themselves," he said.[7]

During the presentation of the defense, two incidents arose which threatened the very trial itself. One involved the irascible juror Horace Smyth. A man named Charles Brodenstein filed a criminal complaint against Smyth for assault and battery, claiming that the elderly juror had beaten Brodenstein's son, 13-year-old George, with a cane for no reason at all.[8]

Smyth's version was that the boy and his friends had been pulling up the ivy on his property and he and Mrs. Smyth caught them doing it. Before that, he said, the boys were miserable nuisances throughout the neighborhood, ringing the doorbells at all hours and throwing debris into open ground-floor windows. A maid of the Smyths had quit over it.

Captain Isaiah Lees of the San Francisco Police Department was alarmed at this turn of events, for it meant that Smyth could be arrested. His arrest would interfere with his duties as a juror and force a mistrial in the Durrant case. (Now they were wishing they had gone ahead with those alternate jurors!) But Brodenstein would not be talked out of his complaint. Eventually, cooler heads prevailed and the angry father agreed to wait until after the trial was over.

Apparently, Smyth had also lost his temper at the courthouse earlier in the trial, striking out at a deputy and telling the sheriff that "if any of his hirelings bothered him in the corridor he would fill them full of lead." Smyth was a walking time bomb.

The second incident was potentially more harmful, and stemmed directly out of the fact that jurors were not sequestered during this trial (they rarely were back then). They went to their offices after court adjourned for the day, then to their homes for the night, then back to court the next morning—all on public transportation.

On one of these occasions, Juror I. J. Truman, a banker by trade, was riding on a streetcar when a friend of his, YMCA Secretary Henry McCoy, got on. Spying the juror, McCoy said jovially, "If you don't hang Durrant, we'll hang you!" As soon as he said it, McCoy realized how imprudent he'd been. Truman did not respond in any way, and the two eventually discussed other topics.

But Truman was bothered by the encounter, even though he knew his friend had said it only in jest. He approached Judge Murphy the next time he was in court and asked to speak with him in private. (Part of Truman's motive for coming forward may have been due to his streetcar companion that day: another juror, Nathan Crocker.) Judge Murphy did not seriously believe that McCoy meant any kind of threat or secret message, but he was afraid of having to declare a mistrial and go through the whole interminable thing again. He issued a bench warrant for McCoy's arrest on contempt of court charges.

When the sheepish McCoy appeared in court and testified as to his much-regretted remark, Murphy gave him a good lecture and fined him $250.[9]

Adolph Oppenheim had said that Theo came to his pawnshop at some point from April 4 to April 10 (and probably before April 8), between 10:00 and 11:00 A.M. Therefore, the defense attempted to produce witnesses who would place Theo elsewhere during those times. They could only do so for April 4 and 5.

Dr. A.W. Hoisholt testified that Theo attended his lecture at the medical school on Thursday, April 4, between the hours of 10:00 and 11:00. However, like Dr. Cheney, he was relying on his roll-book and had no personal knowledge of Theo's presence that day.

A teacher named Oliver Goodell, who had attended Cogswell Poly with Theo, said that on Friday, April 5, his former classmate had come to see him at the California School of Mechanical Arts. Theo had first stopped at the office of the principal, George Merrill, whom he had also known at Cogswell, to get permission to take a tour of the school (a distinctly odd request under the circumstances).

Goodell said that Theo showed up at his classroom door that morning at about 11:15 and stayed at the school until about 12:30. However, he had gotten the distinct impression that Theo had really come to see Lucile Turner, who was a student there. It turned out that Lucile was absent that day. Even with this testimony, it would not preclude Theo's having gone to Oppenheim's pawnshop before going to Lucile's school.

But why did Theo want to talk to Lucile Turner?

The defense was nearly at the end of its case, and the prevailing thought was: Is this all there is? Perhaps a surprise witness waited in the wings. If not, then the consensus was that Theo's attorneys had done little to chip away at the mountain of evidence presented by the state.

There had been attempts at discrediting the more unsavory witnesses for the prosecution (Quinlan, Clarke, Oppenheim, and Phillips), but these were largely unsuccessful. The witnesses against Quinlan were even more disreputable than he was, and had axes to grind besides. For example, one of these had killed a lawyer friend of Quinlan's in cold blood because the lawyer had "betrayed" the witness's married sister.[10] (The witness and his brother-in-law were both acquitted on grounds of justifiable homicide, which illustrates how important a woman's honor was back then.)

There was an attempt to show that the hotel run by William

Phillips in British Columbia was actually a house of ill repute, but it was all just surmise and innuendo. Oppenheim and Clarke were presented as unprincipled and lacking integrity, but with no real proof of this, either—just the say-so of the witnesses.

Dickinson and Deuprey hoped that their other card—the one pointing the finger at Rev. Gibson—would work better.

The defense subpoenaed the intrepid reporter Carrie Cunningham hoping to show that the origin of Mrs. Leak's testimony was actually J. George Gibson. But Dickinson, Deuprey, and even Judge Murphy himself came up against a fortress in the person of Miss Cunningham. She freely admitted she had not heard the story from Mrs. Leak, which agreed with what Mrs. Leak had said on the stand. But as to whom she had heard the story from, she refused to tell. She had promised she would not tell, she said, and she would not.

Judge Murphy was incredulous:

Murphy: Now you are raising quite an issue with the Court. I guess you had better tell, Miss Cunningham.

Carrie: Oh, I cannot tell.

Murphy: You cannot tell?

Carrie: No, sir.

Murphy: Well, Miss Cunningham . . . I do not want to be harsh with you. You probably will find that you are not more powerful than the law or the Court.

But Carrie stood her ground. Murphy blustered at her and threatened her with jail unless she complied, and *still* she did not budge from her position. Then, just as the judge was directing the clerk to issue a contempt citation, Dickinson and Deuprey intervened— it was their question, after all—and asked if the matter could be put over until the next day, as it was already late in the afternoon. Let her think about it overnight, they said, and maybe she'll see the error of her ways. (Bullying hadn't worked; perhaps kindness would.)

The next day, however, the reporter had not moved from her contention that she did not have to answer the question, and would not do so. By then, the newspapers had taken up the battle cry on behalf of reporters everywhere and their duty to their sources. The editorial pages were filled with references to journalistic philosophy and constitutional safeguards.

Murphy had probably read these himself and thought twice about his own position. If the defense continued to insist on the question, as was its right, should he jail the reporter until she answered it? He announced that he wasn't so sure the question was central to the defense, and wanted more time to think about it. He would rule on the Carrie Cunningham situation in a couple of days.

Ultimately, Judge Murphy realized that the question as to who had provided the information was not one that went to the issue of the guilt or innocence of the defendant. It did not impeach the testimony of Mrs. Leak, which *would* have been crucial, but instead was entirely a collateral matter. (It wasn't collateral to the defense, of course, as they were trying to show Gibson's guilty hand in this; but they couldn't say so.) Therefore, Carrie Cunningham did not have to answer the question and would not be cited with contempt. It was a victory for the newspapers.

Rev. Gibson's secretary, Robert Lynch ("prim, pretty, and precise"), was showing up every day in court so he could keep the pastor apprised of any developments that might incriminate him. Deuprey resented having a Gibson spy at the trial, and got Lynch excluded on a ruse: he said he would be calling him as a witness, so he shouldn't be in the courtroom. Lynch fussed and fumed, knowing full well what Deuprey's real motive was, and told the newspapers he hadn't even been in San Francisco at the time of the murders—so how could he have anything to testify to? (Deuprey waited until close to the end of the defense's case, and then called Lynch just to ask him how long he had known Gibson and Carrie Cunningham!)

Gibson himself was subpoenaed, which must have disconcerted him enormously. In fact, his discomfiture showed on the stand in the various poses he affected and his going back and forth from acting "like a frightened rabbit dodging a snake" to "simper[ing] with a cunning sort of leer." He fooled with his hair and his mustache, and in general seemed to be playing to the crowd.

Gibson was called for the purpose of handwriting comparison (he could probably have pleaded the Fifth Amendment on this one, as it was obvious the defense was trying to show that *he* was the murderer, but it doesn't seem to have occurred to him). Nevertheless, he was cagey and suspicious, never granting Dickinson any definite admission as to what samples were his handwriting. "It looks like my writing" is the most he would say, and could not be pinned down to a definite "yes"—even for those samples taken from his own wastebasket!

How Gibson came across to the multitudes can be summarized in this comment by the *Examiner*: "It is not Mr. Gibson's fault that he is an absurd person." It is hard to imagine such a man running a parish successfully; yet, when things went smoothly and there were no great drains on his very limited coping skills, Gibson was a better than average pastor.

A large contingent of witnesses from a wide range of ages and occupations came forward to testify to Theo's good character. In fact, along with an apparent lack of motive for the murder of Blanche Lamont, his good character was the biggest point in his favor: Theo was simply not the kind of person who would do such a thing.

Testimony for good character, however, is a double-edged sword: once it is introduced as part of a case, the other side now has carte blanche to impeach it. The prosecution had used every tool at its disposal to dig up dirt on Theo in the event of just such testimony as was now being presented by his attorneys. If they found anything, it would be brought up in the rebuttal phase—including Lucile Turner's story about the "insulting propostion."

One of Theo's witnesses was Herbert Porter, a former Cogswell classmate and now an undertaker. Barnes questioned him closely about Theo's possible interest in his profession, reflecting the belief that Theo had raped Minnie Williams both before *and* after death, and possibly Blanche Lamont as well. If Theo had inclinations toward necrophilia, Barnes might be able to show this through Porter's testimony.

But Barnes's goal here was thwarted by Porter's answers: Theo had only been to the funeral home twice, and the last time about five years previously. It hardly sounded as if the defendant had a sexual interest in the dead; if he had, it can be assumed he would have "visited" his friend more often.

The defense had only two important witnesses remaining: a young man named Charles Lenahan, who claimed that it was he who had tried to pawn a ring at Oppenheim's shop; and the main attraction, Theo himself.

Charles Lenahan had written to the defense after Oppenheim's testimony at the preliminary examination, saying that he had attempted to pawn a ring a girl had given him (or, more likely, that he had taken from her) so that he and his friend could go to the track. He had clothing very similar to Theo's, he said (and described it), and he was sure he was the one Oppenheim was referring to, as he had gone to the shop on an early April morning and the encounter described by the pawnbroker sounded very much like his own.

Deuprey had promised in his opening statement that a witness would come forward who would show Oppenheim's mistake in identifying Theo, and he was confident that Lenahan would plant a reasonable doubt in some juror's mind. But when the witness took the stand that day, Deuprey was shocked: Lenahan had no mustache! "Where's your mustache?" he asked in astonishment, for the defense was banking on the jury's belief that Lenahan could be mistaken for Theo. "I don't know as I ever had any," was the laconic response.

And that wasn't all. Lenahan controverted nearly every element of the story he had first come forward to tell: He had gone to the pawnshop in the afternoon, not the morning. His coat did not have a blue velvet collar like Theo's, and was much shorter. He did not have a dark hat, but a light one.

Deuprey had no choice but to impeach his own witness with the letter he had written after Oppenheim's testimony. There was nothing in there about the mustache, though, so the defense lawyer couldn't bring forward nine men he claimed had witnessed the bushy growth on Lenahan's upper lip. During his examination of this most disappointing witness, spectators noticed that Deuprey was becoming tongue-tied and occasionally slurring his words. Afterwards, he would be ill for nearly the entire balance of the trial, with what was diagnosed as "rheumatism," but which sounds more like a stroke—probably brought on by the intense stress of this case and its unsatisfying results.

When Lenahan was brought back later in the trial, he said that Deuprey had asked him to grow a mustache and that Detective

Harry Morse (who worked for the defense team) had promised that Deuprey would help with Lenahan's Water Board application if he would consent to testify. Deuprey was not above sharp practices (namely, the Charles Clark gambit and the duplicate strap, the solution to which is discussed in chapter 11), but his astonishment at Lenahan's lack of a mustache was real. He was obviously thrown completely off balance by this, so Lenahan—like West, the cable car conductor—might have been seeking a little notoriety as a Durrant witness.

The thing that struck *Chronicle* reporter Mabel Craft most about the first day of Theo Durrant's testimony was the number of "high society" people who came to the trial.[11] There were so many fancy hats with birds and flowers and other gewgaws that it looked more like a horse show than a murder trial. Everyone was tired of looking at the back of Theo's head; now they wanted to see his face and hear his story. When he took the stand, people stood on chairs and benches (anything to surmount those immense headpieces in the front rows), then quickly got down before Murphy could bang his gavel at them. The result, Mabel thought, was a little like a roomful of jack-in-the-box toys set to go off at different times.

General John Dickinson's examination method, whether on direct or cross, was exasperating. Slow and deliberate, he often paused so long between questions that Judge Murphy had to remind him it was time to ask one. However, it was a method that suited Theo very well, and probably did much to calm him down during his direct testimony. He was equally deliberate with his answers, and sometimes even repeated the question before giving a response.

Dressed in a black frock coat, gray trousers, and a tie, Theo looked like what he had been before his arrest: an up-and-coming young man on his way to being a doctor. He crossed his legs and assumed a professional pose, with his hands steepled in front of him as he considered Dickinson's questions. He was a good witness, thinking before he answered and not volunteering more than he was asked. But he had a stilted, precise way of speaking that was possibly affected: "I acceded to her request" and "I gradually disposed of them" (instead of "eating" them) and "I deviated somewhat from my regular plan."

Dickinson led Theo through his day at Cooper, then on the streetcars to the church (over an entirely different route from that traveled by the other witnesses), and then into the *unlocked* side door at 4:55. Theo opened the library door with his key, took off his jacket and hat, folded them, and placed them on top of a box. Then he went up to the vestibule where he plugged the electrical button so that the gas would be released at half strength, as he did not want to keep coming down to test it by shutting it off and turning it on again. He went to the opening under the lowered ceiling, picked up the forty-pound ladder, and crawled up and over the ceiling to where the sunburners were situated over the auditorium.

Theo described in very minute detail how he took out some papers from the twenty-four glass reflectors of the sunburner, dusted them off, spread some out to lie on so he wouldn't get too dirty (telling exactly where each toe was placed), removed the plates, and progressed to fix the connection that refused to spark. It was a complicated transaction, and the jury was confused. Dickinson gave Theo a pointer so he could explain by means of a diagram. Standing in front of the jury, one hand in his pocket, he looked every bit the young college professor explaining basic electricity to a group of freshmen. He even fielded questions from the jury, handling them adroitly and in a way that could be understood by those who were unfamiliar with electricity. He demonstrated through the use of a model how the contact points were supposed to open to spark the gas, and how he cleaned the tips of each fixture by running a stiff card through them. They even sent to another department for a blackboard so Theo could illustrate more clearly exactly where in the church the burners were located.

Judge Murphy was getting nervous having the defendant out of the witness chair and interacting so closely with the jury. At one point he asked, "Let me ask you if you have got through with this explanation. If so, take the stand." But Theo wasn't quite finished, and the jurors had more questions. Murphy probably felt he was losing control of the trial.

Theo then related how having his head situated over the fixtures caused him to become nauseated with gas, and how he went out of his way to see George King when he could have exited the church unseen. He had heard George playing, he said, from up on the false ceiling, and walked right through the doors and over to

him. George was wrong when he said Theo had stood in the doorway and that George had spoken first.

Dickinson had Theo tell where he was every morning from April
4 to April 10, so that he could not have been the man in Oppenheim's pawnshop. Moreover, he brought out the fact that Theo
had money in several bank accounts—so why would he need the
money from Blanche's ring?

It was an impressive and convincing performance.

Dickinson's direct examination of Theo had taken so long that
Barnes only had about forty-five minutes for cross-examination before court would be adjourned for the day. Wisely, the District
Attorney chose a mellow, nonthreatening approach for the three-
quarters of an hour he had access to Theo on the stand. He didn't
want to get into anything too heavy, and give the defense a chance
to coach the witness overnight. Barnes wanted very much to see
if he could catch Theo off guard.

But the next day was a different story. Barnes was relentless in
his questioning, picking apart everything and making Theo follow
it through (asking, for example, what he had done with the empty
wrapper for the nuts he claimed to have bought at noon on April
3). Most people, when making up a story, fail to think of the tiny
attendant details that can trip them up, and it became obvious that
this was causing Theo to get flustered.

Another gimmick Barnes used was to dart quickly to an entirely
different subject to keep the witness off balance. Just when Theo
might be getting comfortable explaining one set of actions, Barnes
would jump to something that had happened on another day, or
at another location. Theo had no opportunity to relax. And he
began to contradict himself.

When first asked about who would have given him instructions
to fix the sunburners, Theo testified that the normal occurrence
was for Sademan to report problems to one of the trustees, who
would then direct Theo to attend to the repairs. Later, however,
he said that it was Sademan who had told him the sunburners
needed fixing. His response to Barnes's challenge is nonsensical:

Barnes: Did you not state to me this morning that Mr. Sademan would
report to Mr. Davis or Mr. Code and that then these gentlemen
would report it to you, the object of that rule being that the

expense in repairing those things should be limited in passing through the proper hands?

Theo: I did for a certain reason.

Barnes: What was the reason?

Theo: If there was anything materially wrong with them that needed actual repair, that is what I had reference to.

In responding to contradictions, Theo became literal and semantic. For example, upon his arrest, he had told reporters that he arrived at the church between 4:00 and 4:30 on April 3 and began to work on the sunburners. Confronted with this at trial, he claimed that what he really meant was that he had *left school* at that time, and if the reporters had written something else down, why, that wasn't what he had said.

Theo's favorite line was, "I said nothing of the kind." Then, asked what he really *did* say, he would quote the exact thing Barnes had just asked him about, with only a minor change or omission. Dukes and Dodge had testified that Theo told them he was waiting for members of the Signal Corps to come over from Oakland as an explanation for what he was doing at the ferry on April 12. But Theo now claimed he had "said nothing of the kind"; he said he was waiting for "a member" of the Signal Corps. When asked if he told Sademan he was watching for Blanche Lamont to go over to Alameda because of a clue he had gotten, Theo replied that he had "said nothing of the kind"; he never said a thing about Alameda.

Barnes asked Theo if he had told Herman Schlageter that he "believed that she had been led astray and had got into some house of ill fame." "Not exactly those words," was Theo's response. What had he actually said, then? "I said it was possible she may have been led astray and perhaps had been led into some house of ill fame."

Blanche Lamont had told her aunt about the time she went to Theo's house to get the Christmas present he had for her, at which time he put his arms around her after he turned the gaslight off. Barnes asked Theo if he had turned the gaslight off when Blanche stepped into the hall. The gas wasn't on, Theo told him. "Well, didn't you light the gas when you went in?" Barnes asked. "Yes, I did," was the response. (Barnes must have been shaking his head in puzzlement at this point!) "And did you not extinguish it?" "I did not." After a discussion about how dark it must have been in January at that time of day, Barnes asked again if he turned off the gaslight. Theo said that he had, on leaving the house.

Barnes asked Theo about the time he asked Dunnegan, the reporter, to move away from the cell so he could talk to Gil Graham about the notes from Dr. Cheney's lecture. Here is the tortured exchange on this issue:

Barnes:	Did you ask Mr. Donegan [*sic*] that he step aside, that you wanted to speak to Dr. Graham in private?
Theo:	I don't know as I did.
Barnes:	Do you know whether you did or not?
Theo:	I do not know.
Barnes:	Wouldn't you have known it if you had?
Theo:	It was altogether likely I did not.
Barnes:	Might you have done it?
Theo:	I might not; I had no reason to.
Judge Murphy:	The question is, Might you have done it? Just answer the question. It is probably better for you to answer the question.
Barnes:	Might you have done it?
Theo:	I don't see how I could have done it.
Murphy:	You said you might not have done it, as I understood it.
Theo:	I don't see how I can answer it.
Murphy:	I think, Mr. District Attorney, you should ask him whether he did or not.
Barnes:	Did you ask Mr. Donegan [*sic*] at that interview to step aside so that you could speak to Dr. Graham at that time privately? [This is virtually the same question he had started with.]
Theo:	I asked him to excuse us, the same as Mr. Graham did.

It is difficult to figure out Theo's mental processes here. First he says he doesn't recall, then he says he couldn't possibly have said that, then he admits he *did* ask Dunnegan to step aside, but that Dr. Graham asked it also. Judging from his other verbal gymnastics, it's possible that he was quibbling over the phrase "step aside" as opposed to "excuse"—but he would have come across much better if he had stuck to his original "I don't recall."

This exchange is typical of the vacillation Theo went through when questioned by William Barnes, and it didn't help that the wily Eugene Deuprey was sick in his bed during this time. He might have been able to voice some objections that would have given his client some hints about volunteering too much information.

Theo's cross-examination lasted two days beyond that first forty-five-minute segment, and is riddled with contradictions and confusing responses. But the biggest blows to the defense's case came from Barnes's questions regarding two incidents: the supposed clue given him by the stranger concerning Blanche Lamont's whereabouts, and what he told Carrie Cunningham about what he had seen at the church on April 3.

Theo's story was that he was on the west side of Dupont Street (a dangerous position, in that he had denied knowing the location of Oppenheim's pawnshop, which was also on the west side of Dupont) when a strange man approached him and tapped him on the shoulder. "Are you Durrant?" the stranger asked, and when Theo told him he was, the man asked him if he was interested in the disappearance of Blanche Lamont. "Yes, but no more than anyone else," was Theo's strange response (which was probably meant to convey to the jury that there were others who were equally interested in the fair Blanche). He doesn't seem to have figured out that in a real conversation, no one would put such a stipulation on the answer, but would simply say that, yes, I am interested.

The stranger then told Theo to watch the ferries going to the East Bay that day, turned on his heel and walked away. Now, of course, Theo had invented this encounter to explain his presence at the ferry landing on the day that Minnie Williams came over from Alameda and ended up dead in the Emmanuel Baptist Church. He had originally denied being there at all, but too many people had seen him, and Frank Sademan had testified to Theo's self-important statement about following up on a clue about Blanche Lamont. So this is how the prosecution was able to get this into the Lamont trial, even though it was dangerously close to bringing in the Williams case.

However, Theo seems to have felt that it was sufficient to present the tale without more. It is obvious that he didn't think it through.

When Barnes asked him what the stranger looked like, Theo was only able to give a somewhat generic description. He explained his inability to do better by saying that he was too overjoyed with the news either to notice more about the stranger *or* (a more crucial omission, given the fact that Theo was known to have been among the last people to see Blanche that day) follow him to find out his name and the source of his information. The stranger could have let Theo off the hook with the police—yet he did not pursue him.

Theo said he was so thrilled to get this piece of information that he headed right down toward the ferries. But first—he stopped to get his lunch! Why not go right down to the ferry? "I always take my lunch," Theo said primly, and the response caused great hilarity in the courtroom.

Barnes asked him detailed questions about where he stood, which ferries he had watched, etc. When Theo was talking to Dukes and Dodge, did he tell them about the stranger's message? Why, no, it wasn't uppermost in his mind, he said. Yet Dodge had specifically asked jokingly about "the girl you made away with," which should have caused him to remember his purpose there. And then he told the boys that he was waiting for "a member" (as opposed to "members") of the Signal Corps as his reason for being there.

Probably the most telling aspect of this part of the cross-examination was Theo's failure to mention this great clue to Tom Vogel or any of the other young people at the social that night. He had already testified that he thought Tom Vogel would be more interested in Blanche's disappearance than anyone else except for the Nobles, and would probably be among the first to receive any information about her. Now he had to admit that when he got to Tom's that night, he had said nothing about having spent the entire afternoon at the ferries because of the stranger's clue.

Barnes: Why not?
Theo: It did not occur to my mind.
Barnes: It had passed out of your mind?
Theo: Yes, sir.
Barnes: You didn't remember it?
Theo: Not at that time, no, sir.
Barnes: And you did not mention it to anybody there at the meeting?

Theo: No, sir.

Barnes: All friends of Miss Lamont, weren't they?

Theo: I don't know whether they were or not.

Barnes: Well, acquainted with her, weren't they?

Theo: Oh, they all were that were there.

Barnes: And yet you did not mention this fact to any of those people there at that meeting?

Theo: From the simple fact that it did not occur to me to mention it.

Barnes caused a great sensation the first full day of his cross-examination of Theo when he asked him about the envelope he had addressed to his attorneys: "To be opened if I am convicted and returned to me unopened if I am acquitted." Theo said he had never addressed such an envelope, and Barnes warned him about perjury: "Reflect, Mr. Durrant." It was this fierceness on the part of the district attorney that made the press think he had solid information and was not merely bluffing. But what could it all mean?

Judge Murphy spoke for everyone at the end of that first long day of Theo's cross-examination: "I understand the District Attorney is exhausted, and really we are all exhausted. Today has been a very hard day."

But with Barnes's hints about the mysterious envelope hanging in the air, everyone was eager for the next day's court session.

On Theo's second full day of cross-examination, Barnes came back to the Gil Graham episode. Graham had said that Theo at first wanted the notes for comparison, then admitted that he *had* no notes of his own and would need them to establish his alibi. Now Barnes asked Theo about this: Hadn't he already said he had taken notes during the class? Why would he need to compare his notes? Theo said he had forgotten as to whether he had notes or not. As he had with the mysterious stranger whose information could possibly provide an alibi, Barnes pressed Theo as to why he wouldn't have checked to make sure he had his notes as soon as it was known what time Blanche Lamont had gotten on the cable car after school that day. Wouldn't it make sense to assure himself that he could prove he was in class at that time?

Barnes: You knew you were at Cheney's lecture that day?

Theo: I did.

Barnes: You knew where you were seated?

Theo: I did.

Barnes: You had been over your notes with Mr. Glaser on the 10th, had you not?

Theo: I had.

Barnes: And yet on the 14th you did not know whether you had your notes of the 3rd of April, Dr. Cheney's lecture; you didn't know how full they were. And yet you knew the 3rd of April was the day on which this girl disappeared, and you knew that your name was connected . . . with her disappearance? . . . You knew when you were arrested, didn't you, that it was essential for you to establish where you were on the afternoon of the 3rd of April, didn't you?

Theo: Yes, sir. The notes had left my mind completely until [the 17th] . . . But I may say that up until that time I had never heard the word "alibi" and I did not know what it was.

Barnes: You had never heard the word "alibi"?

Theo: I had never heard it in my life.

Barnes angered Theo when he questioned him about the propriety of taking Bromo-Seltzer for asphyxiation, and this criticism of his medical knowledge got a bigger rise out of him than any other line of cross-examination. The district attorney, of course, was trying to show that, with true asphyxiation, the carbonation of Bromo-Seltzer would have been the exact wrong thing to take. But Theo maintained the gas had made him nauseous, which *was* the proper usage for this medicine. While Barnes and Dickinson argued over the scope of cross-examination on this issue, Theo stood up and pointed dramatically at the district attorney: "Your honor, I would like to—." This was as far as he got before Judge Murphy, afraid of the defendant's saying anything incriminating, roared, "Sit down, Mr. Durrant; perhaps it would be better to consult with your counsel if you desire to."

But Theo would not be denied. He obediently sat down, then went ahead with his protest: "There is an entirely mistaken idea as to what I have said or the effect Bromo-Seltzer would have upon me. It is an entirely mistaken idea altogether." In response to

Barnes's questions, however, Theo admitted to "only a general knowledge of it" and that he had discussed it in casual conversation. Pressed as to whom he had this "casual conversation" with, Theo said it was another prisoner, a Dr. West.

Barnes: Dr. West?

Theo: Yes, sir.

Barnes: That is the doctor in the County Jail awaiting trial for the murder of Addie Gilmour?

Theo: I believe so.

Barnes: And you have discussed this matter with him subsequent to your confinement in the County Jail, have you, Mr. Durrant?

Theo: I discussed it with him last night for a few moments.

Finally, the moment arrived when Barnes renewed his questioning regarding what Theo had told Carrie Cunningham. Theo's answers in denial are rambling and disjointed. In spite of the hint he had received the day before, that the district attorney would be bringing this up, he had prepared no explanation for it that made any kind of sense. Instead of talking to Dr. West about the properties of Bromo-Seltzer, he would have been better served in thinking about how he could offset the damage of what Carrie Cunningham had told the prosecution.

Barnes was very precise in his questions, repeating verbatim what Theo had told Carrie Cunningham about seeing Blanche's body on the second landing and there not being any blood. Theo's answer is interesting, and it is hard not to imagine his agitation as he says it: "Those are not the words—those are not the words."

Barnes: What are your words?

Theo: There was a story brought to me by Miss Carrie Cunningham identically equal or like the story concerning the "Sweet Pea Girl," which afterward was printed in the paper, purporting to be a rumor, as she said, that she gathered somewhere about town, saying that I heard a noise while fixing the gas burner up between the ceilings, and that I had followed that noise—looked about to see what it was, and had discovered what you make reference to. [He seems unable to say the words "the body of Blanche Lamont".] I neither affirmed her story nor did I deny it . . . I said to her, "Miss Cunningham, do you intend

publishing this story?" She said, "No." I said, "If you do the
same as you did with the Sweet Pea Girl story, you will get me
into a lot of trouble, and put me to great annoyance." She said,
"I will take my oath I will say nothing . . . until it can be
proven." Now, I ask for the proof to come forward.""

Theo's words could hardly be considered an unequivocal denial
of his conversation with Carrie Cunningham. But his ordeal was
over at last, and when he got back to his seat next to Mamma, he
collapsed into the chair.

Dickinson presented one final witness for the defense: a Dr.
McDonald, who claimed that when elderly ladies read a lot about
exciting subjects such as the Emmanuel Baptist murder case, they
developed fixations that caused them to hallucinate!

The prosecution's rebuttal case cut to the heart of the points
raised by the defense and brutally destroyed them. First, each of
the trustees testified that he had never asked Theo to fix the sunburners. Then, Dukes and Dodge reprised their encounter with
Theo at the ferry landing, insisting that he had said "members"
after all, and not "a member." It was a small point, but it showed
that Theo's quibbling over semantics was not done in good faith.

A chemist testified that the so-called blood on the sole of Gibson's shoe, found by the defense in the pastor's study, was really
oil. Barnes took the opportunity to question the witness about gas
asphyxiation, and whether it would cause nausea and pallor. On
the contrary, he said, it would cause death and a cherry-red color
if anyone had really breathed it for as long as Theo claimed he
had.

Charles Morrison, a reporter, read from the notes of his interview with Theo on April 14: Durrant had definitely said he *arrived*
at Emmanuel Baptist between 4:00 and 4:30. J. S. Dunnegan, Gil
Graham's companion on his visit to the jail, said Dr. Graham had
not asked him to "step aside." Theo alone had done this. And Gil
Graham came back to say that it was Theo who had used the word
"alibi," the word he told Barnes he had never heard before in his
life.

Several physicians repeated what the chemist had said: Asphyxiation by gas causes unconsciousness in a very short time, the only
cure for which is fresh air. And even fresh air won't prevent death

if too much gas has been inhaled. The skin takes on a cherry-red color that does not dissipate for some time.

Finally, Carrie Cunningham took the stand to back up what she had told Edgar Peixotto about her conversations with Theo. There was no talk of the Sweet Pea Girl in those talks, she said, and there had never been a rumor in the Mission concerning what Theo had seen. The "rumor" idea was his own proposal as to how he could avoid having it look as if he had talked to someone, when he had been warned by the perpetrators not to, under threat of harm to Mamma. She had promised him she would not publish the story unless he told her she could, and she had kept that promise. (Theo was so angry at Carrie Cunningham after her testimony that he hung a picture of her in his cell and scrawled "Traitor" across it.)[12]

Interestingly, the prosecution closed its rebuttal without presenting any evidence against Theo's good character. Detectives had supposedly left no stone unturned, digging into his background from the time he was a child, yet had come up with nothing. Nor did the state put on Lucile Turner to tell her story, indicating that Lucile's credibility on this point was in doubt.

The defense had no rebuttal testimony to present.

It was time for closing arguments, but these were delayed for several days, as Eugene Deuprey—the silver-tongued orator of the defense team—was still incapacitated. Judge Murphy allowed a reasonable time, but eventually he had to insist that the trial continue. It was now the end of October, and the trial had begun with jury selection in July.

The speaking order established was for Edgar Peixotto to begin for the state, followed by Dickinson and then Deuprey for the defense, with Barnes finishing up for the prosecution.

Peixotto used his speaking opportunity for drama (melodrama in parts) and oratorical showmanship, but there were times when he got down to brass tacks and dealt with the evidence clearly and effectively. In his opening statement, Deuprey contended that the prosecution hadn't answered the main questions as to where, when, why, and by whom Blanche Lamont was killed. Peixotto would now answer them with the state's theories: She was killed in the belfry by Theodore Durrant on the afternoon of April 3, 1895. The motive was passion and blood lust, the same that had motivated Jack the Ripper and the other monstrous murderers of history.

Peixotto took Theo's good reputation and turned it against him, saying that Blanche Lamont would not have trusted him otherwise. In fact, he used this as the reason why the prosecution did not contest the defense's assertion of his character: to show that Blanche would not have gone with him if his reputation was suspect. (This was a good ploy on the state's part in explaining the failure to challenge Theo's good character; however, they had spent so much time, money, and energy on "digging up dirt" that it seems implausible they would not have used at least some of it, as they could easily have asserted that Blanche would have been ignorant of his true nature.)

Peixotto went through most of the evidentiary points, showing how they all pointed to Theo's guilt. Then he turned poetic, quoting variously from Oliver Wendell Holmes, Shakespeare, and a host of others, including someone named Blanche Higginson, whose nine-stanza story-poem he recited in full:

> The devil he stood at the gates of hell
>   And yearned for an angel above;
> And he sighed, "Come down, sweet siren, and learn
>   The lesson of passion and love."

The devil is apparently quite attractive, but the angel insists that he come up to heaven, as she doesn't want to leave there. He tricks her into helping him, to make sure he gets there safely, and lies to her about how balmy and warm hell is. She leans over to lift him up to her, but he drags her down to himself instead:

> "Don't struggle, sweet angel," the devil he cried,
>   As he bore her on passion's swell;
> "When an angel's arms have embraced me but once,
>   She belongs to the devil and hell."

Peixotto had taken three hours and twenty minutes for his closing argument. Dickinson and Barnes would take even more, and if Deuprey had not been ailing, he would have done the same. It was an era that valued oratorical skills, and the lawyer who couldn't spend at least a few hours giving a summation wasn't worth his salt.

General John Dickinson, as the lesser light of the two defense attorneys, was up next. The press, used to rating both attorneys and theatrical productions, gave him only lukewarm reviews: no thundering moments, no fancy quotations, no dramatic flourishes—just a lot of repetition and a somewhat meek criticism of the witnesses against Theo. Dickinson took all day on Friday, October 25, for his summation, and the following Tuesday morning as well. However, it is more than likely that he was stalling to give Deuprey more recovery time, as it would be crucial for the defense to let its star slugger have an at-bat before letting the jury deliberate its verdict. Not only was the weekend coming up, but Monday would be another of the biweekly "Steamer (Collection) Days" on which court would not be held so that jurors could attend to bill-collecting and other business.

Dickinson's main theme, repeated several times throughout his speech, was "When did he become a monster?" In other words, if Theo's behavior both prior to and after the murder of Blanche Lamont was easy and natural, there was no reason to suppose that he had committed this monstrous crime. And if he had, at what point did the vile element of his personality emerge? Wouldn't there be some evidence of it that we could discern? Dickinson's puzzlement echoed that of everyone who believed in Theo.

The defense attorney went through each of the defendant's actions on April 3 and after, showing how each could be judged from the point of view of the natural and normal behavior of an innocent man, and not merely indicative of guilt, as the prosecution had maintained. And Dickinson had an interesting theory about the so-called "phantom man" who had given Theo the clue about Blanche taking the ferry to the East Bay: It was actually a trick of the police, who were following Theo because they suspected him. They wanted to see how he would behave with such a clue. If he did nothing, that would mean he knew that Blanche would not be taking any ferry boat; if he went to the ferry, however, it should show that he really didn't know where she was.

When Dickinson wound up (finally!) his summation before the noon break on Tuesday, October 29, he indicated that Eugene Deuprey would like to address the jury that afternoon at 2:00.

The corridors of New City Hall were mobbed with people frantic to get into the courtroom that afternoon. Not only was the Durrant case winding down, but the eminent Eugene Deuprey, notable for his oratorical skills, would be speaking on behalf of his client. The crush of men and women was bad enough, but most of them thought nothing of flailing away at those around them in order to force their way to the front of the line.

Juror Thomas Seiberlich, a wholesale shoe manufacturer, made the mistake of not telling the crowd who he was, but insisting that he had a right to get into the courtroom. The raucous throng responded by putting a rope around his neck and threatening to hang him. The police, who were not terribly successful in controlling the mob, had no difficulty handling the small, elderly Seiberlich: despite his protestations, they picked him up and threw him out into the street.

Finally, Seiberlich was able to get across the idea that he was a juror, and the same police who had unceremoniously thrown him outside now provided a human wedge for him ("Well, why didn't you say so before?" they quite reasonably asked him when he revealed his identity at last). Eventually, the juror ended up inside the courtroom a little the worse for wear and breathing so rapidly that observers feared he would have an apoplectic fit.

In the meantime, Judge Murphy was having problems of his own in getting to the courtroom. No one recognized him and, like Seiberlich, he didn't bother telling them. But Murphy was more resilient and also more resourceful than Seiberlich: he carried a large legal tome with him and banged the heads of everyone who blocked his way!

Seiberlich's heart rate had slowed to normal by the time Murphy arrived, and the juror told the judge that he would not come to the courtroom again unless he could come in "like a gentleman." Murphy asked him what he meant, and Seiberlich told him of his experiences with the mob. But Murphy had no sympathy, and even somewhat proudly told of his own difficulties. When Seiberlich repeated his ultimatum that he would not come to court again if he had to suffer such treatment, Murphy roughly responded, "Then the Court will see that you are kept here." But then the judge boomed instructions to the sheriff to start making arrests if the crowd could not behave more civilly.

In the midst of this excitement and anticipation, what could be

more dramatic than the entry of Eugene Deuprey into the courtroom? Bundled in robes and accompanied by his physician, the
ailing attorney was brought in in a wheelchair to plead for the life
of his client. He asked if he could address the jury sitting down
and was granted that privilege.

But Deuprey was not up to his usual stuff, and his summation
was not nearly as dramatic as his entry had been. The crowd was
disappointed, but it was obvious that the attorney was suffering.
Although the press and his physician kept talking about "rheumatism," the references to paralysis and inability to speak lead more
to a diagnosis of stroke than rheumatism.

Deuprey abandoned his usual theatrical approach and opted for
plain speaking instead. He spoke of the dangers of circumstantial
evidence and cited cases of mistaken identity, maintaining that the
state had not really presented anything compellingly indicative of
Theo's guilt. Ultimately, of course, there was nothing that he *could*
say: all the defense really had was Theo's possible presence at Dr.
Cheney's lecture, and his previously good character. It came down
to Theo's "I wasn't there and I didn't do it" versus the testimony
of eight eyewitnesses who said he *was* there.

For his finale, Deuprey focused on Theo's family and particularly
his mother. They believed in his innocence, he told the jury, and
who would know him better than they? Don't punish the Durrants
by destroying this faith; restore him to his loving family:

May you, in your deliberations, come to such conclusion that you will
say to this mother that her boy is the same as he has ever been—a Christian youth, a Christian gentleman, wedded to his home, wedded to all of
the family. Let the flashes of lightning go over land and under seas to
that waiting and anxious sister, to say that her brother Theo is the same
good and upright man that he ever was. Say by your verdict to this
broken-hearted father, crushed by the awful wrong the law has done to
his and to him, that his son is not a monster.

It but remained for William Barnes to speak for the state one
final time before the judge would charge the jury and leave them
to their deliberations. Great things would be expected of the son
of General Barnes, the noted orator, and the courtroom crowd was
not disappointed. The district attorney's summation, which
would—like Dickinson's—take a day and a half, provided an elec-

trifying note on which to end the most famous case in California history.

Barnes began with a scene in which he, as Eugene Deuprey had done in his opening statement, conjured Blanche Lamont from the dead. But, instead of pleading Theo's innocence, she pointed the finger of guilt at him:

I see her now! There she stands behind him at this hour; not praying for vengeance for her deep and remediless wrongs, but with uplifted hands and streaming eyes praying that God will not put it into your hearts, by the mockery of a verdict of not guilty, to set free this monster to prey upon other gentle souls, pollute with vile hands the unsunned snow of other children and defy anew that God of justice whose ministers you are.

Convincingly, Barnes went through each witness and each aspect of the evidence. The witnesses, he told the jury, presented not mere circumstantial evidence, but direct testimony of Theo's presence with Blanche on the day of her murder. He recounted Theo's own statements as to what he did from the time he heard George King first begin to play the piano until he walked through the sliding doors to where George was: cleaning out the burners, running the card through the tips, replacing the glass reflectors, dusting them off, walking back across the ceiling, replacing the ladder, trying the lighting apparatus to see if it now worked, crossing the auditorium, closing the attic door, and then going down the stairs to the infants' classroom. This was an impossible feat to accomplish in the two or three minutes that George said he had been playing before Theo appeared in the doorway.

The defense had maintained that Theo's seeking out George King was evidence of his innocence, as he could have left the church without being seen. But the district attorney had other interpretations. Maybe Theo had left his key to the library in his coat, and when George locked the library door he couldn't get back in. Or maybe he thought he should start fixing up his alibi and who better to try it on than a trusting dupe like George King? Or it could be part of that "criminal atavism" that Barnes claimed tripped up all murderers: God had planted in them a tendency to leave clues behind so they'd get caught!

Throughout the trial, Mamma Durrant had acted nonchalant, unworried, and even inappropriately cheerful. But as the court took a break that final morning, Barnes's words cut deep and she broke down sobbing. Theo put his arms around her in a comforting motion, and Papa somewhat ineffectively waved a fan at her. All eyes in the courtroom were riveted on the family scene in astonishment that the "iron lady" had finally collapsed.

Barnes did not want the jury to take Deuprey's final words to heart about Theo's distressed mother, so when he resumed his summation after the break, he called attention to the emotional display they had all just witnessed. It was normal and natural, he told them, but they were not there to try the case on sentiment; they were to try it on the evidence. Then he reminded them of another grieving mother in Montana as she received the body of her murdered daughter back in April. *That* was the mother they should be thinking about.

Judge Daniel J. Murphy began his charge to the jury after the noon break at 2:00 and finished at 3:30. The jurors listened politely but not raptly to the rules they were to apply, as Murphy explained the concepts of circumstantial evidence ("every link must be proved") and "beyond a reasonable doubt." It was as if they were anxious to be about their business and had to endure this final torrent of words to get there. (During the judge's charge, Mamma stared intensely at each juror, as if she could will them to vote "not guilty.")

Murphy had told the jurors to bring blankets and pillows with them to court, as they would not be allowed to leave until they had reached a verdict. There would be no risk of outside influence on the decision.

By 3:35 the jurors had retired to the deliberation room. The first order of business was to elect a foreman, and they chose Warren Dutton, a man of independent means (a "capitalist"). For their second order of business, they cast a ballot just to see where they all stood before beginning the deliberation process.

Out in the courtroom, Mamma had perked up a bit from her morning breakdown, and she chatted gaily with Theo and her lady friends. Theo sent Papa on an errand of some kind, which was fine with the elder Durrant as he wanted to smoke a cigarette anyway. Everyone seemed to settle in for a long wait.

Back in the jury room, the twelve men were astonished to see that on their first ballot they had all voted the same way: Guilty. Dutton suggested they cast another ballot to see if anyone wanted to recommend mercy, which would mean that Theo would get a life sentence instead of the gallows. But this ballot likewise showed them to be in agreement: Death by hanging.

The jurors were somewhat dismayed. "We can't go back out there this soon," one of them said. "Let's have our cigars first," suggested another. So they all sat down to finish the cigars they had lit upon first entering the room. After six weeks of jury selection and two months of testimony, the decision had not even taken five minutes.

Twenty minutes after the jury had retired, Foreman Dutton informed the bailiff that they were ready to go back to the courtroom. As the news began to filter out to the attorneys, the spectators, and the Durrants, the reaction was intense disbelief: They couldn't have reached a decision already—they must be coming back for clarification of some point. Because if they *were* ready with a verdict, it could only be a guilty one.

Papa was still out in the corridor when the verdict was announced, so when his wife broke down for a second time that day he was not there to console her—or his son, who also burst into tears and flung himself into Mamma's arms. When Theo gained control of himself, he turned to Dickinson and asked if he could stand up and address the courtroom. "No," the lawyer told him, "that would not be a good idea."

Judge Murphy lost no time in commanding the bailiffs to take custody of Theo and setting Friday, November 8, as the day for sentencing. There could only be one sentence; it would just be a matter of setting the date for Theo's hanging.

"Mamma's Sweetheart": Appeals and an Execution

Why didn't I let him [slip] away that day when he was sinking so fast? Then he would have died respected and honored. But now!

—Isabella Durrant, June 6, 1897

Theo's trial was not quite over when Coroner William J. Hawkins received a strange handwritten letter from a man who said his name was George Reynolds. Reynolds's letter, dated October 27, said that he was about to commit suicide by drowning himself in the ocean; but before doing that he wanted to confess to his part in a scheme concocted by Theo's defense team.[1]

Reynolds claimed that he and five others had been recruited by a friend of Theo's to put together some stories that would give Theo an alibi for each of the two murders. A man named Richard Smythe was supposed to say that Blanche Lamont had been at his house on April 5 and had left her book strap behind. Reynolds said he marked up the bogus strap himself and sent it to General Dickinson.

There were also plans to implicate Rev. Dr. Gibson by planting a bloody handkerchief with his initials on it, and an invented story that had Theo accompanying the young men for drinks on the night of April 12 (thereby causing him to be late to the Young People's meeting at Tom Vogel's). Reynolds and the others apparently declined to participate because of having to place the blame on the pastor.

Although no one could be found, dead or alive, with the name of George Reynolds, there were very specific details in the letter regarding the fake strap which were never released to the public, and which no one would have known but the police and the person who put the markings on it. The writer also said he had written the threatening letter to Adolph Oppenheim.

Was this a crank letter invented by one of the many people who tried to intrude themselves into the Durrant case? Or had an attempt been made by the defense to present perjured testimony? It is significant that Dickinson is the one to whom the strap was sent, which lends itself to the possibility that Eugene Deuprey might have cooked up this scheme, much as he had tried to with Charles Clark. If he really believed Theo to be innocent, he must have been desperate to come up with something that would free his client; and, no doubt, he was being pressured by Mamma (who would later claim that the defense had not done enough for her son).

Perjury and tampering with evidence were big problems in the 19th century, and were seldom prosecuted. For lawyers, it seemed to be part of the game to alter or abscond with evidence against their clients, and the prosecution's refusal to allow Dickinson and Deuprey to examine Blanche's rings and book strap in private prior to the trial must be seen in that light. This was not limited to the Durrant case, however, as can be seen in an *Examiner* editorial that decried the failure of courts to take steps to prosecute obvious instances of perjury:

The prevalence of perjury in our courts is notorious. Judges, lawyers, and litigants acknowledge and bewail the frequency with which false swearing is resorted to. Yet no steps are taken to check it. Witnesses go upon the stand and swear without hesitation or blush to palpable lies, and show no disburbance when caught.[2]

This is not to excuse any possible subornation of perjury on the part of Theo's defense attorneys, but to place it in a historical perspective in which it was not that unusual.

And what of the envelope Carrie Cunningham saw addressed to Theo's attorneys? A story came out in the *Examiner* that the defense team had the letter prior to Deuprey's opening statement, and that they had consulted another attorney about the wisdom of opening it while the trial was still going on. They were advised to do so, but when they read the letter, they determined that its contents were simply not believable. The *Chronicle* scoffed at its rival newspaper, saying that Dickinson emphatically denied that he and Deuprey had received any such letter from Theo, or that Theo had ever written one. But the *Examiner* stuck by its story.[3]

Once the trial was over, Carrie Cunningham wrote up a complete account of her conversations with Theo. She did not feel that the whole story had been brought out on the stand (Dickinson, in particular, seemed more interested in painting her as an opportunistic journalist trying to get a story at all costs). She now revealed that Theo had broken down more than once over Blanche's death and, when things were not going well at the trial, asked Carrie if he might not do better by getting rid of his attorneys and pleading guilty. Once, when she asked him some questions about Blanche and what he had seen in the belfry, Theo told her, "You make me feel so peculiar when you touch on that point."[4]

Before he was allowed to go back to his cell in the county jail, Theo was thoroughly searched for anything he might conceivably use to commit suicide. From then on, every visitor and every item he received would be scrutinized so that he would not "cheat the hangman."

Theo began a marathon writing spree that would persist until his execution. His first order of business was to write a letter to the *Call* detailing his feelings upon hearing the guilty verdict. (As he wrote, he called out to a fellow prisoner, "How do you spell 'surprise'?")[5] His letter is a self-conscious piece of writing that is much like "freeze frames" in a video, wherein everything is exaggerated out of proportion to the actual time it would have taken. Theo is trying so hard to sound like a writer that some of it makes no sense at all: for example, "I looked as if I desired to know what they were going to do," and "The change of my thoughts as I came to realize my situation was too sudden for my organism."[6]

Theo attempts to crowd in so many different emotions that they often contradict each other. Here is his reaction to the actual reading of the verdict, which in real time probably took five seconds:

I felt as if a half dozen men were reading it at the same time. I felt as if some one was reading for the benefit of my ears, another to catch my eyes, another to touch my heart, another to uncover that great and deep mystery of doubt which was veiled in my mind. As he uttered the first word I instinctively felt for the worst. A peculiar tremor seized my body, but I controlled myself and gasped to hear the verdict to the last. And as the fatal words were uttered a cold chill passed through me. Instantly all doubt passed away and I became conscious of a new feeling, a terrible foreboding of the ill omen.

But Theo reserved his pull-out-the-stops expressions for the effects of the verdict on Mamma, and the fact that the courtroom crowd had erupted into a howl of satisfaction when it was announced:

[A]s I see her bleeding heart with no one to comfort her I say the fiends incarnate must needs to deport themselves like demons and applaud before this sorrowful scene. Ah! for words, for language, for utterances to express my indignation at such a cruel scene. There is nothing so mean, base, vile, degraded, demoniacal, mammoniacal, devilish, satanic, impish and hellish as to revile the true and honest grief and sorrow of a mother's heart.

In closing, Theo repeated his protestations of innocence, which he would continue to proclaim even "as the spark of life disappears in the unfathomable beyond." In an earlier interview, he revealed what it was he wanted to say to the jury when Dickinson told him to keep still: that he wished to be struck dead if he had ever wronged Blanche Lamont.

As soon as the Blanche Lamont trial was over, the district attorney began to gear up for the Minnie Williams case, which he had indicated he wished to set for trial on November 8—the day of Theo's sentencing. Therefore, the newspapers began to focus their articles on the murder of Minnie Williams. And an astounding new piece of evidence developed.

Frank Young, Minnie's baker friend in Alameda, said that on Thursday, April 11, when Minnie had come into his shop, she seemed down—not her usual lively, kidding self. Young asked if she was upset over her friend Blanche Lamont, who was still miss-ing, and Minnie—after an initial hesitation—murmured that she knew too much about the disappearance of Blanche. When Young asked her to elaborate, she refused, indicating that she shouldn't have said as much as she did. As a reason for why he hadn't come forward with this information before, the baker said (along with so many other witnesses) that he didn't want to get involved.[7]

But there are two things wrong with this story. First of all, how would Frank Young have known that Minnie was a friend of Blan-che Lamont when she had not even indicated such to the Morgans? She told them she knew Blanche from church, but there is no solid evidence that shows the two were friends.

Even if Minnie had told Frank Young, truthfully or untruthfully, that she and the missing girl were good friends, there is a larger obstacle to believing his story: he was *already* involved in the Wil-liams case and had been a witness at the inquest and the prelim-inary examination (because his name and address had been found in Minnie's purse). It would seem that a vital piece of information like this should have been brought out at that time. He couldn't possibly have forgotten about it.

The Frank Young story was a scoop by a *Call* reporter, and it was later denounced by the *Examiner* as untrue. The *Call* was furious at this criticism by the "yellow rag," claiming it was just sour grapes on their part because they hadn't discovered the story. As proof, the newspaper printed an affidavit by the editor of the *Alameda Telegram*, who had been a witness to the interview with the baker—an interview which took place in Young's bedroom, as the reporters showed up after he had gone to bed![8]

The *Call* got even with the *Examiner* a few days later when it exposed as fake the latter newspaper's interview with juror Horace Smyth. Supposedly, Smyth had confided to the *Examiner* that he had gone to the Emmanuel Baptist Church on his own to do some investigating while he was serving on the Durrant jury (which would have been grounds for a mistrial). The *Call* sent a telegram to Smyth asking if it were true, and Smyth wrote back to tell them that he had only gone to the church with the jury, and at no other time. The *Call* commented that "since [Hearst's] departure his Western paper has turned to evil ways." (William Randolph Hearst had recently purchased the *New York Journal* and was back East trying to make it profitable.)[9]

Mamma had been criticized back in April (and most recently in an article by Alice Rix) for her comment about Minnie as "that little servant girl." Now that everyone was being reinterviewed about Minnie Williams, Mamma tried to downplay that statement by claiming that Maud Durrant had wanted them to hire Minnie after the Williamses' divorce—but Mamma had thought she was "too slight" and wouldn't be able to handle housework. (So much for her earlier claim that neither she nor Theo knew Minnie.)[10]

Some lawyers were disturbed by the verdict in the Blanche Lamont case, and felt that, to insure that Theo was really guilty, he should be tried for the Minnie Williams murder. If he were acquitted, this would necessarily shed new light on the Blanche Lamont trial. Public expense, of course, was to be considered, but it was important to proceed before too much time intervened: witnesses could forget, move away, or die.

The prevailing theory was that Minnie was killed because she knew something, so it was considered possible that she had been in San Francisco on April 3 and saw Theo with Blanche—maybe even talked with them. There was a gap in the timeline at the changing of the cars at Powell and Market, and also one between their getting off the streetcar at 21st and Mission and their arrival at the church by 4:20 or 4:25 (Mrs. Crosett had four more blocks to travel beyond their stop, plus she walked slowly—yet, she got home just before 4:00).

Reporters contacted Clark Morgan and his wife Susie, now residents of Tacoma, to see if Minnie might have gone over to the city on April 3. Morgan, anxious to agree to anything that might put another rope around Theo's neck, said that Minnie had definitely gone to San Francisco on the 3rd to see her father and a photographer named Thors.[11] However, the meeting between Minnie and her father, and her appointment with Thors, had taken place on April 5, the day she also made arrangements to stay with Mrs. Voy and her family.

So far, then, there was nothing definitive to show what, if anything, Minnie might have known, or to whom she might have imparted it. The only time she seems to have been in San Francisco was April 5, and at that time, no one other than the Nobles (and, of course, Theo) knew that Blanche was missing—so what could she possibly have learned then? Lucile Turner was absent from school that day and presumably at home ill, but if she had seen Minnie so close to the time of her death, she would not have hesitated to make that known. Minnie did not stay in San Francisco with anyone that night, but went back to Alameda. The next time she came to the city was Friday, April 12, the day she was killed.

Did Minnie really know anything at all? And, if not, why was she killed?

A few days before his sentencing, Theo wrote yet another article, this one for the *Examiner*.[12] Most of it is spent praising Mamma, who told him how to spend his money and what he should be saving for. ("I tell you, my friends, it is well said that a 'boy's best friend is his mother.'") He expresses anger at Alice Rix for what she had said about Mamma and mistakenly supposes a comment she made about an "Aged Baby" to refer to Isabella Durrant (in fact, it referred to Carrie Cunningham, whose small stature, "large, round, innocent hats, wide Eton collars and flowing ties of Scottish plaid" reminded Rix of the " 'Aged Baby' in the Bab Ballads").

Against her better judgment, Alice Rix had gone back to the Durrant trial as it was coming to an end.[13] As she observed Theo's mother, she revised her earlier opinion somewhat: Although Mamma still possessed an "evident taste for the notoriety which she and her family had secured," she no longer seemed "flippant and defiant." Alice felt she was "still as far removed from one's natural conception of sorrowing motherhood as darkness is from dawn," but that by the end of the trial real grief could be seen beneath the mask.

Mamma and Papa had an adventure of their own with gas asphyxiation in the first weeks after the trial.[14] Since Theo's arrest, Mamma was sleeping with the light on for some unknown reason, and had asked a young woman who was visiting them to turn it on when the latter was ready to go to bed (why Mamma did not do so herself is not explained). The visitor pushed in the button, but the spark did not ignite (shades of that sunburner!) and the gas began to escape.

Mamma awoke after midnight and could barely get out of bed because of being overcome with the gas, but eventually managed to get to Papa's room next door, where she found him nearly unconscious. However, instead of opening the window in his room, which would have been the first thing to do, she shook him until he responded, then had *him* get up and open the window! It can only be imagined with what high drama Mamma related this story to the newspapers.

At Theo's sentencing hearing on November 8, he showed a definite reaction to Blanche Lamont's name when the conviction was read by Judge Murphy: his lower lip dropped and his hands fluttered nervously.[15] But there was to be no sentence passed that day, as Dickinson indicated that the defense was preparing the motion for a new trial and needed extra time. Murphy put the matter over for two weeks, and Barnes removed the Minnie Williams case from the calendar until a later time: he wanted a clear path to the gallows for Theo before attempting to try him on the second murder.

Theo was supposed to have gone to San Quentin right after his conviction, but he was worried and anxious about it. Besides, if he left San Francisco, his parents wouldn't be able to visit him as easily. So his attorneys managed to postpone his transfer, and would be successful in doing so for more than a year. In his county jail cell, he spent most of his time reading and writing. Two of the books occupying his time were Robert Louis Stevenson's *A Close Call*, which detailed true cases of innocent men being executed; and Ignatius Donnelly's *Caesar's Column*, a Utopian novel written in 1891 and considered "one of the great crackpot books of the 19th century."[16]

Dr. Gibson, of course, had never visited him since his arrest; but neither had any of the other Baptist ministers. Shortly after his conviction, some members of the Salvation Army asked to pray with him, and a grateful Theo knelt with them on the hard cell floor.[17]

But the kindest and most faithful religious visitors throughout Theo's entire period of incarceration were two priests, a Jesuit named Father Jacquet and a Paulist, Father Osborne.[18] They did not seem to judge him, nor did they try to convert him. Theo had always been interested in theology, and often discussed this with the two priests. From the time it became known that he was being visited by Roman Catholic clergy, the press constantly asked him about whether he would convert. Theo's answer was always the same: I have great discussions with them about the Catholic faith, but I was brought up Baptist and will probably remain such.

In the latter part of the 19th century, an anti-Catholic movement had sprung up, started by a Baptist minister. Euphemistically called the American Protective Association (APA), its goal—as with all organizations designed to persecute a race or religion—was to make sure that Catholics did not get elected to office or otherwise hold positions of power. Because the founder and most of its members were Baptists, Theo was asked if he did not also belong to the APA. But he did not, and his view on religion now seemed to be that "all Christian faiths are good if we live up to the precepts." (After this, a minister would write a letter to the editor complaining that Theo was allowed to talk about religion in the newspaper.)[19]

Now that the trial was over, the play called *Crime of a Century* resurfaced, this time with a brazen subtitle: *The Demon of the Belfry*. (In court, the playwright had tried to claim that the work referred to a crime he had heard about as a child back in Europe, and not to the Emmanuel Baptist murders.) This Grand Guignol production was to be performed at the Alcazar Theater, its participants believing that the guilty verdict effectively lifted Judge Murphy's injunction. The reviewer from the *Examiner* had a terrible experience: "The play is, if possible, worse than the acting." But it was all for naught: The actors weren't getting paid, so they went on strike and the play closed down. It was later determined that the managers had absconded with the funds.[20]

Theo was eventually, after more postponements, brought back to court for his sentencing on December 6, 1895, the day after his class graduated from medical school. A policeman practiced in the art of fancy calligraphy had spent two days drafting the highly stylized death warrant addressed to the warden of San Quentin, which would be read to Theo right before he started on his walk to the gallows. Its final words were "Herein fail not," but Theo was convinced he would never hear them: he would win on appeal, he told reporters—of that he was supremely confident.

In Judge Murphy's courtroom that day sat two of Theo's jurors: the foreman, Dutton, and Thomas Seiberlich, whose unceremonious treatment by the crowd in the last days of the trial had caused him such distress. Papa Durrant was also there, as he was for all of his son's court appearances. (Mamma never came to the sentenc:ng hearings, as she did not like to hear the words condemning Theo to death.)

In passing the death sentence on Theo, Murphy lectured him: "Blanche Lamont was a young and inexperienced schoolgirl, and from the position you occupied in society and particularly to the church in which she was an attendant, you undoubtedly gained her entire confidence and trust." He set February 21, 1896, as the day of execution.[21]

But the long, slow process of appeals had begun (the trial transcript alone comprised three volumes containing 2,700 pages) and both February of 1896 and February of 1897 would come and go before the case would receive a decision from the highest court in the state. During this time, Theo remained in the San Francisco county jail.

Dickinson and Deuprey (Thompson had long ago dropped out, having only been nominally involved to start with) used a barrage of appeal points, most of which were either trivial or falling under the category of "no harm, no foul." Some of the more interesting issues were:[22]

1. that the evidence was entirely circumstantial and insufficient to justify the verdict;
2. that the jury failed to take the defendant's good character into consideration;
3. that the prosecution failed to prove motive;
4. that the jury should have given more weight to the defendant's alibi;
5. that McCoy's comment to juror Truman on the streetcar should have resulted in a mistrial;
6. that the defendant was precluded from a fair trial by the highly sensational newspaper reports.

On March 3, 1897, the California Supreme Court handed down its ruling, denying the appellant (Theo) a new trial and controverting every point raised in the appeal. Its language on the issue of the lack of motive is still cited by courts today:

To the act of every rational human being pre-exists a motive. In every criminal case, proof of the moving cause is permissible, and oftentimes is valuable; but it is never essential. Where the perpetration of a crime has been brought home to a defendant, the motive for its commission becomes unimportant. . . . [P]roof of motive is never indispensable to a conviction. The well-springs of human conduct are infinite, and infinitely obscure.

Regarding the inflammatory press, the court's opinion was that "all men do not forsake reason; some still preserve a dispassionate judgment," and Theo's jury seemed to have been composed of people like this. Besides, if defense counsel thought there was something wrong with the jurors, why did they not exhaust more than three-fifths of their peremptory challenges?

But a concurring opinion by Justice McFarland reflects the uneasiness that many people felt about the attendant publicity in the press, and that perhaps a change of venue would have been appropriate:

I desire to say that the conviction of appellant would have been much more satisfactory if he had been tried in some county far beyond the reach of the threatening atmosphere which surrounded him at the place of his trial. . . . As the case stands it is somewhat difficult to feel sufficiently assured that outside adverse pressure did not have some insensible influence.

However, as it was not an obvious case of abuse of discretion on Judge Murphy's part in denying the change of venue motion, McFarland did not feel it warranted a declaration of error.

Chief Justice Beatty dissented from the decision of the other justices denying Theo a new trial, but did not give his reasons. Was he, too, like McFarland, disturbed by the role of the press?

Once the order of the California Supreme Court was handed down, Theo was brought back to court on April 10 for a new execution date. Judge Murphy had retired by this time and the proceedings were held before Judge George Bahrs, who set Friday, June 11, 1897, as the day for Theo to be hanged. (Executions were always held on a Friday, referred to as Black Friday.)

There was no reason now why Theo could not be delivered to San Quentin, so right after his court hearing, he was taken across the Bay to Marin County and handed over to the care of Warden

W. E. Hale. His carefully groomed, pompadoured hair and his mustache were completely shaved off, Marine style; then he was issued his prison stripes (they were vertical stripes at that time instead of the horizontal ones that came into vogue later), his death row vest to set him apart from the general prison population, and his number: 17260. Of all the indignities that Theo had suffered, or would undergo in the future, probably nothing affected him as much as the shaving of his head.[23]

Theo's attorneys (Dickinson and Deuprey were now joined by a young man named Louis Boardman, Theo's commanding officer in the Signal Corps, who would do much of the physical running around for them) were desperate in their search for some legal means to halt the execution. May was going by and it looked as if Theo would be going to the gallows on June 11. At the end of May, Governor James H. Budd handed down his executive decision that he would not interfere with the verdict by granting clemency. However, in an echo of Justice McFarland's opinion concerning the role of the press, Budd had this to say:[24]

The position of the public press upon the case during its trial, and subsequently, is deserving of serious censure, and did I believe that the newspapers were in any way responsible for the conviction of Durrant, or that in the absence of their comment he might not have been convicted, I would interfere with the judgment in this case, to the extent which I thought the facts justified.

Budd's refusal seemed to mark the end of Theo's final hope. The governor had not even been moved by the urgent plea sent to him from Berlin by Maud Durrant ("a character such as he had could not change so in the short time intervening between the day of my leaving home—February 14 and April 3d—to allow his committing the brutal crime of [sic] which he is charged").[25]

Under ordinary circumstances, Theo would have been taken immediately to the deathwatch cell, which was in a separate building—an old furniture factory—on the San Quentin grounds. However, Warden Hale wanted Mamma to be the one to break the news to her son about Budd's denial of executive clemency before they took him there, and also give the two a chance to visit without bars intervening. In the meantime, they were careful not to let any news of the decision reach him for fear he would try to kill himself.[26]

While Mamma waited for permission to enter the prison, she told a reporter, "It is a sad and painful duty I have to perform. We have stood many things during this trying ordeal, and we must be brave now. My poor Theo must hear the decision from his mother's lips. He has been a brave boy, and he will be brave to the end. Poor Theo, poor Theo." The dramatic moment was not lost on her.

When Mamma arrived in Captain Edgar's office, where the visit would take place, Theo was already there. Her first words to him were, "Mamma's sweetheart," and as soon as she said them he knew the governor's decision. Everyone was astonished when the normally unflappable prisoner broke down and sobbed as his mother comforted and stroked him. After ten minutes, he pulled himself together and she was able to tell him the particulars of Budd's refusal. Theo could not understand why the governor had not responded to his request for a private interview, as he had information to impart about the case (more of the kinds of things he had told Carrie Cunningham?).

Their visit lasted for almost two hours, during which Mamma exhorted Theo to be brave and he agreed that he would. Her theory was that only the guilty break down and act cowardly; the innocent never. She would tell him this again and again, consciously or unconsciously setting the stage for one of the most remarkable gallows scenes in the history of capital punishment.

As Mamma prepared to leave, however, their positions reversed: it was she who became hysterical and Theo who was brave and comforting. (The *Call* reporter cynically noted that "before the door was reached her tears had disappeared[,] the hard dry lines returned to her face, and not a trace of emotion could be detected on her return to the prison office.") "Goodby, my Theodore," she called to him while she was still crying. "Goodby, mother, cheer up," Theo said as he lifted up his little convict hat (it looked like the beanies that college freshmen used to wear).

After Mamma's departure, prison officials got Theo ready for the deathwatch cell which he would occupy until his hanging. Adjacent to the gallows and separated from it by only a thin wall, it consisted of a partitioned section in the middle of the giant warehouse. Stretched across the bars was a wire mesh that was so closely knit it was difficult to see through clearly. From now until his hanging, Theo would have to visit his parents separated by this screen. They could not touch each other, and the mesh prevented anything from being passed through the bars.

And that was the whole point. In the past, prisoners had been able to receive contraband poison that enabled them to commit suicide instead of enduring the ignominious and terror-filled climb to the gallows. One man's mother had even gone so far as to soak a Bible with poison; her son chewed the pages and died.

San Quentin officials were especially wary of Mamma Durrant, whose tendency toward histrionics and unstable behavior led them to think she might try just such a stunt to save her son from a gallows death. It even occurred to them that she might shoot him herself. Consequently, Mamma and everything she brought into the prison were searched with a fine-tooth comb. Prison officials confessed that they were never easy when Mrs. Durrant was around.

Adding to their fear of Mamma and her scenes was her latest announcement, that she intended to be at her son's execution to watch him die. Never had a woman been present at an execution, and Warden Hale did not intend it to happen on his watch. Still, it was her right as his mother, so he was in a quandary as to what to do about it. He tried appealing to Papa, who kept vacillating as to whether he would be there or not. Papa's answer is indicative of what must have been true for their entire married life: "If Mrs. Durrant wants to do something, she will do it."

Warden Hale was convinced that Mamma would create "some tragic action" on the gallows by shooting Theo. There was a rumor floating around the prison that she had stated she would kill him before allowing him to die such a death. But this rumor reckoned without the true nature of Mamma Durrant: She intended to create a martyr out of her son, an innocent boy murdered by the State of California for no reason. In order for her to do this, she would have to allow the hanging to take place.

In the meantime, Mamma was spreading rumors of her own: that San Francisco Chief of Detectives Isaiah Lees had influenced Governor Budd to deny executive clemency to Theo. This rumor even reached Budd, who made sure to telephone Lees and tell him to ignore it. He congratulated the chief on his policy of not commenting on the case one way or the other. The magnanimous

Lees said he didn't blame Mamma for her strong feelings, and he would simply refuse to pay attention to anything she said.

Life in the deathwatch cell was like being in a goldfish bowl. Two guards were assigned to watch Theo at all times, even when he slept. A gaslight in the cell, far above his reach, burned all night long. Although he could not see the door that led to the gallows (it was only about twenty feet from his cell), he could hear the hammering and the preparations on the other side of it.

Theo's guards reported that he spent a lot of time walking rapidly back and forth in a "quick, nervous pace . . . like an animal." He would walk for an hour, then throw himself on his cot. Sometimes he would talk to the guards in a torrent of words, mostly about his past, but never about his case—except to proclaim his innocence.

The warden had black-bordered invitations to the execution made up, which would be sent to dignitaries and members of the press. They quite considerately included instructions as to which ferry boat to take. Theo would be allowed five invitations, two of which were still reserved for his parents.

Dickinson, Deuprey, and Boardman thought they might have one final ace in the hole, however: an appeal through the federal courts on a writ of habeas corpus. Their grounds were that Theo had been convicted on an "information" and not an "indictment" coming out of a grand jury—thereby making the verdict unconstitutional under the Fifth and Fourteenth Amendments. But the 9th Circuit Court of Appeals refused to allow them to file, saying it had no merit and they were just stalling for time (which they were). This time, Papa was assigned to convey the bad news to Theo.

As he entered Warden Hale's office for a permit to see his son, a distraught Papa heard the last part of a conversation between Hale and a young man who was looking for a job with the prison. Hale was telling him that he would look over the application and keep it on file, and Papa thought it referred to a request to watch Theo's hanging. "I guess you will have your curiosity gratified a week from Friday if you can wait that long," he told the young man angrily. The job applicant, who had no idea who Papa was, was thoroughly confused by the outburst.

When Papa first saw the deathwatch cell with its wire mesh, he was unnerved. Theo made a move as if to shake his hand, but then remembered the netting and put his hand down. "Welcome to you, Papa," he said quietly. Papa wept as he told his son about the failure of the appeal in the circuit court, and Theo was likewise upset.

After the visit, an uncharacteristically voluble Papa regaled reporters with a melodramatic version of their conversation. "Yes, father," he said Theo had told him, "I shall be brave. Your son shall not falter in the shadow of death. My innocence gives me courage and hope, and if I must die, my blood will be upon the people of this state. . . . I do not fear death. I will die like a Durrant."

"Dying like a Durrant" was a concept Theo reiterated constantly. Some correspondent seems to have sent him some genealogical information about a Durrant family of nobles that had been courageous in battle. Although these people were not in Theo's ancestral line, he liked the romantic notion of acting in accordance with such a tradition and believed—or chose to believe—that the family of nobles was his own.

After Papa left that day, Theo seemed so depressed that he was almost in a catatonic state: he sat on his cot and stared glassily ahead of him, not responding to the guards. The guards were alarmed and felt he might be "losing it," so Warden Hale assigned a third death watch and instructed them that one officer had to be in the cage with the prisoner at all times.

The deathwatch guards were genuinely worried about Theo, who seemed absolutely despondent. He sent away his dinner (he almost always had a hearty appetite), then lay on his stomach for hours without moving. Occasionally they would hear a groan from him. Eventually, Theo crawled under the covers and tried to pull the sheets over his head. But the guards had strict orders about this and pulled them back. If he covered his arms, they made him put them back on top of the blanket.

The three guards—John Miller, John Jones, and the new addition, Frank Arbogast—became very fond of Theo as they got to know him. He never gave them a hard time, but always obeyed their orders and tried to be cheerful, and even when he couldn't be cheerful, he was never cross or complaining.

Guard John Miller had grown up in the gold country counties

that Theo had bicycled through—Calaveras, Tuolomne, and Amador—and the two spent hours talking about the area.

A dramatic incident occurred when Chaplain Drahms, who had been assigned to the prison, came to visit Theo. Normally, Drahms would accompany a condemned man to the gallows unless the prisoner had someone else he wanted with him. As he had done with many death row inmates before Theo, Drahms advised him to confess his guilt and go before his Maker with a clean conscience; if he were innocent, the chaplain continued, then he would be a martyr—but he shouldn't neglect the opportunity to take care of his soul before going to the gallows.

Theo was emphatic. He raised his hand and said in a loud voice, "In your presence, Chaplain, and before Almighty God, I say I am an innocent man!" The guards were impressed. Here was a man who was twenty feet and a few days from the gallows, calling on God—in front of a minister, no less—to witness his innocence.

"Will your son invite his mother to attend his execution?" an *Examiner* reporter asked Papa Durrant. "Theodore Durrant never disobeyed his mother in his life," Papa explained. "With him her word is law. When she says, 'Theodore, I will be with you in death,' he will say, 'Your command, mother, is my law.' When my wife says to her boy that she will be with him to the end he will simply reply that he will do her bidding. Nothing can change Mrs. Durrant's plans to attend the execution, if it takes place."

Did Theo want his mother at his hanging? Decidedly, he did not ("I would much rather she . . . remain with loving friends at home . . ."), although there were moments when Mamma seemed to have convinced him that he *did* want her there, so she could see that he "died game" ("[I]t would kill her, I think, did she believe I could not face the end with an unfaltering face after the bitter injustice I have suffered."). But that this was entirely Mamma's own idea is evidenced by Papa's words. And who could gainsay her? Papa did not really want to be there himself, but if his wife told him to, he would have to obey as well.

The rationale Mamma gave for what seemed to people in 1897 to be an unnatural desire, was that she would not hesitate to be at his side if he had been in a bad accident, or were suffering from a fatal disease (as, indeed, she had been when he nearly died from meningitis in 1894). She also felt that he deserved her last-minute comfort: "[H]e will know as long as he is conscious of anything in this world, that mamma's sweetheart was not left to die alone."

And she had a further motive as well: "It is to claim the remains of my loved one. The moment the law has finished with him, he is mine, and as sacred to me as every darling boy is to his mother. Mine, mine he will be then—all mine! No one can come between us then."

But luck—and the law—were with Theo that June. His attorneys were granted an automatic appeal to the U.S. Supreme Court after their application for a writ of habeas corpus was denied. And, as the Court would not be in session again until October, Theo had, for the moment, no execution date hanging over his head. He was taken from the deathwatch cell back to his regular one on death row.

Needless to say, the Durrants were ecstatic and filled with a new sense of hope that Theo might be ultimately victorious and returned to his home. But, in the long run, the intense seesaw ride of the next seven months would prove crueller than a quick execution in June would have been.

Theo passed the time in reading novels, historical works, poetry, and the Bible. He wrote voluminous letters to his sister in Berlin— not in the pompous, inflated style of his letters to the newspapers, but in a style that was warm, witty, and tender. It is in these letters, poignant against the backdrop of his impending execution, that we get a glimpse of the real Theo Durrant and why he was, as Maud says, "a favorite" with everyone. He rarely referred to his situation, however, and he might have been writing from his college dormitory or from his medical office after the last patient had left for the day.[27]

Theo's larger literary exploits included his autobiography (carried away in chapters by Papa during visits) and a 70,000-word rambling, romantic, frankly awful novel entitled *Azora*. An excerpt of it was published in the *Examiner*'s Sunday section.[28] *Azora* contained two threads that ultimately came together toward the end: one involving the title character, who may have been modeled after his sister, Maud; and the other involving a love triangle and the arrest of one of them for a murder he did not commit. Although it looks very much as if Harley Hamerton is guilty (smoking gun and all that), the evidence against him is purely circumstantial. Only a deathbed confession by the guilty party saves him from the gallows. The *Examiner*'s critical comments on this novel are sarcastic and merciless.

As the months went on, the senior Durrants seem to have grown more and more accustomed to the limelight, and even came to revel in it. They did everything they could to raise money for their son's defense, and this often included special interviews or writing articles. Once, they hired a man to run a kinetoscope, a Thomas Edison invention that was a precursor of the movie camera, to take pictures of Theo in the garden at San Quentin. According to Warden Hale, Papa got down on his knees and wept, begging Hale to allow them to take the moving pictures. The warden assented, and Theo was filmed picking, smelling, and then scattering flowers in the prison garden. Most of the $1,000 the Durrants received from selling the film went to pay costs of the defense.[29]

Where *was* the money coming from for Theo's defense? The Durrants had very little money, and their mortgage was already in arrears. It was only their profound trouble that kept the finance company from foreclosing on their home.[30]

Some of the funding came from Theo's Signal Corps comrades, most of whom contributed to his defense. There were rumors that Mayor Sutro was providing money, but these were false. The real source of the financing was General John Dickinson, who not only worked without a fee throughout the entire case, but spent a good deal of his own money on it. (Some of the appeals bonds, for example, were $500—an enormous sum in 1897.) Why would he do this? Because Theo's National Guard commanding officer believed implicitly in the innocence of his client, and was firmly convinced that he had not had a fair trial.

Eugene Deuprey, who had no prior connection with Theo, was more practical. Much of the defense fund really went to pay him, and he also took over the defaulting mortgage to the home on Fair Oaks. (He would have to bring it out of arrears in order to sell it.) Deuprey was also the more legally astute of the two defense attorneys and more used to the criminal process.

In November 1897, a telegram was sent from the California attorney general in Washington, D.C., triumphantly announcing that the U.S. Supreme Court was rejecting Theo's appeal for a new trial. He ordered District Attorney Barnes to bring Theo into court for a new execution date. Even though Barnes thought he should wait for official word from the Supreme Court itself, he regarded Attorney General Fitzgerald's telegram as an equivalent substitute.[31]

Alice Rix was trying to be kind, but sometimes it was difficult. She had been assigned to be with Isabella Durrant during Theo's last hours, and she knew what a horribly excruciating time this would be for any mother. If only Mrs. Durrant were more—well, more like a normal mother. There were times when her behavior repulsed Alice in the extreme. Luckily, her feelings were tempered by her own strong beliefs that the death penalty was a barbaric system that should not be imposed on anyone—not even on Theo Durrant.

Rix had been observing Mamma ever since Theo's arrest in April 1895, and thought her "a strange woman, a stranger mother." But when the journalist went to the Durrant home on Fair Oaks on the night the attorney general's telegram had arrived—Monday, November 8, 1897—she was moved to pity when she saw the "little shrunken wraith of a woman," her hair now turning white and her despair sitting on her like a cloak.

Mamma said that she had tried to keep up a cheerful appearance for Theo's sake, although many people (including Alice Rix, but Mrs. Durrant did not point this out) misunderstood and characterized her as macabre. "I made up my smiles many times at the courtroom door," she said bitterly.

On the boat to San Quentin the next day, Mamma had perked up considerably. In the middle of her conversation with Alice Rix, however, she recognized Chief Jailer Sattler from San Francisco, and promptly went into hysterics, correctly guessing that he was there to serve notice that Theo was to be taken back to court for a new execution date.

"Tell me the truth," she begged him. "You are going to take him today?" "No," Sattler told her, "not today." He didn't have the heart to tell her it would be the next day. Still, Mamma thought something else was going on. "I fear, I fear something," she kept saying to Alice Rix. "There is something I do not know! Something they are keeping from me—something." She had the idea that they would take Theo out and hang him right away, and she went nervously among the officials and reporters at San Quentin to find out what was going on. "Will no one help me? No one?" Finally, someone showed her the warrant, which was merely for a court date.

When the two women were ushered in to see Theo, Alice was impressed with how good he looked, compared to the prison pallor he had at the trial. He had gained weight, too, and seemed healthier, which he credited to the good meals, the outdoor exercise, and Marin County sunshine. In fact, Theo was sorry he had resisted going to San Quentin for so long—if he had known what it was really like, he would have told his lawyers he wanted to go right away.

Although Theo was upset at the Supreme Court's decision, he exuded a calm resignation that he said came from his faith in God. As he talked with Alice Rix, Mamma wept furiously, frequently interrupting him for yet another demonstration of maternal excess. At one point she cried out, "Theo, my darling, my baby!" and pulled his head down to her shoulder. Alice noticed that he tried to put up a mild resistance, but then let Mamma indulge herself.

Theo was explaining to Alice that he tried to have courage, to hope that everything would work out for him, and the newspaperwoman responded that she could see from Mamma where he had inherited his strength.

"She is my mainstay," Theo told her, "after Christ." But Mamma had no intention of taking second billing to Christ. "Theo!" she cried out sharply. "After none! I come first! I must come first! You belong to me! I will give you to Christ when it is over, but while you are here, you are mine—mine, dear, mine!" This outburst shook Theo's calm, and Alice noticed how very young and frightened he looked.

"Be brave," the reporter said to him as they were leaving. "I will be brave until the very end," he told her. But when he got back to his cell, he threw himself on his bed and wept for a long time.

Outside the prison, Mamma told Alice that Theo had been nervous talking about the coming execution, but that he was not "unnerved." It seemed to be of the utmost importance to her that he not break down: "They are looking for it—for a sensation; but they will be disappointed about everything they expect." Would Theo take poison? Alice hinted. "Never!" was Mamma's response. "They think that I will give it to him. When my boy is murdered, his blood will be not on my hands but on the people of this State."

The next day in court, Judge Bahrs shocked everyone when he set November 12—a mere two days away—for the execution. Mamma's instincts had not been far off when she thought they would take her son away immediately and hang him. At what they assumed would be the final court hearing were juror Horace Smyth and ex-Judge Daniel Murphy. Spectators crowded the courtroom once more, standing on chairs, benches, and tables to get a look at Theo. Nobody obeyed the bailiff's order to sit down.

On the boat back to San Quentin, Alice Rix rode with Theo and Papa. Theo was curiously calm knowing he would die in two days, and at times achieved a somewhat grandiose way of speaking, "the voice of the zealot, the voice of those who speak 'in meeting.' " Another Catholic priest had come into his life, Father Edward Lagan, although Theo told Alice that he was not prepared to convert to Catholicism, but would continue to "pride myself on independent thought, the one privilege a man can call his own."

Theo grew philosophical as he talked with the reporter: "You begin by being bitter and revengeful and then as the months go by and you have only your thoughts and your God for close companionship, all the affairs of the world seem to grow small and insignificant and the bitterness dies out of your heart, and you can do what you never believed you could be capable of."

He wished he could say something that could convey his immense gratitude to his father, he told her. "His devotion, his patience. There is no reward for it here." And his final words that he wished Alice to convey to her readers: "I die an innocent man and I forgive my enemies."

Back at San Quentin, Theo spent some time with Papa calmly going over his last requests: He did not want an autopsy. (Many physicians were anxious to see if there was some biological explanation to the mystery of Theo Durrant and wanted a chance to look at his brain.) He did not want the rope that hanged him to be cut up and sold for souvenirs, so he asked Papa to see that it was burned. He wanted his body to be put in a casket and turned over to his parents. He did not want anyone, other than his parents and the prison officials, to see him after he had been hanged.

Theo had many questions about how the execution was to be carried out, and the guards told him whatever he wanted to know.

He thanked them for all their kindnesses, thanked the warden as well, then burst into tears. But soon he had himself under control again and was ready to climb the stairs once more to the old furniture factory and enter the deathwatch cell. As he reached the top step, he paused a moment and looked around for a last time at the beautiful California hills and the sunlight sparkling on the Bay. Then he turned abruptly and went through the door.

The method of execution by hanging is this:[32] On the morning he is to be hanged, the prisoner (or "executee") is awakened and served breakfast. At San Quentin in 1897, he also doffed his prison garb and put on a suit of civilian clothes. Instead of shoes, he put on slippers.

Approximately twenty minutes prior to the time set for execution, the warden comes into the cell to read the indictment to the prisoner. The prisoner, if he wishes, can waive this reading. The guards then come to strap his arms to his sides, and they all go out in a procession, led by the warden, then the clergyman chosen by the prisoner. It is also recommended that some form of sedation be given to the prisoner. In 1897, this would have been whiskey; today it is diazepam (valium).

At the gallows stairs, two of the guards accompany the prisoner up to the platform, and one stays below unless needed. As soon as the prisoner is standing on the trapdoor, the guards fasten straps around his ankles. This is to prevent the natural flailing around of the limbs when the body falls. Oftentimes, a prisoner is weak-kneed at this point and physically unable to stand—or, alternatively, refuses to cooperate in the procedure. For times like these, there is a "standing board" to which the prisoner is strapped and which will allow him (or force him) to stand on the trapdoor. In 1897, this board was made of wood. Today, it is made of steel tubing and is called a "collapse frame."

When the prisoner is standing over the trapdoor, the hangman places the rope around his neck and tightens it, making sure that the thick knot is firmly situated directly behind the left ear. The object of hanging is not to choke the prisoner to death, but to break his neck so that death is swift and relatively painless. The rope, made of three-quarter-inch Manila hemp, must be measured to the prisoner's height, and stretched to prevent coiling.

The drop distance is calculated based on the prisoner's weight, to ensure sufficient force to break his neck. If the distance is too short, he will strangle; if it is too long, he will be decapitated. The rope length is determined by the distance he will drop, plus the distance of his chin from the scaffold crossbeam. Theo probably weighed about 140 pounds by 1897, and therefore his drop distance would be just over seven feet. The heavier the prisoner, the shorter the drop distance.

After the rope has been tightened around the prisoner's neck, the black hood is placed over his head. When the executioner or the warden gives the signal, the trapdoor is dropped. At San Quentin, the trapdoor had three ropes connected to it, and the ropes twisted around and led to a hidden compartment above the gallows where three men stood. Each had a knife, and at the hangman's signal (right arm raised), would cut the rope in front of him. Only one rope dropped the trap, but it was thought that the men would rest easier not knowing for sure if theirs had been the rope to send a man into eternity.

Theo awoke on the morning before his execution after a good night's rest. He had eaten his dinner with no problem, chatted amiably with his guards, and—as far as the deathwatch officer in his cell could tell—slept like a baby.

Two Sisters of Mercy came to pray with him that morning, but after they left, Theo became agitated once again, pacing furiously in his cell as he waited for his final visit from Mamma. (She had finally come to her senses and decided not to witness the execution, although she did want Papa there.) On the other side of the partition, audible preparations were taking place on the gallows structure.

As Theo paced, a loud knocking came at the door of the former factory. The guards admitted a messenger with a note from Captain Edgar: the California Supreme Court had granted a stay of execution. Theo fell to his knees in a rapture, tears in his eyes: "I prayed for life and it has been given to me. My trust is in the Lord."

Alice Rix and Mamma were en route to San Quentin when a messenger stopped the horse-drawn bus they were on to tell her the news. At first, the other passengers thought she was to be told that Theo had committed suicide, but when they heard of the stay, they rejoiced for her in spite of their feelings for the Demon of the Belfry. "I'm glad for her, anyway," one of them said. "Think what she came for, and then to hear this."

Outside the bus, Mamma was laughing hysterically, and one of the women took hold of her gently and brought her back in. She looked, if anything, in worse shape than she had before the news. When they got to the warden's office, Alice was afraid Mamma would collapse. She was babbling uncontrollably and incomprehensibly. "It was a little terrible to see," Alice wrote.

Theo's face reflected a strange, joyful glow. "Dearest," he told Mamma, "I have undergone a great religious experience in the last twenty-four hours. I thank God that this great light came to me in my hour of darkness. It was this wonderful faith that sustained me and gave me courage. We owe my deliverance to the justice and mercy of God." He went on to say that each stay of execution made him think that time would be granted for the "unraveling of those horrible crimes" of which he had no knowledge.

If it was all an act, it was an incredibly convincing one.

The premature telegram sent by the attorney general and the precipitate execution date were the reasons for the California Supreme Court's granting of the certificate of probable cause.[33] Judge Bahrs should have done nothing until officially informed by the U.S. Supreme Court of its decision; furthermore, there was a requirement that at least ten days pass between the sentencing date and the execution date. They would have to go back and do it again.

In his haste to get to San Quentin to serve the papers and stop his client's execution, Eugene Deuprey tripped and fell on a mooring cable on the dock, spraining his thumb and hurting his nose. But his victory in keeping Theo from the gallows yet again must have done much to dispel his discomfort.

Before Theo's next court date another dramatic incident occurred to muddy the waters of the Durrant case: the appearance of a letter purporting to be from the real killer of Blanche and Minnie. A man named Joseph E. Blanther had committed suicide in a Texas jail, but before doing so he had slipped a handwritten confession into the pocket of a cellmate. The cellmate didn't discover the letter until eight months later(!), at which time he passed it along to the prison authorities.[34]

Was it a forgery? The dead man's bank and his lawyers said it wasn't. But was it true? Blanther seems to have been a con artist who traveled throughout the United States under various names and taking up with various people. He accumulated two wives along the way, and also killed a Mrs. Langfeldt in San Francisco (he included this confession in his letter). It was generally known he had killed Mrs. Langfeldt, but Blanche and Minnie?

Chief Lees burst the balloon of all those who wanted to cling to the Blanther letter (notably Mamma) by coming forward with proof that the con man had not been in San Francisco until *after* the Emmanuel Baptist murders. But the Blanther confession entered the lore of the Durrant case.

When Rev. J. George Gibson had been interviewed after Deuprey's opening statement at Theo's trial, he said this to reporters: "What do I know? Mr. Deuprey has not the genius to find out. Had he made a friend of me instead of an enemy, he would have succeeded better. . . . If he had only taken me into his confidence, as he did the other witnesses in the Mission, how different his case would have been."

What Gibson actually meant by this was that he would not have remained neutral in the case and would not have resisted the efforts of the defense—rather, he would have stood by Theo as a friend and supported him. However, many of Theo's backers felt that this statement implied guilty knowledge on the part of the minister. In mid-December 1897, Theo wrote an open letter to Dr. Gibson, published in the *Examiner*, in which he begged the pastor to tell what he knew about the crimes.[35]

After the letter appeared in the newspaper, the police warned Dr. Gibson to watch his back. They had an idea that some of Theo's friends would murder him, then plant a suicide/confession note on him to save the condemned man. They advised him not to eat in restaurants, not to go out at night, and not to talk to any of Theo's supporters. The amiable Lynch had left San Francisco by this time, so Gibson engaged yet another young man of the parish to move in with him.[36]

On December 15, 1897, Theo made his last trip to court. He stood impassively as the judge declared January 7, 1898, as his execution day, and gazed longingly at the blue sky, the sun streaming in the window, and a small piece of grass he could see across the street. He was so oblivious to what was going on around him that Papa had to whisper at him, "Sit down!" while the attorneys wrangled with the judge over legal points.[37]

"Ain't he young!" declared one of the hundreds of curious spectators in the courtroom to her companion. "I'm kinder sorry for him."

"Are you?" her friend answered. "I ain't!" And she laughed.

As the howling mob ran after the wagon that took Theo back to the ferry, Alice Rix was impressed with the efficiency and speed with which the police got him away, one bright spot in "the most frivolous and cruel of American legal farce."

At Christmastime, two weeks before Theo's execution, another sensation emerged. Several prominent San Franciscans had come forward to say that, some time after the trial, they had heard juror Horace Smyth—he of the short fuse—bragging that he had special knowledge during the trial that Theo was a "moral monster" and that he "came by it honestly" (i.e., that he had inherited it). Smyth indicated that he voted "guilty" based on these stories more than on the evidence that was presented in court. Dickinson had Smyth brought in on contempt of court charges and, if he were found guilty, it might mean a new trial for Theo.[38]

The stories told to Smyth concerned Theo's incestuous relations with both Mamma and Maud, stories which had been in currency in San Francisco during and after the trial. In the affidavit filed by Dickinson, these stories were outlined in graphic detail—but, unfortunately for modern researchers, were not reproduced in the newspaper articles. Not even the *Examiner* would go that far.

At the hearing, however, Smyth maintained under oath that, although he had heard the stories, he only learned of them after the case was over. Apparently, the tales outlined in both the affidavit and on the stand were common fare in San Francisco, as the *Chronicle* reporter said that, as disgusting as they were, there were no new sensations there.

Smyth was found not guilty of contempt, but Dickinson immediately filed a slander suit against the "peppery" juror in Papa's name, in the amount of $50,000. This airing of private laundry in the press and the courts, whether the allegations were true or not, gives some indication of how desperate the Durrants were for money, and also hints more than a little at their lack of understanding of appropriate behavior.

Nothing seems to have come of the suit. Dickinson and Deuprey tried to use it as a reason why Theo should be granted another stay of execution (he would be needed to testify at the slander trial), but the ploy did not work. As it turned out, Smyth, the self-styled "capitalist," had no money, and this may be why the suit was dropped.

As Theo's execution day grew closer, the Durrants grew more frantic. Mamma went to see Rev. Gibson to beg him to disclose what he knew, but he refused to see her (after what the police had told him, he probably thought she was there to shoot him). Papa hounded Chief Lees at the police station, babbling about new evidence. After visiting Theo one day in the deathwatch cell, Papa told reporters that in a few days "the truth of the dreadful murders would be made known" and that Theo would be exonerated. In her home, Mamma moaned constantly: "Mamma's sweetheart. Mamma's Theo."

New black-bordered invitations were issued for the January 7 execution. The warden got wind of counterfeits being made and vowed to check every single one at the door.

The Durrants found themselves up against a new problem: no cemetery or crematory would accept the body of the condemned murderer. After the Goldenson execution, there had been reprisals against the Odd Fellows for accepting his body for burial, and no establishment wanted that to happen because of its consent to bury or cremate Theo Durrant.

Theo had wanted to be buried rather than cremated, but Mamma soon disabused him of that notion. First of all, there was the problem of depredation of the body by angry citizens or by ghouls. But most of all, Mamma wanted to keep her boy by her forever.

A woman from Council Bluffs, Iowa, wrote to offer her own burial plot for the Durrants to use for Theo, and young attorney Louis Boardman said they could have his space in a San Francisco cemetery.

In the deathwatch cell, Theo had violent mood swings between high hopes and deep despair. When the latter was upon him, his guards said, he writhed on the floor in agony. Sometimes he would pick up his Bible and stare vacantly at one page for an hour. At other times, he wrote furiously for hours on end. The guards said that when visitors came, Theo would pull himself together and act nonchalant, but after they left he would be on the floor again bemoaning his fate.

And now he wanted to discuss his case. Over and over he analyzed the trial for his guards, pointing out what he saw as the flaws in the prosecution's case and claiming that the whole thing was a conspiracy against him that was designed to protect the real perpetrators. Throughout his diatribe, Theo proclaimed his innocence, so much so that he convinced Captain Jameson, the head of the death watch, that he had not killed Blanche Lamont (Theo does not seem to have discussed the Minnie Williams case).

Two clergymen connected with the prison, Chaplain Drahms and Rev. William Rader, came separately to visit Theo. As he had before, Drahms urged him to confess his sins. This time, Theo became extremely offended and tossed him out. Later, Mamma told Drahms that she did not want him to visit Theo again unless he were convinced of his innocence. Drahms never came back until just before the execution, at which time Theo apologized for his outburst and said he wished to part amicably.

Rader had come by a couple of times and Theo asked him to accompany him to the gallows. But now, a few days before his execution, something happened between them to cause bitterness on Theo's part and Rader, too, was evicted. The minister never revealed exactly what happened, but apparently Theo—in an unguarded moment—said something that convinced Rader of his guilt. After the statement was out, Theo claimed Rader had trapped him. Unfortunately, the minister never made public what it was that Theo had said—possibly to protect the Durrants—but he did share it with Eugene Deuprey.

The day before Theo's execution can only be described as a circus—not the fault of the media, for once, but because of the behavior of Mamma and Papa. General Dickinson had hoped to give the family some peace and privacy to visit with each other that final day, and therefore had told the warden to forbid access to all reporters. Warden Hale ruled that no reporters would be admitted unless Theo asked for them. And, to curtail any dirty tricks on the part of the press, he stipulated that if one reporter managed to sneak in, he would let them all in. No newspaper wanted to be the cause of getting scooped by a rival, so the reporters dutifully hung around outside the prison hoping to waylay anyone with information.

In the meantime, a young Oakland minister named Edwards Davis had come forward to offer his spiritual assistance to the Durrants, now that Theo had dismissed Drahms and Rader. Davis was a slightly pudgy, flamboyant, publicity-loving preacher who wore his hair in a longish, Oscar Wilde style, and had once offered to perform a marriage in a lion's den. (Today, Edwards Davis would probably be a successful televangelist.)

In a sneaky subterfuge, however, Rev. Davis had been secretly hired by the *Examiner* to get an interview with Theo under the auspices of providing him with spiritual counsel. The minister would be able to walk right in under the noses of the prison officials and other reporters, and the *Examiner* would—once again—scoop its rivals. It is unclear whether the Durrants knew about this directly (they later claimed they did not), but some clues that should have tipped them off were that the newspaper had provided the three visitors (Mamma, Papa, and Davis) with a carriage, and had also hired bodyguards (professional prizefighters) to mingle with the prison crowd and see that they weren't bothered.

When the Durrants and Davis emerged from their visit with Theo, reporters converged on them to get some quotable items for their newspapers. However, the pressmen were unceremoniously shoved aside by the prizefighters, who had been told to bustle the trio back into the carriage without allowing them to talk to anyone. Someone recognized the bodyguards as being connected with the *Examiner*, and then things turned ugly. Davis was roughed up in the ensuing brawl and squealed in terror, while Papa tried to be forceful: "Does no one have any respect for a man of God?" he yelled at the crowd. Eventually, Davis and the Durrants were back in the carriage, a little the worse for wear, and spirited away from the prison.

But now the pact had been broken, and Warden Hale declared that one reporter from each newspaper would be allowed to see Theo, if he wished it. And he wished it.

As the reporters talked with Theo through the netting of the deathwatch cell, Mamma sat outside the cage in a rocking chair to monitor the topics. If he ventured into areas that she considered "dangerous" (some of the reporters were convinced she was afraid he would confess), Mamma would say in a warning voice, "You've said quite enough, Theo."

But what sickened and horrified everyone were Mamma's not-so-subtle hints that the newspapers should pay the Durrants for Theo's interview: "Everything that Theo says now is worth a great deal. We have received good offers from all the Eastern papers." She was willing to barter her son's last hours on earth for money instead of allowing him a more tranquil ending, and if he went along with it, it was because her desires were ever the focal point of his existence. (No one offered to pay, however, and Theo kept on talking regardless.)

Warden Hale was disgusted. "Don't talk to me of sympathy for these people," he told reporters angrily. "They have been trying to run the execution. They behave to me as if they were proud of all this."

Pride, indeed, seemed to be one of Mamma's primary emotions, as she grandiosely speculated that Theo would be the greatest martyr in California history and she agreed with him that his wrongful execution would end capital punishment in the state. She reminded him that Christ, too, was misunderstood and executed.

Theo himself was strangely altered that last day. Gone was the agitation, the frenzied pacing, the tormented rehashing of his case. In their place was an almost ecstatic state of calm acceptance, an eagerness, almost, to face death. The *Chronicle* reporter noted that his face glowed as he spoke, primarily on religious topics. "I can not exactly understand the calm that has been given to me," Theo told him.

Again declaring his innocence, Theo said, "It seems as if I were two persons, so distinct are my physical and spiritual natures." Commentators—and, indeed, the *Chronicle* reporter as well— have tried to read into this statement an acknowledgment of a split personality, a Jekyll and Hyde existence. But this takes it somewhat out of context, as he was referring to the gap between his spiritual desires (wanting to be with God) and his physical fear of death.

(Theo was not blessed with a great amount of insight into himself, so it is fruitless to attempt to make more of it.)

For his last interview, Theo quite fittingly chose Alice Rix. "I am extraordinarily happy," he told her, and indeed, she could see that he was curiously elated. He said he felt "uplifted by some power not my own" and that he felt no sorrow except for his family. (Prison guards wondered if he had been hypnotized—it all seemed so unnatural.)

Theo told Alice that he had decided to send for Father Lagan so he could be baptized a Catholic, as he had come to respect that faith and wanted to die in it. Then he proclaimed his innocence once again—the message he wished her to convey to the world on his behalf—and said "good night" instead of "good-bye."

That Theo's state of ecstasy was not an act can be seen in his last letter to his sister, Maud, which he wrote at about midnight after everyone had left. Although he spends much time talking about the weather and how happy the farmers were to get the long-overdue rain (!), he also talks about his buoyancy: "I feel way above ordinary things and trouble seems to have been lifted from my soul."[39]

It could be that Theo still held out hope that Deuprey would be successful in his latest assault on the U.S. Supreme Court, or that Dickinson—who was visiting the governor at his sickbed—would get Budd to grant a stay of execution so he could be tried on the Williams case. He does talk of such hope at the end of his letter to Maud. And when the prison doctor had checked him over that night (finding that his pulse was a normal seventy, within hours of execution), Theo told him that a cut on his lip (from the barber) would go away "in a few days." So it may be that he was oblivious to the reality he faced. It would not be the first time.

But the real proof would come the next day.

On the last morning of his life, Theo Durrant arose after an unbroken sleep and devoured a hearty breakfast: steak, potatoes, eggs, ham, tea, and toast. He spent a lot of time fixing his clothing and tying his tie. When he saw the socks they had brought for him, he was dismayed. He wanted dark ones, he said, and his guards obliged. He got permission to wear a stand-up collar, which would have to be removed before the rope was put around his neck. And he turned down the offers of whiskey to help settle his nerves. He would go to the gallows without sedation.

All of this can be seen as either overweening vanity, or a desire to put the best face on his ignominious end—and probably a little of both. Theo would not have wanted to face his detractors looking as if he minded being executed. He had the idea, drummed into him by Mamma, that innocent people are calm and unafraid, whereas the guilty break down in despair. Poor Theo! He never understood that the attitude he tried so hard to present to the world was the very one that made everyone believe he was capable of murdering two young women in cold blood.

Father Lagan came and administered the sacraments: Baptism, Confirmation, Penance, Holy Eucharist, and Extreme Unction (the rite for the dying). Many cynics thought Theo had converted because of the sacred inviolability of the Catholic confessional: Father Lagan would be forever bound to keep secret any admission of guilt. But the guards said that Theo raised his voice at one point, exclaiming, "No! I will not confess the murders, because I am not guilty." And Father Lagan later said he believed Theo to be innocent.[40]

Theo's farewells to his parents were curiously lacking (on his part, anyway) in their previous excesses of maudlin grief. He shook hands warmly with Papa, whose eyes were filled with tears. Theo's sister had sent him a locket containing her picture, intending it for a New Year's present, but the Durrants thought it would upset Theo too much to see it. Now, however, Papa gave it to his son, who put it in his pocket and said, "Now we are together forever."[41]

Mamma threw herself upon him, exclaiming, "Theo, my Theo, my dear boy, my darling," and the like. She kissed him "passionately" (according to the *Chronicle*) and clung to him. But soon he gently removed her arms from around his neck, took her hands, and placed them inside Papa's. Then he closed his own hands around those of his parents and quietly said, "Good-bye."

Father Lagan recited the prayers for the dead as the procession made its way to the door of the execution room. Over the previous week, Theo's guards had thought he would break down, and Amos Lunt, the hangman, had ordered the standing board to be readied for use. But no board would be needed today: Theo mounted the stairs with alacrity, even ahead of the guards assigned to hold him up.

Up on the scaffold, Amos Lunt got ready to drop the rope over Theo's head. The hangman had been drinking whiskey since breakfast to fortify himself for this deed—probably because it was important for such a high-profile execution to go smoothly. Lunt didn't want any hanging horrors to be fodder for the press. But he didn't notice any nervousness in the man he was about to send to meet his Maker—not even a tremor.

As Lunt held the rope over the condemned man's head, Theo told him, "Don't put that rope on, my boy, until after I talk." Too late—the rope was around his neck. Theo smiled a little sheepishly, then said, "Well, don't tighten it then." With his arms pinned to his sides and his legs strapped as well, Theo attempted a dignified stance and addressed the crowd below with an obviously memorized speech:

Do you wish me to say anything? Well, I would like to say this: I have no animosity against any one, nor even against those who have persecuted me and who have hounded me to my grave, innocent as I am. I forgive them all. They will receive their justice from the Holy God above, to whom I now go to receive my justice, which will be the justice given to an innocent boy who has not stained his hands with crimes that have been put upon him by the press of San Francisco; but I forgive them all.

I do not hold anything against the reporters. I do not look upon them now as enemies. I forgive them as I expect to be forgiven for everything that I have done, but the fair name of California will forever be blackened with the crime of taking this innocent blood, and whether or no they ever discover the committers of this crime matters little to me now, for I, before the whole world, announce my innocence for the last time, and to those who have insinuated that I was going to spring a sensation of any kind, I must say there is no sensation other than that which I have said. Those who wish to consider it a sensation may do so, but I am innocent of the crimes charged to me before God, who knows the heart and can read the mind. I am innocent.

Theo might have gone on with his speech, but an unnerved Amos Lunt took advantage of a slight pause after his last word to drop the black hood over his head and raise his hand in signal. The trap dropped open, and Theo plummeted through it with a loud crash. His neck was snapped immediately, so it was not likely that he suffered other than a momentary pain.

Eleven minutes later, Theo Durrant was officially declared dead.

Amos Lunt, who had previously hanged thirteen men without a qualm, and who had declared to Alice Rix in a November interview that it never bothered him to do his job, had a slight nervous breakdown after Theo's execution. He had never seen anyone so calm on the scaffold, and the thought crossed his mind that he was hanging an innocent man.

Several of those who stood at eye level to where the body hung under the scaffolding felt sick and had to leave.

During Theo's speech, which was delivered in a clear, unwavering voice, Papa seemed to be trying to get his son's attention. He held his arms out in front of him and opened his mouth as if to cry out. But Father Lagan, up on the scaffold, had effectively placed himself so that Theo could not see Papa below him. After the trap dropped, William Durrant buried his head in the shoulder of the young attorney from Deuprey's office who had accompanied him. Then he screamed defiantly, "How's that for a brave boy?"

San Quentin officials arranged Theo's body, with its blackened and swollen face, in a prison coffin. But when Papa came to collect it, he was furious: the Durrants had supplied a coffin, and he demanded to know why Theo had not been put in it. Finally, the mixup was settled and the body was placed in the right coffin, then taken to a small room off the gallows area.

When Mamma was admitted to the room to see her dead son, she threw herself on the coffin, crying out, "My boy, my boy, my precious darling, they have murdered you," over and over. She kissed his lips, and in general put on quite a scene.

There is one more gruesome story that comes out of this encounter, related in macabre detail by the *Call* and summarized by the *Examiner*.[42] Apparently, the convict in charge of the rooms in the furniture factory asked Mamma if she would like some tea as she and Papa sat next to the coffin looking at their son. Mamma said she would, but the convict came back with a kind of British version of tea, including cold meat and other food items.

A table was set up for the Durrants not three feet from the coffin, and the food set upon it. As they stood watching Theo's parents enjoy their food, the convicts heard Mamma say, "Papa, give me some more of the roast."

With this chilling little story, the *Call* more than made up for its decision—alone among the newspapers—not to include sketches of the hanging. This version of the incident is always included in accounts of the case. In fairness to the Durrants, however, it must be asked why the convict chose to respond to Mamma's desire for a cup of tea with a groaning board of food dishes if he thought it would be inappropriate for the grieving parents to eat anything.

The *Examiner* felt that the Durrants were so relieved that Theo did not break down and confess that their appetites had come back with a vengeance. And there may be some truth to this. Mamma's interviews throughout the ordeal always included the firm conviction (a directive to Theo?) that her son would never confess, would never break down. Surely, in their private discussions, she imbued him with the necessity of holding his head up and not giving his "enemies" any reason to think he might be guilty.

Theo himself, whatever his inclinations might have been to confess, must have felt that he had given his family enough grief without adding a confession to it. In 1957, a death row inmate at San Quentin, convicted on circumstantial evidence as Theo Durrant had been, was told by the prison psychiatrist that if he admitted his guilt, the governor might grant him executive clemency and commute his sentence to life. "Doc, I can't admit it," Burton Abbott told him. "Think of what it would do to my mother. Doc, she could not take it."[43]

As for what Theo had unwittingly revealed to Rev. William Rader, Joseph H. Jackson relates that after the execution, Eugene Deuprey told Edgar Peixotto not to be troubled about his part in Theo's conviction, as he had "confessed his guilt to the priest in San Quentin."[44] Now, this could not have referred to Father Lagan for three reasons: First, a priest can never reveal anything that has been told to him in the confessional; second, the guards overheard Theo proclaiming his innocence to the priest; and third, Father Lagan specifically expressed his personal belief in Theo's innocence— which he would never have done if there had been an admission of guilt in the confessional. On the other hand, Rader said that he not only believed Theo to be guilty, but *knew* him to be such as the result of a conversation they had at San Quentin.

The *Examiner* paid for the carriage that took the Durrants and the casket back to Fair Oaks Street after the execution. It was placed in the front parlor in a sort of shrine, while a crematorium could be found that would consent to accept Theo's body. (Since

Theo had died a Catholic, officials at Holy Cross Cemetery said he could be buried there, but Mamma wanted him cremated.)[45]

At the house, Mamma spent her days talking to her dead son and kissing his lips. Although the marks of the hanging (except for the rope burn around the neck) eventually disappeared, his eyes and mouth had never been completely closed. And, as there was no embalming because of the planned cremation, signs of decomposition soon set in. (Luckily, it was the month of January, which even in temperate San Francisco, is chilly.)

Outside, morbid onlookers gathered by the hundreds to watch the house and all who entered or left it. For souvenirs, they picked flowers from bushes in the yard.

At last, a compassionate crematorium in southern California consented to cremate Theo: Reynolds & Van Nuys in Pasadena. The casket was sealed in an airtight shipping container and, in the dead of night to avoid spectators, the undertaker and the Durrants went to the railway station for the trip. (The undertaker was Theo's former Cogswell classmate who had testified to his good character at the trial: Herbert Porter.)

At the crematorium, Mamma wanted to spend more time with Theo before consigning him to the flames. She also ordered that everything else be burned up in the furnace—the casket and its shipping container—so that nothing could be distributed for souvenirs. After another tearful good-bye and a farewell kiss, she watched through the glass window of the retort as Theo's body entered the two thousand-degree flames. When it was all over, the Durrants collected the urn and went back to resume their lives in San Francisco.

Despite the almost universal rejoicing in San Francisco and elsewhere that the Demon of the Belfry was well and truly dead at last, there must have been many who felt that "nothing in his life became him like the leaving it."[46]

Killer Angel: Murder in the Emmanuel Baptist Church

This case has never been fathomed. There is a mystery deep
and intricate which I believe some day will be revealed. . . .
Some people imagine I can clear the mystery, but this is a
mistaken idea.

—Theo Durrant, November 12, 1897

What happened to Theo Durrant to turn him from a mild-
mannered, gentlemanly medical student into the slayer of Blanche
Lamont and Minnie Williams? What happened to cause a young
man of such great promise to go so terribly wrong? Was he a sexual
psychopath finally acting out on fantasies he had harbored for
years beneath a false religious exterior?

That Theo was *not* a psychopath is readily evident in his relations with his family and friends, in his ability to empathize with
others, in his ability to stay focused on school and employment,
in his kindness to animals, and in a total absence of any suggestion
of cruelty prior to the murders.[1]

Modern criminologists believe that the best predictor of future
violence is past violence,[2] but there was none of that in Theo's
background. Detectives and reporters spent a great deal of time

and effort trying to find examples of aberrant behavior, going as far back as his childhood, yet came up empty. Had anything been found, even if it had not been presented at trial, it would have been written up in the newspapers.

Although Theo's taking of Blanche's rings and Minnie's purse after he murdered them could be seen as typical behavior of the serial killer (the keeping of trophies or "souvenirs" for the purpose of reliving the crime), his treatment of these items doesn't fit the pattern.[3] He tried to pawn what he considered to be the most expensive of Blanche's rings (the one with the chip diamond), and when this failed, he sent them all back to her family.

Minnie's purse was stuck in his coat pocket, either at her own request, or because he wanted to see if it contained money, or—the likeliest reason—because he wanted to make it look as if Minnie had been killed by a mugger. He left the overcoat hanging in the Durrants' front hallway; if he had taken the purse as a trophy, he would have removed it from the inside pocket and taken it upstairs to his room. He would not have left it in such a public area, where Mamma (who probably routinely went through his things) could have come across it. Also, his reaction when told that the police had found the purse was one of "Uh-oh. I forgot to get rid of that darned thing."

So the murders of Blanche Lamont and Minnie Williams were most likely the beginning and the end of Theo's murderous career. To explain the explosion that caused them, we need to examine three areas: neurology, biochemistry, and the genetic and behavioral influence of his parents.

NEUROLOGICAL INFLUENCES

In April and May 1894, just a year before the Emmanuel Baptist murders, Theo Durrant lay dying of bacterial meningitis (called "brain fever" at that time).[4] Even with today's antibiotics, not available back then, the fatality rate for meningitis is as high as 30 percent and the incidence of brain damage in those who survive is 40 percent.[5] These figures are *with* antibiotics, and were no doubt much higher in 1894 without them.

A 1997 study of forty-one murderers by Professor Adrian Raine of the University of Southern California indicated significant neurological damage in the impulse-control areas of the brain, damage that may cause a predisposition to violence.[6]

Likewise, a twenty-five-year study of murderers on death row by a psychiatrist and a neurologist yielded similar results: the subjects all exhibited signs of neurological damage to the impulse control centers of the brain:

When we disconnect the pathways between our reptilian brain and our frontal cortex, we no longer have good control of our anger. Accidents and injuries often do just that kind of damage. If the connection between our frontal lobes and limbic system are disrupted, how responsible are we for flying off the handle? It's a hard call.[7]

Clearly, Theo's bout with meningitis would not have left him without some brain damage. And there are at least two indicators that the Durrant children may have inherited neurological weakness from one or both parents: the death of little Edward from "infantile convulsions" and the notation on Maud Durrant's death certificate that she had suffered from "cerebral arteriosclerosis with chronic brain syndrome." Those inherited defects, if they existed, would have been exacerbated by the meningitis and its resultant swelling of the brain.

Theo's fit-like "nightmares" in City Prison could have been due to neurological short circuits, but as they were only reported as occurring twice, there is not enough evidence to come to a more definite conclusion.

BIOCHEMICAL INFLUENCES

It is practically certain that Papa Durrant suffered from manic depression. His impetuous trip to Philadelphia on the "green goods" scheme in December 1894, and his subsequent week-long bout with depression; his curious fits of abstraction; his inability to remain steadily employed; and the delegation of his household tasks (such as the ordering of the coal) to his son, all point to this. In addition, there are some references in Maud Durrant's diaries to Papa's strange behavior (unspecified), as if it were a regular occurrence.[8]

Manic depression is now known to be highly heritable, particularly through the father's side. Whether Theo exhibited signs of it before his meningitis is not known, but it is certain that he did afterward. For most patients, manic depression surfaces in their twenties, exactly when it seems to have done with Theo.

The wild mood swings Theo experienced after his arrest, particularly during his time at San Quentin, could be seen as the natural result of incarceration and impending execution. However, Lucile Turner—who had only known him since his illness—said that even before his arrest he was subject to "gloomy spells," during which it was best to leave him alone.[9]

The *DSM-IV* (*Diagnostic and Statistical Manual of Mental Disorders, Fourth Edition*) outlines the symptoms of the manic, or elevated, mood phase of this disease:[10]

1. Inflated self-esteem or grandiosity;
2. Decreased need for sleep;
3. More talkative than usual;
4. Flight of ideas;
5. Distractibility;
6. Increase in goal-directed activity (either socially, at work or school, or sexually), or psychomotor agitation;
7. Excessive involvement in pleasurable activities which have high potential for painful consequences (unrestrained buying sprees, sexual indiscretions, or foolish business investments).

Theo often talked about staying up late into the night (to study, to work on drawings, etc.). In fact, on the night of Minnie's murder, he said he had come home late after the party at Tom Vogel's and stayed up to work on his senior thesis for med school, even though he had to get up at 5:00 A.M. to go on his Signal Corps weekend. And he probably told the truth in this. His success in medical school, despite his struggles, was undoubtedly the result of many such nights.

Theo's grandiose thoughts, wherein he saw himself as a martyr and the means by which capital punishment would be eliminated in California, are indicative of a self-involved personality; but they could also be manifestations of manic depression. Hyperreligiosity, the constant pacing, the paranoid thoughts, the euphoria that preceded his execution, the occasional fits of irritability, even the abstracted behavior during his trial—all of these are part of the disease.

And Theo's constant talking about women, which he seems to have started the year before the murders, is also indicative of manic depression. A survey of nurses involved with manic-depressive patients found that in the manic phase these patients "talked about sex" or were "sexually preoccupied" to a marked degree.[11]

THEO'S UPBRINGING

There can be no doubt that, whatever else may have affected him, the Durrant family was the seat of much of Theo's trouble. Both of his parents exhibited considerable mental instability, and Mamma's obsession with him must have had a profound influence on his relations with women. Papa's physical absences from the family, his mental absences due to abstraction (from whatever cause), his inability to function consistently as the head and breadwinner of the family, and Mamma's setting up of her son to take his place, all had a damaging effect on Theo's psychic development.

There was an undercurrent of incest that ran through Theo's relations with his mother and his sister that, even if never overt, caused him to focus his entire emotional life on these two women. He seems to have tried to break away and forge relationships with women outside the family, but the damage to his psyche may have been too great. Theo is depicted as sensitive, and the evidence supports this. It would have taken a more callous nature than his to emerge unscathed from this emotionally crippling influence.

Were the incest allegations correct? We can never know for sure. At the very least, Mamma Durrant was flirtatious and seductive with her son; and there is his plea to his sister not to reveal the fact that he had "slept with" their mother (see chapter 3). However, Theo was a prude, a romantic, and an idealist when it came to women, and as late as 1893 he was still a virgin. Hence, it is probable that the Victorian mentality of the day misinterpreted the relationships in the Durrant household—unhealthy though they undoubtedly were—as full-blown incest.

Maud Durrant, who takes a back seat in the press through the years of Theo's trial, incarceration, and execution, is portrayed by those who knew her before her departure for Berlin as a gentle, ladylike person. Yet, she did not turn out this way. In Felix Cherniavsky's book, *The Salome Dancer*, her letters, her diaries, and the incidents related by others reveal a selfish, often mean-spirited person, and almost certainly a pathological liar. In spite of Theo's adoration of her, she does not seem to have had any real desire to come back home to see him, even when she knew his execution was imminent. Maud was more concerned with interrupting her career and with the negative attention she might have received in San Francisco.

All of this is to say that Maud did not escape unscathed from the unstable Durrant household. She, too, was damaged. Her brother's execution cannot be seen as the event that caused a complete turnaround in her personality; no one changes that drastically as a result of one traumatic experience. She must have had those traits to begin with, however infrequently they manifested themselves prior to January 1898.

The mental weakness exhibited by the entire Durrant family may have had its source in inherited genetics, as well as in learned behavior. Again, from such a distance and absent other evidence, we can never know for sure.

THE PRECIPITATING EVENT

Criminal behaviorists look for a significant event, a stressor, that causes an individual to cross the line into murder. These events are always of great magnitude: the breakup of an important relationship, the loss of a job, the death of a loved one.[12] In Theo's life, the stressor was the departure of his sister Maud on February 14. It was no accident that Blanche Lamont was murdered a mere seven weeks later.

Maud herself may have guessed as much. In her diary, she notes that if she had been there, this would not have happened;[13] and it is likely that she suffered a great deal of guilt over the effect of her absence on her brother.

THE EMMANUEL BAPTIST MURDERS

Obviously, we will never know exactly what happened in the church between Theo and his two victims on April 3 and 12, 1895. But it is possible to speculate on what *might* have happened, based on what is known about Theo, his victims, and current findings in medicine and psychology.

Not even District Attorney Barnes believed that Theo set off from his home on April 3 with the intention of killing Blanche Lamont.[14] Although Barnes did think his intention was to meet up with her for purposes of seduction, this is probably not true. From all reports, Blanche and Theo had little to do with each other since the end of January—so why would he suddenly decide on Wednesday, April 3, to accost her on her streetcar stop? Besides, she was running late (he could have lied about this, but then her aunt and her sister would have made it known that Blanche had left in plenty of time), and he could easily have missed her if she hadn't been. It is only her uncustomary lateness that brought them together that morning.

There are two reasons why Theo might legitimately have been going to see George King on his way to school that morning. One was that George needed help carrying down the cabinet organ from the auditorium, and Theo wanted to tell him he'd be at church that afternoon. Another was exactly what Theo always claimed, only with a little twist: Frank Sademan had been complaining about the big chandelier in the lobby, that it was giving off a little gas and didn't light properly. Theo might have wanted to fix the stopcock on the chandelier that day, and wanted to make sure George would be there to help him by turning the gas on and off. When he needed to explain his presence *upstairs* in the church, he merely transferred the location of the repairs.

However, on his way to Capp Street, Theo saw Blanche Lamont waiting on her car stop. He may have asked her to go with him to George King's, or he may have abandoned that mission to accompany her. Either way, she most likely did *not* ask him to go with her, as he would claim later; he would have taken this on himself.

Once on the car together—and this must be emphasized—Blanche and Theo were very much enjoying each other. In fact, every single witness who saw them that day said the same thing: They were having a good time; they were absorbed in their conversation; they were laughing; they were not in any hurry.

If there is a mystery in this case, it lies in the behavior of Blanche Lamont. She had scorned Theo's advances, she had laughed at and made fun of him to her family, and she had not had much to do with him in more than two months. Yet, the way she related to him on April 3 went beyond the bounds of mere social politeness. Not only that, but the very ambitious, very conscientious Blanche Lamont was so involved with him that day that she either completely forgot about her music lesson with Professor Schernstein, or she decided to skip it in favor of spending time with Theo Durrant. What could explain this behavior?

The answer may be found in some of the manifestations of the manic phase, which Theo was almost certainly in that day (his nervous pacing for an hour, witnessed by Mary Vogel, gives it away). Here is what Dr. Kay Redfield Jamison, noted expert on the disease and herself a manic depressive, has to say about it:

When you're high it's tremendous . . . Shyness goes, the right words and gestures are suddenly there, the power to captivate others a felt certainty. There are interests found in uninteresting people. Sensuality is pervasive and the desire to seduce and be seduced irresistible. Feelings of ease, intensity, power, well-being, financial omnipotence, and euphoria pervade one's marrow.[15]

Anyone who has ever known a bipolar person can attest to the irresistible magnetism of the manic phase. If Theo were in it when he encountered Blanche Lamont, he must have presented himself as extraordinarily glib, charming, and witty. She may not have seen this side of him before (all things considered, they had really not spent that much time together), and she may have thought to herself that he deserved a second look as a suitor. Perhaps she even flirted with him a little—the implication is there in the witnesses' statements.

So, by the time Theo got to Cooper that morning, he may have been "high" on her reaction to him as well as on the manic phase itself. He would have found it difficult to sit through lectures because of his natural restlessness and his thoughts of Blanche. Indiscretion is ever the hallmark of the manic phase, and he decided he would wait for her after school and see exactly how receptive she might be to him. She had mentioned to him that morning that she needed a book, *The Newcomes*, and he had told her he had a copy. Why not use that as his excuse now? He would say that the copy was in the church library because he had donated it, and they could just swing by and check it out.

Blanche had probably told him in the course of conversation

what time her new school let out. Theo showed up early, not so much because he was afraid of missing her, but because he was too "antsy" to sit still at school. She was probably not expecting him, but her reaction on seeing him showed that she was pleased he was there.

On their way to the church, Theo might have expounded on the delights of *The Newcomes*. How he must have loved that book! It would exactly fit his idealistic, romantic nature. And there were characters that matched himself, Blanche (or his sister, Maud, with whom he significantly identified her), even Rev. Gibson. So, as they walked along, *sauntering* toward the church (both Martin Quinlan and Caroline Leak noticed this), he was quite possibly enthralling her with the saga of this family of heroes, rogues, scoundrels, and ne'er-do-wells, and the compelling tale of two lovers kept apart by a well-meaning but snobbish grandmother. Blanche would have found his account (and maybe him) irresistible; maybe she couldn't wait to start reading it. At the very least, she would have been overjoyed to be getting a free copy, as she had told her aunt she didn't want to pay for it.

Once inside the little library, perhaps Blanche stood looking at the books on the shelves while Theo pretended to look for *The Newcomes* (it was actually at his house). Then, he might have—as he had that January when she came to 1025 Fair Oaks to get her Christmas present—come up behind her and put his arms around her, mistakenly taking her friendly response, and maybe her flirtatiousness, to indicate that she would welcome a sexual advance.

Blanche's immediate reaction would probably have been anger or outrage—or, even worse, laughter. Perhaps she even threatened to tell others about this—certainly her aunt, and possibly Theo's mother. His standing in the community would be ruined, and above all he would never want Mamma to find out. Did he act out in a manic rage? Or did he try to keep her quiet, blocking her way until she agreed to say nothing of the incident?

Whatever the dynamic between them in the library at this point, the situation quickly escalated beyond his ability to control it, or himself. It is likely that Theo choked her at this point, maybe initially to keep her from screaming, or simply out of rage. However, she was probably not dead yet. He told Carrie Cunningham that "she was killed on the second landing" and, as this was an attempt at a confession, it must be seen as true. Backing him up are the drops of blood found on the second landing of the belfry, the natural result of strangulation.

Let us suppose, then, that Blanche passed out from the choking, or from one of those strange cataleptic spells she may have been subject to (if these were real, they were stress-related).[16] Theo probably thought he had killed her. *Now* what could he do? George King would be arriving soon, and there was a service there that evening.

So he picked her up and carried her to the belfry. His panic would have given him adrenaline to carry someone his own weight, and he probably threw her over his shoulder like a sack of flour to free his hands and make it easier to negotiate the turns on the belfry stairs. But when he got to the second landing, Blanche began showing signs of coming to. She wasn't dead! Too late, though: What would she think about his carrying her to the belfry in an unconscious condition? There was no way he could explain, so he would have finished right there what he thought he had finished downstairs.

Theo would not have had time to remove Blanche's clothes and hide them. He probably only had time to disable the door so no one would be tempted to visit the belfry before he could finish. (We know he did that much, because the gasfitter noticed it on Thursday morning at 10:00.) Then he went downstairs to confront George King.

George's testimony, and the rumors of what he told his friends in the Mission District, indicate that Theo was suffering, not from gas asphyxiation, but from emotional shock. He had never intended to hurt Blanche, and now she was dead. He must have found it impossible to get his mind around it.

Dr. Jamison and others say that after the manic phase the patient does not always remember, or remember completely, what he has done. Confronted by friends and family, he will deny it—because he does not remember. However, it cannot be said that Theo forgot completely what he had done, even if some of it may have been hazy to him later (Dr. Jamison says of one of her episodes, "Once I think I shoplifted a blouse . . . Or maybe I just thought about shoplifting, I don't remember, I was totally confused.")[17] His later attempts to hide Blanche's clothes, pawn her rings, and defuse suspicion from himself all militate against a total amnesia.

On the other hand, is it not possible that the deed was so horrible that he was shocked out of his manic phase immediately afterward and was then faced with the enormity of what he'd done? The evidence would be right there in front of him—no possibility of placing the blame elsewhere—yet, how *could* he have done it? This was not like him at all.

In this may lie the source of Theo's persistent, and often convincing, protestations of innocence (and probably the reason why he does not always include Minnie in these protestations): "The person who committed this deed is not the person I know myself to be. Therefore, I did not do it. It was an unexplainable aberration that I do not intend to acknowledge; it is no part of me." Perhaps over time he even convinced himself that it was not he who killed Blanche Lamont, or that it had been an accident.[18]

It is not likely that Theo raped Blanche. Dr. Barrett thought not, and psychologically he may have even been impotent with regard to her because of his association of her with his sister. This might have been true even if she had accepted his advances, and that raises another interesting scenario: What if Blanche *did* respond to him? Would he have been horrified at her fall from the pedestal (where he kept most of the women he knew)? Did he kill her because of that, as he threatened to shoot Maud if he found out she had gone to the indecent Grotto?

Whatever happened that day in the Emmanuel Baptist Church, there is no doubt that Theo had not intended the result, and no doubt that he felt sorrow over Blanche's death—whatever he told himself about how she came to it.

What might George King have kept secret about that day? He probably did not lie about the gas smell, because it was well known that the lobby chandelier leaked gas. What he lied about was the library door. George said that he had found it open, and when he went in to check the gas jet, he did not notice Theo's hat and coat there. This is probably true. What is most likely *not* true is that George then locked the door behind him.

Theo must have taken off his hat when he went into the church (manners dictated this), but his coat would have stayed on if he and Blanche were only going to check out a book and leave. After she passed out or died and Theo realized he'd have to carry her to the belfry, he would have taken his coat off and maybe thrown it on the floor somewhere (he would have been desperate, and also in a desperate hurry), and George may not have noticed it when he went in later.

Theo didn't think to take his key with him to the belfry; it was in his coat pocket. Later, he sent George to the drugstore for the Bromo-Seltzer for two reasons: because he really did need it (he was nauseated); and because he had to get George out of the church so he could quickly retrieve his hat and coat from the floor of the library (or from wherever else in the church he had put them) and arrange them neatly on the box as if they'd been there all along, as if nothing of a violent nature had caused him to re-move them.

Theo could easily have convinced George that the lie was a little one, but one that would help his case. George's statement that he locked the door and Theo opened it with his own key took away the state's contention that he needed to seek George out because he had to get to his coat and hat. But what he really needed was to put his hat and coat *in* the library, in a place they could be readily seen. Then it was only natural to "suggest" that George was confused about not having noticed them when he first went in.

Another possibility is that George locked the door and Theo did not have his key with him, that he asked to borrow George's key and then sent him to the drugstore. Later, he would tell George to omit the part about borrowing the key.

On the other hand, if Theo really did keep his key with him and George really did lock the door, then that means that Theo merely unlocked the door to replace the hat and coat, then relocked it and met George in the lobby as he returned from the drugstore. But this scenario would leave George with no guilty knowledge, and that is not likely.

If George did not lock the door, or if Theo had his key with him, why would he approach George at all when he could have left the church unseen? He may have been in such a state of shock that he was not thinking clearly; and George, after all, was one of his best friends. George said Theo stood in the doorway for some time without saying anything, and this supports a theory of shock. If Theo were thinking clearly, however, he might have realized that an unsuspecting dupe like George would provide a perfect backup to his alibi about the gas.

Theo's story about fixing the sunburners could be so precise and so detailed because he *had* worked on them—the janitor had seen him do it at least five times. But he hadn't done it on April 3.

When Theo walked George home, going out of his way to do so, it wasn't to prevent his friend from returning to the church; it was to clear his own head and try to regain a semblance of composure. Perhaps the whole thing had an air of unreality to it ("Did this really happen? When I go back to the belfry, will the body still be there?"). On his way home, he took the time to chat with some people he knew, instead of saying, "I'm late for dinner. Got to run!"

Ted Bundy, certainly one of our more prolific serial killers, said that his first murder shocked him so much that he felt the need to throw himself into his normal activities so that he could *feel* normal, that maybe it hadn't happened after all.[19] If a man who would go on to murder dozens, perhaps even hundreds, of women could have this reaction to his first murder, then certainly Theo— who was not a serial killer—would have had a similar reaction. His going about his normal routine after murdering Blanche—talking to neighbors, going to church, attending his classes—was undoubtedly an attempt at reestablishing his equilibrium, even though at the time it was deemed cold-blooded.

When Theo got home that night, he was unable to eat. And how coincidental that the Durrants had received a letter from Maud that very day! He grabbed it like a lifeline and read it to his parents.

At some later time, after Thursday morning, Theo went back to the belfry to take Blanche's clothes off (if he had not done so already) and hide them around the rafters. His loving treatment of her body must be seen as a sign of his remorse, and he may have even "visited" with her when he went back to hide the clothes. ("It's a viewing pose," says mortuary scientist Darrell Harman. "He spent some time looking at her.")[20]

During this second trip, Theo permanently disabled the door, making it impossible for anyone to get into the belfry (including himself) without kicking down the door. Then he crawled from the belfry to the false ceiling, and down through the opening.

By Friday, April 5, Theo must have been going crazy. The Nobles had not said anything about Blanche's being missing, and he must have wondered about their silence. That day, he tried to pawn her ring, possibly thinking it was worth something. He had money in the bank, true, but Mamma kept a close watch on it and those funds were earmarked for his education. Why didn't Theo just throw the rings away? That would have eliminated two witnesses against him at his trial. And an even more foolish move was sending them to Mrs. Noble, which he probably did to focus the blame on George King and Professor Schernstein. This shows he was not thinking clearly.

George King's grandfather, Rufus Moore, had an interesting story to tell. When everyone at Emmanuel was worried about Blanche, Moore made a comment to Theo about the music professor, not knowing that he was an old man, and hinting that maybe the two had eloped after the months of proximity over the violin lessons. Theo, who may have also been unaware that the professor was elderly, responded, "Blanche did not care for men in that way."[21] (Did he think her rejection of him equated to a rejection of all men?) This conversation occurred prior to his sending the rings with the professor's name on the wrapper, and possibly inspired it.

After Theo went to Oppenheim's pawnshop, he went to Lucile Turner's school. He was probably going to make it look as if he just chanced upon her rather than sought her out—hence the elaborate ruse about taking the tour of the school. But why did he want to see Lucile Turner?

By this time, it is entirely possible that Theo Durrant was in such a state that he needed to confess to someone. He had to get this off his chest, although he may not have been ready to implicate himself. Theo did best with women, and his usual confidante (Maud) was not available (of course, if she had been, Blanche would not have been killed). Lucile was unsophisticated and would not question him too much; moreover, she would be sympathetic, as she usually was with him.

But Lucile was not in school that day, and Theo must have been frustrated. Who could he turn to? And he thought of Minnie Williams.

Theo did not know that Minnie Williams would be in the city that night or he would undoubtedly have tried to hook up with her then. Instead, the next day (Saturday), he went across the Bay to Alameda, where he was seen by Patrolman Dennis Welch. The conversation he had with Minnie that day is the one to which she referred when she spoke with Clark Morgan about "the same topic as last time."

What would that topic have been? In all probability, it was the same as, or similar to, the story he later told Carrie Cunningham: that he had seen Blanche's dead body and the perpetrators had threatened Mamma and forced him into submission. Nobody else knew, he would tell her, and he was afraid to go to the police.

But instead of sympathy and support, what Theo would have gotten from the practical Minnie Williams would have been an angered outburst that *of course* he should go to the police. What was he thinking? She may have even been so foolish as to suggest that if *he* didn't do it, she would contact them herself.

Now, this would never do. On April 6, as far as Theo knew, the Nobles had not even reported Blanche as missing. If Minnie were to go to the police with this tale, then it would come right back to him. He pleaded with her for the life of his mother, but she was adamant. And he was desperate.

On Sunday, April 7, Tom Vogel informed Theo at church that Blanche was missing, and that Detective Anthony wanted to interview him. That evening, he went to Tom Vogel's house and answered some questions, admitting to Anthony that he and Blanche had ridden to school together that morning. It must have unnerved him incredibly to be connected with her disappearance so soon.

But disappearance was one thing and murder entirely another. For all Theo could tell, Blanche would never be discovered in the belfry until she had turned into an unrecognizable skeleton. With no clothes to identify her, they could never be entirely sure it was she. And that meant they could never successfully prosecute Theo for her murder, no matter how much they suspected him. But Minnie could lead them right to the belfry before decomposition took place.

The next day, Monday, April 8, Theo skipped his classes at Cooper, getting Harry Partridge to answer for him, and went back to Alameda to try to convince Minnie to change her mind. He invited her to San Francisco to see a play that evening, probably thinking that wining and dining her might do the trick. It is unlikely he would have extended such an open invitation right on her front porch if he had plans to murder her in the city during their date.

But Minnie was not interested in going to the city. Besides, she did not intend to open up this conversation again—she would remain adamant that Theo should do the right thing by going to the police and reporting Blanche's murder. Once the killers were caught, Theo and his family would have nothing to fear from them. She told him she would talk to him at the Young People's party on Friday night.

Theo must have been in agony all week, wondering if the axe would fall on him. Blanche's disappearance was the talk of the Mission, if not the city, and on Friday Minnie would be coming over to add her two cents! Would she reveal what he had told her?

By Friday, Theo had concocted a plan (just as Minnie loved to do) that he thought would work to keep her from the party and get her into the church. And now he *did* intend to kill her, because he could not see any other way out of it. It was imperative that Mamma and Maud *never* hear anything about what he might have done to Blanche, and he would do anything to keep their adoration intact.

What would most appeal to Minnie Williams? We know that she loved meddling and gossip, and Theo knew this, too. Here's what he might have said to her as he intercepted her after waiting all afternoon at the ferry terminal:

Let's sneak into the pastor's study and see if we can find evidence that definitely shows him to be the murderer. He and the others will be at the social tonight, so we can do this without being caught. If we go to the police now, it will just be my word against his—and he's a minister of God. I need to find some definite proof before I say anything.

Minnie would have jumped at this exciting opportunity to spy and maybe catch a murderer. The Voys noticed she was in particularly good spirits that evening, *and* she never mentioned going anywhere before attending the party at Tom Vogel's. Since we know she went right from the Voys' to meet Theo at the church, she deliberately kept this from her friends—which indicates a secret rendezvous. And this rendezvous could not have been for a sexual encounter, when so many previous opportunities were not taken advantage of. Why would she consent to that now when she was expected at Tom Vogel's shortly? Nor could their meeting have been for the purpose of taking her name off the membership list. Minnie had been very vocal about wanting to take care of this, and the subject even came up at the Voys' that evening. Why, then, would she keep her meeting with Theo secret if it only meant an end to her worrying about dues?

This theory would also account for two things that have puzzled commentators since Minnie's murder: her failure to take the flowers to the church, when she had brought them over expressly for that purpose; and her failure to change into the new dress, which her dressmaker made specifically for the Young People's meeting. Minnie must have realized that the flowers would only get in her way on a sleuthing mission at the church, and she wouldn't have time to arrange them before the 8:00 meeting. As for her new dress, she would not have wanted to get it dirty or torn if she thought she'd be exploring the dusty upper levels in search of clues.

When Mrs. McKay saw Theo and Minnie, the girl seemed to be pleading with him, and he was calling her a little coward. Yet she wasn't angry. If the espionage theory is correct, then Minnie could have gotten cold feet ("What if he comes back and catches us? It's too dangerous. We should leave it to the police."). Eventually, however, Theo calmed her down and they went into the church.

What happened next was probably a blitz attack once they got into the little library (ostensibly to put their coats there, no doubt). Theo rendered her unconscious, then went about staging an elaborate scene that would make it look as if an intruder had beaten, stabbed, raped, and then robbed Minnie. He even broke the new lock on the library door.

It is quite possible that earlier in the day he had tried to see if he could get back into the belfry by using the chisel from the pastor's study; if he had been successful, he might have killed Minnie the same way he did Blanche and hidden her up there. But the chisel didn't work, so he was forced to improvise. (Would he have really put her up there, though, with his adored Blanche? Would he not have considered that a sacrilege?)

Theo must have thought that he would be the last person suspected as the perpetrator of the butchery in the library, and this is why he took such pains with its gruesomeness. He had to make it look as awful as he could imagine in order to distance himself—the person he was known to be—from the kind of person who could commit such a crime. Under ordinary circumstances, the body would have been discovered on Sunday by whoever would be taking over Theo's usual job of handing out hymnals while he was away on his National Guard weekend. He probably never dreamed that Minnie would be found on Saturday.

Some of the staging may also reflect Theo's very real anger at Minnie. He had taken up with her because he thought he could safely lose his virginity with this woman whom he had no intention of marrying. Yet, she would not oblige him. She was probably somewhat bossy, and why should he put up with that? He got enough of that at home. She most likely gave him grief about his attentions to Blanche Lamont, whom he *did* want to marry, and he may have heard some of the gossip she was spreading about him and Blanche, perhaps even feeling that Minnie was trying to ruin Blanche's reputation. Moreover, Mamma had convinced him that Minnie was not worthy of him.

Did Theo rape Minnie? And, if so, was it the result of passion or part of the staging? Because of the lack of specific evidence from the autopsy report, we can't know for sure. It would be helpful, for example, to know if there was only penetration (indicating the use of something other than his penis) or if semen was also present. Certainly, rape—or the appearance of it—fit in with Theo's staging plans, and this might have presented him with the opportunity for sexual experience (and release) he had been looking for. But he was such a prude about women that it is distinctly possible that he found himself unable (physically or mentally) to do it.

The prevailing opinion among Victorians was that rape—especially when it took a woman's virginity—was an even worse crime than murder. If Theo had refrained from raping his victims, he could still consider himself "a gentleman," and this may also be what lies behind his statements that he "never harmed those poor girls."

Theo would never have staged such a gory scene with Blanche's body as he had with Minnie's. And he would never have taken the time to arrange Minnie as respectfully as he had Blanche. Afterward, the remorse he would express to reporters referred only to Blanche, with the occasional inclusive "those poor girls" thrown in. He never mentioned Minnie by name after his arrest.

Was Theo in a manic state when he killed Minnie? This murder seems calculating, whereas that of Blanche seems almost accidental, a situation that got out of control. Still, the people at the party said he joined in the games and was "unusually lively" that night.

Ironically, the Durrants had received another letter from Maud that day, and Theo took it to the party to read.

Minnie could not have known anything about the murder of Blanche Lamont unless Theo himself told her, and it is unlikely that he would have made a full-blown confession to her. The "third-party" story served the purpose of getting it off his chest and involving someone else in his tale—as he had tried to do with Carrie Cunningham.[22] Only, with Minnie it would have backfired. (Carrie pretended to go along with him to get the story; it is obvious she didn't believe him.)

Lucile Turner never saw Minnie after the pastor's reception on March 22; if she had, she would have told the reporters and the attorneys, because it would have made her more important in the case. Her statements that Minnie "was suspicious" of Theo were designed to make it look as if Lucile were privy to special knowledge; but any utterances about suspicion would have to have been made before April, and most likely referred to Minnie's feeling that Theo was dating other girls.

The baker Frank Young's story about Minnie knowing too much about Blanche's disappearance is probably untrue, although it could fit what Theo might have told her about what he saw in the church on April 3. However, the fact that Young never came forward with the story at the time of his court appearances in April and May indicates that this event probably never happened.

What happened to Theo Durrant, then, was the weird convergence of all these problems, medical and emotional, on April 3, 1895. Dr. Jamison says that at some point in the manic phase, "everything previously moving with the grain is now against—you are irritable, angry, frightened, uncontrollable, and enmeshed totally in the blackest caves of the mind."[23]

Theo had idolized his sister, and then he had idolized Blanche Lamont because she reminded him of Maud. When Maud left him without a support system, and then Blanche resisted his advances, he snapped. His impulse control centers had been further weakened by the meningitis, and he was unable to stop himself from killing her. Perhaps he just put his hands around her throat to silence her, and found himself squeezing harder and harder . . . until at the end, on the second landing of the belfry, there were seven clear fingernail marks on the right side of her throat, and five on the other.

Under these circumstances, the murder of Blanche Lamont is understandable. The murder of Minnie Williams is inexcusable, but given the great control that Mamma had over his life, and his excessive fear of having her find out about Blanche, it was probably inevitable.

Even under today's laws, an insanity plea would not have helped Theo (and he would never have consented to one even if it had). However, a modern court presented at a sentencing hearing with evidence of neurological and biochemical damage would probably not impose the death penalty.

Today we know a good deal more about the chemistry of the brain and the body, about genetic inheritance, and about mental instability that has its roots in all of these, as well as in the dynamics of the family environment. In other words, Theo Durrant was a victim of both nature and nurture. The wonder of it is that he was able to surmount them for so long to become the kind of man he was before it all caved in on him. Which of us can declare with conviction that, under like circumstances, we would escape unscathed? Let that person cast the first stone.

Many inmates on death row "find God" as they await the long appeals process before their execution; and perhaps some of these are even legitimate conversions. But Theo Durrant never "lost" Him. His religious devotion was not fake, nor a clever device used to seduce women (as some would claim). He must have been as confused about what happened to him on April 3 as everyone else who had difficulty believing it, and probably felt that a cruel trick had been played on him.

None of this can excuse what Theo did to the two young women who were once his friends. But he was not the monster most people thought he was in 1895, nor the sex fiend he has been portrayed as since then. In *The Newcomes*, a hypocritical minister criticizes a genuinely good man who is seen as irreligious and undeserving of heaven when he dies. Thackeray, however, clearly thinks otherwise, and perhaps not even Theo Durrant was denied divine grace by a God more merciful and forgiving than we are:[24]

Does a week pass without the announcement of the discovery of a new comet in the sky, a new star in the heaven, twinkling dimly out of a yet farther distance, and only now becoming visible to human ken though existent for ever and ever? So let us hope divine truths may be shining, and regions of light and love extant, which Geneva glasses cannot yet perceive, and are beyond the focus of Roman telescopes.

Epilogue

So we beat on, boats against the current, borne back cease-lessly into the past.

—F. Scott Fitzgerald, *The Great Gatsby*

How did those involved with the Emmanuel Baptist murders—the witnesses, the friends, the family members—live out the rest of their lives after the trial and the execution of Theo Durrant? Did their involvement in the case scar them? Or did it merely become a quaint story to tell their grandchildren years later?

For the immediate families of the two victims and their killer, there must have been a constant ache of loss and bewilderment. After the trial, after the appeals, after the execution—after the Durrant case had slipped from the front pages, and finally from the newspapers completely—the Lamonts, the Nobles, the Williamses, and the Durrants would still be faced with the task of carrying on with their lives as best they could.

THE EMMANUEL BAPTIST CHURCH MEMBERS

The church itself survived the threats of destruction from an angered San Francisco populace, but it never regained the affluence it had enjoyed before that terrible Easter Saturday in 1895. Emmanuel Baptist struggled along under Rev. J. George Gibson until 1909 and Rev. W. M. McCart after that, and was eventually torn down in 1915.[1]

Many stories have been told since 1898 of Rev. Gibson's alleged confession of the crimes Theo Durrant was executed for, of his commitment to a mental hospital, and of his eventual suicide there. None of this is true. In 1910, an ailing Gibson moved back to Chico to live with his sister and her family. He died there of heart disease on October 25, 1912, at the age of 55, and is buried in the Chico Cemetery.[2]

Gibson's friend and secretary, Robert Newton Lynch, left San Francisco after the trial and did not return to California for six years. In 1900, he received a degree from the Southern Baptist Theological Seminary in Louisville, Kentucky, then spent two years at London's Regents Park College where he received a degree called Associate of Theological Senate. Lynch served as pastor in Petaluma, California, from 1903 to 1909. In 1907, at the age of 32, he married 19-year-old Elizabeth Riley, with whom he had three children. He eventually left the ministry and served a long and distinguished career as a businessman and an officer of the state chamber of commerce. Lynch's extensive biographical sketch in *The History of San Francisco* mentions nothing of his life in California prior to 1896, and nothing of his connection with Rev. Gibson or the Durrant case. He died on June 5, 1931, at the same age as his mentor: 55.[3]

Frank August Sademan, the former janitor, died January 8, 1923, and is buried in San Francisco's Presidio National Cemetery. His stepson, James, continued his thieving ways. At the age of 18, he broke into his parents' home and stole money, as he had done many times in the past. Fed up with James's incorrigibility and at the end of their rope, Frank and Mary Agnes Sademan had him arrested for burglary. There is no mention of James in Mary Agnes's obituary of 1927, which means he had died by then or was estranged from the family. The state does not keep records of incarceration for burglary after a certain time, but it is likely that James spent some time behind bars.[4]

Elmer Alonzo Wolfe, upon whom Theo's defense counsel tried to cast suspicion for the murder of Minnie Williams, married his date of that evening, Miriam Lord. They had two children. Miriam, who was Minnie Williams's friend and one of the discoverers of her body, died in 1955 at the age of 80. Elmer followed her in 1956 at the age of 85.[5]

Elmer's brother, Clarence Navarre Wolfe, ran a successful lumber and hardware company in San Francisco, which he began in 1900 and retired from in 1960. Clarence died in July 1966, at the age of 93.[6]

Thomas Augustus Vogel stayed in San Francisco and continued his career as a dentist, earning many honors throughout his life. He married, had two children, and was blessed with many grandchildren. However, he never told them about the central role he played in the Durrant trial, nor that he had known the defendant and both victims quite well. Tom Vogel died in San Mateo, California, on September 16, 1951, at the age of 78.[7]

Dr. William Z. King died suddenly of a heart attack at the home of his daughter, Flora, in Oakland, on May 7, 1910. His wife, Ophelia, lived to be 106, dying in Los Angeles in 1958.[8]

George King's sister, Flora (whom Theo thought he saw outside the Emmanuel Baptist Church after Minnie Williams's murder), married attorney Percy Clay Black in 1902 and had one child. The Blacks eventually moved to prestigious Rodeo Drive in Beverly Hills, where on March 19, 1944, at the age of 63, Flora committed suicide by taking an overdose of barbiturates. The cause was said to be her ill health.[9]

George's sister, Annette (Nettie), married Theodore Jenkins and died in Santa Monica on December 2, 1975, at the age of 90.[10]

George R. King did not attend college as he had planned, instead serving in various companies as a clerk. At the time of Theo's trial he was working for his uncle Clement Wilder's advertising company, and later he worked for his father and then his brother-in-law, Percy Black. A short marriage ended in divorce, and there were no children. In February 1913, George moved to an apartment in Oakland, and a month later, on March 5, 1913, he died there of tuberculosis at the age of 36. Like his friend Theo, he was cremated.[11]

Flora Sara Upton, Theo's one-time fiancée, managed to avoid the spotlight of publicity from the trial. She eventually went on to Stanford University, where she met her future husband, William A. Waterman, five years her junior. They moved to Tulare County in 1910 and raised four children. Flo Upton Waterman died on October 1, 1949, at the age of 79. Her family never knew about her involvement with Theo Durrant.[12]

Edna Lucile Turner got married on November 29, 1897, at the age of 19—just a little over a month before Theo was executed. Her husband was 27-year-old Charles Watson Moore, the brother of George King's mother, who for some unexplained reason also had two aliases: Clement Wilder and Clement Moore. It is remotely possible that Clement Wilder was actually the *son* of Ophelia Moore King and not her brother. She was 18 when he was born, and the Moores had no other children. In the 1870 census for Tonica, Illinois, Charles Moore is noted as having been born in New York City in March of that year. (The Moores must have left for Ohio right after this in order to be settled in Tonica by the summer, when the census was taken.) However, Charles/Clement reports his date and place of birth as January 1870, in Tonica, Illinois—which is what he was probably told. All this secrecy must have had a purpose.

Lucile either divorced Clement Wilder and remarried before 1910 (she does not appear in the census under Turner, Wilder, or Moore), or died in one of the short periods of time when no death records exist. Her husband remarried, divorced, and died in 1938 of pneumonia and malnutrition.[13]

THE ATTORNEYS

Eugene Nelson Deuprey was never healthy after the Durrant case and died of a heart attack only five years after his most famous client's execution, on October 4, 1903, at the age of 55. His grandson has never heard of the Durrant case.[14]

John H. Dickinson died around 1904.[15]

Like his fiery defense counterpart, District Attorney William S. Barnes died young. He had a stroke on March 5, 1910, and died eight days later at the age of 44. Barnes is buried in the Presidio National Cemetery.[16]

Edgar D. Peixotto took advantage of the fame bestowed upon him by his first big trial, and entered private practice shortly thereafter—as a defense attorney. He was active in the Republican Party, serving as a delegate to the national convention in 1896 and 1900. In 1904, he married Malvina Nathan, "internationally known as one of the West's outstanding beauties," with whom he had two children. Edgar Peixotto died on June 24, 1925, at the age of 57.[17]

BLANCHE LAMONT'S FAMILY[18]

Most of Blanche Lamont's family went on to have long, productive lives. One who did not was her only brother, Rodger, who was killed in a freak shooting accident in 1904 at the age of 17. Rodger and a group of friends were on their way back from a trip to Yellowstone Park when his gun fell out of the wagon and discharged, sending a bullet through his lungs. He lingered for a day before he died and was able to talk to his mother and his sister, Grace, who had traveled to his bedside. Like the funeral for his sister, Blanche, Rodger's was immense, ornate, and attended by almost all Dillon residents. He is buried with his parents and his sister in Mountain View Cemetery.

One can only imagine the pain and grief suffered by Julia Lamont who, in the space of a dozen years lost her husband, a daughter, and her only son. Yet, she carried on, a woman of incredible inner strength. There is a notice in the *Dillon Tribune* of December 27, 1895, about a doll contest held by a local merchant. Residents cast votes for little girls in the town to win the doll, and one of the top vote-getters was 5-year-old Marie Lamont. Surely, Julia (and possibly Grace as well) made sure that the little girl, who would not have understood about the murder of her sister eight months previously, participated in the contest with the other children. It is a poignant testimony to Julia's realization that, in spite of the horrible tragedy of Blanche's murder, life must go on. Julia Lamont died at the home of her daughter, Maud, in Spokane, Washington, in 1928. She was 78.

Blanche's oldest sister, Grace, served for many years as postmistress of the Dillon Post Office and supported the rest of the family. After 1910, Grace and her mother moved to Spokane, Washington, where Maud and her husband were living. When she was in her forties, Grace Lamont married John Logan, the widower of one of her close friends. She died in a nursing home in Clallam County, Washington, in 1953, at the age of 81.

Maud Lamont never became a teacher. After the trial she worked as a clerk in the Dillon Post Office, and in 1902 she married Joseph Dewitt Hicks, a bookkeeper working for the government on the

Flathead Indian Reservation near Missoula. Maud and her husband eventually moved to Spokane, Washington, and later lived in Klamath Falls, Oregon. They had several children. Maud died in a nursing home in Spokane in 1958 at the age of 83.

Little Marie Lamont attended Simmons College in Boston and became a librarian. She married a college professor and lived in Hawaii for many years. Marie died in 1987 at the age of 97.

Blanche's uncle, Charles G. Noble, died in 1914 at the age of 60, and Aunt Tryphena died in Los Angeles in 1938 at age 82. Their son, Karl, died before 1914, and Paul died in San Diego in 1946 at age 57.

MINNIE WILLIAMS' FAMILY[19]

The names of Minnie's mother and siblings were never mentioned in the newspapers. A search of the newspapers nearest the town of Beamsville in Ontario, Canada, likewise proved fruitless: even though they carried accounts of the case (with varying degrees of accuracy), not one of them gave the names of the Williams family.

An article at the time of Theo's execution stated that Minnie's mother had been driven mad by her daughter's murder and was at that time in a mental institution in Canada. However, this sounds more like one of the many rumors that sprang up around this case, and cannot be taken as definite without more proof.

Minnie's father, Albert E. Williams, stayed in San Francisco, calling himself a "mining engineer."

Minnie had been buried in Laurel Hill Cemetery in April 1895. When San Francisco passed its ordinance against burials inside the city limits, bodies from Laurel Hill and other cemeteries were dug up and taken down to Colma. The Little Quakeress is now in a mass grave with 35,000 bodies in the Laurel Hill section of Cypress Lawn Cemetery in Colma.

Minnie remains the forgotten victim. With a nearly anonymous background (Blanche's life was detailed in the newspaper, while Minnie's never was), the shameful breakup of her parents, her employment as a servant, and the hints of her imprudent behavior, she was not portrayed as sympathetically as was Blanche, the aspiring teacher. And the fact that her case was never tried insured that Minnie would forever take a back seat to Blanche—the very thing that had angered and humiliated her in life.

Minnie's final ignominy was the anonymous burial in a mass grave, no headstone to mark her presence, and far away from family and friends. Even the usual designation of this case as "the belfry murder" ignores the reality of her death.

THEO DURRANT'S FAMILY[20]

The Durrants—Mamma, Papa, and Maud—reinvented themselves after the final act faded away. Isabella and William stayed in San Francisco until after the 1906 earthquake, although they changed their surname to William's middle name: Allan. Over in Europe, Maud did the same.

A year after Theo's execution, Mamma followed through on her original intention of going to Germany to visit Maud . . . and stayed for a year and a half! Papa remained in San Francisco to watch over the urn containing Theo's ashes. When Isabella came back, she enrolled her husband in a correspondence course to study optometry and, although he graduated, there is no indication that he ever practiced it.

Mamma and Papa moved to Los Angeles sometime after 1906, although Mamma frequently traveled to Europe for extended visits to Maud. When Papa died in 1917 of cancer of the stomach, Mamma listed his occupation as "optician" on the death certificate.

Mamma lived until 1930, when she died at the age of 78 while on a visit to Maud in England. Maud was so distressed by her mother's death that she retired from public life for two years.

What happened to Theo's ashes? Were they lost in the 1906 earthquake, as has been reported by some? Or did the Durrants take them to southern California and bury them quietly down there as they always intended? It is hard to imagine that they would have abandoned them, and so it is more likely that the ashes ended up in Los Angeles. The autobiography that Theo was working on at San Quentin, carried away in chapters by Papa during his visits, has never turned up.

The strangest post-execution saga surely belongs to Maud Durrant, now known as Maud Allan. Following her mother's suggestion that she somehow channel her grief over Theo's troubles and use it to her advantage, Maud decided to abandon her lifelong study of the piano and turn herself into an interpretive dancer. Although she considered her art original, she was actually following the model established by another San Franciscan, the better-known Isadora Duncan.

Still, Maud Allan had her fanatic devotees, notably among effete European homosexuals. Her "Vision of Salome" (performed in a scant costume that for the Edwardian era was considered little better than nothing at all) was based on a play by Oscar Wilde, whose trial for homosexuality had taken place around the time of Theo's arrest in April 1895.

Maud Allan became a star at the turn of the century, mostly in Europe, and almost always did her Salome dance to full houses. She became rich as well as famous and, like the fictional Trilby in 1895, spawned a lucrative marketing spinoff:

Maud Allan statuettes were sold in Bond Street, her classical sandals were worn by society ladies, and jewellers copied her costume jewellery with beaded necklaces and bosses worn as breastplates.

But no one knew the truth about her brother. In fact, Maud never told anyone that she had a brother.

In 1918, a Joseph McCarthy-type member of Parliament named Noel Pemberton Billing accused Maud Allan of heading up a lesbian clique of famous women, which he sarcastically entitled "The Cult of the Clitoris." He alleged that the "blackmailability" of famous homosexuals in Great Britain was helping Germany to win the war. Billing had published this in a newspaper, so Maud took him to court on charges of criminal libel.

When she took the stand, "dramatic in red-feathered picture hat and black cloak," Billing (who was conducting his own defense) produced Thomas Duke's book, *Celebrated Criminal Cases of America*, and got her to admit that Theo Durrant was her brother. The implication was that immorality ran in her family, and truth is a defense in libel cases. For that and other reasons, Maud failed to clear her name at the trial and Billing was not convicted.

The irony of it was that Maud *was* a lesbian, or at least bisexual. In 1938, while driving her current lover, a wealthy Pasadena widow, she crashed the car, killing the lover and seriously injuring herself.

Maud Allan died in a Los Angeles rest home in October 1956, of a coronary thrombosis. Among the contributing causes of long-standing duration was cerebral arteriosclerosis with chronic brain syndrome.

Maud had apparently made herself out to be younger than she really was, as her death certificate lists her date of birth as August 27, 1880—seven years after her actual birth.

In her (mostly fictional) autobiography, *My Life and Dancing*, Maud never mentions the existence of a brother in her life. However, she relates the story of a doll she had as a young child. The doll had fallen off the table while Maud was playing with her:

I found the poor dear lying unconscious on the floor, with her arms and legs broken. Could a mother imagine anything more dreadful? I ran to rescue her, but while tenderly lifting the poor little body, the sawdust streamed to the floor. I dropped her as quickly. I ran screaming to mother. 'Oh, my dolly is blooding!'

The name of Maud's doll was Minnie.

MISCELLANEOUS

Alice Ballard Macdonald Rix and her husband, Edward Austin Rix, disappeared from California by 1900, and could not be found in New York, either. A short story by a writer named Alice Rix surfaced in 1924 in the British-based *New Magazine*, so she may have relocated there—if, indeed, it is the same person.

Carrie Cunningham may have married by 1900, as she does not appear under her own name in the census.

After the 1906 earthquake, several members of the National Guard were arrested for looting in the burned Chinatown area. Although most were from the First Brigade, two of them were from Theo's Second Brigade.[21]

In 1999, the Hearst Corporation's *Examiner* bought the *San Francisco Chronicle*, thereby ending one of the greatest journalistic rivalries in the history of newspapers.[22]

In 1951, a mystery writer named Anthony Boucher got together with several other fellow writers to produce a work called *The Marble Forest* (also known as *The Big Fear*). They didn't want to list all their names on the book, so they chose a collective one: Theo Durrant.[23]

Notes

Abbreviations have been used for the following newspaper citations:

SFC = The *San Francisco Chronicle*
SFE = The *San Francisco Examiner*
Call = The *San Francisco Call*

All other newspapers are written out in full.

CHAPTER 1: IN PLAIN SIGHT

1. The testimony of Henry J. Shalmount can be found in *SFC, SFE*, and *Call*, September 13, 1895. Shalmount's name had as many as six variations in the newspapers and in Peixotto's official summary, but the city directories of the time spell it as indicated herein.

2. Herman Schlageter's testimony is in *SFC, SFE*, and *Call*, September 13, 1895. His age comes from the California Death Index.

3. Mary Vogel's testimony is in *SFC, SFE*, and *Call*, September 17, 1895. Her age, place of birth, and parentage are from the 1900 census.

4. Minnie Edwards's testimony is in *SFC, SFE*, and *Call*, May 2, 1895 and September 13, 1895. See also "The Identification of Durrant," *SFE*, April 16, 1895.

5. The testimony of May Howard Lanigan and Alice Pleasant Dorgan is in *SFC, SFE,* and *Call,* May 2, 1895 and September 13, 1895. Alice's comment to May is in "The Identification of Durrant," *SFE,* April 16, 1895. The cable car line that is the subject of their testimony (from the bay to Market Street) is the same one in existence today. The only other line, a shorter one, goes up and down California Street and crosses this one at Powell. The gripmen on both lines must still let go of the cable at this intersection and pick it up on the other side.

6. The testimony of Mrs. Elizabeth D. Crosett can be found in *SFC, SFE,* and *Call,* September 17, 1895. Information about James Lyman Crosett comes from the Manuscripts Collection of the California Historical Society, available online at http://www.calhist.org/Support_Info/Collections. Accessed July 24, 1999. The rest of the information comes from "She Tried to Keep Her Secret," *SFE,* September 14, 1895.

7. In the *SFE* of September 14, 1895, there is a reproduction of the "phone book" of the Independent Social Telegraph Line, revealing the names and codes for everyone hooked up to it. Elizabeth Crosett is listed.

8. This information comes from Maud Durrant's diary and is quoted in Felix Cherniavsky, *The Salome Dancer: The Life and Times of Maud Allan* (Toronto: McClelland & Stewart, 1991), pp. 28–29. (The Durrants changed their surname to William's middle name, Allan, after Theo's execution.) Maud goes on to speculate as to whether Jim's grandmother would have come forward to testify against Theo if she had accepted Jim's proposal.

9. Quoted in District Attorney Barnes's closing argument. See Edgar D. Peixotto, *Report of the Trial of William Henry Theodore Durrant* (Detroit: The Collector Publishing Co., 1899; New York: Notable Trials Library Edition, 1996), pp. 176–77.

10. "He Passes the Church Door," *SFE,* September 18, 1895.

11. For a detailed description of the Nicholson pavement process, see *City of Elizabeth v. American Nicholson Pavement Co.,* 97 US 126 (1877).

12. This seems strange for a young man who was considered such a gentleman, and Mrs. Durrant uses this as one argument as to why the man with Blanche Lamont could not have been Theo. However, a book of manners from the era states that "if crossing a street with a lady who has his arm, it is better not to disengage the arm, and go round upon the outside. Such effort evinces a palpable attention to form and that is always to be avoided." Blanche and Theo had just crossed to the other side of the street, which would now put him on the inside. See John H. Young, *Our Deportment or the Manners, Conduct, and Dress of the Most Refined Society* (Detroit: F. B. Dickerson & Co., 1882), pp. 151–52. Elsewhere, the same volume states that "a gentleman . . . may take either side

of the walk," but that he customarily has her on his right side unless the street is crowded (p. 149).

13. The testimony of Martin Quinlan is in *SFC, SFE,* and *Call,* May 2 and September 18, 1895.

14. Blanche's height is usually stated as 5'7", which would have been taller than most women back then. Theo Durrant was noticeably shorter by as much as two inches, and he gives his height as 5'5⅛" (measured by county jail officials). However, San Quentin records indicate that he was an inch taller, and they would have to be accurate for the grisly purpose of determining the correct rope length for execution (see *Operation and Instruction Manual for Execution by Hanging in the State of Delaware,* 1990, available at http://www.theelectricchair.com/hanging_protocol.htm). So it may be that Blanche was as tall as 5'8".

15. The testimony of Caroline Leak is in *SFC, SFE,* and *Call,* September 18, 1895. Her name is variously spelled as "Leak" and "Leake," but she is listed as "Leak" in city directories. The "imprudent" reference is from "The New Witness Against Durrant," *SFE,* August 17, 1895.

16. "Skillful with the Scalpel," *SFE,* April 21, 1895.

17. "Piling Up Evidence," *Call,* April 18, 1895. George King's testimony at the trial in September specifically mentions James Sademan as one who needed to be kept out of the library.

18. George told many of his friends about Theo's severe trembling and shivering as if with cold ("A Different Story from the Mission," *SFC,* September 19, 1895), but he was never asked about this on the stand. Shivering is a sign of emotional shock, as is pallor and nausea, which Theo also exhibited.

None of the newspapers capitalized Bromo-Seltzer, which was at that time (as now) a brand name. Consequently, *direct quotes* from those sources will reproduce the spelling as it was written, but other references to this product will spell it correctly.

19. George's original testimony at the inquest (*SFC* and *SFE,* May 2, 1895) was that he met Theo in the vestibule. But at the time of the trial the defense attorneys had convinced him that Theo was possibly lying on the podium in the classroom.

20. The testimony of George R. King is in *SFC, SFE,* and *Call,* May 2 and September 19 and 21, 1895.

21. This is Theo Durrant's version of what he did on the way home (*SFC, SFE,* and *Call,* October 10, 1895) substantiated by Mrs. Hearn in "Durrant's New Witness," *Call,* October 20, 1895.

22. From the testimony of Mrs. Isabella Matilda Durrant, *SFC, SFE,* and *Call,* September 26, 1895.

23. "[M]y sister . . . doesn't know a tiny bit how Teddy loves her. He

never half appreciated her worth till I found her gone." Letter from Theo to his sister, 1896, quoted in Cherniavsky, p. 79.

CHAPTER 2: MISSING!

1. Unless otherwise indicated, the information in this chapter comes from the testimony of Tryphena Noble and Maud Lamont, which can be found in *SFC, SFE*, and *Call*, September 11 and 12, 1895. Some of the proposal information can be found in "Proposed to Miss Lamont," *SFE*, April 21, 1895; and "Durrant Again Accused," *Call*, May 2, 1895.

2. "Some Police History," *SFC*, November 2, 1895. The fainting spells are never mentioned anywhere else, although they are never denied by the family. The autopsy revealed a normal heart, so if the spells were real, they must have had a neurological basis. See chapter 12, infra, for further discussion of this.

3. Information from the U.S. Census, 1900, the City of Dillon, Montana, and the niece of Blanche Lamont.

4. Illinois State Archives, Muster and Descriptive Rolls of Illinois Civil War Units. David R. Lamont was a "one-year man," enlisting in February 1865 at age 17 and mustering out in January 1866. Although he never rose above the rank of private in his brief service, he later enlisted in the Montana National Guard and reached the rank of captain ("A Wild Rumor," *Butte (Montana) Daily Miner*, April 16, 1895). Newspaper articles usually referred to him as Captain Lamont. See also the U.S. 1890 Special Census of Civil War Veterans and the Civil War Pension Index.

5. Rockford College Archives.

6. This information comes from the Personals columns of the *Dillon (Montana) Examiner*, August 8, 1893, and January 3 and May 9, 1894.

7. "Blanche Lamont's Career," *SFE*, April 15, 1895. However, the family never specified what illness Blanche had and the *Dillon Examiner* for August 29, 1894 only mentions "her recent illness."

8. Blanche's youngest sibling, Marie, told her daughter about the limited marital prospects in Dillon for young women who didn't want to marry lumberjacks or ranch hands. (Personal correspondence with the author.)

9. *Dillon Examiner*, June 20, 1894.

10. Today, this school is Western Montana College of the University of Montana. Although it was founded by the legislature in 1893, it did not open its doors until the fall of 1896. (See the *Dillon Tribune* for January 1, 1896.) However, there was the Montana Normal Training School in nearby Twin Bridges, and the fact that neither Maud nor Blanche attended it indicates that they were interested in more than just an education.

11. I am reading between the lines of newspaper articles such as "Missing Blanche Lamont," *SFE*, April 13, 1895, and from the fact that Blanche was still recuperating from her illness when she arrived in San Francisco. It is unlikely that her mother would have sent her without a great deal of pressure on Blanche's part.

12. These pictures, one of which is reproduced in this book, are located in the Whatcom County Museum of History and Art in Bellingham, Washington. The other picture is reproduced in an out-of-print series done by Time-Life in 1978. The series was entitled *The Old West*, and Blanche's picture can be found in "The Women" on pp. 82–83.

13. "Missing from Home," *SFC*, April 10, 1895; "She Has Not Returned," *SFC*, April 11, 1895; "Has Left Friends and Home," *SFE*, April 10, 1895; "Blanche Lamont's Double," *SFE*, April 11, 1895; "She Has Not Been Found," *SFE*, April 12, 1895; "Missing Blanche Lamont," *SFE*, April 13, 1895.

14. The testimony of William Richard ("Dick") Charlton can be found in *SFC, SFE*, and *Call*, September 13, 1895.

15. There was some dispute as to whether this scene actually occurred, with the Durrants insisting it did, and Maud and her aunt insisting that they couldn't remember any such incident. However, Maud and Mrs. Noble were very reluctant to admit any previous liking for Theo and on the stand tried to distance themselves as much as they could from any association with him. But, as Mrs. Noble regarded him very highly up until April 14, 1895, and as the girls would in the natural course of things be introduced by their aunt, the encounter was probably as the Durrants presented it.

16. It was never explained why Blanche attended the Boys' High School (Lowell) instead of the Girls' High School. It may be that the latter did not have the kinds of courses she needed.

17. Stanford University Archives; *Dillon Examiner*, September 5, 1894.

18. "At Blanche Lamont's Home," *SFE*, April 15, 1895. This article, and the same one in *SFC*, was actually copied from one of the Dillon newspapers. Although the article goes on to say that the "dental student" was probably Durrant (who also rode a bike), it was really more likely to have been Tom Vogel, who had only been a practicing dentist for five months. At the time Blanche wrote the letter to her sister, she was not on good terms with Theo, and she was spending time with Vogel.

19. "She Has Not Returned," *SFC*, April 11, 1895.

20. "Lured by a Book," *SFE*, April 15, 1895.

21. "Blanche Lamont Had a Warning," *SFC*, October 18, 1895.

22. "Glad He Is to Die," *Call*, November 3, 1895. No one else ever mentions that Theo had trouble reading (he certainly did a great amount of it) or could not "pronounce even common words correctly." Perhaps

he was overly self-conscious and nervous in Blanche's presence. He did, however, have a spelling problem.

23. In modern paperback format, *The Newcomes* is nearly 800 pages. Nineteenth-century editions of this work were usually done in multiple volumes and, judging from the sketch of the defense attorney holding it at the trial, the one Theo brought to the Nobles' house must have been only the first of a multivolume set.

24.

Q [*Dickinson*]:	During the time that you have been in the city you have been attending school also?
A [*Maud Lamont*]:	No, sir. I taught one week. I taught in the kindergarten one week. (*SFC*, September 12, 1895)

25. I am speculating here, based on the fact that the girls need not have gone to San Francisco for their education and that their absence from the home would have been a hardship for their widowed mother; and also on Maud's somewhat petulant testimony as to what happened with the letters in Blanche's trunk, which indicates that a grief-stricken Julia Lamont was irritated with Maud (did she blame her for Blanche's death?):

Q:	Where is that trunk and where are those letters?
A:	The trunk is at home.
Q:	Do you mean in your auntie's house?
A:	No, sir; in Montana.
Q:	And the letters also?
A:	Yes, sir, unless they were burned up.
Q:	Well, were there any letters burned up?
A:	Mamma burned up some.
Q:	After your return to Montana?
A:	Yes, sir.
Q:	Did you and your mother make an examination of the letters, and so forth, after you arrived home?
A:	No, sir.
Q:	Did your mother?
A:	No, sir.
Q:	Well, how did she determine what to burn up?
A:	I don't know—she just burned everything up; well, I don't know whether she did or not.
Q:	Well, do you know that she burned any up?
A:	No, sir, I am not positive.

Q:	Then why did you make the statement a few moments ago?
A:	Because she burned some of mine.
The Court:	Because she burned some of yours—was that your answer?
A:	Yes, sir.
Dickinson:	At what time did she burn some of yours?
A:	I don't know—soon after I got home. (*SFC*, September 12, 1895)

It is a strange scene depicted here. Why would Julia burn the letters of either daughter? Did they reveal too much? Was she angry that they had gone to San Francisco in the first place and wanted no reminders of it?

26. "Durrant and the Lady Reporter," *SFC*, October 13, 1895. As far as I can determine, no commentator has mentioned the possible courtship of Blanche Lamont by Tom Vogel. Yet, the members of Emmanuel Baptist—including Theo, who wanted to marry Blanche—consistently acknowledge the fact that, next to the Nobles and Maud, Tom would be the most interested in news of Blanche, and would be most likely to hear it before anyone else. There is an undercurrent of Tom's having the right to mourn Blanche's disappearance that is second only to the right of her family.

27. Personals, *SFE*, April 10–12, 1895.

28. "Missing from Home," *SFC*, April 10, 1895; "She Has Not Returned," *SFC*, April 11, 1895; "Has Left Friends and Home," *SFE*, April 10, 1895; "Blanche Lamont's Double," *SFE*, April 11, 1895; "She Has Not Been Found," *SFE*, April 12, 1895; "Missing Blanche Lamont," *SFE*, April 13, 1895.

29. "Some Police History," *SFC*, November 2, 1895.

30. The traditional German spelling of this name would have been written as "Schoenstein" and pronounced as "Shernsteen" or "Shernstine." The writer was evidently aware of the pronunciation, but not of the way the professor spelled his name.

CHAPTER 3: THE DURRANTS OF TORONTO

1. Unless otherwise indicated, information on the Durrants comes from the testimony of Isabella Durrant, *SFC*, September 26, 1895; "Durrant's Trial Delayed," *SFC*, August 24, 1895; and Isabella Matilda Durrant, "Why I Shall Be Present at the Execution of My Son,," *SFE*, June 6, 1897. There is no Dredger in the 1871 Ontario Census, so the name may be reported incorrectly.

2. Ontario Marriage Certificates, lib. 10, folio 242, 1870. The certificate lists the date as June 20, although Mrs. Durrant places it at June 30. Some commentators have erroneously placed the marriage year as 1871, thereby adding illegitimacy to the list of strikes against Theo.

3. Ontario Birth Certificate No. 013105 (Theo); No. 028033 (Maud); and No. 35675 (Edward). Ontario Death Certificate No. 017593 (Edward). Some commentators have spelled her first name as "Beulah," so it was probably pronounced to rhyme with it. Her name is given as Ulah Maud Alma Durrant in the affidavit to the elder Durrants' libel suit against juror Horace Smyth (see "Out of One Trouble and Into Another" *SFE*, December 30, 1897).

4. I will be using the more inclusive term "manic-depressive illness" rather than the smaller subset currently known as "bipolar disorder." See Frederick K. Goodwin, M.D., and Kay Redfield Jamison, Ph.D., *Manic-Depressive Illness* (New York: Oxford University Press, 1990).

5. Maud Allan, *My Life and Dancing* (London: Everett & Co., 1908), p. 29.

6. Although Isabella Durrant gives the name of the woman they rented the rooms from on 5th Street, she significantly omits the fact that the residence at 305 Fell Street belonged to her husband's parents (San Francisco City Directory, 1889). Hayes Street address is from the 1880 U.S. Census.

7. During the trial, the houses on Fair Oaks were undergoing renumbering. Hence, there are at least three different addresses given for the Durrants' home: 1025 (its original listing), 425, and 421.

8. Cogswell Polytechnical College moved from San Francisco to the Peninsula after the 1906 earthquake, and until the mid-1990s was in Cupertino. It is currently located in Sunnyvale.

9. "Preparing an Alibi," *SFE*, April 19, 1895.

10. "Durrant at Cogswell," *SFE*, April 19, 1895. For an interesting look at the telegraph craze in the nineteenth century, see Tom Standage, *The Victorian Internet* (New York: Walker Publishing Co., 1998).

11. Stanford University Archives has Theo registered as a student for 1891–1892, but it is possible that he didn't attend at all. Mrs. Durrant says he enrolled, but got a job offer instead ("Why I Shall Be Present at the Execution of My Son," *SFE*, June 6, 1897). On the other hand, "Facts of His Life," *SFC*, April 15, 1895, states that he *did* go, and he is not listed in the 1892–1893 San Francisco City Directory. The information for the directory would have been collected in April 1892.

12. "Why I Shall Be Present." Mrs. Durrant never states that it is her idea, but given the facts and her relationship with her children, I am guessing that it was.

13. "Inquiries at the College," *SFC*, April 15, 1895 (detailed notes that other students borrowed); "Durrant's Denial," *SFC*, April 15, 1895 (stayed up late working on thesis); "Hoisholt's Opinion," *SFC*, April 17, 1895 (attendance); "Went to Stockton," *Call*, April 17, 1895 (failed exams).

14. Isabella Durrant, "Why I Shall Be Present."

15. "A Quick History of Bicycles," available at http://www.pedalinghistory.com/PHbikbio.htm; for his purchase of a bicycle for Maud, see the testimony of Edward A. Bunker, reported in *SFE*, October 9, 1895.

16. "Death Watch Removed," *Call*, June 5, 1997 (Amador, etc., trips); "Evidence for Durrant," *SFE*, August 21, 1895, relates an incident during the Yosemite bicycle trip where Theo and his companion allegedly cheated innkeepers. In "Twelve Men Chosen for the Trial of Durrant" (*SFC*, August 30, 1895), Theo claims that the person reporting this only visited two or three innkeepers and that he can explain those negative reports. At the same time, he gave his attorneys the hundreds of positive testimonials he collected from the others he visited.

17. "Durrant's Skull," *Call*, April 17, 1895.

18. Testimony of W. H. T. Durrant, *SFC*, October 11, 1895.

19. The information in this section as to Theo's jobs and personal traits comes from Isabella Durrant, "Why I Shall Be Present." There had been rumors that Theo had tortured and maimed small animals as a boy, but this is unlikely in view of these stories, as well as the fact that the Durrants had a family dog, Dan, for many years (see "Dejected, Desolate," *SFE*, January 3, 1898). The PBS program, "The 1900 House," which aired in June 2000, is the source of the information on the high price of eggs (22 cents a dozen in the United States in 1900) and the fact that many people raised chickens because of this. Information on the Golden Rule and the Emporium is from "Golden Rule Bazaar to Go," *Call*, July 1, 1897.

20. In sketching a self-portrait while in prison, Theo placed himself in the full dress uniform of the California National Guard's Signal Corps. (See photo inserts in Cherniavsky.)

21. For information about the Pullman strike (American Railway Union) of 1894, see William W. Ray, "Crusade or Civil War? The Pullman Strike in California," *California History* 58: 20–37.

22. "Blanche Lamont Found Dead in Emmanuel's Belfry," *SFC*, April 15, 1895. Information about Theo's weight comes from his direct testimony, reported in the newspapers of October 10, 1895.

23. Information about Theo's activities at Emmanuel Baptist comes from his testimony at the trial (October 10–12, 1895) and from Rev. J. George Gibson's testimony at the inquest (April 25–26, 1895).

24. "His Last View," *Call*, June 1, 1897.

25. Text under picture in *SFC*, September 7, 1895. This gives his age for the *Pinafore* performance as 7, but also states that it was a fundraiser for the Metropolitan (Baptist) Temple (Rev. Isaac Kalloch's church). In that case, the age is wrong, as the Durrants did not arrive in San Francisco until December 1879, when Theo was 8.

26. "Opening of the Durrant Murder Trial," *SFE*, July 23, 1895.

27. "Her Alameda Home," *SFC*, April 14, 1895 (objected to his dating Minnie); testimony of Isabella M. Durrant, reported in newspapers of September 26, 1895 (habit of kissing her); "Durrant's Own Story," *SFE*, November 6, 1895 ("I shall never, never forget how my dear mother would sit with me and talk of how this and that should be done, and what this and that dollar or half-dollar should be spent for, or why it should be saved, etc."). Mamma's letters to Maud in Berlin are full of this kind of advice (see Cherniavsky, passim), and it can be assumed that she was in the habit of dishing it out to both children on a regular basis.

28. Theo testified that he went downtown to order coal on April 8, 1895. The insinuation is that this was one of his usual tasks, and no doubt he was responsible for many more. Information about Joseph Browder comes from Mamma's testimony, *SFC* of September 26, 1895, San Francisco city directories, and the California Death Index.

29. See handwriting facsimile on page 2 of *SFE*, April 15, 1895. Papa's scheme is detailed in "Durrant Believed in Dreams," *SFE*, April 16, 1895, and the statement alleging he knew all along that the "investment" involved counterfeit money is in "Advised Durrant to Confess," *SFC*, October 17, 1895.

30. "Durrant Talks of Christmas," *SFC*, December 23, 1895.

31. Felix Cherniavsky's uncle was the executor of Maud (Durrant) Allan's estate, and after her death he destroyed some of Theo's letters to protect her memory. The uncle told Mr. Cherniavsky that in one of them Theo begged Maud not to tell anyone that he had "slept with Mamma" (personal e-mail to the author from Felix Cherniavsky, June 30, 1999). It is doubtful that the term "slept with" had the same meaning in the 1890s as it does today, so it was probably a literal, though only slightly less disturbing, statement. The information about the Durrants having separate bedrooms comes from Isabella Durrant's testimony and from "Nearly Killed by Gas," *SFE*, November 12, 1895.

32. "Mania about Women," *SFC*, April 16, 1895. Another possibility is that his constant talking of women was a form of "protesting too much" to cover up a lack of sexual attraction for them.

33. "He Kept Close Vigil," *Call*, April 17, 1895. The Queen Charlotte consists of red wine, grenadine, and lemon-lime soda served over ice in a collins glass (see http://www.webtender.com).

34. "Durrant's Religion, *SFE*, April 17, 1895. Supposedly, Theo had somehow rescued an Emmanuel Baptist girl from "ruin" at the hands of another man, and this girl related the story to Isabella Durrant ("Nearer the Gallows," *Call*, April 22, 1895).

35. "Facts of His Life," *SFC*, April 15, 1895 (smoking incident at Cooper); "First Night in Prison," *SFE*, April 15, 1895 (denies smoking).

36. "Durrant's Religion," *Call*, April 17, 1895.

37. Theo Durrant's testimony, reported in newspapers of October 11, 1895. In Blanche's narration of this incident to her aunt, she never expressed puzzlement at Theo's gift of a padlock, so possibly some of their conversations concerned the lack of privacy in their respective homes.

38. "Why I Shall Be Present" (never played with boys); "In Two Households," *SFE*, April 17, 1895 ("room as particular as a girl's").

39. "Juno robusto" appears in DA William S. Barnes's closing argument, reported in *SFE* and *SFC* on November 1, 1895. Information on James Lick is from the 1896–1897 San Francisco City Directory; Lucile's presence in the library is from the testimony of George R. King, reported in *SFC*, September 19, 1895.

40. "A New Witness for Durrant," *SFC*, September 2, 1895.

41. Information on Flora Sara Upton comes from "Points on the Accused," *SFE*, April 15, 1895, US Census for 1880 and 1900, and from her obituary in the *Tulare Advanced Register*, October 6, 1949.

42. "Minnie Williams and Durrant," *SFE*, April 16, 1895; "The Inquest," *SFC*, April 18, 1895; "Her Alameda Home," *SFC*, April 14, 1895.

43. "Gloomy Prospect for Durrant," *SFC*, May 2, 1895 (Theo had no respect for Minnie); interviews with her friends indicate that she went out frequently without supervision, spoke of questionable matters with Clark Morgan, and visited a man's hotel room alone.

44. "Her Alameda Home," *SFC*, April 14, 1895.

45. "Coroner's Inquest," *SFC*, April 17, 1895.

46. "Clews Still Lead to Theodore Durrant," *Call*, April 18, 1895.

47. The proposal incident has been documented in chapter 2, supra.

48. "Work of the Police," *SFC*, April 14, 1895; "His Ghoulish Vigil at the Church," *SFC*, April 18, 1895; "The Inquest," *SFC*, April 18, 1895 (she didn't slam the door in his face); "Durrant and His Lady Friends," *SFC*, April 24, 1895 (she talked freely to him about her problem).

49. See Isabella Durrant, "Why I Shall Be Present," and Cherniavsky, p. 35.

50. "An American Girl and Her Great Sorrow," *SFE*, June 20, 1897. Information about Minnie's presence and Theo's gift of a journal comes from Cherniavsky, p. 36.

51. "Points on the Accused," *SFE*, April 15, 1895.

52. "His Mind in a Whirl," *SFC*, April 15, 1895.

53. "Durrant's Letters to Helen Henry," *SFE*, August 20, 1895. The reporter writing the article tried to stir up scandal by suggesting that the letters were improper and suggestive. However, not only did Helen and her mother refute this, but Captain Lees (who was never sympathetic to Theo) ridicules the story in "Points against Durrant," *SFC*, August 21, 1895.

54. "Four Jurors Have Been Sworn," *SFE*, August 1, 1895.

CHAPTER 4: THE LITTLE QUAKERESS

Only the *Examiner* provided an official transcript of the police court proceedings. The *Chronicle* mostly summarized testimony, with an occasional section reproduced by a reporter, but there were inaccuracies if the reporter did not hear it correctly. The *Call* primarily summarized, often in a Question and Answer format that was not exactly reproduced from the actual testimony. For these reasons, the *Examiner* must be considered the authoritative source of police court testimony.

1. Testimony of Susan Morgan, *SFE*, April 23, 1895; and Clark Morgan, *SFE*, April 17 and 23, 1895.

2. Nothing was ever specified as to what was wrong with Minnie except for a bout of lumbago (see "What Was It Minnie Williams Knew?" *Call*, November 8, 1895). But several articles mentioned her as having something wrong, including one that said she would not have lived long because of "organic disorders" (see "Blacker Grows the Cloud over Emmanuel Baptist Church," *Call*, April 15, 1895), and Theo himself referred to her as "sickly" ("Durrant Talks," *Call*, April 17, 1895). Clark Morgan said when she first came to live with them in May 1894, she was not able to work for a while (Clark Morgan testimony, *SFE*, April 17 and 23, 1895). And Dr. Barrett, who performed her autopsy, said she was "undernourished" (testimony, *SFE*, May 1, 1895).

3. Testimony of Clark Morgan.

4. "Her Alameda Home," *SFC*, April 14, 1895.

5. The information in this section comes from the interview with Jennie Turnball, reported in "Her Alameda Home," *SFC*, April 14, 1895.

6. "Her Alameda Home," *SFC*, April 14, 1895. It is my interpretation that Minnie was shrewd, based on the various reports of her behavior. Other commentators have referred to her as "sly" (see, for example, Hildegarde Teilhet, "The Demon in the Belfry," in Allan Bosworth et al., *San Francisco Murderers* (New York: Duell, Sloan, and Pearce, 1947).

7. "Her Alameda Home." I am assuming this is the same man referred to by Albert Williams, infra.

8. "Miss Williams a Domestic," *Call*, April 14, 1895. Minnie's secretiveness can be seen in the fact that, although she was dating Theo and spoke of him quite often to both Morgans, neither of them ever saw him more than once—and only Susan saw him at their home in Alameda, despite their frequent dates in that city.

9. "Woman Murdered in a Church," *SFE*, April 14, 1895. Because of the great discrepancy between these reports and Minnie's actual behavior, I am assuming the Little Quakeress personality belonged to a pre-divorce Minnie, when she was more carefree and not dependent on

herself for survival. See also "Blacker Grows the Cloud over Emmanuel Baptist Church," *Call*, April 15, 1895:

There was no girlish romance in her composition. She had witnessed the miserable causes that had separated her parents, had herself suffered the hard pangs which the discovery of a lover's duplicity had forced upon her, and had been driven from a position of comfort to perform menial service for a livelihood. *Thus had she been made wise and hard beyond her years, and withal her character was firm and self-reliant.* (emphasis mine)

10. Testimony of Dennis Welch, *SFE*, April 27, 1895.

11. "Her Alameda Home," *SFC*, April 14, 1895.

12. Testimony of Clark H. Morgan, *SFE*, April 17, 1895: "He called there last summer—fall—and took her out to walk; they went out on the electric cars, and she said to a very secluded part of Fruitvale, as I understood it—a part of the country she was familiar with and he wanted to see."

13. "Horrible Tragedy in a Church," *SFC*, April 14, 1895.

14. The information in this section comes from the testimony of Clark H. Morgan (*SFE*, April 17 and 23, 1895) and that of A. E. Williams (*SFE*, April 18, 1895). Minnie talked about Theo to Susan Morgan as well, but not about the Fruitvale incident.

15. "Miss Williams's Father," *SFC*, April 14, 1895.

16. "A Horrible Tragedy in a Church," *SFC*, April 14, 1895. It is my conjecture that Minnie might have tried to become friends with Blanche Lamont, based on the many reports that they were friends. It would have been in her interests to do so, and Blanche also probably represented the class Minnie aspired to. Blanche, on the other hand, had her own agenda, in that the only girls of Emmanuel Baptist she had much to do with were Daisy Wolfe and Grace Corwin, both daughters of the highest-ranking members (see "Blanche Lamont's Career," *SFE*, April 15, 1895). Daisy Wolfe's stepfather, Charles Taber, had been a San Francisco city supervisor and was the chief trustee at Emmanuel Baptist.

17. "A Horrible Tragedy in a Church," *SFC*, April 14, 1895. In his testimony (*SFE*, April 18, 1895), Albert Williams said that some girl had told Minnie something Theo had done, and Minnie was not happy about it. This could well have been Lucile Turner. Tom Vogel's testimony strongly indicates that Lucile was prone to exaggeration: first, in his clarification of her story about Theo's offer to examine her; and second, in his insinuation that, although Lucile claimed Minnie had told her she was suspicious of Theo, this did not necessarily mean it was true.

18. Testimony of Dennis Welch, *SFE*, April 27, 1895.

19. Testimony of A. E. Williams, *SFE*, April 18, 1895.

20. Testimony of Frances Willis, *SFE*, April 20, 1895. Dennis Welch is the only one to testify to Theo's presence in Alameda on Saturday, April 6. Previous to his testimony on the 26th, there was a report (apparently by the Alameda Police) that Theo had registered at the Park Hotel on the night of April 6 under the name of B. M. Warner. However, the next day the real B. M. Warner came forward and said he had been at the hotel that day (see "Durrant Not in Alameda," *SFC*, April 21, 1895). As Welch would have known of the mistake by the time of his testimony the following week, he was obviously sticking by his story that he had seen Theo on April 6.

21. Testimony of Clark Morgan, *SFE*, April 17 and 23, 1895.

22. Testimony of Florence Voy, *SFE*, April 18, 1895.

23. See A. E. Williams's testimony, *SFE*, April 18, 1895: "I didn't pay very much attention to it at the time she told it." When asked about a girl who told Minnie something about Theo, he couldn't give the name: "I don't know that I asked her." Asked what the girl said, he replied: "She didn't tell me what the other girl said. I didn't ask her."

There is also the following exchange between Clark Morgan and a *Chronicle* reporter:

Q: What old subject do you suppose she referred to?

A: That I cannot tell. When the child told me of her meeting with Durrant on Monday, I did not pay much attention to the matter. In fact, it went in one ear and out the other. . . . I used to hear her stories but asked few questions. ("The Alameda Links," *SFC*, April 16, 1895)

And Jennie Turnball's interview with the *Examiner* resulted in this comment: "Once Miss Williams spoke of having a chance to marry a middle-aged man right away, but she talked in her jocular way and her friend paid no attention to the matter." ("Minnie Williams and Durrant," *SFE*, April 16, 1895). That Minnie was not reluctant to divulge what was happening in her life can be seen in the fact that she seems to have revealed her family's troubles to everyone she knew.

24. Testimony of Clark Morgan, *SFE*, April 17, 1895 (had a new dress made); "The Second Church Murder," *SFE*, April 30, 1895.

25. Testimony of P. S. Chappelle, *SFE*, April 17, 1895.

26. Testimony of Charles A. Dukes and Clarence W. Dodge, *SFE*, April 20 and 24, 1895.

27. Testimony of Frank A. Sademan, *SFE*, April 17 and 24, 1895. Information about the Sademan family comes from the California Death Index and the obituary of Mary Agnes Sademan, *SFC*, January 13, 1895. James's problem behavior and status as stepson are described in "A Father Has a Son Arrested," *Call*, January 25, 1898. See chapter 13, infra.

28. Testimony of Adolph Hobe, *SFE*, April 25, 1895. His age comes from the California Death Index.

29. "Woman Murder in a Church," *SFE*, April 14, 1895. Information about the other daughters is from the 1900 Census. The flowers Minnie brought have presented a problem, in that she stated to Clark Morgan that she was going to take them to the church for Easter. However, none of the many witnesses who saw her at the ferry or in front of the church saw anything resembling a parcel or a box of flowers. The Voys *did* see the flowers, so she must have had them at the terminal. But, instead of taking them to the church, Minnie seems to have arranged them in vases around the Voy home, according to the article cited here. As with the new dress, Minnie simply seems to have changed her mind. Alternatively, she may have opted against the flowers and the dress as a result of her conversation with Theo at the ferry (see chapter 12, infra).

30. "Dr. Perkins' Story," *SFC*, April 14, 1895.

31. The information in this section comes from the testimony of Mary Ann McKay, *SFE*, April 23, 1895.

32. The information in this section comes from the testimony of Charles T. Hills, *SFE*, April 18, 1895.

33. "Seen by Two Bicyclists," *SFE*, April 17, 1895.

34. Testimony of James P. Hodgdon, *SFE*, April 23, 1895.

35. Testimony of Albert O. McElroy and Bert James Minner, *SFE*, April 26, 1895.

36. "A Second Chain Forged," *SFE*, November 5, 1895; "The Murder of Minnie Elora Williams; What is Known and What is Mystery," *SFE*, January 7, 1898.

37. Testimony of Struven and Fitzpatrick sisters, *SFE*, April 23, 1895. In an interview, Louisa Struven said she and her sister had seen Theo and Maud go by on their way to school (see "They Saw Durrant," *SFC*, April 22, 1895). However, on the stand none of the sisters indicated that she had ever seen him before.

38. This was a badly-written contemporary work by Jacob Taussig, entitled *The Letter F; or, Startling Revelations in the Durant* [*sic*] *Case*. See Joseph Henry Jackson and Lenore Glen Offord, *The Girl in the Belfry* (Greenwich, CT: Fawcett Books, 1957), p. 62.

39. California 1900 Census.

40. This section comes from the testimony of Thomas A. Vogel, *SFE*, April 18 and 26, 1895. At first, he said Theo told him about being at the armory with the Signal Corps and trying to catch his horse. Later, he said he could not be sure exactly what Theo had said as to why he was late and needed to wash his hands.

41. "The Story of Pastor Gibson," *SFE*, April 15, 1895 ("he seemed more jolly and full of life than usual"); see also "His Mind in a Whirl," *SFC*, April 15, 1895 ("He seemed to be in the best of spirits"—Thomas Vogel).

42. "What the Police Know," *SFE*, April 15, 1895. Information on how the games are played comes from *Good Housekeeping's Book of Home Entertainment* (Cleveland: World Publishing Co., 1961), pp. 112–13.

43. Unless otherwise noted, the information in this and the next section comes from the testimony of Elmer A. Wolfe, *SFE*, April 15, 19, 20, and 27, 1895.

44. Elmer Wolfe's marriage to Mary Snook (1889) is noted in the Science Fiction Call Index database, available online at http://feefhs.org/fdb2/sfcalli.html. Information about his son and his behavior comes from "Wolfe Must Explain," *SFE*, April 19, 1895.

45. That Miriam Lord was not just a casual date and that Elmer might have been distracted by her is proven by the fact that they later got married and had two children. See obituary for Miriam Lord Wolfe, *SFC*, January 17, 1955.

CHAPTER 5: HOLY WEEK HORRORS

1. Testimony of Rev. J. George Gibson, *SFE*, April 17 and 18, 1895. "Busted" quote, cleaned up by the *Examiner*, appears in "Emmanuel's Pastor on Witness Stand," *Call*, April 25, 1895.

2. U.S. Census, 1880 (Kings in Chico); "Dr. Gibson at Chico," *Call*, April 15, 1895 (success at fund-raising).

3. "The Story of Pastor Gibson," *SFE*, April 15, 1895 ("He acted like a man whose whole life had been run in one groove.").

4. "Emmanuel Church to be Abandoned," *SFE*, April 16, 1895; "Strange Church Music," *Call*, April 16, 1895.

5. Text from under picture on front page of *Call*, April 19, 1895. The stance was a standard elocution pose (see p. 116 of Time-Life's "Prelude to the Century" in the Our American Century series, 2000).

6. "The Story of Pastor Gibson," *SFE*, April 15, 1895.

7. The information in this section comes from the testimony of Lila Berry, Catherine Stevens, and James Sademan, *SFE*, April 18, 1895; Lila Berry's age is from the California Death Index. Mrs. Nolte's name was also spelled as Nolt in the newspapers, but was mostly spelled Nolte in the city directories.

8. Testimony of Rev. J. George Gibson, *SFE*, April 17 and 18, 1895; "The Pastor's Story," *SFC*, April 15, 1895.

9. Testimony of Harry Snook, *SFE*, April 18, 1895.

10. Testimony of Thomas A. Vogel, *SFE*, April 18, 1895.

11. "Woman Murder in a Church," *SFE*, April 14, 1895.

12. "Her Alameda Home," *SFC*, April 14, 1895; "The Alameda Links," *SFC*, April 16, 1895.

13. Testimony of Thomas A. Vogel, *SFE*, April 18, 1895.

14. "Shield from Blood Spurts," *SFE*, April 19, 1895; "Evidence is Strong against Durrant," *Call*, April 19, 1895.

15. Testimony of Sgt. W. F. Burke, *SFE*, April 18, 1895; see also "A Horrible Tragedy in a Church," *SFC*, April 14, 1895.

16. Testimony of Dr. J. S. Barrett, *SFE*, April 20, 1895.

17. "Woman Murder in a Church," *SFE*, April 14, 1895; "The Pastor's Story," *SFC*, April 15, 1895.

18. "Missing Blanche Lamont," *SFC*, April 14, 1895.

19. "The Second Chapter of Horror," *SFE*, April 15, 1895. Unless Gibson already suspected Theo Durrant of Blanche's murder, there can be no reason for him to make such a statement. At that point, the other witnesses who had seen Theo and Blanche approaching the church had not yet come forward.

20. Testimony of Clark H. Morgan, *SFE*, April 17, 1895; "Looks Bad for Durrant," *SFC*, April 15, 1895.

21. "Mrs. Durrant's Statement," *SFC*, April 15, 1895; testimony of Sgt. W. F. Burke, *SFE*, April 18, 1895.

22. Cheviot is a fine, soft wool, heavier than serge. It comes from the Cheviot sheep. ("Wool," available at http://www.fabrics.net/wool.htm; accessed September 6, 1999.)

23. Testimony of Clark H. Morgan, *SFE*, April 17, 1895.

24. "Tighter Grows the Chain around Durrant," *Call*, April 17, 1895.

25. Testimony of Frank A. Sademan, *SFE*, April 17, 1895; "Durrant Had a Key to the Church," *SFE*, April 15, 1895.

26. Testimony of Detective Edward L. Gibson, *SFC*, September 6, 1895.

27. "The Second Chapter of Horror," *SFE*, April 15, 1895.

28. Testimony of Arthur B. Riehl and Edward Gibson, *SFE*, April 17, 1895; see also "Her Body Found," *SFC*, April 15, 1895, and "The Second Chapter of Horror," *SFE*, April 15, 1895.

29. Robert K. Ressler and Tom Shachtman, *I Have Lived in the Monster* (New York: St. Martin's Press, 1997), p. 7. See also John E. Douglas et al., *Crime Classification Manual* (San Francisco: Jossey-Bass Publishers, 1992): "Undoing frequently occurs at the crime scene when there is a close association between the offender and the victim or when the victim represents someone of significance to the offender." Examples of undoing cited by the authors include the "folding of the hands over the chest so that the victim appears to be sleeping peacefully, washing up, cleaning the body, covering the victim's face, or completely covering the body with something" (p. 251).

30. Testimony of Charles G. Noble, *SFC*, September 7, 1895.

31. "Crowd at the Morgan," *SFE*, April 15, 1895.

32. Mortuary records of the city and county of San Francisco, August 1, 1894–June 30, 1896. Although Barrett's testimony says he performed

the autopsies on Sunday, April 14, the mortuary records state that both bodies were received on Wednesday, April 17, along with thirty-two others that same day. However, as the newspapers reported it on the 15th, it is unclear what the date in the records refers to.

33. "At the Morgue," *SFC*, April 15, 1895.

34. "The Identification of Durrant" and "Crowding to See the Victims," *SFE*, April 16, 1895 (Blanche's three classmates taken to the morgue to identify her); "Startling Evidence," *SFC*, April 16, 1895 (her deformed foot).

35. "The Crime of a Century," *SFE*, April 15, 1895 (calla lilies); "Tears for Her Clothes," *SFE*, September 11, 1895 (people at the crime scene).

36. Testimony of Starr Dare, *SFC*, September 7, 1895.

37. Text under picture on front page of *SFE*, April 19, 1895.

38. "Discoveries in the Church," *SFE*, April 17, 1895.

39. Testimony of Maud Lamont, *SFC*, September 12, 1895. (The Delsarte pamphlet from May Duncan's School was Defendant's Exhibit AAW12.) Devised by Francois Delsarte, this system "combined rhythmic but decorous gymnastics with gestures indicating specific emotions" ("My History Is America's History": http://www.myhistory.org/history-files/articles/theatrical_dance.html; accessed July 4, 2000). It is ironic that Blanche would contemplate this form of dancing, a precursor of Maud (Allan) Durrant's dance form.

40. "Tighter Grows the Chain around Durrant," *Call*, April 17, 1895. Police at the time claimed that the writing was Theo's, but he would hardly have had time to think up and print the maxims on the ride to the church. Moreover, none of the witnesses who saw him on the various cars testified to his writing anything, and in her cross-examination, Maud Lamont says it looks like her sister's writing (see Testimony of Maud Lamont, *SFC*, September 12, 1895).

41. "The News by Sun Flashes," *SFE*, April 16, 1895; "Tidings Flashed," *Call*, April 17, 1895; "Dr. Perkins Confident," *SFE*, April 20, 1895.

42. "Flashed on the Sunlight," *SFE*, April 15, 1895. Normally, Theo's somewhat passive response would indicate what modern criminologists refer to as "guilty man syndrome": The guilty man thinks that if he is calm and unperturbed, he will appear innocent, whereas innocent people are usually very vocal and insistent on their lack of involvement. However, the message sent via heliograph would have alerted him and taken away the element of surprise, so it's hard to tell about his reaction. But the message didn't say *what* he was to be arrested for, and if he were truly innocent, it would seem that more of a shocked response would be in order.

CHAPTER 6: THE PRINCE OF CITY PRISON

1. This peppy, Gilbert-and-Sullivanesque tune can be heard on the CD *Moonlight Bay: Songs As Is and Songs As Was*, performed by Joan Morris and William Bolcom on Albany Records (1998).

2. The account of Theo's arrest can be found throughout the April 15, 1895 issues of all three newspapers.

3. "Durrant's Jaunt to Court," *SFE*, May 30, 1895.

4. Detective Anthony's notes were spared destruction in the 1906 earthquake and fire and discovered in Sacramento by author Joseph Henry Jackson when he was researching his *The Girl in the Belfry* (Greenwich, CT: Fawcett, 1957). However, they cannot now be found in either the California State Archives or the State Library in Sacramento. Theo's statement to Anthony is on p. 22 of Jackson's book.
The information about women's purses comes from a letter to the editor, *SFE*, May 2, 1895.

5. "Arrest of Durrant," *SFC*, April 15, 1895.

6. Detective Anthony's notes, in Jackson, p. 22.

7. "Flashed on the Sunlight," *SFE*, April 15, 1895.

8. "Delayed for Deuprey," *SFE*, October 16, 1895; "Three O'Clock on the Third," *SFE*, September 13, 1895. Populists were against big railroads and big banks.

9. The account of the ferry incident can be found in " 'Lynch Him!' The Cry," *SFC*, April 15, 1895, and "Scene at the Ferry," *Call*, April 15, 1895.

10. "What Durrant Has to Say," *SFE*, April 15, 1895; "The Noose Tightens," *SFE*, April 16, 1895; "Behind the Bars," *Call*, April 15, 1895.

11. "Did He Kill Ware?" *SFC*, April 15, 1895; "Ware and Durrant," *SFC*, April 17, 1895; "He Did Not Know Ware," *Call*, April 18, 1895; "The Ware Theory Baseless," *SFE*, April 19, 1895; "Close to Ware's Assassin," *SFC*, August 22, 1895.

12. "Mrs. Ella Forsyth," *SFC*, April 16, 1895; "Mrs. Forsyth Not a Member," *SFE*, April 16, 1895; "Mrs. Forsyth Heard From," *SFE*, April 18, 1895.

13. "Tried to Kill Her," *SFC*, April 16, 1895.

14. Ad from *SFC*, April 16, 1895.

15. "Five Inquests Finished," *Call*, April 21, 1895; "Durrant in the Prison," *SFE*, April 19, 1895.

16. "Latest Detective Theory," *Call*, April 19, 1895; "A New Theory in the Murder Case," *SFC*, April 21, 1895; "Four New Witnesses Are Found," *SFC*, April 22, 1895.

17. "A Light in the Study," *SFE*, April 20, 1895 (church rumors); Taber's letter can be found in the *Chronicle* ("Dr. Gibson's Church," April 23),

the *Call* ("Emmanuel Church," April 24), and the *Examiner* ("Statement from Mr. Taber," April 23).

18. "As to Hypnotism," *Call*, April 20, 1895. It is impossible to convey the extent of Trilbymania in 1895. As is done in our own day, there were even purchasable by-products, such as spoons, brooches, and even ice cream! There are several streets and cities in Florida that are named after the characters in *Trilby*. This 1894 novel by George du Maurier is available in a paperback reprint edition by New York's Dover Publications (1994), with the original illustrations by the author. For a look at *Trilby* as a sociological phenomenon, see Emily Jenkins, "*Trilby*: Fads, Photographers, and 'Over-Perfect Feet,' " in *Book History* 1.1 (1998), 221–67. See also "Trilbymania Has Arrived," *SFE*, April 28, 1895.

19. "Mania about Women," *SFC*, April 16, 1895. A paperback version of *Psychopathia Sexualis* is available from The Paperback Library (New York, 1965).

20. From the front page of *SFE*, April 20, 1895; "look at his mouth; that tells the story" is overheard in the crowd by Miss Rouse in "The Woman of It," *SFC*, July 26, 1895; see also "Durrant's Skull," *Call*, April 17, 1895.

21. The picture of the ears appears in *SFE*, November 19, 1897.

22. The pelvic problem can be found in "Durrant Injured," *Call*, April 19, 1895, and the telegram in "Chambliss Takes a Hand," *SFE*, April 25, 1895. The pain and high fever may have been connected with meningitis, which Theo contracted around April of that year.

23. "There Were Two Durrants," *SFE*, April 16, 1895.

24. "His Disposition," *SFC*, April 19, 1895 (bizarre behavior); "Skillful with the Scalpel," *SFE*, April 21, 1895, and "A New Witness for Durrant," *SFC*, September 2, 1895 (respectful behavior).

25. "She Will Not Be a Witness," *SFE*, September 16, 1895.

26. "The Prisoner's Pleasures," *SFE*, April 17, 1895.

27. "Durrant's New Cell," *SFC*, May 5, 1895.

28. "[I]f I even smile, the reporters say I'm getting flippant, and if I look serious they say I'm sullen. I don't know how to please them." ("Twelve Men Chosen for Trial of Durrant," *SFC*, August 30, 1895); "It is hard to please everybody. If I should put on a long face, they would say I had lost hope, and if I looked bright, they would charge me with flippancy. So I try to take a course midway between the two, and still I catch it." ("Durrant is Hopeful," *Call*, July 28, 1895).

29. "A Fearful Vision," *SFC*, April 16, 1895; "Cried Aloud in His Sleep," *SFE*, April 16, 1895; "Probably Feigning," *SFC*, April 17, 1895; "More Horrid Dreams," *SFE*, April 17, 1895.

30. "Flashed on the Sunlight," *SFE*, April 15, 1895 ("I liked Miss Lamont greatly. She was so much like my sister . . . so active and jolly."); "First

Night in Prison," *SFE*, April 15, 1895 ("I knew Blanche Lamont very well and thought of her as I have of a thousand girls and my own sister."); "How He Spent Sunday," *SFE*, April 29, 1895 (cries over Blanche and expresses sorrow; goes into raptures over his sister's beauty); "Why Durrant Was Silent," *SFE*, November 1, 1895 ("No one feels more sorry for poor Blanche than I. If she had been my own sister I could not experience more intense suffering than I do when I dwell on the fate of that poor, unfortunate girl.").

31. "Clarke the Witness," *SFC*, August 3, 1895.

32. This tale fits the classic model of the urban legend (see Professor Jan Harold Brunvand's collection and commentary on this version of the folk tale in *Too Good to Be True: The Colossal Book of Urban Legends*, 2000, from W.W. Norton). The "mysterious woman" in the Durrant case was always "a friend of a friend" and sometimes even further removed from the narrator. It's the kind of story that makes people gasp or titter when they hear it—or read it—but the fact remains that, as with all urban legends, *the event never happened*. See "The Mysterious Woman," *Call*, September 13, 1895. ("The prosecution . . . no longer believes that there is such a person. . . . In each instance [the rumors] are run down by detectives, who have thus far proven in every case that there was no foundation for the story. . . . [T]he police and the District Attorney [have come] to the conclusion that the mysterious woman is a myth.") Commentators since 1895 (with the notable exception of Joseph H. Jackson) have either carelessly or deliberately chosen to repeat the story as true when both the police and the prosecution specifically stated that the "mysterious woman" did not exist. See, for example, Thomas S. Duke, *Celebrated Criminal Cases of America* (San Francisco: The James H. Barry Co., 1910). Duke was the chief of police in San Francisco and should have known better; he is also responsible for the perpetration of yet another legend, which will be addressed in chapter 8, infra. See also Hildegarde Teilhet, "The Demon in the Belfry," in Allan Bosworth et al., *San Francisco Murderers* (New York: Duell, Sloan, and Pearce, 1947); Dorothy Dunbar, *Blood in the Parlor* (New York: A. S. Barnes & Co., 1964); H. S. Stuttman, *Crimes and Punishments: The Illustrated Crime Encyclopedia* (Westport, CT: H. S. Stuttman, Inc., 1994); Jay Robert Nash, *Bloodletters and Badmen* (New York: M. Evans, 1995); and Colin and Damon Wilson, *The Killers among Us, Book II* (New York: Warner Books, 1995). This is just a small sampling of the many works presenting this myth as true.

Ida Clayton, named in the text, *was* a real person; but through a convoluted series of events she was at one time identified as "the friend of the friend" who had undergone the experience at the hands of Theo. It turned out she knew nothing, but occasionally her name is mentioned by commentators as the woman who actually saw him naked in the church. For a detailed description of how this shy schoolteacher became connected to this racy rumor, see "Durrant's Suggestion," *SFE*, September 9, 1895; "Mrs. [*sic*] Clayton's Story," *SFE*, September 10, 1895; "That Mysterious Witness," *SFC*, September 8, 1895; "Durrant Expresses Himself as to the Mysterious Woman," *SFC*, September 9, 1895; "Miss Clayton Returns," *SFC*, September 10, 1895.

33. "A Desolate Church," *Call*, April 21, 1895; "The Church Haunted," *Call*, November 10, 1895.

34. "The Future of Emmanuel" and "Emmanuel Church to Be Abandoned," *SFE*, April 16, 1895. For information about the Kalloch-De Young incident, see Jerome A. Hart, "The Kearney-Kalloch Epoch," available online at http://www.sfmuseum.org, and the *San Francisco Chronicle* April 24–30, 1880, and March 2–26, 1881. See also "Emmanuel Church To Be Abandoned," *SFE*, April 16, 1895, and Dunbar at p. 51. Robert Graysmith's quasi-fictional work, *The Bell Tower: The Case of Jack the Ripper Finally Solved in San Francisco* (Washington, DC: Regnery Publishing Co., 1999), treats the shooting extensively. An interesting side note is the fact that it was suspected that the deYoung shooting was a plot concocted by Milton Kalloch's father, Mayor Isaac Kalloch. One of the people supposedly involved in this plot (if such existed) was Flo Upton's uncle, Dr. George E. Davis, who was the mayor's personal physician. (See "The Servant Ransome's Home," *SFC*, April 25, 1880.) However, it is possible that Milton Kalloch was *not* the pastor of Emmanuel Baptist.

35. "The Fate of the Church," *SFE*, April 17, 1895; "Church in Danger," *Call*, April 19, 1895.

36. "Exposed to Public View," *SFE*, April 17, 1895; "To the Grave," *Call*, April 17, 1895.

37. "Mourn Their Loss," *Butte (Montana) Daily Miner*, April 20, 1895; "Blanche Lamont Found Dead," *Dillon (Montana) Tribune*, April 19, 1895.

38. "Symbols of Purity," *SFC*, April 18, 1895; "Rest, Marian Williams," *SFE*, April 18, 1895. In 1902, an ordinance was passed in San Francisco to prevent further burials within city limits. The ordinance was challenged, but declared constitutional in *Laurel Hill Cemetery v. City and County of San Francisco* 216 US 358 (1910). The bodies interred in Laurel Hill Cemetery were removed to Laurel Hill Mound in Cypress Lawn Memorial Park, Colma, California, in 1940, and buried in a mass grave there.

39. "Minnie Williams and Durrant," *SFE*, April 16, 1895.

40. "Rest, Marian Williams," *SFE*, April 18, 1895; "The Funeral," *Call*, April 18, 1895.

41. "A Doomed Edifice," *Call*, April 18, 1895. Theo said of Rev. Gibson:

"He is a very excitable man and loses his head if he is hurried or has to do anything quick." ("First Night in Prison," *SFE*, April 15, 1895).

42. "Church Doors Shut," *SFC*, April 19, 1895; "Pastor Gibson's Moods," *SFE*, April 19, 1895.

43. "The Doctor Fought," *SFE*, April 20, 1895; "Searching for the Murderer's Garments," *Call*, April 20, 1895.

44. Information on Robert Newton Lynch comes from "Gibson's Understudy," SFC, August 15, 1895 and from Lewis Byington, ed., *The History of San Francisco* (Chicago: S. J. Clarke Pub. Co., 1931), 27.

45. Mrs. Durrant's letter appeared in "A Mother's Prayer," *Call*, April 17, 1895. Robert Lynch's response on behalf of Gibson appears in "Gives His Reasons," *SFC*, April 21, 1895, and "Rev. Dr. Gibson Explains His Position," *SFE*, April 21, 1895.

46. Information on John H. Dickinson comes from Leigh H. Irvine, *A History of New California* (Lewis Publishing Company, 1905), pp. 366–68 and "Durrant's Counsel," *SFC*, April 20, 1895. (Leigh Irvine was one of the San Francisco newspaper reporters who interviewed Theo on his first night in prison. He was later a witness for the prosecution at the trial.)

47. Information on Eugene N. Deuprey comes from "Sudden Death of Eugene Deuprey," *Stockton Independent*, October 6, 1903.

48. "Evidence in a Letter," *SFE*, April 20, 1895 ("hang a dozen men"); "Durrant May Sue Chief Crowley," *SFE*, May 15, 1895 (Rogues' Gallery picture).

49. "Startling Evidence," *SFC*, April 16, 1895; "Must Stand Trial," *Call*, May 3, 1895.

50. "They Saw Durrant," *SFC*, April 22, 1895; Testimony of Emma Struven, *SFE*, April 24, 1895.

CHAPTER 7: THE INQUEST, AND A TRIAL BY "NOOSE"PAPER

Only the *Examiner* provided an official transcript of the police court proceedings. The *Chronicle* mostly summarized testimony, with an occasional section reproduced by a reporter, but there were inaccuracies if the reporter did not hear it correctly. The *Call* primarily summarized, often in a Question and Answer format that was not exactly reproduced from the actual testimony. For these reasons, the *Examiner* must be considered the authoritative source of police court testimony.

1. "If Women Went to Congress," *SFC*, November 10, 1895.

2. "Fin de Siècle Fun, *SFE*, May 1, 1895 (editorial page).

3. See "Bloomers in Billville," *SFE*, August 6, 1895:

The women down at Billville have got the bloomer craze:
They're ridin' round on bicycles an' blockin' all the ways.
They say it makes 'em healthy, an' they're goin' for it strong.
An' the men are bakin' biscuits an' cussin' all day long!
　　Bicycles an' bloomers—
　　　Never saw the like;
　　Never is no tellin'
　　　Where lightnin's goin' to strike!

4. "The New Era," *SFE*, August 11, 1895.

5. "Her Bifurcates Too Scant," *SFE*, September 7, 1895. See also "Frost on the Bloomer," *SFE*, July 31, 1895; Alice Rix, "The Women Who Wear Them: An Argument," *SFE*, August 25, 1895; Alice Rix, "Bloomers Are Now Passing," *SFE*, October 13, 1895; Bill Nye, "Bloomers Are Good Things," *SFE*, October 13, 1895; "The Rev. Dr. Cryor's Attack on Bloomer Costumes Resented by Cyclers," *SFE*, December 8, 1897.

6. International Bicycle Fund, "Bicycle History: USA," available at http://www.ibike.org/historyusa.htm.

7. "Are Written in Blood," *Call*, April 22, 1895.

8. "Must Stand Trial," *Call*, May 3, 1895.

9. "San Francisco's Shame," *SFE*, April 16, 1895; "Where the Responsibility Lies," *SFE*, April 18, 1895.

10. "Some Practical Joker," *SFE*, April 16, 1895.

11. "Thought It a Joke," *Call*, April 20, 1895.

12. "After Durant [*sic*]," *SFE*, April 14, 1895.

13. "An Eccentric Student," *Call*, April 16, 1895.

14. "She Distrusted Durrant," *SFC*, August 19, 1895.

15. The *Examiner* letters appeared in issues of April 20–May 7, 1895.

16. Letters to the Editor, *Call*, April 20, 1895.

17. "Cranks Developed," *Call*, April 26, 1895.

18. "Durrant in the Prison," *SFE*, April 19, 1895.

19. "The Missing Clothes," *SFE*, April 18, 1895.

20. "She Is Confident," *Call*, April 20, 1895; "A Bloody Shoe," *Call*, April 21, 1895.

21. Unless otherwise indicated, the information on Minnie Williams's inquest and preliminary examination comes from all three newspapers, April 17–May 1, 1895.

22. Peixotto, p. 214. However, his summary says Minnie was "outraged *probably* before and after death" (emphasis mine), so the report must not have been conclusive. And, in an interview with the *Examiner*, Dr. Barrett, the autopsy physician, said that Minnie was "assaulted *before* the injuries that killed her" ("Woman Murder in a Church," *SFE*, April 14, 1895; emphasis mine).

23. Testimony of Herbert C. Porter, October 9, 1895.

24. "San Francisco City Hall and Hall of Records," from the website of the Museum of the City of San Francisco, available at http://www.sfmuseum.org/hist2/c-hall.html.

25. Information on William S. Barnes comes from "Popular Lawyer Succumbs to Apoplexy," *SFC*, March 14, 1910; information on salaries comes from the 1895–1896 San Francisco City Directory.

26. "Hills Attempts Suicide," *Call*, May 3, 1895; "Hills Sought Death," *SFC*, May 3, 1895.

27. Unless otherwise indicated, information on Blanche Lamont's inquest and preliminary examination comes from all three newspapers, May 2–4, 1895.

28. Gynecological information, which was not printed in the newspapers, comes from Peixotto, p. 5. The statement about Blanche's not being raped comes from "Crowd at the Morgue," *SFE*, April 15, 1895.

CHAPTER 8: KNEE-DEEP IN THE HOOPLA: THE ROAD TO TRIAL

1. "Durrant's New Cell," *SFC*, May 5, 1895.

2. "Durrant's Change of Cells," *SFE*, May 5, 1895. However, the *Chronicle* says that Walter "Kid" Shear was a burglar.

3. "Durrant's Jaunt to Court," *SFE*, May 30, 1895.

4. When the district attorney announced his decision to try Theo Durrant on the Blanche Lamont murder first, everyone was surprised, as it seemed that the Minnie Williams case was the stronger of the two. (It was not until after this decision was made that the strongest witnesses in the Lamont case—Mrs. Crosett and Mrs. Leak—came forward.) However, although it was never stated, it is likely that the prosecution felt that, of the two victims, Blanche Lamont would present a much more sympathetic figure to a jury.

5. "Durrant May Sue Chief Crowley," *SFE*, May 15, 1895. For Theo's willingness to have his picture taken, see "Durrant's Change of Cells," *SFE*, May 5, 1895.

6. "An Exhibition of Temper," *SFE*, April 27, 1895; "Murder in the Belfry," *SFE*, April 28, 1895. Mamma may be referring to the slop pail incident in her (undated) letter to Maud in Berlin: "Theo's exhibition of temper last night will do him no good, but you know him of old, whatever he has to say he will say at any cost" (Cherniavsky, p. 34).

7. "Durrant's Notes on That Lecture," *SFC*, October 7, 1895.

8. "One Secret of His Defense," *SFE*, August 28, 1895.

9. "Emanuel's Doors Again Open," *SFC*, July 15, 1895. Information about Dr. King comes from "Durrant Expresses Himself as to the Mysterious Woman," *SFC*, September 9, 1895.

10. Unless otherwise stated, all information concerning jury selection comes from all three newspapers, July 22–August 30, 1895.

11. Alexander Goldenson, 19, lived next door to the sexually precocious Mamie Kelly, who seems to have been importunate at best, stalking him at worst. Goldenson, frustrated by the situation, shot Kelly when she confronted him yet again about not paying attention to her (see Duke, pp. 84–84). After Goldenson was executed, the mortuary receiving his body came in for much negative publicity and some vandalism; this experience would later cause repercussions for Theo's family (see chapter 11, infra).

12. For an explanation of the ongoing controversy, see "Another Offer to Mr. De Young," *SFE*, November 29, 1895.

13. Duke says (p. 122) that Rosalind Bowers later lived in a Sutter Street "house" under the name of Grace King, where she tricked a wealthy but drunken Edward Clarke into marrying her.

14. Charles Clark enters the newspaper articles beginning July 28, 1895, and stays until August 8 with his admission that he made a casual remark to Deuprey about seeing Blanche on a streetcar prior to April 3.

15. Carrie Cunningham's article (unsigned) is "Saw Blanche Lamont Lured to Her Death," *SFC*, August 16, 1895.

16. "Durrant Talks in His Cell," *SFC*, August 22, 1895.

17. Carrie Cunningham testified to this at the trial, but there were a few facts that didn't come up there. After the trial, she wrote an article for the *Examiner*, where she was then working (because the *Chronicle* didn't pay bonuses for scoops, and she had gotten several): "What He Told Miss Cunningham," *SFE*, November 2, 1895. See also "Durrant's Story To His Lawyers," *SFE*, October 26, 1895, which discusses the possibility (reported by a defense team "insider" as a fact) that Theo's lawyers actually read the letter he had shown to Carrie and later presented to them. In the letter, Theo referred to the murderers as Rev. Gibson and "a young man prominent in the affairs of the church," which would seem to implicate George King (Elmer Wolfe was not involved with the church at this time). The *Examiner* refers to this person as Theo's "closest friend," which would also indicate George King.

18. The picnic picture and the reference to the improper conduct are in *SFE*, August 20, 1895 ("Durrant's Letters to Helen Henry"). Some further clarification comes in "Durrant's Straw Ride," *SFC*, September 14, 1895. In both "Durrant's Suggestion," *SFE*, September 9, 1895, and "Durrant Ill At Ease," *SFE*, October 13, 1895, there is a reference to a photograph to be introduced against Theo's character. Although the *Examiner* had published that very photograph in August it is obvious the reporter is not making the connection (another indication that "evil is in the eye of the beholder").

19. Duke, p. 122.

20. Wilson and Wilson, p. 80.

21. For the decision, see *Dailey v. Superior Court*, 44 Pac. Rep. 458 (1896). For a discussion of the case, see "Right to Produce a Play Based Upon the Facts of a Criminal Case Pending Its Trial: The Expression of One's Sentiments through the Medium of a Play Held to be Within the Constitutional Guarantee of Right of Free Speech and Therefore Not Subject to Injunction Proceedings," 30 *American Law Review* 597 (1896).

22. Of the 1,300 men called, 490 made it to the jury box for examination. (See Peixotto, p. 3).

CHAPTER 9: THE CASE FOR THE PROSECUTION

1. Alice Rix, "With the Other Women at the Durrant Trial," *SFE*, August 11, 1895.

2. Alice Rix, "The Women Who Wear Them: An Argument," *SFE*, August 25, 1895; "Bloomers Are Now Passing," *SFE*, October 13, 1895.

3. Unless otherwise stated, all accounts of the prosecution's case come from *SFE*, *Chronicle*, and *Call* of September 1–25, 1895. The *Chronicle* was using the transcript prepared by Judge Murphy's court reporter, so theirs must be considered to be the official one.

4. Jackson and Offord, p. 70.

5. "Sudden Close of Durrant's Defense," *SFC*, October 23, 1895.

6. Personals section, *Dillon (Montana) Tribune*, November 8, 1895.

7. Both the *SFE* and the *Call* sketched the duplicate strap, on which was clearly printed BLANCHE LAMONT. As neither Aunt Tryphena nor Maud Lamont indicated a problem with the spelling, this should answer the question as to how Blanche spelled her first name.

8. The first names of Charlotte, Clarence, and Ellen—not given in the newspapers—were provided by city directories, the California Death Index, and obituaries.

9. There were many variant spellings for this saloon, which does not appear in the city directories: Giovanetti's, Giavanotti's, Gianetti's. However, the transcript provided by the official court reporter used Gionetti's.

10. Readers of Irish descent will recognize this delightfully sardonic word ("himself") used as a nominative pronoun to refer to anyone in authority—or anyone who *esteems* himself as an authority. "Herself" is also used, usually by husbands.

11. Darrell Harman, C.E., is a certified embalmer and funeral director who also taught autopsy procedures to interns at Boston's Massachusetts General Hospital. He says that blocks are *never* used in autopsies, but are often used by morticians when preparing a body for viewing. In such

cases, the blocks are placed on either side of the head, similar to what had been done with Blanche (personal interview, December 8, 1999).

CHAPTER 10: THEO TAKES THE STAND

1. "Refused to Read the Durrant Trial," *SFE*, October 10, 1895; "Mrs. Rogers Vanishes," *SFE*, October 25, 1895; "Off with Her Sister," *Call*, October 25, 1895.

2. "Durrant on the Brain," *Call*, October 14, 1895.

3. "She Will Not Be a Witness," *SFE*, September 16, 1895.

4. Defense testimony appears in all three newspapers from September 26–October 24, 1895. Theo's testimony is covered in the issues of October 10–12.

5. "Rev. J. George Gibson Pays His Respects to Eugene Deuprey," *SFC*, October 1, 1895; "The Voice of Gibson," *SFE*, October 1, 1895.

6. The doctor's name is sometimes mistakenly written as William Fitz Cheney. However, the official records of Cooper Medical School, now housed at Stanford University, report his middle name as Fitch.

7. See "Prays for Him Nightly," *Call*, September 20, 1895. This phenomenon was not peculiar to the nineteenth century. A program produced for HBO television in December 1999 ("America Undercover: Women Who Love Killers") presents five murderers, the most notable of whom is Richard Ramirez (the "Night Stalker"). All of them had hundreds of women who wrote to them after their arrests, showed up in court, and in some cases married them. One sheriff commented that there were lots of women at Ramirez's trial every day, many of them good looking, well dressed, and well educated.

8. "Juror Smyth Gets into Trouble," *SFC*, October 15, 1895; "Smyth's Sharp Blow," *SFE*, October 15, 1895.

9. "Mr. M'Coy's Expensive Joke," *SFE*, October 4, 1895.

10. The word "betrayed" in this context always meant seduction followed by abandonment. However, the woman was married, so possibly it implied an affair or even a rape.

11. Mabel Craft, "The Prisoner's Alibi Story Told Cautiously in a Dreary Monotone," *SFC*, October 10, 1895.

12. "With Durrant But Once," November 15, 1895.

CHAPTER 11: "MAMMA'S SWEETHEART": APPEALS AND AN EXECUTION

1. "Planning Alibis for Durrant," *SFE*, October 29, 1895; "It Is Yet a Mystery," *SFE*, October 31, 1895.

2. "A Time for Severity," *SFE* editorial, November 11, 1895.

3. "Durrant's Story to His Lawyers," *SFE*, October 26, 1895; "Durrant's Lawyers Deny a Wild Tale," *SFC*, October 27, 1895.

4. "What He Told Miss Cunningham," *SFE*, November 2, 1895. Carrie Cunningham had been employed by the *Chronicle* at the time of these interviews and up until the day before her testimony on the witness stand, when she went back to her old employer, the *Examiner*. The reason for the switch, she said, was that the *Chronicle* didn't pay extra for scoops. Obviously miffed, the *Chronicle* ridiculed her for believing the tall tale fed her by Theo, which he was claiming he had invented to keep her from bothering him. (See "An Exploded Mystery," *SFC*, November 2, 1895.)

5. "The Murderer Talks," *Call*, November 2, 1895.

6. "What Durrant Felt While Waiting for the Fatal Verdict," *Call*, November 6, 1895.

7. "Motive for Minnie Williams' Murder," *Call*, November 7, 1895.

8. "Minnie Williams' Words," *Call*, November 9, 1895.

9. "Another Mare's Nest," *Call*, November 9, 1895; "Mr. Hearst of New York," *Call*, November 10, 1895.

10. "Mrs. Durrant Still Hopes," *Call*, November 6, 1895.

11. "What Was It Minnie Williams Knew?" *Call*, November 8, 1895; "Penalty of Knowledge," *Call*, November 9, 1895.

12. "Durrant's Own Story," *SFE*, November 6, 1895.

13. "Alice Rix Sees the Durrant Trial," *SFE*, October 27, 1895.

14. "Nearly Killed by Gas," *SFE*, November 12, 1895.

15. "Theodore Durrant Was Not Sentenced," *Call*, November 9, 1895.

16. Donnelly, a somewhat successful politician, was a believer in the Atlantis myth and was called the "Prince of Cranks." However, the book Theo was reading, published in 1891 (*Caesar's Column*), a story of America in the year 1988, accurately predicted television, radio, and poison gas. See http://www.britannica.com, and Marjorie Braymer, *Atlantis: The Biography of a Legend* (New York: Atheneum, 1983).

17. "Durrant Knelt and Prayed Aloud," *SFE*, November 4, 1895.

18. "Durrant on Religion," *SFE*, November 6, 1895.

19. "The American Protective Association," from *The Catholic Encyclopedia*, available online at http://www.csn.net/advent/cathen/01426a.htm; "Durrant and Religion" (letter to the editor), *SFE*, November 13, 1895.

20. "Demon of the Belfry," *SFE*, November 7 and 12, 1895; "It Made Them All Laugh," *Call*, November 12, 1895; "A Demon but No Ghost," *SFE*, November 19, 1895.

21. "The Doom of Durrant," *SFE*, December 11, 1895.

22. *People v. Durrant*, 116 Cal. 179 (1897).

23. San Quentin Inmate Records; *SFC, SFE,* and *Call* for April 11, 1897.

24. "The Governor's Decision," *Call*, June 1, 1897.

25. "Pleaded for the Life of Her Guilty Brother," *SFE*, November 12, 1897. (Maud had actually sent the letter in June for the execution date of June 11, 1897, but it was not printed in the newspapers until November.)

26. Articles on Theo's first session in the death-watch cell can be found in all three newspapers for June 1–13, 1897.

27. Cherniavsky, p. 105 and passim.

28. Theodore Durrant, "Azora," *SFE*, November 19, 1897.

29. "Revolting Scenes at the Prison's Gates," *SFC*, January 7, 1898; Cherniavsky, p. 106.

30. "Still in the Fight," *Call*, November 3, 1895. For an interesting look at Kinetoscopes, see Ray Phillips, *Edison's Kinetoscope and Its Films: A History to 1896* (Westport, CT: Greenwood Press, 1997).

31. Articles on Theo's second session in the death-watch cell can be found in all three newspapers for November 8–12, 1897.

32. Information on hanging comes from the 1897–1898 newspapers and from Fred A. Leuchter Associates, Inc., *Execution by Hanging Manual Prepared for the Department of Corrections of the State of Delaware*, 1990, available online at http://www.theelectricchair.com/hanging_protocol.htm. Only the states of Delaware and Washington offer the option of hanging.

33. *People v. Durrant*, 119 Cal. 54 and 119 Cal. 201 (1897).

34. "Blanther as the Fiend of the Belfry," *SFE*, November 24, 1897; "An Offer of Assistance to Durrant," *SFE*, November 25, 1897.

35. "Durrant's Appeal to the Rev. Mr. Gibson," *SFE*, December 13, 1897.

36. "Dr. Gibson Warned by the Police," *SFE*, December 14, 1897.

37. Articles on Theo's final session in the death-watch cell and on his hanging can be found in all three newspapers for December 15, 1897–January 8, 1898. Alice Rix's interview with the hangman is in "Lund [*sic*] Tells How a Man Should be Hanged," *SFE*, November 21, 1897. Rix was horrified at Lunt's complacency about his job, and the article is filled with subtle criticisms of him and of the death penalty. She must have enjoyed the fact that he was shaken to the core at last.

38. "Durrant Case Opens in a New Place," *SFC*, December 25, 1897; "Two Proceedings for Durrant Today," *SFC*, December 28, 1897; "Deuprey's Sensation Arrives," *SFC*, December 29, 1897; "Juror Smyth is Cited for Contempt," *SFE*, December 25, 1897; Juror Smyth Got Angry and Said Things," *SFE*, December 29, 1897; "Out of One Trouble and into Another," *SFE*, December 30, 1897.

39. Cherniavsky, pp. 127–28.

40. "Father Lagan Believes Durrant Was Guiltless," *Call*, January 11, 1898. See also, "Durrant Did Not Confess," *Call*, January 9, 1898.

41. "His Iron Nerves Unshaken to the End," *SFE*, January 8, 1898. In this interview, Mamma says that Theo put the locket around his neck, but "Where Will Durrant Rest," *SFC*, January 9, 1898, says it was put in his pocket. It is doubtful the prison authorities would have allowed him to put anything around his neck prior to the execution.

42. "A Ghastly Banquet," *Call*, January 8, 1898; "His Iron Nerves Unshaken to the End," *SFE*, January 8, 1898.

43. Harry Farrell, *Shallow Grave in Trinity County* (New York: St. Martin's Press, 1997), pp. 300–301.

44. Jackson and Offord, p. 183.

45. Articles on the search for a crematorium and on the cremation itself can be found in all three newspapers for January 9–15, 1898. Theo's body lay in his parents' house, unembalmed, for five days before it was sent to Pasadena.

46. William Shakespeare, *Macbeth*, act I, scene iv.

CHAPTER 12: KILLER ANGEL: MURDER IN THE EMMANUEL BAPTIST CHURCH

1. These qualities are specifically *not* found in the psychopathic individual. Typically, as children, they are cruel to animals and like to set fires. (See *DSM-IV*, §301.7(c); Stephen Michaud with Roy Hazelwood, *The Evil That Men Do* (New York: St. Martin's Press, 1998), p. 13 and passim; John Douglas and Mark Olshaker, *The Anatomy of Motive* (New York: Scribner's 1955), pp. 57, 108, and 145.

2. John Douglas, "Battered Barbie: An Ominous "Sign" May 30, 2000 (APB news.com).

3. John E. Douglas et al., *Crime Classification Manual: A Standard System for Investigating and Classifying Violent Crimes* (San Francisco: Jossey-Bass, 1992), pp. 124–25.

4. Isabella Durrant said that Theo's paternal grandparents had given him their chickens to raise when they were moving to Los Angeles in June 1894, and that he was convalescing from his illness at this time. As the meningitis lasted seven weeks, this indicates that he was sick during the months of April and May—just one year before the murders.

5. Stephen Leib, "Brain Damage Caused by Bacterial Meningitis is Prevented by Readily Available Antioxidant Drugs," presented at Interscience Conference on Antimicrobial Agents and Chemotherapy," September 26–29, 1999, San Francisco, California. Available online at http://www.newswise.com/articles/1999/9/ICAAC09.ASM.html.

6. Adrian Raine et al., "Brain Abnormalities in Murderers by Positron Emission Tomagraphy," *Biological Psychiatry* 1997; 42: 495–508.

7. Dorothy Otnow Lewis, M.D., *Guilty by Reason of Insanity: A Psychiatrist Explores the Minds of Killers* (New York: Fawcett, 1998), p. 288.

8. Cherniavsky, p. 33.

9. "His Mind in a Whirl," *SFC*, April 15, 1895.

10. *DSM-IV (Diagnostic and Statistical Manual of Mental Disorders, Fourth Edition)*, p. 318.

11. Frederick K. Goodwin, M.D., and Kay Redfield Jamison, Ph.D., *Manic-Depressive Illness* (New York: Oxford University Press, 1990), p. 310.

12. Robert K. Ressler and Tom Shachtman, *Whoever Fights Monsters* (New York: St. Martin's, 1992), pp. 100–102.

13. "Why was I not at home to be with him those fatal days?" (Cherniavsky, p. 69).

14. William S. Barnes, closing argument: "Mind you, gentlemen, I do not say that on that morning he had made up his mind to murder her." (See *SFC*, October 31, 1895.)

15. Kay Redfield Jamison, Ph.D., *An Unquiet Mind* (New York: Alfred A. Knopf, 1995), p. 67.

16. Compton's Online Encyclopedia defines catalepsy as

a physical state in which the muscles of the face, body, and limbs take on a condition of suspended animation; a trancelike or unresponsive state of consciousness, which is also called anochlesia. It may last for several hours. The body position or expression does not alter and the limbs remain in whatever position they are placed (waxy flexibility). It is associated with hysteria, epilepsy, and schizophrenia in humans; may also be caused by brain disease and some drugs. (http://www.optonline.com/comptons/ceo/10430_Q.html

17. Jamison, p. 74. Yet another possibility is the amnesia that results from extreme stress: "Conventional psychiatric explanations of stress and trauma [agree] that a dissociative state is induced at the moment of greatest tension, and this causes a blackout" (Ressler, p. 123).

18. Theo's almost hysterical insistence that there was "no blood, no blood" in his "confession" to Carrie Cunningham may have stemmed from the feeling that he had not meant to kill Blanche. For him, the presence of blood would signify violence and great bodily harm.

19. Stephen G. Michaud and Hugh Aynesworth, *Ted Bundy: Conversations with a Killer* (New York: Signet, 1989), p. 93.

20. Personal interview, December 8, 1999.

21. "Blanche Lamont Had a Warning," *SFC*, October 18, 1895.

Another, although remote, explanation for Blanche's murder is that Theo was not attracted to women and was trying to suppress homosexual feelings by being sexually aggressive with Blanche. If she scorned him ("Blanche did not care for men in that way") or made a slighting reference to his masculinity, he might have reacted in rage.

Throughout this saga, there are hints that Theo might have had homosexual leanings: his tendency toward effeminate behavior in dress and manner, his feeling more comfortable with women, and his constant talking about women the year leading up to the murders (protesting too much). While he was in jail awaiting trial, Theo wrote to his sister Maud about a dream he had about their mutual friend Nell Partridge (Harry's sister). I felt it might contain some important clues about Theo's attitude toward women, so I had a syndicated columnist and dream analyst, Nancy Huseby Bloom, look at it. I did not give her his name or his circumstances because I did not want to influence her interpretation; nor did I say anything about my suspicions as to his possible homosexuality. Here is Theo's dream, related in Cherniavsky's book:

I had the greatest dream you ever heard about [Nell]. I dreamed we were all at a picnic and were about to return home and she had left us. I turned back and saw Nell coming towards me and she was eating what appeared to be rubber balls, but they were rubber balls with whiskey in them. I smelled it when she came up close and she was 'full as a goat'. Whew but wasn't she tho.

I looked in astonishment and she began to reel and it began to rain and she appeared to be dressed in a beautiful bathing suit which by the action of the rain was all washed off leaving her a la statue. I was in a great way as to what to do, but in looking down I discovered I had a blanket in my hands which I used to encircle her, then taking her up in my arms I looked for a place to go. I seemed to have left the picnic grounds and was behind a fence which shut off a lake. It was terribly warm and the sun beat down on the lake and in a corner by the fence, yet it rained.

I found a lot of straw or hay and made bed and at this juncture the rain ceased and sun became hotter so I laid her upon the bed and she began to steam and in a moment the blanket all steamed away (again a la statue recumbent). The heat diminished and I was in a terrible stew. I didn't know what to do. She got up and came and put her arms around me and clung to me. I then made her a skirt of straw not being able to remove a stitch of my clothes for some reason or other and in a few minutes we found a flying machine into which we got and were landed upon her own roof at home from which I carried her down and into her house. Wasn't that a great experience? [Theo then enjoins Maud not to tell this to anyone "over there or here" and instructs her to destroy the letter; he probably thought it would not be a good idea to reveal a dream about himself and a naked woman.] (79–80)

Here is the analysis provided by Nancy Huseby Bloom:

On the surface, it seems it could be regarding his own repressed sexuality (he wanted to cover her up, and he couldn't get his own clothes off). The rubber balls are interesting . . . a set of gonads? They are filled with whiskey, which can be viewed as an aphrodisiac or a substance that loosens up the psyche to let forbidden thoughts come in.

The magical quality of the dream makes me think that this woman is his own sexuality, and he's trying to cover her up. I think he might be gay—the rubber balls, his inability to make love to her. . . . She wants his embrace, and if she is his repressed sexuality, he can't really accept it. He still wants to cover her up, although this time with a grass [*sic*] skirt. (e-mail to author, August 10, 1999, used by permission)

22. Authors Michaud and Aynesworth (*The Only Living Witness* and *Ted Bundy: Conversations with a Killer*) got Ted Bundy to talk in great detail about his crimes by employing the third-person device: Bundy described the "hypothetical" serial killer who would have committed the murders.

23. Jamison, p. 67.

24. William Makepeace Thackeray, *The Newcomes: Memoirs of a Most Respectable Family* (London: Everyman, 1994), p. 648.

CHAPTER 13: EPILOGUE

1. San Francisco city directories through 1910. Information about the tearing down of the church comes from Jackson, *The Girl in the Belfry*, p. 185.

2. Chico Cemetery Index. Death certificate for John George Gibson.

3. Lewis Byington, ed., *The History of San Francisco*, pp. 27–29.

4. California Death Index. Obituary for Mary Agnes Sademan, *SFC*, January 13, 1927. James's arrest for burglary appears in "A Father Has a Son Arrested," *Call*, January 25, 1898. James Sademan does not appear in the California Death Index, 1905–present, which could mean several things: he died before 1905; he died out of state; or he went back to his birth surname.

5. California Death Index. Obituary of Miriam E. Wolfe, *SFC*, January 17, 1955.

6. California Death Index. Social Security Death Index. Obituary for Clarence N. Wolfe, *SFC*, July 9, 1966.

7. This information comes from the California Death Index, the obituary for Dr. Thomas A. Vogel, *SFC*, September 17, 1951, and the grandchildren of Thomas Vogel.

8. California Death Index. Obituary for Dr. William Z. King, *SFC*, May 8, 1910. Death certificate for William Z. King.

9. Death certificate for Flora K. Black. Los Angeles County Coroner's Report.

10. California Death Index. Obituary for William Z. King.

11. San Francisco city directories. Death certificate for George R. King.

12. Information about Flo Upton comes from the California Death and Birth Indexes, the obituary for Flora S. Waterman, *Tulare Register*, October 6, 1949, and her grandchildren.

13. California census records and San Francisco city directories. Marriage announcement in *SFC*, December 5, 1897 (where Lucile's husband is listed as Clement Wilder); marriage announcement in *Call*, November 30, 1897 (where her husband is listed as Charles Moore). Death certificate for Clement Wilder, also known as Charles Watson Moore, also known as Clement Moore. Coroner's records exist for all sudden or premature deaths (which Lucile's would have been) from July 1901 through December 1, 1904, and Lucile does not turn up here. She could have died between May 1900, when the 1900 census was taken, and July 1901; or between December 1904 and January 1905, when the California Death Index begins. Or she could have remarried and died under another name, in which case she would have died prior to 1940, as no combination of her name and date of birth produces a result on the 1940–1997 database.

14. Information comes from Eugene Deuprey's obituary, *SFC*, October 5, 1903, San Francisco coroner's report, and Deuprey's grandson.

15. Dickinson does not appear in the California Death Index, 1905–1997, yet he was still alive at the time of the writing of his biography in *History of the New California*, published in 1905.

16. Obituary of William S. Barnes, *SFC*, March 6, 1910.

17. Information about Edgar Peixotto comes from his biography in *History of the New California*, 1905, pp. 706–707, and the California Death Index. Information about his wife comes from her obituary in *SFC*, August 18, 1953.

18. Information about Blanche Lamont's family comes from the census records for Montana and Washington, Washington Death Index, marriage certificate for Maud Lamont, death certificates for Julia Carmichael Lamont, Grace Lamont Logan, and Maud Lamont Hicks, news reports from the *Dillon Tribune*, and from Blanche's niece. Information about Rodger's fatal accident is from his death certificate, the funeral record, and the following newspaper articles: "Was Fatally Shot," *Dillon Tribune*, September 2, 1904; "Trip Came to Sad End," *Dillon Examiner*, September 7, 1904; and "The Last Sad Rites," *Dillon Tribune*, September 9, 1904. Information about Maud's husband comes from "A Thanksgiving Wedding," *Dillon Tribune*, November 29, 1901 and "Took Home a Charming Bride," *Dillon Examiner*, December 4, 1901.

19. I searched the Ontario Birth Index to find Minnie's birth certificate, which would have yielded her mother's name. However, there is no entry for her, which could mean that she was not born in Ontario Province. A marriage entry for an Albert E. Williams and Minerva Swayze may be correct, but it did not take place in Beamsville, where Mrs. Williams was

supposed to be from. Information about Albert Williams comes from San Francisco city directories. He does not show up in the California Death Index.

20. Information about the Durrants comes from San Francisco city directories, death certificates for William and Maud, Maud's obituary ("Maud Allan, Dancer of Decades Ago, Dies," *Los Angeles Times*, October 8, 1956), Maud's autobiography (*My Life and Dancing*), Felix Cherniavsky's *The Salome Dancer*, and Philip Hoare's *Oscar Wilde's Last Stand*. Cherniavsky's book is essential for an understanding of the relationship among the Durrants, and contains several excerpts from Theo's letters and Maud's diaries. Hoare's book recounts the libel trial of Noel Pemberton Billing.

21. "Looting by the California National Guard Following the 1906 Earthquake" (letter from Judge Advocate Willliam P. Humphreys of the second Brigade to the Assistant Adjutant General of the second Brigade), Museum of the City of San Francisco. Available online at http://www.sfmuseum.org/1902.2/ngc.html. Accessed June 8, 1999.

22. "Hearst Corp. Buying S.F. Chronicle," *Moscow-Pullman Daily News*, August 9, 1999.

23. "Anthony Boucher," available online at http://www.ansible.demon.co.uk/writing/boucher.html. Accessed November 18, 2000.

Selected Bibliography

Allan, Maud. *My Life and Dancing*. London: Everett & Co., 1908.

American Psychiatric Association. *Diagnostic and Statistical Manual of Mental Disorders, 4th ed*. Washington, DC: American Psychiatric Association, 1994.

"Bicycle History: USA," in *International Bicycle Fund*. Available online at http://www.ibike.org/historyusa.htm. Accessed May 18, 1999.

Byington, Lewis, ed. *The History of San Francisco*. Chicago: S. J. Clarke Publishing Co., 1931.

California Birth and Death Indexes.

The Catholic Encyclopedia. "The American Protective Association." Available online at http://www.csn.net/advent/cathen/01426a.htm. Accessed June 19, 1999.

Census records for the province of Ontario, Canada, 1871.

Census records of the federal government for California, Montana, and Washington.

Cherniavsky, Felix. *The Salome Dancer: The Life and Times of Maud Allan*. Toronto: McClelland & Stewart, 1991.

Chico Cemetery Index.

City of Elizabeth, New Jersey v. American Nicholson Pavement Co., 97 US 126 (1877).

Civil War Pension Index.

Douglas, John E. and Mark Olshaker. *The Anatomy of Motive*. New York: Scribner's, 1999.

Douglas, John E., et al. *Crime Classification Manual*. San Francisco: Jossey-Bass, 1992.

Duke, Thomas S. *Celebrated Criminal Cases of America*. San Francisco: The James H. Barry Co., 1910.

du Maurier, George. *Trilby*. New York: Dover Publications, 1994.

Dunbar, Dorothy. *Blood in the Parlor*. New York: A. S. Barnes & Co., 1964.

Farrell, Harry. *Shallow Grave in Trinity County*. New York: St. Martin's Press, 1997.

Fred A. Leuchter Associates, Inc. *Execution by Hanging Manual Prepared for the Department of Corrections of the State of Delaware*, 1990. Available online at http://www.theelectricchair.com/hanging_protocol.htm. Accessed August 24, 1999.

Good Housekeeping's Book of Home Entertainment. Cleveland: World Publishing Co., 1961.

Goodwin, Frederick K., M.D., and Kay Redfield Jamison, Ph.D. *Manic-Depressive Illness*. New York: Oxford University Press, 1990.

Hoare, Philip. *Oscar Wilde's Last Stand*. New York: Arcade Publishing, 1997.

Illinois State Archives. Muster and Descriptive Rolls of Illinois Civil War Units.

Irvine, Leigh H. *A History of New California*. San Francisco: Lewis Publishing Co., 1905.

Jackson, Joseph H., and Lenore Glen Offord. *The Girl in the Belfry*. Greenwich, CT: Fawcett Books, 1957.

"James Lyman Crosett." Manuscript collection of the California Historical Society. Available online at http://www.calhist.org/support_info/Collections. Accessed July 24, 1999.

Jamison, Dr. Kay Redfield. *An Unquiet Mind: A Memoir of Moods and Madness*. New York: Alfred A. Knopf, 1995.

Jenkins, Emily. "*Trilby*: Fads, Photographers, and 'Over-Perfect Feet,'" *Book History* 1.1 (1998), 221–67.

Lane Medical Library. Archives and Special Collections, Stanford University Medical Center, 1883–1903.

Leib, Stephen. "Brain Damage Caused by Bacterial Meningitis is Prevented by Readily Available Antioxidant Drugs." Presented at Interscience Conference on Anti-microbial Agents and Chemotherapy, September 26–29, 1999, in San Francisco, CA. Available online at http://www.newswise.com/articles/1999/9/ICAAC09.ASM.html. Accessed August 12, 2000.

Lewis, Dorothy Otnow, M.D. *Guilty by Reason of Insanity: A Psychiatrist Explores the Minds of Killers.* New York: Fawcett, 1998.

Michaud, Stephen E., and Hugh Aynesworth. *Ted Bundy: Conversations with a Killer.* New York: New American Library, 1989.

Michaud, Stephen E., with Roy Hazelwood. *The Evil That Men Do.* New York: St. Martin's Press, 1998.

Morris, Joan, and William Bolcom. *Moonlight Bay: Songs As Is and Songs As Was.* Albany Records (compact disc), 1998.

Mortuary records of the City and County of San Francisco, 1894–1904.

Ontario, Canada, Birth, Death, and Marriage Indexes.

Peixotto, Edgar. *Report of the Trial of William Henry Theodore Durrant.* Detroit: The Collector Publishing Co., 1899; reprinted by the Notable Trials Library, 1996.

Procter, Ben. *William Randolph Hearst: The Early Years, 1863–1910.* New York: Oxford University Press, 1998.

"Quick History of Bicycles." Available at http://www.pedalinghistory.com/PHbikbio.html. Accessed January 12, 2000.

Raine, Adrian, et al. "Brain Abnormalities in Murderers by Positron Emission Tomagraphy." *Biological Psychiatry* 1997; 42: 495–508.

Ray, William W. "Crusade or Civil War? The Pullman Strike in California." *California History* 58: 20–37.

Ressler, Robert K., and Tom Schactman. *I Have Lived in the Monster.* New York: St. Martin's Press, 1997.

———. *Whoever Fights Monsters.* New York: St. Martin's Press, 1992.

"Right to Produce a Play Based upon the Facts of a Criminal Case Pending Its Trial." 30 *American Law Review* 597 (1896).

Rockford College (Illinois) archives, 1889–1892.

San Francisco, California, city directories, 1889–1910.

San Francisco Call Index. Database. Available online at http://feefhs.org/fbd2/sfcalli.html.

San Quentin Inmate Records. California Historical Society Archives.

Standage, Tom. *The Victorian Internet.* New York: Berkeley Books, 1998.

Stanford University Archives, 1890–1894.

Teilhet, Hildegarde. "The Demon in the Belfry," in Allan Bosworth et al., *San Francisco Murders.* New York: Duell, Sloan, and Pearce, 1947.

Thackeray, William Makepeace. *The Newcomes: Memoirs of a Most Respectable Family.* London: Everyman Library (J. M. Dent), 1994.

Time-Life, Inc. "Prelude to the Century," in Our American Century series. New York: Time-Life, Inc., 2000.

von Krafft-Ebing, Dr. Richard. *Psychopathia Sexualis, with Especial Reference to the Antipathic Sexual Instinct: A Medico-Forensic Study,*

translated by F. J. Rebman. New York: Paperback Library, Inc.,
    1965.
Wilson, Colin, and Damon Wilson. *The Killers among Us, Book II: Sex,
    Madness, and Mass Murder*. New York: Warner Books, 1995.
Young, John H. *Our Deportment, or the Manners, Conduct, and Dress
    of the Most Refined Society*. Detroit: F. B. Dickerson & Co., 1882.

Index

About the Author

VIRGINIA A. McCONNELL, a native of Syracuse, New York, has degrees from The College of St. Rose in New York, Purdue University, and Golden Gate University School of Law. She has taught high school in upstate New York and in Sacramento, California, and has practiced law in San Francisco. Currently, she teaches English, Literature, Speech, and Criminal Justice at Walla Walla Community College's Clarkston Center in Washington and lives on 30 acres of land in Idaho. She has been researching crimes from the past for many years and would like to become the "Ann Rule of Victorian true crime." Her 1999 debut, *Arsenic Under the Elms* (Praeger), earned a starred review in *Kirkus Reviews*.